Women Who Love Psychopaths

*Inside the Relationships of Inevitable Harm
with Narcissists, Sociopaths, & Psychopaths*

Sandra L. Brown, M.A. with
Jennifer R. Young, L.M.H.C

Third Edition

Important Notice

The purpose of this book is to provide accurate and authoritative information about the subject matter covered. The author (and any contributors) has made every effort to ensure the information is correct and complete. However, neither the publisher nor authors are engaged in rendering professional advice or services to the individual reader. This book is not a substitute for mental health treatment. If you require such advice or treatment, you should seek the services of a competent mental health professional.

The material in this book is intended to help women identify dangerous, potentially dangerous, and pathological relationships with disordered men. Every effort has been made to provide accurate and dependable information regarding his potential disorder and the relationship dynamics. The contents of the book have been compiled through professional research and by mental health professionals. However, the reader should be aware that professionals in the field have differing opinions.

Therefore, the publisher, author(s), and editors, as well as the professionals quoted in the book, cannot be held responsible for any error, omission, professional disagreement, or dated material. The author(s) and publisher assume no responsibility for any outcome of applying the information in this book in a program of self-care or under the care of a licensed practitioner. If you have questions about the application of the information described in this book, consult a licensed therapist. If you are in a violent or potentially violent relationship, please call a domestic violence hotline or law enforcement.

Cover design: Barry Briggs
Published by Mask Publishing, Balsam Grove, NC
www.saferelationshipsmagazine.com

Library of Congress Catalog Number 2008924208
ISBN 9798388504838

*C*ontents

*D*edication

Joyce was more than the most radical mother anyone could hope to have, more less me. More than a potter, more than a painter of nudes, more than a drinker of crappy wine from boxes, more than a rider of her motorcycle, she was a survivor who grabbed life by the male anatomy and refused to let go until she found a wonderful new life in recovery that would redeem the years lost in someone else's pathology.

Joyce was married for twenty-five years to someone with narcissistic traits and whose bigger than life fame in the music world hampered her own unique talents and distorted her concept of who she was. Following that marriage, Joyce 'upgraded' to a psychopath and lived through a ten-year marriage rampant with infidelity, alcoholism, gaslighting and financial theft. The relationship's aftermath resulted in identity-crushing dissonance.

Without the benefit of outside counseling (I was not yet in the field), Joyce developed great insight into her own personality, the risks it had placed her in, and the damaging effects with which she had been living, and created unique techniques to manage her mounting cognitive dissonance. Many of these 'Joyce-isms' are used today by *The Institute for Relational Harm Reduction* and taught to both survivors for recovery and therapists for use with clients. With thirty-five years of her life lost in another person's pathology, Joyce was determined, in her remaining years, to 'get a great life' big enough for her personality, and a life that would heal the wounds that pathology left behind. She knew it had to be self-satisfying enough for her so that she would never be tempted by pathology's initial charms.

Her phenomenal bounce-back story is told in the final segments of our online course, *The Living Recovery Program*™, which is full of her wisdom, determination, and the acquisition of the amazing life that was indeed as great as she was. I remember Joyce's final hours with a mixture of pain and awe. It was just a few hours before her death; twilight was falling, and happy hour grew near   Joyce loved her own happy hour, with her cut crystal glasses and her Jack Daniels and water. So, I slipped away to the liquor store and bought a small bottle. I roused her from the near-comatose state she was trying to slip into.

When her eyes opened, she saw the bottle of Jack held in front of her eyes, she smiled and looked around sheepishly. "Am I allowed to have that?"

I almost laughed. "You're dying! You're in hospice. You could have pot if you wanted it. Yes, of course you can have it!"

"Crank up this bed!" she ordered. Straightening her crumpled hospital gown and rolling her shoulders like a Hollywood starlet, she growled in a voice ravaged with lung cancer, "You know I always loved a good party."

I poured her drink into an institutionalized Styrofoam cup with a bendy straw, hardly the deserving finality of a toast to her life with her preferred cut crystal glasses. I placed it in her hand. My husband got his cup and I got mine.

And with her remaining life energy, she raised her cup and said, "I want to toast my life. My life in all its recent fabulosity is proof that even sixteen good years, lived right, is enough. I have had a great life! I have been greatly loved by family and friends, and, in my last years, I found and lived a life full of love. Who could ask for more?"

Joyce's toast to her own life in a way that could honor and celebrate sixteen good and authentic years was one of those moments that has been seared into my soul and in which I saw recovery like I had never seen it before: a life recaptured and lived *fully* without regrets after the ravages of pathology.

Her life and wisdom have been passed on in the work we do, and it is to her wisdom, and radically astonishing full and joyful life, that this book is dedicated.

Purposeful Repetition

From thirty years of working with survivor partners, we understand that trauma makes it unusually difficult to retain and remember information. A pathological love relationship impacts the mind in destructive ways, which are discussed more fully later in this book. Core concepts regarding personality disorders, relationship dynamics, super traits, and aftermath symptoms, therefore, are *reiterated* throughout the book specifically for the purposes of retention. This same approach is used in all the services provided by *The Institute*, giving the mind plenty of access to core information in a manner that allows it to absorb and retain that information.

Gender Focus

Our work has largely been with women—not by design, but by the fact that 99 percent of survivor partners who have contacted us for services over thirty years have been female, with male partners. Developing an appropriate treatment approach, research methodology, and education plan should be reflective of the population we *serve*. Therefore, the presentation of the information in this book is geared toward women. While men are also victims of Cluster B/psychopathic partners, and whose pain and symptoms are similar, if not identical, to those of women, there is very little data gathered about male survivors, which is unfortunate, and hopefully will be addressed in other studies. This book, then, is written primarily for those women with issues most frequently addressed by *The Institute*.

Pathological Love Relationships and their aftermath symptoms are certainly mental health and *not* gender issues; both genders are affected by psychopathic relationships. The language used in this book, however, addresses the population who comprise the clear majority of our clientele and our readership.

$\mathcal{F}$oreword

If you're reading this book, you likely fall into one of the following groups:

- You're in a relationship that doesn't quite feel right, and you've begun to wonder if your partner has psychological problems that may be contributing to the confusing events you're experiencing.
- You've been, or currently are, in a relationship with someone whom you suspect, or who has been identified as having a Cluster B/psychopathic disorder.
- You're a friend or family member of someone whom you think is in a dangerous relationship with a person who could have psychological problems.
- You're a therapist who wants to understand more about Pathological Love Relationships.

You are not alone in your search for information about these toxic and destructive relationships. In fact, when we last looked, there were over eight hundred websites, social media venues, blogs, and books about Cluster B/psychopathic partners. With that much information out there, what will you find in *this* book that's different and, hopefully, more helpful?

The first book about love relationships with psychopaths was the First Edition of the book you are reading right now, written over a decade ago.[1] Little did we know that it would be the catalyst for eight hundred venues offering to help others understand these relationships of 'inevitable harm.' That shows a wide recognition of the absence of any information on the subject, and the rush by others to provide more of it—in eight hundred ways. But this sudden excess also highlighted a previously ignored field of counseling in desperate need of a clinical voice and an understanding of not just the *descriptions* of toxic relationships but the theories and research behind them. And mere descriptions hardly address the totality of the experience, or the harm done by it.

Massive in size and scope, these eight hundred other venues of information still did not address what we had been doing in the field for over thirty years—studying pathologically toxic relationships, providing therapy to survivor partners, conducting research, and developing both workable theories and survivor treatment approaches. All this work began before the creation of the first edition of this book in 2008 and now is culminating in the third edition you are reading.

The book you're reading now, like previous editions, is written for partners seeking to decipher the possible lurking pathology at the root of their relationship dynamics. It's also for friends and family who don't understand why their loved one entered such a relationship and why she has trouble leaving it, and for therapists looking for a simple, yet comprehensive, overview of pathology, theories, and the traumatic aftermath that survivors experience.

The book describes the disorders behind the mayhem, not in the flowing story form favored by the many other venues, but in straightforward science-based language which answers the questions that partners, family, and professionals need addressed to dismiss erroneous notions of hope for the relationship's continuation, treatment and eventual success.

Parts of the book include informal assessments for partners to review diagnostic criteria that is used by professionals to determine possible disorders. The book also delineates the unusual relationship dynamics that produce the profound aftermath symptoms found in most survivors.[2] More importantly, it discusses the first and only research into the personality traits found in partners who are targeted.[3] The book assists partners, family, and professionals in finding the appropriate trauma-informed care to avoid the simplistic and inaccurate recovery assumptions that have proliferated in literature and now via the Internet.

What we really hope this book will be able to help you achieve, as either a survivor or a professional, is a huge reduction in cognitively dissonant questions like "Why does he do that?" and "Why is it so difficult to disengage from this relationship?" It's not that these questions don't have answers— they do. But by reframing the way you think about the pathological partner, and yourself, through accurate pathology education, your path to recovery becomes illuminated. We hope this book will be a light on your path.

Foreword Endnotes

1   Brown, Sandra L. and Leedom, Liane J. (2008). *Women Who Love Psychopaths: Inside the Relationships of Inevitable Harm. First Edition*. Health and Well-Being Publications, LLC.

2   Brown, Sandra L., *The Institute* (2006). Survivor symptom survey. Agency raw data.

3   Brown, Sandra L. and Young, Jennifer R., *The Institute* and Purdue University (2014). Outcomes of Research: Personality descriptors of women who have been in relationships with antagonistic men with borderline, narcissistic, antisocial, and psychopathic disorders. Raw data from a 600-person research.

Acknowledgments

By Sandra L. Brown, M.A.

A life's work, much less a book, does not happen in a vacuum. The work is a product of all I have experienced and those I have shared this journey and career with, beginning with why I even ended up in the field. And so, I recognize my father Frank Brown, whose murder stirred something so deeply that could never be let go of…

And to my mother, Joyce Brown, whose wisdom in her own recovery from a Pathological Love Relationship has given not only techniques for survivors but also inspiration for their journey and by whom I felt deeply loved and encouraged to take the world by storm.

To my own children, Lindsay and Lauren, and grandkids, Aliyah, Bryce, Paige, Amaree, and Kamdyn who motivate me to make this a safer world for them.

To Carol Parker, L.M.H.C. who spent 10 long years training, teaching, guiding, supervising and bringing me the best training of trauma through her sage wisdom. I would not know what I know without you.

To the staff at *The Institute* who live so passionately the "pass it forward" philosophy, who have given unselfishly of their own recovery to other survivors, and who are the mojo of the work *The Institute* has been privileged to do. Many volunteers have given over the years and we give honor to that work—the hours of love poured out for new emerging survivors. Thank you to all the volunteers who coordinated retreats, handled social media, edited articles, or supported others.

And then there is the staff who have worked tirelessly for our goals and mission—who provide the support that has grown *The Institute*, and to those that have passed on—Susan Murphy-Milano.

And to Jennifer Young, L.M.H.C., who arrived at *The Institute* as a young grad student, who caught the big picture of Pathological Love Relationships and who spent years side by side with me honing the theories, doing the research, working on clinical techniques for recovery, and guiding the survivors in a stable recovery method. She has proven herself as a talented therapist and a rock star innovator.

To Dr. Doug Samuel of Purdue University for his belief in our hunches about the Super Traits and the guidance and perseverance in the research project.

And to the invaluable help of Penny in the conversion of an unreadable manuscript to something I hope will stand the test of time. And to Darlene, Sherri and June for helpful cleaning and tweaking of this book.

And to the visionaries of our Association Board who believe that the future quality of survivor's care is in the necessity of therapeutic training, who have stepped forward to carry that mantle of stewardship to those who will come after those of us who have worked in this field.

Much respect and thanks to Dr. George Simon, Claudia Paradise, Bree Bonchay, Sherri Renner, Carl Gacono, and Jennifer Young for their exceptional work and help in bringing this project to life.

And to those who have emotionally and spiritually supported me personally, not just through the writing of this book but in life—who have been a friend to me through years of caring for my soul—Margaret Langes, Karen Lauriden, Bill Brennan, Ric Blair, Jenny Durbin, Sherri Renner, Chris Hatch, Judy Moore and those who are now gone but whose rich friendships were towers of support in my life—Toni Roop and Susan Murphy-Milano. And to friend and medicine-woman Lorraine Eldridge who tries to keep my body going.

And most importantly, to every survivor who has taught me and inspired me to understand—

I am a product of every seed of every relationship sown into the soil of *The Institute*.

Acknowledgments

By Jennifer R. Young, L.M.H.C.

To my husband Dave, my love, your compassion and kindness has been the light I will always follow.

To my son Ben, I admire your generous spirit so much. May the life ahead of you be filled with the kind of riches that will move your soul and strengthen your heart.

To my village, my extended family (Lili, Bill, Cheryl, Chris, Greg, Melana, Amy, Jay, and Dennis), my dear, sweet friends and my coworkers, I have learned so much from you, and I truly thank you for lifting me up when I needed it most.

To Sandra, my mentor and friend, I am so grateful for the hours and hours of discussion and collaboration and for your insights and focus. Thank you.

Most importantly, to my mother, Sally Farris, who passed away before this book was finished. She was a single mother who worked hard every day to ensure my life was just a little better than hers. But it was her life that always inspired me. Her character, her heart, and her love of the world have made me who I am, and I am forever grateful.

It has always been the survivors who have shown me the way. Each step in the process of my understanding of the pieces of a pathological relationship have been guided by the strength, dignity, and grace of those who have experienced these horrors. Thank you for taking risks to move into recovery. I wish, for each of you, to find the peace you deserve.

Introduction

*T*he Undetected Victim

People are very interested in *extremes*—the worst anything, whether it be mass tragedies, political messes, or outrageous celebrity behavior. So, it's hard to imagine that something like the private and personal lives of people capable of some of the most extreme danger to others have somehow eluded the world's curiosity.

There is a trio of disorders belonging to a specific population which have little to no conscience. The trio consists of The Charming Psychopath, The Personable Narcissist, and The Edgy Bad-Boy Antisocial Personality Disordered, which are referred to as the 'Dark Triad.' Oh, sure these charmers and their bad-boy escapades garner *some* curiosity. For instance, an entire genre of books has been created around them—thrillers that contain every psychopathic and deviant behavior imaginable. Certain national news media lives and breathes to document The Dark Triad's extreme behavior, which create tantalizing media clips. Serial killer websites and fan clubs worship the ideology of no conscience. Researchers also share a skewed fascination with this type of pathology and spend millions of dollars per year studying and restudying the same mangled mind for just one more obsessional peek at what makes these people tick.

The interesting fact is that, for all the fixated fascination and the repetitious research, no one has attempted to examine the intimate details of how this trio interact and live behind closed doors with their love interests. The tortured partners of the Dark Triad garner little or no public interest, even though they are the very ones who have lived and survived psychology's highest challenge—mental mutilation via an extreme, although fascinating, pathology.

Sadly, it is not just pop culture that has missed what a narcissist's, antisocial's, or psychopath's personal life can reveal. Even the pathology researchers, who focus excessively on this level of extreme pathology, have somehow neglected to study the intimate partners of the Dark Triad. If the world is all about *extremes*, why isn't the extreme victim studied? How can there be such little information about the partners of some of the most extreme, and pop-culturally interesting extremists?

==

We wondered that too, thirty years ago, when we began working with the partners and children of the Dark Triad. It was clinically shocking to see that such serious trauma had not been readily recognized in an entire population of victims. With the cultural fascination of every narcissistic celebrity, every impulse-disordered professional athlete, every antisocial criminal, and every fascinating psychopath, the question remained, "Why have the victims flown under the radar of pop culture and psychology? Why are they not recognized?"

==

Because others were not recognizing the disorders of the Dark Triad, the victims, their relationships, and their traumatic aftermath, these relationships went largely undetected. The reason *why* the relationships and their victims are unrecognized are related to both education and how we identify victims and their abusers.

A Lack of Public Pathology Education

When was the last time you read a *New York Times* article about your likelihood of dating one of the 1 in 100 persons who have no conscience? When did you ever see a government poster in a health clinic that warned that 60 million people are negatively impacted by the 1 in 5 persons who have severe pathological personality disorders? Did your kids get *How to Spot a Dangerous Dark Triad Partner Before You Get Involved* in the dating portion of health class? Did your college student get a checklist of symptoms in the *Do-Not-Date a Narcissist* portion of freshman orientation? Are there any billboards (like those for depression or breast cancer) advertising *How to Detect Antisocial Personality Disorder?* No. No one has funded that billboard campaign. Are there fliers in the restrooms of bars right next to the condom machines stating, "If you are being harmed in a relationship by a psychopath, call this number"? Has a celebrity spokesperson ever taken this issue for his or her cause, or sponsored a Pathology-Aid concert by Willie Nelson to fund victim education and treatment? Nope.

At least 60 million (but possibly as high as a 100 million) people in the United States alone are impacted by someone's dangerous and severe disorders of narcissism, Antisocial Personality Disorder, and psychopathy. The Dark Triad of disorders is estimated to cost *$560 billion* per year, mostly in medical and mental health costs to their victims who have been traumatically impacted. This triad of disorders impairs every societal system (legal, medical, mental health, victim services/law enforcement, and social services) and represents a staggering cost to our lives, both financially and personally. Whether they are ever identified as abusers, perpetrators, or criminals, this disastrous trio are still those who dramatically damage entire societal systems and create interpersonal chaos through the women they claim to love, the children they bear, and the psyches they harm. These are the disorders which are at the heart of high conflict law cases, which drag on for years. They are the disorders most likely to result in child alienation or abduction, stalking and cyber stalking, and which are at the top of the list for intimate partner homicides. And yet they are still poorly identified.

The Dark Triad of disorders belong to those who, if they are ever arrested, pass through the revolving door of failed court-ordered treatment, batterer intervention, and mediation. If they are not arrested, they continue to transform high functioning partners to females in near-fetal positions needing social service assistance as they watch their former careers circling the drain.

This is a triad of disorders as effective in organized, personal terror as any highly-impactful organized crime group, whose destruction to our societal bottom line is unmatched even by meteorological disasters, and yet we have no public pathology education program to warn of this societal and personal plague.

Before we make judgments about women who have fallen into relationships with a member of the Dark Triad, we need to realize that no one has taught us how *not* to become a victim of them. Those whose supposed specialty is victim education know almost nothing about these disorders. And while there is no organized public pathology education program to alert us to the impending nature of these personality problems, let's recognize that *The National Enquirer* and other sensationalist tabloids plastered with celebrity pathology is hardly the place for any victim to learn the true essence of a powerful disorder.

In the absence of real public pathology education, the media are not an accurate educational substitute. Media outlets' portrayals of leaked private infidelities, and reality shows that glorify grandiosity are not public pathology education. This type of pathology exposure has created a public who likely cannot name even five behaviors associated with the disorders of narcissism, Antisocial Personality Disorder, or psychopathy. Most non-victims think that the only people who have these types of behaviors are serial killers. They are unfamiliar with pathology's true, and not-so-rare nature, and likely think they probably have never met one of these unforgettable people.

A Lack of Professional Pathology Education

If the public can't avoid what they don't know, they also can't get help for what they can't name. For victims of low-conscienced partners to be helped, they must identify what they need help for. Victims tell us the same story repeatedly: that because of a lack of information, they could not figure out what was wrong with him, or the relationship. They spent months scouring books, paying a fortune going from counselor to counselor, and spending hours searching the Internet trying to figure out what was at the core of his behavior. The inability to identify his disorder was at the source of their search for help.

But not only is there no public pathology educational system, there is also a profound absence of *accurate* professional information about these low-conscienced disorders. Professionals from whom victims might seek information about these disorders were not well educated in the Dark Triad. Victims trying to recover might seek information about their disordered partners from

- A marriage and family therapist while they were trying to repair the relationship
- Domestic violence if things got abusive
- A support group, when she hadn't made up her mind to stay or go
- Her own personal counselor when the relationship ended
- A church for spiritual support
- A book for guidance on *how-to-spot*
- The Internet for information

The disorders of low-conscience have been poorly understood in several arenas, including those listed above, which happen to be the very places victims attempted to get assistance. This begs the question again: "If these disorders are so interpersonally destructive, why aren't they better known?

Should it be *this* hard for a victim to find out what disorder her partner has, or what his behaviors point to?"

Over the years, we have wondered why information about disorders that fall into categories referred to by the DSM5 (Diagnostic Statistical Manual, a mental health diagnostic tool) as the 'dramatic and erratic,' and previously called 'the dangerous and severe' disorders, did not warrant increased public safety education regarding their potential effects. We are warned about food and environment contaminants; relational contaminants are just as dangerous. We are warned about the public-health risks of not using condoms; equally important to know are the public-health risks of interacting with people with disorders already labeled 'dangerous and severe.' We are warned about how to protect yourself from rape or attack. Why not be warned of the safety risks related to a partner with little or no conscience?

From graduate school to domestic violence agencies to the law enforcement and legal system, the lack of information and understanding about these disorders is continuing to affect the lives of millions.

If therapists don't recognize these disorders, they can't advise their patients. If domestic violence agencies don't identify these partners as having low conscience, they can't prevent victim fatalities. If court systems don't spot members of the Dark Triad, they will continue to give custody to a profoundly disordered parent or deny Restraining Orders [in some areas these are called Orders of Protection] for abusers with poor impulse control. If individuals can't identify people with these disorders, they will continue to partner with them. The list of victims, in the wake of the low-conscienced, will and has continued to grow.

A Lack of Recognizing the Victims

It seems obvious that if we can't recognize this menacing triad of disorders, we likely will not be able to recognize their victims. An additional issue is that the victim of the Dark Triad is not always a typical victim. While she is likely to fly under the treatment radar due to the profession's lack of pathology education, she is also mislabeled, due to the way in which victims are defined and categorized and by whom.

Since the 1970s and the onset of the domestic violence awareness

14

movement, the details of what violence does to a person have been well documented. For that reason, services exist today for survivors to heal from many forms of abuse. There remain generalizations about victims, however, that are causing the partners of those with extreme pathology to go unrecognized.

There has been an underlying assumption that if victims experienced relational abuse of any form, they would fall within the standard profile of a domestic violence victim. This profile assumes basic emotional and historical characteristics, along with certain responses to abuse. It then categorizes these victim features to create a snapshot of a 'victimized person.' These types of profiles were generated mostly from the victims who utilized services related to domestic violence. Research and studies were conducted with victims who were in shelter care, counseling from a domestic violence-related agency, or a domestic violence support group environment. But not all victims use these services.

Thirty years ago, we began wondering about the victims who never utilized domestic violence services, and who remained largely unstudied. How are the victims who don't utilize services (and may not need those types of services, or may require other types of services) different from shelter-care populations? Are there victims who have different emotional and personality make-ups than those who fit the standard victim profile? Could these differences account for why a whole subgroup of victims rarely used victim services?

There doesn't seem to be a curiosity by others (on the rare occasion that these victims are recognized) as to *why* these women were attracted to, and tolerant of, the most disordered and dangerous partners. The women are labeled simply as *codependent* or *relationship addicted* or victims of *learned behavior*, but no studies had been conducted to understand *what* might be at the heart of normal women getting involved with seriously disordered partners.

Do victims of Pathological Love Relationships have clues in their personalities that may show a predisposition toward being the type of person who is an ideal target for a prospective pathological partner? Can we come to understand whether personality might impact how a woman responds to a partner's advances or how she chooses partners? Or can personality traits impact the way she categorizes or misses red flags that indicate danger? Are there people whose tolerance levels may be higher for having a pathological partner and which are unrelated to codependency? How can we help victims who have unusual groupings of characteristics, temperaments, and personality factors that might be negatively influencing their patterns of selecting relationships?

A Lack of Research about the Victims of the Dark Triad

It is hard to get the attention of victim service providers, self-help approaches, the media, or the public for that matter, if nothing is *known* about a problem. In the case of women who love psychopaths and narcissists, however, what's puzzling is how did they *not* garner attention.

One of the main reasons for this is a lack of any research-generated information about the *victims* of narcissists, antisocials, and psychopaths, which is shocking given the million-dollar research fascination with the whole topic of the Dark Triad. But there is almost nothing written clinically about how their relationships affected their partners and families, which could have drawn attention to this unrecognized population. It should seem evident that if there is no impetus for understanding these types of relational dynamics with these types of personalities, victims can neither be helped nor taught to help themselves. Professionals, also, cannot help victims if they themselves are unable to identify those victims or develop the approaches that this type of victim needs.

If the public or those in the mental health systems believe that all abuse victims in relationships are the same, that their relationship patterns are generated from the same type of abusive partner, that all trauma is the same, that there are no contributing factors to make one victim's experience different from the next, then the differences that exist regarding the victims and relationships of extreme pathology are going to remain unidentified. Very little research will be undertaken, leading to almost no information gathered about this subgroup of victims or specific treatment created for them.

It is not a far leap, then, to assume that if there is a lack of awareness that this subgroup of victim exists, and there have not been special reasons to study them, and they have not been researched to be understood, then there certainly will not be programs designed to meet their unique needs. This chain of invisibility has kept the survivors of pathological partners out of sight and out of the range of meaningful help.

Why are victims of narcissists, antisocials, and psychopaths often lumped together with other victim populations who do not share some of the unusual personal factors, relational experiences, or traumatic symptoms? Why are generalized approaches to helping them not based on their trauma-specific symptoms and needs? Why have the issues of the victim's personality traits and other risk factors that impact her patterns of selection, relationship dynamics, risk level, and exiting difficulties not been identified?

A Lack of Awareness in Victim and Abuser Services

Even how the Dark Triad is viewed and undiagnosed may be a culprit in how these victims remain largely unaccounted for. Within the domestic violence and batterer intervention communities, the low-conscienced partners (who have been violent) also have a general profile of behaviors which are associated with the motivation behind abuser's actions. Much like the victims who have been generalized by these same communities, so have Dark Triad abusers been generalized who have passed through these systems for services.

The Domestic Violence and Batterer Intervention communities' profiles associated with what makes any abuser tick are related to power, control, low self-esteem, and learned battering behavior. (In these victim/abuser communities, the reasons are, unfortunately, not related to the power-packed pathological disorders.) These abuser identifiers are explained by the victim/abuser community's teaching tool called *The Power and Control Wheel* whose theory dates to the 1970s. But Dark Triad partners whose behaviors are not always readily identified on The Power and Control Wheel, fly under the radar of detection, as does their disorder. Those victim/abuser programs are not taught how to spot them and are not communities who include Dark Triad disorders as part of *causes* for violence. When low-conscienced partners fly under the radar, no doubt their victims do, too.

Some of the issues that The Institute has followed include whether certain abuser disorders increase risk in the victim, and if certain disorders exist that are associated with victim mortality risks. It follows, then, that the disorders of some abusers may cause them to seek certain traits in victims, and if so, it's important to identify those disorders and why the abusers are attracted to certain traits.[1]

The Dark Triad of disorders is understood clinically to be those most associated with intimate partner homicides. Still, there is no process for identifying these pathological disorders when a pathological partner enters a batterer intervention program, or when stories mirroring Nicole Brown Simpson's murder continue to emerge. Agencies that deal with the Dark Triad must be better equipped to identify its victims and help the victims understand the danger of having a relationship with a partner without a conscience.

A Lack of the Known Features of the Successful Dark Triad

There is yet another reason why the victim is not recognized. These dark and pathological disorders do not always make it through the doors of a batterer's program, a police station, or the courthouse. Some of the features related to the Dark Triad are what Dr. Robert Hare—the world's leading expert on the darker disorders— calls *The Disorder of Social Hiding*. These pathological partners frequently hide behind the mask of sanity or the veil of professional status and are often referred to as successful narcissists or psychopaths. This does not simply mean success in career status (although that is often applicable); it also means the disorder can remain undiagnosed and not recognized for the interpersonal harm the person is causing.

The survivors of 'successful' pathological partners face the almost impossible challenge of convincing law enforcement, courts, custody evaluators, and therapists that this person who is anxiety-free, dressing in $3,000 tailored suits and Italian loafers, with CEO hanging on his office door, has the lurking disorder of someone with no conscience. Why? Nowhere is there the scary movie depiction of the highly deranged. Instead the mask of a cool, calm, and collected professional exists, disarming all those around him who don't realize this much pathology packed into a suit is really a disorder of social and relational hiding.

A leading researcher of the pathology spectrum suggests that the number of successful members of the Dark Triad in the business field is approximately four times greater than in the general population and are not as easily identified as the criminal types. In fact, many people with one or more of these disorders gravitate to prestigious careers that massage their narcissism and reward their lack of conscience as they bolt up the career ladder, taking out anyone in their path. Some careers are a natural fit for the character and conscience deficits common to the Dark Triad.

It is interesting to contemplate whether the successful psychopath seeks an equally successful partner. These people, who find great pleasure in flying under the radar of detection, must equally enjoy the cat-and-mouse game of remaining undetected in relationships, especially with bright and successful women.

A Lack of the Classification of a Pathological Love Relationship

Without the ability to identify those with a Dark Triad disorder, it is unlikely that Pathological Love Relationships will be noticed either; after all, it is the abuser of the relationship who draws attention to the relationship's dynamics. Those with the low-conscienced disorders of social and relational hiding can go decades without their deviant behavior ever being identified, especially if there is no physical violence that would warrant investigation and/or intervention.

Many factors are unique to the low-conscienced and their relatively normal partners. Combinations of personality traits in both partners create intense and often combustible dynamics that are misattributed to unrelated factors. His traits of social appeal coupled with her unstudied personality traits of empathy, tolerance, agreeableness, and conscientiousness (discussed later in the book) make for an unusual presentation of relational features ripe for misunderstanding.[2]

These misunderstandings have run the gamut from ascribing paranoia to the victim, to assessing the psychopath as calm and rational, to defining the issue as one of relationship addiction and codependency, to not recognizing a problem at all. But the fact remains that the victim is undetected when her relationship *looks* like something else.

We wondered if there were personality traits in unusual combinations that might predispose a victim to engage in pathological relationships. Were some of the covert relationship dynamics related to his pathology or to her combination of personality traits? Do Pathological Love Relationships have different patterns than those described in domestic violence settings or marriage and family counseling? Are these relationships unique in any way that has not been studied?[3]

A Lack of Differentiating the Trauma and Aftermath as Atypical

The extreme end of the human spectrum is where disordered partners cross over from being one-time batterers to another category of pathology, where having a conscience and remorse is absent. Extreme psychological torment happens mostly in situations involving prisoners of war, cults, and organized crime. However, the experience is also similar for victims of extremely pathological partners.

And why wouldn't it be? War criminals, cult leaders, and crime lords are all known for their lack of conscience and dangerous behavior, which is what makes their soul-destroying psychological impact sometimes even more devastating than physical assault. While the world has shuddered at film images of what a lack of conscience looks like, we haven't given much thought to what being in the presence of this much pathology does to those around them. While we would expect that what those in the Dark Triad would do to someone is far more extreme than what those with a conscience would do, we seldom think about what happens to the victims of narcissists, antisocials, and psychopaths.

For intimate partners and their children who live years and decades with this twisted and deformed psyche, the aftermath effects of exposure to the disorder linger. There have been few to no studies of the aftermath of harm caused to those living in a home with a dangerous pathological disorder, so it's nearly impossible to understand its impact and how that pathology distorts the view of how victims come to sees themselves, others, and the world.

What happens to normal people when coupled with the extreme abnormal partner? Just what does psychological gaslighting and terrorism do to victims over the course of months, years, or decades? How might this abuse create a type of victim different from those seeking services at a shelter? How might their trauma appear differently than other less pathological, yet still abusive, partners?[4]

Victims of those with a lack of conscience don't always appear with black eyes and trembling demeanor. The unique substructure of their personality can create an unusual tolerance of and adaptation to extreme pathology. The victims' own personal successes have created resources that allow them to bypass community services, thus flying under the radar as the stereotypical domestic violence victims, which are the victims who are most studied. If care providers only look for the overt trauma, these victims can be missed; their atypical trauma may not fit the exact criteria for Post-Traumatic Stress Disorder or other trauma disorders consequently they may go unrecognized as trauma victims.

What about the victims whose trauma reactions do not match the typical descriptions of trauma, or what is called 'Battered Women's Syndrome'? What about those whose unique combination of reactions are atypical? Can a victim's personality and relational dynamics impact her reactions and responses? Are there any personality traits that make reactions to trauma different, or predispose a victim to expose herself to more trauma? Do pathological partners impact others differently?

Societal Myopia

The myopic view of the Dark Triad has focused on all things dark, while missing what that darkness and remorselessness leaves behind. The extremity of pathological behavior, as a cultural fascination, trumps the desire for knowledge about the disorders. It leaves an entire society at risk for the manipulations and mayhem of the unseen force of this pathology. The miseducation of the public regarding pathology has created unhelpful and generic views of victims and abusers. These are the cracks through which victims have fallen. Those who have experienced the most extreme disordered partners this world offers are usually those whose cries for help have fallen on deaf ears and blind eyes. Systems that should have educated the victim did not. Services that should have reached her did not. Programs that should have healed her did not.

For all the world's interest in all things extreme, one of the most extreme things has been left largely unexamined. But that ends now.

$\mathcal{N}$ormal Women, Abnormal Relationships

Diana was a former prosecutor and judge who worked at the Governor's office and whose dashing narcissist was a JAG (military Judge Advocate General) officer. Dena was a university professor whose psychopathic husband was in high level management in a Fortune 500 company. Susan was a college president whose antisocial disordered husband was an attorney for a major NBA team. These are real women whose real-life Pathological Love Relationships are probably like the stories of those survivors who are reading this book.

Diana, Dena, Susan, and others like them have the types of stories that captured our attention—bright, corporate women whose highly polished skill sets landed them very notable jobs but who could, on the other hand, be attracted to, tolerant of, and gaslighted by severe and dangerous partner pathology. We believed that at the core of these warm, open, trusting, and resourceful women were personality traits that impacted each woman's ability to read signs of personal danger. The very normal traits that are valued in society such as empathy, loyalty, and optimism, which contributed to these women's success in many other areas of their life, in excessive quantities became their undoing with a pathological partner.

The stories of the women we have been privileged to help have shattered the myth that women who love men with a Dark Triad disorder are women who themselves suffer from mental illness, or are victims with a lengthy violence history, or are needy and dependent.

The incongruences we discovered caused us not only to question what we believe as fellow human beings but also what we believe as mental health professionals and researchers. We think that by studying women who love psychopaths we may be able to understand what traits, in their excesses, predispose a person to imminent danger.

It's time for a new view of these very misunderstood relationships.

Introduction Endnotes

1   Brown, Sandra L., The Institute (2008). Trait targeting theory in Pathological Love Relationships. Prepared for The Institute's Therapist Training Program and Manual: Treating the Aftermath of Pathological Love Relationships.

2   Brown, Sandra L., The Institute (2016). Misidentification of Super Traits in Pathological Love Relationships—Stop Calling it Codependency. Prepared for Women Who Love Psychopaths. Third Edition; and The Institute's Therapist Training Program and Manual: Treating the Aftermath of Pathological Love Relationships.

3   Brown, Sandra L., Bridgework Counseling Center (1996). Relational Dynamics of Personality Disordered Relationships: A Historical Qualitative Research Study. Report prepared for Bridgework Counseling Center.

4   Brown, Sandra L., The Institute (2006). Survivor symptom survey. Agency raw data.

Section One

Puzzle Piece #1™

A Partner with a Cluster B / Psychopathic Personality Disorder

Figure 1.1
Puzzle Piece #1™

Chapter One

The Disorders of Relational Harm Puzzle Piece #1™

*R*elational Harm

What is in the heart of every survivor is the haunting question of who can cause this much damage to another, and why. This single question encompasses much of the turmoil survivors experience. On many levels, survivors who want to heal, instinctively know that to heal is to understand the disorder that has produced so much soul destruction. However, the answer that holds the power to heal, unfortunately, is not one clichéd sentence that will wrap them in a warm balm of soothing recovery but is instead the excavation of deep knowledge and an understanding of the power of pathological disorders that helps to heal the ravages left behind.

This book details the ravaging harm that occurs within, and from, relationships with Cluster B/psychopathic disorders, which is referred to as 'relational harm'. The word harm in all its generic generalities is quite specific in the outcome of its behavior in pathological relationships. The specifics include the expansive harm of emotional, physical, psychological, sexual, financial, spiritual, and self-perceptual injuries that are acquired in a pathological and toxic relationship. While the Dark Triad (NPD, ASPD, and Psychopathy) is likely to harm any it meets, it is within intimate relationships where the severity of harm is experienced exponentially by the survivor partners. All pathological relationships cause relational harm which becomes manifested in personal harm.

This book chooses to utilize the word "pathological" in connection with the word "relationships" because it helps differentiate that he has a 'dangerous and severe' disorder noted as a form of pathology and separates these relationships from those that are merely dysfunctional relationships due to other, more commonly thought of, causes. 'Pathological relationships' are a separate category in need of recognition.

To answer the questions posed in the introduction of the book—how strong and competent survivors can be utterly mangled by pathologically toxic partners—we need to understand the pathology that makes someone capable of such psychic destruction. It is no small task, then, to understand and accept the reality that lurks in what is often a covert relational time bomb. To that end, this book catalogues the breadth, the depth, and the reasons for the profound debilitation of relational harm, which begins by recognizing the four elements found in all pathological and toxic relationships.

Puzzle Pieces of a Pathological Love and Toxic Relationship

For this book to achieve the goal of 'public pathology education for all,' readers must learn what constitutes a Pathological (or Toxic) Love Relationship so they can spot these disorders and recognize, avoid, or leave the relationship. *The Institute* has identified four elements that make up a Pathological Love Relationship (PLR).[1] These elements help to *identify* the disorder in one partner, the subsequent relationship dynamics, the unusual traits of the survivor partner, and the aftermath trauma that results from the relationship.

We believe these four elements are the *identifiers* of any PLR. Since PLRs in the past have been invisible, as discussed in the Foreword and Introduction of this book and which have created 'puzzling' and misinterpreted assumptions, *The Institute* uses the analogy of puzzle pieces. When all four puzzle pieces are connected, they create a whole picture of PLRs which aids in solving puzzling questions about the relationship and recovery. The book is broken down into the *Four Puzzle Pieces of a Pathological Love Relationship*™. Each puzzle piece, and the chapters connected to it, explains one of these four elements. The first four chapters address Puzzle Piece #1™—A Partner with a Cluster B/Psychopathic Disorder.

These chapters, related to the first puzzle piece, examine the disorders capable of serious harm to others and how the survivor's partner developed such a powerful disorder. While this chapter (and Chapter Two) gets a little psychologically technical, please try to hang in there through this explanation as it is central to understanding the extreme risks involved in these relationships and the resulting aftermath of those who have experienced relationships with narcissists, antisocials, and psychopaths. So, to help you assess your partner's pathology potential, we have designed some chapters with worksheets that will walk you through pinpointing potential lurking pathology and the behaviors associated with it.

The question is: If the disorders are *that* bad, why aren't they better recognized?

It is exactly this lack of recognition that has prevented survivors from finding the necessary help for recovery and has aided in the disinformation about pathology's societal and relational menace.

Add to the existing informational crisis the fact that even the psychology field is often not in agreement on what to think about this cluster of malfunction which creates a critical incident of unidentified psychological manglers on the loose. The field of psychology has failed to come to agreement as to how to identify the cluster of pathology comprised of narcissists, psychopaths, antisocial behavior, and even borderline personality disorder not simply diagnostically, but more importantly, within hidden relationship dynamics when the disorder might not yet be suspected. This failure has led to a great degree of unidentified people who in turn cause psychological damage to others.

This is more than extremely unfortunate because survivors rely on the field of psychology for congruent and consistent information and education about these disorders. But the professional field has been divided on several issues which have kept a consistent form of public pathology education from being available. It has been difficult for them to agree upon -

- Who fits the definition of these disorders
- How and why the disorders are likely created
- Whether these disorders are mildly treatable but not curable or not
- What specific harm they do to their partners partially because of their low treatability

The psychological category these disorders fall into are called 'Personality Disorders,' meaning, that during the personality's development, a deficit or distortion occurred, creating a disorder. *How* those deficits, distortions, and damage happened will be covered in a later chapter.

The Diagnostic and Statistical Manual of Mental Disorders 5 (referred to as the DSM5) is the psychology field's template for measuring mental health. It lists criteria for hundreds of types of mental health, developmental, and personality abnormalities. It is within the DSM5 that we can define what these disorders *are*, and it is within the relationships that we can see what they *do*.

The challenge has been, and continues to be, getting an entire psychology field on the same page about this group of disorders that constitutes some of the most serious of all disorders. For reasons that range from inter-field political battles about existence, definitions, and treatability, to a variety of theory beliefs, even the DSM5 has wrestled with its own conceptual ideas about personality disorders. Likewise, therapists have grappled with their own ideas about these disorders while often overlooking the destruction that happens to people *in* relationships with these disorders because the DSM talks about personality disorder symptoms but not the *effect* on others.

The good news is that the most recent DSM demonstrates insight into many factors related to the disorders that will hopefully and eventually influence the consistent identification of the disorders, especially in relationships, and education to survivors by therapists about the disorders. The publication of the DSM5 has, in fact, taken a step in the right direction regarding Personality Disorders by also presenting information on how the disorders manifest themselves in the lives of the partners. We will be discussing these important additions in the DSM in this chapter.

*T*wo Views of Personality Disorders

Categorical View

The DSM5 has offered two views, or descriptions, of Personality Disorders. The first view is the traditional model and description of the disorders that has been listed in the DSM (with minor changes) for decades. It is referred to as the Categorical View and sees each disorder as separate with distinct symptoms. It has been hard for survivors to find this view useful, since it feels to them like it forces them to choose *between* disorders—the partner is this *or* that. For instance, they either are a narcissist *or* an antisocial personality. However, the Categorical View did not clearly explain the fact that the individual might fit into multiple diagnoses, which is normally the case in personality disorders. This is the view that therapists had used until the new DSM5 came out.

Dimensional View

The new view, called 'The Alternative Model,' is an example of how the field is starting to understand the complexity and overlapping nature of personality disorders outside of the *either/or* view. The Alternative View is also referred to as the 'Dimensional View' and sees personality disorders as often sharing (or overlapping in) similar symptoms and not easily fitting in to those cut-and-dried categories associated with the Categorical View.

We at *The Institute for Relational Harm and Public Pathology Education* have always believed that most pathological partners display several symptoms from several different disorders. They don't have one singular disorder; rather they have a complex weaving of symptoms from several disorders and from several categories of disorders, not just disorders of the personality. One of the reasons why these partners are so dangerous is, in fact, that they have so many different types of disorders. It is this Alternative Model that we will be utilizing in this book to define and discuss personality disorders.

$\mathcal{P}$ersonality Disorders as Clusters

In the Alternative or Dimensional Model, there are six personality disorders, (Psychopathy is considered separately) that reflect the way an individual's personality has been damaged, distorted, or is deficient, which means it is *disordered,* in areas related to his/her -

- Emotional stability
- Self-perception
- Behavior
- Interpersonal functioning (which is how the individual acts in relationship to, and with, others)

The six personality disorders can be divided into three clusters. They are called clusters because their symptoms have overlapping similarities. This overlap of symptoms is a reason why survivors have had a hard time trying to figure out which disorder the partner may have. The survivor may read a group of symptoms about one disorder and see the partner's behaviors in it and then read another disorder's symptoms and equally see the partner's behavior there, too.

The disorders are set in clusters because they *share* symptoms. It is common to see symptoms in more than one category of personality disorders precisely because the symptoms *are* similar

The Cluster A Group is referred to as 'The Odd or Eccentric Disorder' and includes[2]:

- Schizotypal Personality Disorder

The Cluster B Group is referred to as 'The Dramatic and Erratic Disorders' and includes[3]:

- Antisocial Personality Disorder
- Borderline Personality Disorder
- Narcissistic Personality Disorder

The Cluster C Group is referred to as 'The Anxious or Fearful Disorders' and includes[4]:

- Avoidant Personality Disorder
- Obsessive-Compulsive Personality Disorder (not to be confused with Obsessive-Compulsive Disorder which is an anxiety disorder.)

Although all the personality disorders listed above imply some problems which would occur in relationships due to the deficits and distortions that exist in all personality disorders (which will be discussed later), *The Institute*, and this book, primarily focuses on Cluster B Disorders, which have proven to be distinctly more damaging and manipulative. This book is about the Cluster B disorders descriptively called by the DSM as the 'dramatic and erratic' disorders.

Blending DSM Explanations

The term Cluster B is associated with the traditional Categorical Model of Personality Disorders and is widely known by that term amongst survivors and therapists. For teaching purposes in this book, we are utilizing the term Cluster B and the concept of clustering as described in the Categorical Model while *also* discussing the new additional information from the Alternative Model. The Alternative Model has added important distinctions in its terminology that help survivors see their partners' deficits and distortions in new ways that explain why their relational dynamics were the way they were. For teaching purposes, we are *blending* concepts from both models which will help survivors more clearly understand the disorders. We believe utilizing the known concept of clusters *with* the new broader explanations in the Alternative Model gives the most thorough understanding of personality disorders. Therapists should read the Alternative Model in the back of the DSM to follow along.

Psychopathy

Additionally, there is one more disorder related to disorders of 'inevitable harm' and pathological (and toxic) love relationships that will be discussed at length in this book: Psychopathy.

Psychopathy is an anomaly of sorts. While it appears to have similar symptoms to Antisocial Personality Disorder, experts maintain that psychopathy is a different disorder altogether. Psychopathy experts believe that due to its psychological, neurological, genetic, and biological differences, it warrants a separate disorder category. It is included in this book because of its distinct overlap with Cluster B disorders and symptoms. The symptoms of psychopathy are discussed later.

What IS a Personality Disorder?

To understand the destruction a Cluster B personality can do to the relationship and the survivor partner, one must start with what a personality is and what in it can become disordered.

Everyone's Personality

A personality, in general, is expressed in how a person thinks, feels, relates, and behaves. It is often described as a person's character, or his/ her emotional, social, and behavioral qualities. It is perhaps what we are most aware of when we are in a relationship with someone. We say they have a 'kind' personality or an 'obnoxious' personality. Most often, people relate personality to how someone behaves, although thinking, feeling, and relating are also aspects of it.

Beyond kind or obnoxious, personalities have an important function, especially in our relationship to others. When a personality is healthy, it can accurately interpret what is happening with others. It can notice what others think, feel, and how they behave. It can also interpret how their own personal qualities affect other people either positively or negatively.

Disordered Personalities

However, in personality disorders, the filter for interpreting their own and other people's reactions to them is skewed. Personality disorders are related to the poor functionality of the personality's -

- Cognition (Thinking)
- Emotions (Feeling)
- Interpersonal abilities (Relating)
- Behavior (Behaving)

===

Survivor Note:

If you think about your partner, you may have noticed that how he thought, felt, related, and behaved was different than other people. Since thinking, feeling, relating, and behaving are all functions of interactions in intimate relationships, interactions with a person with a personality disorder are disturbed, disruptive, and ultimately dangerous.

===

$\mathcal{T}$he DSM5 Alternative Model of Personality Disorders

Assessing Potential Pathology

A survivor's inability to understand the skewed filter in their personality-disordered partner produces the question, "What is wrong with him?" To assess potential personality pathology in a partner, the DSM5 Alternative Model can be followed, as it defines personality disorders in a manner that highlights the problems in the personality and gives insight into why a survivor was so severely impacted. To assess personality problems, we are going to utilize the following pages, which are set up as worksheets for you. More information later in this chapter will help you understand how to utilize the information and insights you have gathered from these checklists. Since the language that describes these concepts is written for mental health professionals, it has been simplified for ease of understanding.

Criterion A: Level of Personality Functioning[5]

A personality 'disorder' implies that the personality is dysfunctional compared to how a personality normally functions. The problems are related to -

- How a personality-disordered person sees himself
- How he relates to others, and
- How the level of dysfunction impacts his behavior, including his behavior within relationships

To understand the problem in the personality, the Alternative Model first examines how the personality-disordered person views them self and how this disordered "self" acts with and toward others. How bad or dysfunctional someone thinks, feels, relates, and behaves is rated from low to severe. A chart presented later helps compare just *how* severely problematic the pathological partner's personality truly may be. (See Tables 1.1 through 1.5)

The Alternative Model begins by defining two areas which are evaluated relating to the problems of the self. One is self-identity and the other is self-direction.

Self-Functioning

1. Self-Identity

Self-identity is defined as -

- The experience of oneself as unique, with clear boundaries between the self and others
- The stability of self-esteem and the ability to accurately appraise one's strengths and weaknesses (called self-appraisal)
- The capacity for, and ability to, regulate a range of emotional experiences.

2. Self-Direction

Self-direction is defined as -

- The pursuit of consistent, rational, and meaningful short-term and life goals
- The use of productive behavior that is positive, helpful, and intended to promote social acceptance and friendship (called internal pro-social behavior)
- The ability to self-reflect adequately (i.e. to practice accurate self-examination)

Negative Impact in Personality Disorders

When there are problems in the personality, it means the distorted way in which he sees himself (either in inflated or deflated ways), his inconsistent self-esteem that fluctuates with situations, and the inability to experience a wide spectrum of emotions will have a negative outcome in any relationship because of this inconsistency in his self-identity.

The inability to have meaningful life or relationship goals, the inability to have positive relationships, and the inability to accurately examine his own behavior in the relationship will curtail the *quality* of what can be achieved in a relationship due to the self-direction problems.

Survivor Note:

*In many ways, the relationship can only be as healthy as the functionality of the self. For personality-disordered people, the unhealthy **self** is the disorder, and there is little to no health to bring into building a normal relationship.*

The next item that is evaluated for problems in the personality has to do with Interpersonal Functioning with others through adequate empathy and capacity for intimacy.

Interpersonal Functioning

1. Empathy

Empathy is defined as -

- The awareness and recognition of others' experiences and desires

- The tolerance of differing perspectives
- The understanding of the effects of one's own behavior on others

2. *Intimacy*

Intimacy is defined as -

- The depth and duration of connection with others
- The desire and capacity for closeness
- The mutuality of regard reflected in interpersonal behavior[6]

Negative Impact in Personality Disorders

Both empathy and intimacy are tied to the ability to have successful relationships with others. The dysfunction of these parts of the personality means they don't bring adequate or healthy enough amounts of empathy and intimacy to a relationship with which to be successful or even normal. The Alternative Model's view of personality disorders is the first time the DSM has acknowledged that there are serious problems with personality-disordered people that will affect *others* in relationships with them and not just symptoms in the disordered person that affect only themselves. This is because deficits in empathy and intimacy have a negative influence on those in relationships with the disordered partner.

The deficits in empathy mean he has an inability to understand or relate to other people's emotional experiences or what causes emotional states, for instance, in the survivor. When his perspectives differ from the survivor's, he cannot put himself in her shoes to understand why she feels the way she does, especially when it relates to his behavior. The Alternative Model notes empathy as being *crucial* to normal personality functioning, and the absence of it is what creates not merely dysfunction but a *disorder*.

Intimacy is the byproduct of a healthy relationship. It is what people strive for in relationships and the very reason for entering relationships—to build intimacy with others. Dysfunctional or inadequate intimacy means the very thing a survivor is striving for in a relationship cannot be attained, as the disorder prevents deep connection, and the duration of intimacy itself is likely to be short-lived despite the length of the relationship. The Alternative Model indicates that sometimes the disordered person doesn't even desire true closeness, and on the occasion that they might desire it briefly, they do not have the true *capacity* for having or *maintaining* closeness. The inability to have mutual regard for others, as seen in how they treat others, will be addressed in the relationship dynamics described in another chapter.

Survivor Note:

These are more than relational flaws that can be fixed by couples counseling and are a relational fatality that guarantees what will happen in relationship failure and, ultimately, the aftermath survivors will experience.

Healthy vs Unhealthy

The Alternative Model establishes the core building blocks of interpersonal (and relationship) success based on self-identity, self-direction, empathy, and intimacy. These four skills are needed to maintain a healthy intimate relationship. Without these, other persons are bound to be harmed by the disordered personality's lack of these skills and is, in fact, exactly why survivors are indeed harmed.

The Alternative Model of Personality Disorders measures these self and interpersonal skills by rating how poorly the disordered person relates to himself and to others. This is seen on a continuum ranging from little or no impairment to moderate, severe, or extreme impairment. The Alternative Model also names other milestones to predict probable pathology:

- The lack of skills in two basic areas of human functioning—the ability to relate to yourself and to others—is a high predicator of probable personality pathology.
- It is impairment in personality functioning that predicts whether a personality disorder exists.
- It is how severe the impairment *is* that predicts whether the person has more than one personality disorder.[7]

$\mathcal{T}$he Self and Interpersonal Functioning Continuum[8]

The following chart offers an opportunity to view how a professional would assess the level of impairment in a disordered partner's self and interpersonal functioning. For a personality disorder to be considered existent, the disordered partner would need to score at least in the moderate impairment range or above.

In utilizing the charts below, review all the charts *first*, then choose which chart reflects the level of your partner's primary functioning level during the relationship. The charts are in order from least impairment to most impairment.

Table 1.1

Level 0: Liflle or No Impairment

Self	
Identity (Boundaries)	**Self-direction (Goals)**
• Has ongoing awareness of a unique self; maintains role-appropriate boundaries. Has consistent and self-regulated positive self-esteem, with accurate self-appraisal. • Is capable of experiencing, tolerating, and regulating a full range of emotions.	• Sets and aspires to reasonable goals based on a realistic assessment of personal capacities. Utilizes appropriate standards of behavior, attaining fulfillment in multiple realms. • Can reflect on, and make constructive meaning of, internal experience.

Interpersonal	
Empathy	**Intimacy**
• Is capable of accurately understanding others' experiences and motivations in most situations. • Comprehends and appreciates others' perspectives, even if disagreeing.	• Maintains multiple satisfying and enduring relationships in personal and community life. • Desires and engages in a number of caring, close, and reciprocal relationships.

Interpersonal	
Empathy	Intimacy
• Is aware of the effect of his own actions on others.	• Strives for cooperation and mutual benefit and flexibly; responds to a range of others' ideas, emotions, and behaviors.

. . . .

Table 1.2

Level 1: Some Impairment

Self	
Identity (Boundaries)	Self-direction (Goals)
• Relatively intact sense of self with some decrease in clarity of boundaries when strong emotions and mental distress are experienced. • Self-esteem diminished at times with overly critical or somewhat distorted self-appraisal. • Strong emotions may be distressing, associated with a restriction in range of emotional experience.	• Excessively goal-directed, somewhat goal-inhibited, or conflicted about goals. • May have an unrealistic or socially inappropriate set of personal standards, limiting some aspects of fulfillment. • Able to reflect upon internal experiences, but may overemphasize a single (e.g., intellectual, emotional) type of self-knowledge

Interpersonal	
Empathy	Intimacy
• Somewhat compromised in ability to appreciate and understand others' experiences; may tend to see others as having unreasonable expectations or a wish for control.	• Is somewhat compromised in ability to establish depth and satisfaction in enduring personal and social relationships. • Although capable of establishing intimate relationships is somewhat compromised in ability to have meaningful communication especially during emotional or conflictual experiences.

Interpersonal	
Empathy	Intimacy
• Although capable of considering and understanding different perspectives, resists doing so. • Inconsistent in awareness of effect of own behavior on others.	• Has unrealistic expectations which hampers cooperation and is compromised in ability to respectfully communicate with others or tolerate differing feelings, thoughts and behaviors.

· ·

Table 1.3

Level 2: Moderate Impairment

Self	
Identity (Boundaries)	Self-direction (Goals)
• Excessive dependence on others for identity definition, with compromised boundary delineation. • Vulnerable self-esteem controlled by exaggerated concern about external evaluation, with a wish for approval. Sense of incompleteness or inferiority, with compensatory inflated, or deflated, self-appraisal. • Emotional regulation depends on positive external appraisal. Threats to self-esteem may engender strong emotions such as rage or shame.	• Goals are more often a means of gaining external approval than self-generated, and thus may lack coherence and/or stability. • Personal standards may be unreasonably high (e.g., a need to be special or please others) or low (e.g., not consistent with prevailing social values). Fulfillment is compromised by a sense of lack of authenticity. • Impaired capacity to reflect upon internal experience.

Interpersonal	
Empathy	**Intimacy**
• Hyper-attuned to the experience of others, but only with respect to perceived relevance to self. • Excessively self-referential; significantly compromised ability to appreciate and understand others' experiences and to consider alternative perspectives. • Generally unaware of or unconcerned about effect of own behavior on others, or unrealistic appraisal of own effect.	• Capacity and desire to form relationships in personal and community life, but connections may be largely superficial. • Intimate relationships are largely based on meeting self-regulatory and self-esteem needs, with an unrealistic expectation of being perfectly understood by others. • Tends not to view relationships in reciprocal terms and cooperates predominantly for personal gain.

. . . .

Table 1.4

Level 3: Severe Impairment

Self	
Identity (Boundaries)	**Self-direction (Goals)**
• A weak sense of autonomy/agency; experience of a lack of identity, or emptiness; Boundary definition is poor or rigid: may be over identification with others, overemphasis on independence from others, or vacillation between these. • Fragile self-esteem is easily influenced by events, and self-image lacks coherence. Self-appraisal is un-nuanced: self-loathing, self-aggrandizing, or an illogical, unrealistic combination.	• Difficulty establishing and/or achieving personal goals. • Internal standards for behavior are unclear or contradictory. Life is experienced as meaningless or dangerous.

Self	
Identity (Boundaries)	**Self-direction (Goals)**
• Emotions may be rapidly shifting or a chronic, unwavering feeling of despair.	• Significantly compromised ability to reflect upon and understand own mental processes.

Interpersonal	
Empathy	**Intimacy**
• Ability to consider and understand the thoughts, feelings, and behavior of other people is significantly limited; may discern very specific aspects of others' experience, particularly vulnerabilities and suffering.	• Some desire to form relationships in community and personal life is present, but capacity for positive and enduring connection is significantly impaired.
• Generally unable to consider alternative perspectives; highly threatened by differences of opinion or alternative viewpoints.	• Relationships are based on a strong belief in the absolute need for the intimate other(s), and/or expectations of abandonment or abuse. Feelings about intimate involvement with others alternate between fear/rejection and desperate desire for connection.
• Confusion or unawareness of impact of own actions on others; often bewildered about peoples' thoughts and actions, with destructive motivations frequently misattributed to others.	• Confusion or unawareness of impact of own actions on others; often bewildered about peoples' thoughts and actions, with destructive motivations frequently misattributed to others.

Table 1.5

Level 4: Extreme Impairment

Self	
Identity (Boundaries)	**Self-direction (Goals)**
• Experience of a unique self and sense of agency/autonomy are virtually absent or are organized around perceived external persecution; Boundaries with others are confused or lacking. • Weak or distorted self-image easily threatened by interactions with others; significant distortions and confusion around self-appraisal. • Emotions not congruent with context or internal experience. Hatred and aggression may be dominant affects, although they may be disavowed and attributed to others.	• Poor differentiation of thoughts from actions, so goal-setting ability is severely compromised, with unrealistic or incoherent goals. • Internal standards for behavior are virtually lacking. Genuine fulfillment is virtually inconceivable. • Profound inability to constructively reflect upon own experience; Personal motivations may be unrecognized and/or experienced as external to self.

Interpersonal	
Empathy	**Intimacy**
• Pronounced inability to consider and understand others' experience and motivation. • Attention to others' perspectives is virtually absent (attention is hyper-vigilant, focused on need-fulfillment and harm avoidance). • Social interactions can be confusing and disorienting.	• Desire for affiliation is limited because of profound disinterest or expectation of harm. Engagement with others is detached, disorganized, or consistently negative. • Relationships are conceptualized almost exclusively in terms of their ability to provide comfort or inflict pain and suffering. • Social/interpersonal behavior is not reciprocal; rather, it seeks fulfillment of basic needs or escape from pain.

Once you have determined the potentiality of an existing personality disorder, the next checklist will help you identify specific *types* of personality disorders that the pathological partner might have.

Criterion B: Evaluation of Specific Personality Traits[9]

This criterion identifies specific symptoms associated with personality disorders. To simplify the understanding of these traits, we are applying the DSM5 Alternative Model's list of personality traits as it relates to this book's target group: The Cluster B Disorders of Antisocial Personality Disorder, Narcissistic Personality Disorder and Borderline Personality Disorder (rewritten for ease of understanding).

(Psychopathy will be covered later in the chapter by reviewing Dr. Robert Hare's testing instrument, the Revised Psychopathy Check List—PCL-R).

If the partner scores a moderate or higher degree of impairment on the Personality Functioning Scale above, then the next step is to determine if he meets criteria for one or more Cluster B disorders.

Antisocial Personality Disorder (ASPD)

To meet the criteria for Antisocial Personality Disorder, the partner must first be determined to have moderate or greater impairment on the Level of Personality Functioning Scale, illustrated previously, as well as six (6) or more of the following traits:

☐ Manipulativeness: Frequent use of subterfuge to influence or control others; use of seduction, charm, glibness, or ingratiation to achieve one's ends. (Subterfuge is the deceit used to achieve one's goals.)[10]

☐ Callousness: Lack of concern for feelings or problems of others; lack of guilt or remorse about the negative or harmful effects of one's actions on others; aggression; sadism.

- [ ] Deceitfulness: Dishonesty and fraudulence; misrepresentation of self; embellishment or fabrication when relating events.
- [ ] Hostility: Persistent or frequent angry feelings; anger or irritability in response to minor slights and insults; mean, nasty, or vengeful behavior.
- [ ] Risk Taking: Engagement in dangerous, risky, and potentially self-damaging activities, unnecessarily and without regard for consequences; boredom proneness and thoughtless initiation of activation to counter boredom; lack of concern for one's limitations and denial of the reality of personal danger.
- [ ] Impulsivity: Acting on the spur of the moment in response to immediate stimuli, acting on a momentary basis without a plan or consideration of outcomes, difficulty establishing and following plans.
- [ ] Irresponsibility: Disregard for, and failure to honor, financial and other obligations or commitments; lack of respect for, and lack of follow-through on, agreements and promises.

Survivor Work Page Question:

How many of the above traits did you list your partner as having? _____.

With which level of functioning (from the previous chart) did your partner most closely align? _____

If your partner received a moderate, severe or extreme rating on the level of functioning chart and scored six or more on this list of traits, then he has the potential to have Antisocial Personality Disorder.

Narcissistic Personality Disorder (NPD)

To meet criteria for Narcissistic Personality Disorder, the partner must first be determined to have moderate or greater impairment on the Level of Personality Functioning Scale as listed above, as well as both of the following:[11,12]

- [ ] Grandiosity: Feelings of entitlement, either overt or covert; self-centeredness; firmly holding to the belief that one is better than others; condescension toward others.

☐ Attention Seeking: Excessive attempts to attract and be the focus of the attention of others; admiration seeking.

Survivor Work Page Question:

How many of the above traits did you list your partner as having? _____.

With which level of functioning (from the previous chart) did your partner most closely align? _____

If your partner received a moderate, severe or extreme rating on the level of functioning chart and scored both traits, he has the potential to have Narcissistic Personality Disorder.

Borderline Personality Disorder (BPD)

Survivor Note:
Why We Included Borderline Personality Disorder

Borderline Personality Disorder is one of the disorders within the Cluster B 'Dramatic and Erratic' grouping. Since the clusters have traits that often overlap, Borderlines can exhibit traits from ASPD, NPD, or both. For that matter, Narcissism can have overlaps with Borderline or ASPD, and vice versa with ASPD. We have included Borderline Personality Disorder as one of the 'relationships of inevitable harm' because it does, in fact, carry traits that overlap the other three disorders. Borderlines appear on the reduced-self and intimacy spectrum and are found to have neuro-abnormalities that are also seen in the other Cluster B and psychopathy disorders.

Let's look at the symptoms of Borderline Personality Disorder to see its contribution to the relationships of inevitable harm.

To meet criteria for Borderline Personality Disorder, the partner must first be determined to have moderate or greater impairment on the Level of Personality Functioning Scale as listed above, as well as four or more of the following traits, at least one of which must be Impulsiveness, Risk Taking, *or* Hostility.[13]

☐ Emotional Instability: Unstable emotional experiences and frequent mood changes; emotions that are easily aroused, intense, and/or out of proportion to events and circumstances.

☐ Anxiousness: Intense feelings of nervousness, tenseness, or panic, often in reaction to interpersonal stresses; worry about the negative effects of past unpleasant experiences and future negative possibilities; feeling fearful, apprehensive, or threatened by uncertainty; fears of falling apart or losing control.

☐ Separation Insecurity: Fears of rejection by and/or separation from significant others, associated with fears of excessive dependency and complete loss of autonomy.

☐ Depression: Frequent feelings of being down, miserable, and/or hopeless; difficulty recovering from such moods; pessimism about the future; pervasive shame; feelings of inferior self-worth; thoughts of suicide and suicidal behavior.

☐ Impulsiveness: Acting on the spur of the moment in response to immediate stimuli; acting on a momentary basis without a plan or consideration of outcomes; difficulty establishing or following plans; a sense of urgency and self-harming behavior under emotional distress.

☐ Risk Taking: Engagement in dangerous, risky, and potentially self-damaging activities, unnecessarily and without regard to consequences; lack of concern for one's limitations and denial of the reality of personal danger.

☐ Hostility: Persistent or frequent angry feelings; anger or irritability in response to minor slights and insults.

Survivor Work Page Question:

How many of the above traits did you list your partner as having? _____.

With which level of functioning (from the previous chart) did your partner most closely align? _____

If your partner received a moderate, severe or extreme rating on the level of functioning chart and scored four or more on this list of traits, at least one of which must be Impulsiveness, Risk Taking, OR Hostility, then he has the potential to have Borderline Personality Disorder.

Psychopathy[14]

The revised Psychopathy Check List (PCL-R) is a different diagnostic system from the DSM5. It is a specialized instrument implemented only by those specifically trained in its use. The Check List ranks the person on four factors related to psychopathy:

- Their interpersonal reactions and behavior
- Their emotional, or 'affective' qualities
- Their lifestyle
- Their antisocial behavior

To diagnose psychopathy, the PCL-R is utilized along with an interview with the disordered person and outside collateral information obtained from others, such as partners and/or official mental health or criminal records. While a specially trained professional would need to assess the partner, survivors can get a look at the type of symptoms related to psychopathy for their own understanding and education from the Psychopathy Check List-Revised (PCL-R).

To meet criteria from the PCL-R (shown below), which does not include personal interviews or outside collateral records, the person needs to possess more than half of these characteristics.

Facet 1: Interpersonal

- ☐ Glib/superficial charm
- ☐ Grandiose sense of self-worth
- ☐ Pathological Lying
- ☐ Cunning/manipulative

Facet 2: Affective (Emotional)

- ☐ Lack of remorse or guilt
- ☐ Emotionally shallow
- ☐ Callous/lack of empathy

Facet 3: Lifestyle

- ☐ Need for stimulation/proneness to boredom
- ☐ Parasitic lifestyle
- ☐ Lack of realistic, long-term goals
- ☐ Impulsivity

☐ Irresponsibility

Facet 4: Antisocial Behavior

☐ Poor behavioral control
☐ Early behavioral problems
☐ Juvenile delinquency
☐ Revocation of conditional release (broke probation/parole)
☐ Criminal versatility

Other Items

☐ Many short-term relationships
☐ Promiscuous sexual behavior

Psychopaths or Antisocial Personality Disorder?

Psychopaths are often lumped together with Antisocial Personality Disorder (ASPD) because the two are often *assumed* to be the same disorder. However, researchers of psychopathy (specifically Hervey Cleckley and Robert Hare) disagree. While psychopathy does share some of the worst of the behavioral features of Antisocial Personality Disorder, it has *additional* traits that are unique, which include genetic and neurological abnormalities, biological markers, and psychological symptoms. Where ASPD is associated with illegal and/or criminal behavior, psychopathy (as originally described by Cleckley) is *not* limited to criminal behavior. Cleckley's[15] original emphasis was on a personality style, not just among criminals, but also among successful individuals in the community. This helps the public to expand its recognition of psychopathy outside of the Antisocial Personality Disorder *criminals.*

Hare, in his co-authored book *Snakes in Suits,* notes the differences between law-abiding (although not moral) psychopaths and law-breaking psychopaths. He notes that successful, white-collar psychopaths who don't behave violently or criminally remain largely undetected, wreaking havoc in the personal lives of those who love them. Hare, who created the Psychopathy Check List Revised (PCL-R) listed above, has worked most of his career within the prison system dealing with criminal psychopaths. He noted that he could have had just as successful a career working with the corporate psychopaths on Wall Street.

A Word About Sociopaths

Sociologists and those in the field of social work and psychology have used the words *sociopath, sociopathic,* and *sociopathy* when referring to traits that appear in the spectrum of these low-conscience disorders associated with psychopathy and Cluster B personality disorders. They chose these terms to reflect *how* the development of the low-conscienced individual occurred. In their view, the social or family environment in which the pathological partner was raised created the distortions and deficits that then created the disorder. This includes learned conditioning by having exposure to a pathological parent, abuse, neglect, gang exposure, or other antisocial environments.

Technically and clinically, there are no DSM *criteria* used to determine if someone is, in fact, a 'sociopath.' When sociopaths are discussed, the symptoms used to describe their emotions and behavior sound like those found in Antisocial Personality Disorder, or even Psychopathy. *The Institute* has noticed that people use the word when they don't want to call someone a 'psychopath,' as if 'sociopath' were a milder term, if not displaying milder symptoms. If you hear others use the word 'sociopath,' they are referencing symptoms related to the group of low-conscience disorders probably related to Antisocial Personality Disorder or Psychopathy.

In writing this book, we acknowledge others' use of the word, but we ourselves are sticking to the relevant disorders of Cluster B and Psychopathy, where research and testing instruments exist that detect the disorders.

Summary of a Partner's Potential Pathology

Survivor Work Page Questions:

Based on the checklists provided above, my partner demonstrated the potential for potentially meeting the criteria for the following personality disorders:

Self and Interpersonal Functioning:
- ☐ Little or No Impairment
- ☐ Some Impairment
- ☐ Moderate Impairment
- ☐ Severe Impairment
- ☐ Extreme Impairment

Evaluation of Specific Personality Traits:
- ☐ Antisocial Personality Disorder
- ☐ Narcissistic Personality Disorder
- ☐ Borderline Personality Disorder
  OR
- ☐ Psychopath (based on Hare Checklist)

Now that we understand what a personality disorder is, let's find out other factors that can intensify the disorder's effect on him and on those around him.

Chapter One Endnotes

1   Brown, Sandra L., & Young, Jennifer R. *The Institute* (2016). Pathological love relationship four components: An analysis of consistent factors. Prepared for *Women Who Love Psychopaths. Third Edition.*

2   Esterberg, M. L., Goulding, S. M., & Walker, E. F. (2010). *Cluster A Personality Disorders: Schizotypal, Schizoid and Paranoid Personality Disorders in Childhood and Adolescence. Journal of Psychopathology and Behavioral Assessment,* 32(4), 515–528. https://doi.org/10.1007/s10862-010-9183-8

3   Crawford, T., Cohen, P., & Brook, J. (2001). *Dramatic-erratic Personality Disorder Symptoms: I. Continuity from Early Adolescence into Adulthood. Journal of Personality Disorders,* 15(4), 319–335. https://www.ncbi.nlm.nih.gov/pubmed/11556699

4   Dervic, K., Grunebaum, M. F., Burke, A. K., Mann, J. J., & Oquendo, M. A. (2007). *Cluster C Personality Disorders in Major Depressive Episodes: The Relationship Between Hostility and Suicidal Behavior. Archives of Suicide Research,* 11(1), 83–90. https://doi.org/10.1080/13811110600992928

5-13 *Alternative DSM-5 Model for Personality Disorders.* (2013). FOCUS: *The Journal of Lifelong Learning in Psychiatry,* XI(2), 189–203. https://focus.psychiatryonline.org/doi/abs/10.1176/appi.focus.11.2.189?journalCode=foc

14   Brazil, K. J., & Forth, A. (2016). *Hare Psychopathy Checklist (PCL).* In *Encyclopedia of Personality and Individual Differences.* https://link.springer.com/referenceworkentry/10.1007/978-3-319-28099-8_1100-1

15   Cleckley, H. (1941). *The Mask of Sanity.* Mosby.

Chapter Two

Additional Disorders of Relational Harm Puzzle Piece #1™

Survivor Quick Review

- The preceding chapter discussed Cluster B and Psychopathic Disorders, which include Borderline, Narcissistic, and Antisocial Personality Disorders, and/or Psychopathy, and the impacts of these disorders on the partner in a relationship.
- The pathological partner has deficits in thinking, feeling, relating, and behavior.
- These deficits negatively affect the pathological partner's personality functioning as it relates to self-identity and self-direction.
- These deficits negatively affect the pathological partner's interpersonal functioning as it relates to empathy and intimacy.

*I*ntensification Effects

Depending on its severity, a personality disorder can have devastating consequences to the partner within the relationship. But the affected person hardly ever possesses one single disorder. Instead, most persons with a personality disorder have more than one personality disorder, each carrying their own negative impact on the *already* existing disorder. But in addition to having more than one personality disorder, most will have *other* mental health problems contributing to the severity of what is being acted out in the relationship.

Understanding the many layers of disorders and symptoms contributing to the severity of personality disorders is like peeling an onion—pulling back layers of psychological impact, each layer overlapping with other disorders, which create the factors that intensify the personality disorder. To peel the onion, we will look at the different layers of problems associated with personality disorders.

Intensification through the Overlapping of Personality Disorders

The first layer and intensification happen within the personality disorder itself. As mentioned in the previous chapter, personality disorders are called *clusters* precisely because of the symptoms that overlap with other personality disorders. The worksheets presented in Chapter One are designed to identify whether a partner has more than one overlapping personality disorder. Disorders are considered overlapping when certain symptoms are similar within each disorder. Each disorder includes its own version of self-identity issues, reduced conscience/empathy, impulsivity problems, etc. The more overlaps of similar symptoms in each personality disorder (if a person has more than one), the more likely you are to see those symptoms manifest strongly in the person's behavior.

This overlap can be seen, for example, in the symptom of impulse control that is a common trait in Borderlines, Narcissists, Antisocials, and Psychopaths. For instance, if a partner has Borderline Personality Disorder and Psychopathic traits, you will see a much stronger presentation of impulse control as a resulting behavior, since impulse control problems are part of each of those disorders. This is just as true for other shared symptoms such as unstable emotions, reduced conscience, etc. Look back at your work sheet and see how many personality disorder types your partner potentially had. This will indicate how many overlapping personality disorders he potentially has.

An example of overlapping clusters is illustrated in the following diagram:

Figure 2.1
Cluster B Personality Disorder Overlap © *The Institute* **2006**

Survivor Note:

Each person with pathology is different, so the symptoms of each disorder can vary as well as the impact of the combination of the person's personality disorders. Each pathological partner will not have an equal quantity of varying symptoms, so the size of the circles in Figure 2.1 may be smaller or larger. Most pathological partners have traits or symptoms of several of these disorders. The more overlap of the same type of symptoms, the more severe the display of the disorder is likely to be.

The next section will discuss other issues that can cause additional severity in the pathological partner through a process of intensification.

Intensification through the Overlapping of Personality Disorder Symptoms with Other Mental Health Disorder Symptoms

Not only do personality disorders overlap with each other and with psychopathy, they also coincide with other mental health disorder symptoms. This also intensifies symptoms within the personality disorder that a survivor is likely to experience in the relationship.

Mental health issues are different than personality disorders, and they are considered *additional* types of disorders that possibly affect the partner. Mental health issues may consist of mood disorders such as depression, anxiety, bipolar disorder, compulsive-addictive disorders, or other disorders.

Survivor Note:

*The pathological partner who meets the criteria for more than one disorder, whether it's a personality disorder or a mental health disorder, would be considered as having a **co-occurring diagnosis**, and indicates the probability of even more complications for those in a relationship with him.*

The types of mental health issues most associated with personality disorders include -

- Addictions affiliated with substances (drugs or alcohol)
- Compulsive Disorders affiliated with sex, pornography, gambling, spending, food, etc.

- Mood Disorders affiliated with depression, anxiety, bipolar disorder, or other cycling mood disorders
- Impulsivity disorders affiliated with anger, rage, and irritability

A person with a low-conscience disorder might have a personality and mental health inventory that looks something like this -

✓ Antisocial Personality Disorder
✓ Narcissistic Personality Disorder
✓ Borderline Traits
✓ Substance Abuse Disorder
✓ Sexual Compulsivity
✓ Mood Disorder

This 'combo pack' of disorders adds not only to the complexity of trying to have a normal relationship with someone with such high pathology but also adds exponentially to the lethality risk for anyone in a relationship with them. Mood disorders such as bipolar disorder, for instance, carry their own risk and impulsivity problems, as does any compulsive or addictive disorder. These, then, increase the complications of successful treatment and relationships.

Survivor Work Page Question:

My partner may have had additional mental health issues such as:

_____

Why Consider the Overlap at All?

Overlaps are identified because they help pinpoint the *severity* of symptoms that will likely be experienced both by the partner with the disorders and the survivor who will receive the brunt of unmanaged symptoms. This is important, for instance, with a partner who is violent. A simple descriptor of the label 'violent' hardly defines the risk without looking at all the contributing disorders he has that are likely to influence an act of violence.

Survivor Note:

Overlaps help identify risk and can help therapists or survivors act preven-
tatively when there are many sources generating a particular symptom. It
assists in predicting the likelihood of repeating patterns of behavior.

For instance, a partner with impulsivity problems and who has more than one personality disorder is likely to have extreme impulsivity problems, because this is a reoccurring trait in each of the personality disorders he has. But a partner might have several disorders that include both personality disorders *and* other mental health disorders, each which generates the symptom of impulsivity. If a partner has two or three of the disorders that have impulse control problems associated with them, there is significant risk in the relationship, resulting from their high level of impulsivity. Overlapping disorders with similar symptoms might look like this:

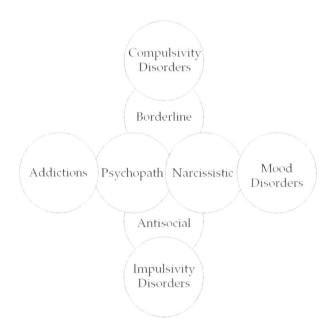

Figure 2.2
Personality Disorders Overlapping
with Mental Health Disorders © *The Institute* **2010**

This diagram shows that there are several disorders, not merely one single source, from which a symptom like impulsivity, for instance, may be generated. Any of the personality or additional mental health disorders can generate this symptom, and to some degree, they are all contributing to it, which makes impulsivity in a relationship highly likely.

How one thinks, feels, relates, and behaves exists in personality disorders but also in other mental health problems.

- Similar symptoms, such as shallow intimacy, exist in personality disorders, but also in issues such as addiction.
- Self-direction symptoms exist in issues such as bipolar disorder, but also in personality disorders.
- A lack of conscience, empathy, and remorse may exist while a person is actively involved in addiction, but it also manifests in Cluster B personality disorders/psychopathy.

Similarly, these intensified symptoms also affect how they are experienced by others in the relationship with a pathological partner.

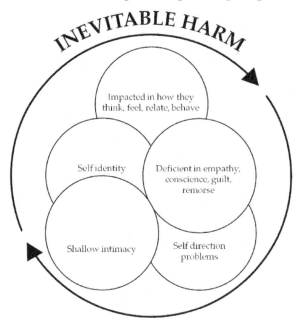

Figure 2.3
Overlap of Symptoms © *The Institute* **2010**

Survivor Note:

It's important to understand that there are many ways that personality disorders are enhanced and intensified by additional overlapping disorders and symptoms, making personality disorders some of the most complicated and relationally risky disorders in the DSM5.

Survivor Work Page Question:

Which overlaps do you potentially see in your pathological partner's disorders?

My partner has overlaps with _____

*W*hy It's Important to Understand *Just* Traits

Some disordered partners are diagnosed with, or implied to have, psychopathic, antisocial, narcissistic, or borderline *traits*, sometimes called *features* as opposed to the full-blown diagnosis of a Cluster B personality/psychopathy disorder. It's important to understand what narcissistic traits are, for instance, or how they differ from a full diagnosis and why this difference is important.

A person who only exhibits 'traits' has fallen just slightly short of meeting enough symptoms to warrant a full-blown diagnosis of that personality disorder. For instance, ASPD must have six symptoms from the DSM5 checklist to warrant a diagnosis of Antisocial Personality Disorder. If the person has only four symptoms, he/she would be said to have 'traits' of the disorder—meaning that some of the symptoms are indeed present, but the number falls just short of the amount needed to fully diagnose them with the disorder.

Many survivors misunderstand the importance of the traits criteria and may assume that fewer symptoms or traits equal probable safety. They believe that if their partner doesn't have enough checkmarks on the psychopathy checklist or the DSM5 lists for ASPD, NPD, or BPD for an official diagnosis, he is not dangerous and, therefore, the relationship is not risky since he wasn't diagnosed with the full-blown disorder.

It only takes a few traits or features of pathology, however, for most survivor partners to be able to eventually experience the negative impact of psychopathy or pathology on their relationship. Traits, or *deficits*, as the DSM defines them—in the core areas of personality such as self-identity, self-direction, empathy, and intimacy—are surely going to negatively impact the relationship, whether they exist in a full-blown diagnosis or fall short of one. For instance, Antisocial Personality Disorder requires six of the following:

1. Manipulativeness, use of seduction, charm, and subterfuge
2. Lack of concern for feelings of others; lack of guilt or remorse, sadism
3. Dishonesty, misrepresentation of themselves
4. Anger, sensitivity to slights, insulting, vengeful
5. Risk taking, doesn't regard consequences, avoids boredom through risky activities
6. Impulsivity, not considering outcomes, acting on the spur of the moment to immediately satisfy gratifications
7. Irresponsibility with commitments, agreements, promises

Assume a person has symptoms 1 through 5. He would not be diagnosed as having Antisocial Personality Disorder because he does not have six symptoms, but he might be diagnosed as having 'antisocial features' (or traits). Manipulativeness, lack of empathy, dishonesty, anger, and risk taking are all parts of the symptoms that *did* meet the criteria and can be expected to be part of the relationship dynamics. His lack of having a full-blown diagnosis of ASPD does not mean he doesn't have the other five relationship-destroying symptoms. Pathology does not have to come with a full and definitive diagnosis for survivors to be seriously harmed by its impact. Therefore, we believe that traits matter and need to be considered seriously when understanding what causes inevitable harm.

Survivor Note:

Having traits can be just as negatively impactful and can still qualify a relationship to be viewed as a Pathological Love Relationship.

$\mathcal{T}$he Low-Conscience Spectrum

As seen by the symptoms discussed in Chapter One in the list of Personality Functioning and the list for Borderline personality, Narcissism, Antisocial personality, and Psychopathy, each of the Cluster B disorders and Psychopathy carries with it a likelihood of harming those who are in relationship with people possessing these disorders because the disorders themselves are so profound and extreme. Regardless of which disorder is present, there are implications to consider:

- Each of these disorders manifests distortions and deficits related to how the person thinks, feels, relates, and behaves.
- The person possessing one (or more) of these disorders is crippled by self-identity issues.
- Each of these disorders prohibits the disordered person from adjusting their self-directional compass to exhibit consistent positive behaviors in relationships.
- Each of these disorders prohibits or inhibits empathy, conscience, guilt, and/or remorse.
- Each of these disorders allows for only the shallowest ability to express intimacy.
- Each of these disorders is branded with the eventuality of inevitable harm being caused in the relationship.

The consistent aftermath symptoms addressed in the rest of this book are universal among survivors who were in a relationship with a person with a Cluster B disorder and/or Psychopathy.

It is a little wordy to talk, for example, about an *Overlapping-Borderline-Narcissist-Antisocial-Psychopath*. To the survivor and her recovery needs, terminology doesn't matter since each disorder in varying combinations does the same thing to everyone. While it is important for a survivor to understand what a personality disorder is, what it does, and to what degree a partner might possibly be affected, this phraseology needs to be boiled down to a manageable phrase so that the following chapters can be understood without too much difficulty.

If, as therapists, we had to choose only one symptom of this group of disorders that exemplified what makes them so dangerous, dismantling, devious, and diminishing, the symptom we would pick is *low (or no) conscience*.

Why this symptom? A conscience is a stamp of our humanity. It is what steers insight, intimacy, and behavior. Conscience impacts guilt, remorse, empathy—all the important factors of a relationship. If a person does not have sufficient conscience, someone is going to get hurt—and it's not likely to be the pathological partner.

All the Cluster B/psychopathy disorders heavily disrupt the areas related to conscience: remorse, guilt, and empathy. Therefore, we have lumped together the disorders and created an umbrella term that expresses the most dangerous trait of all—Low Conscience. This is called The Spectrum of Low-Conscienced Disorders.

Psychopathy
Sociopathy
Antisocial Personality Disorder
Narcissistic Personality Disorder
Borderline/Borderpath Personality Disorder
Combinations of these

Figure 2.4

Low-Conscienced Spectrum Umbrella © *The Institute* **2006**

Viewed in this way, whatever terminology is used to describe the cluster of symptoms possessed by the pathological partner, the symptoms fall within the spectrum of one or more of the disorders in which the affected person exhibits low conscience; this is another way of predicting 'inevitable harm.'

While these disorders each have their own unique aspects (and researchers enjoy discussing their differences), what we have found is that most victims don't find the differences that notable in their own aftermath experiences. Harm is harm; PTSD is PTSD. Cognitive dissonance, intrusive thoughts, financial ruin, flashbacks, obsessions—it all feels mind-numbing when the survivor is going through it. To split hairs over whether the partner is a particular type or mixture of low-conscience disorder doesn't matter much to a survivor.

Any of the disorders of the Low-Conscience Spectrum (and combinations of the disorders) fall clearly in the category of relationships of inevitable harm. However, we chose to use the term *psychopath* in the title of the book because it is the terminology most associated with extreme harm. Our society is still in flux, struggling with the concepts, descriptions, and verbiage associated with this group of disorders. Creating an inclusive language of all the disorders of inevitable harm under one umbrella allows us to discuss the same group of disorders of the Dark Triad and their inevitable and harmful outcomes.

We have included Borderline Personality Disorder in the list of Low-Conscience disorders because it is listed in the DSM5 as part of the Cluster B Disorders (and the disorder is often notably damaging to relationships). The Dark Triad, however, refers to the higher end of the Low-Conscience Spectrum: narcissism, antisocial personality, and psychopathy.

$\mathcal{D}$iagnosis or Reasonable Assumption

The first two chapters provided detailed information about personality disorders and their symptoms. The information regarding the DSM5 in this chapter is designed to help mental health professionals understand these disorders—the key words here being *mental health professionals*. While the information can help survivors to educate themselves about whether there are symptoms consistent with pathology that should be explored further with a mental health professional, the pathological partner must be assessed by a mental health professional to be accurately diagnosed. This would involve a verbal clinical interview and may include additional psychological testing. Many pathological partners do not stay in treatment long enough to receive an adequate diagnosis, or they may refuse testing altogether. But just because your partner hasn't been diagnosed doesn't mean he does not have a personality disorder.

The Institute only works with survivors of pathological relationships; we do not meet the pathological partner. To help survivors guard against further relational and potentially lethal harm, we must work with the survivor to achieve a level of acceptance of a possible diagnosis of a Cluster B/psychopathy disorder if it's applicable. Without the ability to interview or test the potentially pathological partner, we utilize the DSM5 symptom checklists and allow the survivor to provide historical information about the partner's symptoms and behavior. While we cannot definitively arrive at a diagnosis for the partner, we can make some reasonable assumptions about possible pathology that can be shared with the survivor. At the very least, the DSM5 and psychopathy checklist educates partners about what pathology might look like in others. At most, we may have accurately captured the potential of a disorder that can be further explored by other professionals. Therefore, we approach the outcomes of a symptom list compiled by the survivor as 'reasonable assumptions' for pathology consideration.

*J*ust How Likely Are You to Have a Pathological Partner?

Pathology, in its many forms and disorders, is not rare. One out of five people has a personality disorder and one in a hundred has a form of psychopathy. If you are reading this book, it is likely you or someone you know has been harmed by a psychopath or a Cluster B disordered partner. Pathology not only negatively affects intimate personal relation-ships, it harms other relationships such as those with friends, bosses, em-ployees, family members, or other professionals in the disordered per-son's life. The fact is, we all have pathological people in our lives. And for most people, the pathology isn't spotted until the harm has been done.

According to psychopathy researchers and *The Institute*'s own experi-ence of working with the victims of psychopaths, the psychopaths who never get caught are a far larger population than what's usually been estimated. Those who do not cross the line of overtly breaking the law, or who are smart enough to avoid arrest and detection, fly under the radar of identification. They simply don't come physically identified like Charles Manson, with a swastika tattooed between their eyes. Psycho-paths are such excellent imposters that they can live their entire lives behind what Hervey Cleckley called the "Mask of Sanity"—looking nor-mal *enough* never to be detected. A psychopath is likely to dupe nearly everyone. Only those who, over time, have negative experiences with the psychopath end up meeting the true 'man behind the mask.' The rest of society is likely to believe they have never met a psychopath, when in fact they probably have and didn't know it because psychopaths are hard to detect and recognize.

How many psychopaths and variations of psychopathy are out there? Those who aren't in prison are largely overlooked and go uncounted because they go unrecognized. They are roaming freely in your city, sitting next to you in class, working at your company, and may be dating your sister. According to some experts, the numbers could be as high as three to four percent of the population. This means that possibly eight million individuals (six million men and two million women) in the United States are psychopathic—possessing a disorder or group of traits serious enough to cause damage to others.

Beyond the potential eight million, even more people demonstrate some forms of low conscience. Since therapists usually restrict this diagnosis to those with criminal behavior, many clinicians may miss diagnosing a full-blown psychopath hiding behind a well-constructed and non-criminal "Mask of Sanity." At most, the therapist who falls under the spell of the mask will only see the psychopath as 'a little selfish' or 'self-focused.' Without a traceable criminal history, the psychopathic partner is likely to fly under an assessor's radar.

These numbers, however, do not account for the *other* disorders associated with low conscience and inevitable harm in relationships. What about Borderline, Narcissism, and Antisocial Personality Disorders? How many of them are out there ruining relationships?

It's estimated that BPD, NPD, ASPD, and Psychopathy together could total up to 45.6 million people in the United States alone.

Here are the U.S. statistics:

Table 2.1
Approximate Number of People in the United States
with Personality Disorders

Personality Disorder	% of Population*	Millions of People*
Borderline	5.9%[1]	19
Narcissistic	6.2%[2]	20
Antisocial	1%[3]	3.3
Psychopathy	1% (low end)[4]	3.3 (low end) or 6 (high end)

* Approximate

Then the math gets complicated because, as we mentioned, some people have more than one of these disorders. More importantly, how many victims are impacted by this much pathology in our country?

If all the ASPDs, the NPDs, the BPDs, and Psychopaths are grouped together and *assigned* as few as five people harmed by each pathological person -

===

60-100 million people in the United States alone will be negatively affected by the disorders of low conscience. © *The Institute* 2012

===

This number doesn't include the number of children negatively influenced by pathological parents, or even the chronic exposure to other pathological adults. This leaves a huge portion of the population who may require help healing from exposure to someone else's pathology. Remember: one in five people has a personality disorder. One in a hundred has a form of psychopathy. This preponderance of relationship-destroying disorders is evidence of the need for public pathology education—and more help for victims.

A lack of properly-trained clinical professionals is by far the biggest impediment to survivors' recovery. With millions of low-conscienced individuals churning out victims by the multi-millions, it's time this country does something about public pathology education. This book, at the least, can begin the process of understanding what pathology is and what it does in relationships.

Now that you understand more about personality disorders, and you can reasonably assess whether your partner may have a group of these disorders, let's answer the burning question we know you've been wanting to ask: How did he get this disorder and what can we do about it?

Chapter Two Endnotes

1   Grant, B. F., Chou, S. P., Goldstein, R. B., Huang, B., Stinson, F. S., Saha, T. D., ... Ruan, W. J. (2008). Prevalence, correlates, disability, and comorbidity of DSM-IV borderline personality disorder: results from the *Wave 2 National Epidemiologic Survey on Alcohol and Related Conditions. The Journal of Clinical Psychiatry, 69*(4), 533–45. https://doi.org/10.4088/JCP.v69n0404

2   Stinson, F. S., Dawson, D. A., Goldstein, R. B., Chou, S. P., Huang, B., Smith, S. M., Grant, B. F. (2008). Prevalence, correlates, disability, and comorbidity of DSM-IV narcissistic personality disorder: results from the *Wave 2 National Epidemiologic Survey on Alcohol and Related Conditions. The Journal of Clinical Psychiatry, 69*(7), 1033–45. https://doi.org/10.4088/JCP.v69n0701

3   Lenzenweger, M., Lane, M., Loranger, A., & Kessler, R. (2007). *DSM-IV Personality Disorders in the National Comorbidity Survey Replication. Biological Psychiatry, 62*(6), 553–564. https://www.ncbi.nlm.nih.gov/pmc/articles/PMC2044500/

4   Hare, R. D. (1999). *Without Conscience: The Disturbing World of Psychopaths Among Us.* Guilford Press.

Chapter Three

What Causes Pathology?
Puzzle Piece #1™

Survivor Quick Review

People with Cluster B disorders and/or Psychopaths have overlaps that intensify their disorders.

- The pathological partner's disorders could overlap with the disorders within Cluster B and/or Psychopathy.
- Their personality disorders could overlap with other mental health disorders.
- Their personality and mental health disorders could overlap with shared symptoms within the personality and mental health disorders.
- Overlaps that cause intensification create relationships of inevitable harm.

Now that we have identified what constitutes a personality disorder, the additional elements of Puzzle Piece #1™ will help us focus on the creation of these disorders and how they came to be.

What Happened?

Once a survivor understands the depth of pathology implied in the Low-Conscience Spectrum, she compassionately and understandably wants to know what it was that created this much dysfunction. Sometimes that compassion can come from believing that, if she can understand the causes of pathology, there might be a *cure* that will make Mike the Monster turn into Nick the Normal. In this chapter, we'll discuss why that isn't likely to happen. First, however, it's important once again to define some terms. There's just as much controversy over what to *call* pathology as what *caused* pathology. It would be much easier if there were just one clear cut answer for how a partner develops low conscience, a bundle of impulsivity, and relational malfunction, but this isn't the case.

As described earlier, what makes pathology so destructive is the layers of disorders at play—personality layers, mental health layers, addiction layers, impulsivity layers, etc. Each one of those layers of disorders have its own causes. For instance, the cause of a mood disorder (which could be part of a pathological person's whole package of disorders) is not the same as the cause of the personality disorder he may also have. Mental health and personality disorders are different disorders, so there isn't a *single* reason for a complex syndrome of behaviors comprised of several disorders.

Depending on the book you read, the counselor you talk to, or the survivor website you haunt, you will find several perceived reasons for the development of personality disorders. We'll look at a few of these and then discuss what we at *The Institute* have come to believe. While it is beyond the scope of this book to identify what causes the various types of mental health disorders that create the layers in large-package syndromes like this, we will specifically discuss the causes of personality disorders which create much of the problems in Pathological Love Relationships.

In the Beginning

Most people have heard the 'nature versus nurture' debate regarding personality disorders. Simply put, this theory holds that one of the following is true to explain a personality disorder:

The person was born that way (Nature).
The person was *not* born that way, but their environment made them that way (Nurture).
The person was born that way AND their environment made it worse (Nature *and* Nurture).

The problem with these theories is that people believe that one choses *either* the nature theory *or* the nurture theory as possible reasons for the development of personality disorders and don't recognize that *both* theories are often attributable.

Psychology is an evolutionary science; that is, what we have come to

70

know is always changing. This is especially true in the last few decades. With the advancements in technology, neuroscience, research, and testing, the field of psychology has allowed us to broaden our understanding of the mind, various disorders, and how disorders are created. All these advancements enhance what the field has come to believe about how and why certain disorders are created.

Research in different areas has begun to shed light on the complex tapestry of our individualistic mental health, such as what happens when we are young with personalities that are just developing; how mood and other mental health problems can affect the mind; how the neurology of the brain impacts the mind's functionality; and how psychology and neurology are intricately and inextricably connected.

Before psychology had all the technology and advancements in neuroscience that we have now, the field had older theories that focused primarily on early childhood development. Every symptom seemed to stem from a sort of Freudian analogy of early childhood disasters related to bad parenting, interrupted bonding, abuse, or neglect. While childhood disasters *are* notably at the core of many adult psychological problems and can be one of the causes in personality and other disorders, they are not the *only* cause in personality disorders. In fact, there are likely even more powerful influences in the development of personality disorders than just the theory that personality disorders are made, not born, or vice-versa.

So, while we are going to talk about the Nature versus Nurture debate, let's start with what we already know about the effect of our life experiences and influencers (the *nurture* portion of the debate) on personality development.

*T*he Nurture Debate

In the Nurture Theory, what is important to our development are our experiences and life events. Let's review some of the factors that contribute to the case to be made for the theory that we are a product of how we were nurtured through experience and interpersonal relationships.

Unatached/Unbonded Soul Neglect

The same group of sociologists that believed, as discussed in an earlier chapter, that environment creates *sociopaths* are also the same group that understandably believes in the immense power of the social and family environment. Sociologists believe that a person's social and family environment greatly influences who they become.[1] In fact, so great is this influence, especially early on when the child is young and his/her personality structure is still developing, that a devastating environment can permanently harm the child, thus causing personality disorders.

Most of us are familiar with the documentaries about the method in which countries like China and Russia have handled the problem of orphaned babies. The dismal footage of hundreds of identical cribs lined up end to end, filling large institutionalized rooms with nurses walking the rows putting a bottle in each crib without holding the babies, made us instinctively aware that something bad was likely to happen to babies who were fed but never held. Because of the universal belief that this kind of neglectful environment affected a child's developing personality—and soul—an outpouring of people all over the world scrambled to adopt and save these babies from unidentified but perceived impending disorders.

The social and family environment of these babies was marked by a lack of human bonding, the absence of touch, and emotional neglect. For some children, this resulted in severe problems later in their development. These unattached and unbonded children, as the syndrome is termed, highlighted the reality that what happens, or doesn't happen, in a child's life can leave an indelible scar upon a personality that leaves permanent ramifications.

Abuse/Neglect/Social Environment

In addition to soul neglect, physical, emotional and or sexual trauma also damages a child's developing psyche.[2] One can readily see just how applicable these destructive abusive environments are in producing the low-conscience spectrum of disorders. In fact, so strong is the influence of social environment on a child that sociologists refer to a person with no conscience as a *sociopath* as opposed to a *psychopath* because they believe they have been socially created within their abusive families, as opposed to being created by the natural causes (i.e. biology and genetics) related to psychopathy.

We are decades into the study of the effects of abuse and trauma on children to know that these experiences can, and often do, create severe emotional, physical, sexual, and spiritual developmental crises that impact a child's life, including the development of personality disorders. In fact, Borderline Personality Disorder has strong ties to abuse as its core cause in nurture theory.

Learned Conditioning and Pathological Parenting

The theory that personality is the product of one's external environment is also highly predicated on the concept of 'learned conditioning.' Children who grew up experiencing the admonition of pathological parents are more likely to be, at the very least, emotionally and psychologically vulnerable by these parenting tactics.[3] The child's self-image and world view are sculpted by the input that also forms their concepts of others. A parent with narcissism or psychopathy has distorted views of themselves, others, and the world. Children can come to see the world through their pathological parents' eyes and internalize those pathological views, which become adult belief systems and even behaviors.

Pathological parenting and learned conditioning are most likely combinations of abuse, neglect, and, to some level, nonauthentic attachment and bonding and can produce significant damage to a child. Nonauthentic bonding is the absence of deep connection, and, instead, the parent sees the child as an object that should meet the parent's needs. Nonpathological parents fight hard in court for custody of their child(ren) to limit the child's exposure to the other parent's severe pathology.

===

Survivor Note:

Learned conditioning is optimal when parents are healthy and their impact on a child is positive. When the parent is pathological, learned conditioning is devastating to a child's development.

===

A lack of bonding or attachment, abuse, and negative learned conditioning are all examples of what toxic environments do to the developing personalities of children.[4] Several studies have demonstrated that traumatic life events, such as abuse and parental psychopathy, are risk factors for developing Borderline Personality Disorder. It's imperative that a child's early development be safeguarded because harm and neglect have lasting impact. The personality structure is developed only once and the damage that is done creates a domino effect well into adulthood. (Inner child work is not a repair therapy for a damaged personality system.)

Developmental Stages

Erik Erikson, a developmental psychologist who subscribed to the theory that personality is affected by outside influences, sculpted a view about personality development through the stages of life and suggested that 'developmental tasks' must occur for a personality to form without problems and deficits, such as personality disorders. He believed that each developmental task built on the preceding task to form a normal and healthy personality structure. Things that impacted one developmental task would have a trickle-down effect, creating problems that eventually severely impacted other developmental tasks in the chain.[5]

For instance, the first developmental task a baby completes is bonding. If the baby does not bond successfully, the next developmental step is likely to be adversely affected because of the first uncompleted process. In this theory, then, Cluster B disorders are related to issues of attachment or bonding as well as other disruptions in early development.

Erikson's theory on the necessary stages of development takes us from the cradle to the grave, stacking successfully completed developmental tasks on top of each other to create the tower of a healthily constructed personality. Various symptoms in personality disorders are often viewed through the lens of what *did not* happen during this critical period of personality development. These malformations within personality disorders create what is often referred to as 'holes in the soul.[6] '

These theoretical holes and the deficits they represent become evident when adults have the emotional mindsets and skill sets of teenagers. It is why personality disordered people are not often believed to be older than about fourteen years of age emotionally.

Imbued in the under-developed personality are

- A lack of healthy bonding
- Skewed abandonment issues
- High thrill-seeking needs
- Impoverished thinking related to right and wrong, reflecting faulty moral decision making
- High impulsivity and the inability to learn from consequences

These traits sound more like those of a teenager than a normal adult. These uncompleted developmental tasks manifest themselves in demonstrations of irresponsibility, boredom, and thrill seeking which plague the low-conscienced adult's life. Their adult reflections mirror the *stuck* aspects of their teen mentality. For instance -

- Their chronic infidelity points to their inability to develop normal attachments and bonding.
- For some personality disorders, the intense abandonment and the need to keep constant tabs on their mate point back to a lack of development in early childhood.
- Risk taking in many areas of life reflects their teen-like thrill seeking and impulsivity, and their lack of learning from punishment shows impulsivity and insight problems.
- Their behaviors of stealing, lying, and conning point to their undeveloped moral decision-making ability.[7]

In this aspect of the nurture debate, these uncompleted developmental tasks do not merely create emotional holes but social and interpersonal skill deficits in the child. Sadly, the world does not stop because a child is not getting his psychological or physical needs met. Life continues, and so must the child. His emotional growth adapts around his deficits, much like a tree grows around an obstacle in its path. The tree adapts by creating bulging and knobby protrusions that jut out in odd places and, despite whatever might be in its way, the tree continues to grow and develop. Today it is dwarfed here, arthritic there, extended in this section, and protruding in that section. It survives to tell a story of its own mangled journey.

The absence of what the child needed emotionally, psychologically and physically may form a deficit. Over the long term, these deficits create disorders, such as personality disorders and other forms of pathology.

The Low-Conscience Spectrum of Cluster B Disorders is most often viewed singularly from this theory.

*T*he Nature Debate

If the nurture debate doesn't ring true for you, perhaps you will find answers that hit the mark in the nature debate.

Before current advances in research allowed for discoveries about the genetic and neurological aspects of personality disorders, it was hard to determine, given the lack of scientific means, just what contributed to the disorders of low conscience and the behaviors that went with it. The consensus was that people were simply *born that way.*

The implied understanding of a disorder was that it was an *innate* aspect of the personality. The word *innate* gives us a clue about the implied permanence of the disorder - *innate* is defined as 'existing in one from birth; inherent in the essential character of something' and a 'relatively unmodifiable behavior pattern.' Today we tend to use the phrase *hard-wired*, since we now often refer to our minds in computer-related terms.

Genetics — More Nature Debate

The debate that people are born with a predisposition for pathology is related to the issue of genetics. Genetics is the study of heredity — a biological process where a parent can pass on genes through DNA to their children. Part of this debate is incomplete without looking at what role genetics plays in personality disorders and psychopathy.

It is important to understand the role genetics plays because, until we had a better understanding of it, behavior, even if affected by personality disorders, was thought to be mostly willful. Or, those who subscribed to the idea that personality is affected by external nurturing forces, believed people behaved in negative ways because they were abused, and their behavior was a reaction to trauma. The study of biology will introduce us to another way of viewing what is driving pathology. But first, let's pose a question.

Can biology impact psychology?

So far, we've looked at the influence of parenting on children when one or more of the parents has a pathological disorder. This influence is mostly seen in how children of pathological parents come to see their world, themselves, and others. But pathological parents affect *more* than just a child's world view and a shared dysfunctional environment. They pass on DNA. Pathology, in a very real sense, often starts with biology.

Survivor Note:

This is important to understand for people in relationships with a partner who has one or more of the Cluster B/psychopathy disorders because waiting for therapy to change someone's DNA is like waiting for nature to change the color of their eyes.

In many cases regarding people with Cluster B Disorders, genetics *is* at play—just how much, and to what extent, is problematic to pinpoint. But it is important to note that all Cluster B and Psychopathy disorders show some genetic factors as one of the reasons for the causes of the disorder. In fact, research indicates that Cluster B disorders have genetic as well as environmental (nurture) reasons.[8]

This suggests that the reason for the personality-related pathology comes from both biology and external influences; both genetics and pathological parenting/abuse/neglect are likely factors. But it also explains why decades of therapy that was focused on the issues resulting from neglect, abuse, and learned conditioning did not remediate the disorders. Decades of recent therapy approaches, and medications, have been utilized with disorders of the Low Conscienced but still have not produced any consistent and permanent positive changes in the behavior or emotions of affected people. In other words, therapy and/or medication did not cure the disorder.

==

Survivor Note:

If Cluster B/psychopathy disorders were largely only the result of issues of abuse and neglect, therapy would remediate the behavioral, cognitive, and emotional problems inherent in these disorders. But after decades, therapies are still being developed today for these disorders, trying to address the same problems other therapies have tried and failed to cure.

That's because therapy does not remediate genetics.

==

Inheriting a Personality Disorder

The measurement of the likelihood of the traits of personality disorders being passed on in DNA is called *heritability* and is taken from the concept of inheriting traits as one would for other medical disorders that are often passed on.

These heritability factors are as high as[9]

- 25.1% for Narcissistic Personality Disorder
- 37.1% for Borderline Personality Disorder
- 40.9% for Antisocial Personality Disorder

In fact, studies on personality disorders have shown that genetic components as well as personality disorders run in families, and that most personality disorders appear to result from genetic factors and temperament traits related to 'poor behavioral/impulse control' and 'poor emotional control.[10]'

We know that these temperament traits are *also* part of the Cluster B/psychopathy temperament in general and are likely to apply to Narcissistic Personality Disorder (NPD), Antisocial Personality Disorder (ASPD), and Psychopathy as well. More importantly, 'unstable interpersonal relationships' and 'interpersonal hypersensitivity' (emotional control) that the DSM noted as deficits, were also cited as not just the result of pathological parenting or even abuse, but, *instead* a genetic trait.[11] Embedded in the crazy-making dynamics of the PLR relationship can be a genetic trait that is producing the behaviors and emotions to which the survivor is exposed.

Survivor Note:

For decades the mental health field has been looking at relationship instability as an issue in Cluster B disorders that are connected to issues in early childhood, but the field has missed the connection of **relationship instability as a genetic trait.**

Relationship instability, often seen in voyeuristic and exploitative reality daytime television programs when they shout, 'he's not the baby daddy,' might not therefore be merely learned conditioning within families, but also may be as inherent in the family as the color of their eyes.

Before we think this complex problem is all nature issues, though, Joel Reid, MD cautions that all personality disorders cannot be reduced to a neuro biological cause. This reminds us that both nature *and* nurture, in combination, can have strong effects on personality development.

Neuroscience as Part of the Nature Debate

Today, Magnetic Resonance Imaging (MRI), Functional Magnetic Resonance Imaging (fMRI), and Positron Emission Tomography (PET) scans help illustrate that personality disorders are, in part, based in biology.

Neuroscience views the *mind* as a psychological structure for the emotions, separate from the *brain* as an organ. This separation allows us to look at the brain to see what can go horribly wrong and result in the Low-Conscience Spectrum disorders.

Where psychology has spent a century focused on the very nurture-oriented causes of pathology, we have missed the very real potential of brain problems as a contributing factor in the existence of these disorders.

Survivor Note:

The brain has all the same proclivities of being born with challenges, abnormalities, and differences as any other part of the body. But if a disorder is not overt, or if it is well compensated for by I.Q. or manipulation, it may be missed. Biology does, in fact, impact psychology.

Brain imaging of various disorders in people with Low-Conscience Spectrum disorders note similar problems with -

- Brain Formation
- Brain Activity
- Brain Circuitry
- Brain Chemistry

Brain research articles give credence to the theories that Cluster B and psychopathy disorders are triggered in part by brain problems. Note the following article titles which all show the impact of these biologically based problems across the Cluster B/psychopathy spectrum:

- Neural foundation to moral reasoning and antisocial behavior[12]
- Into the Mind of a Killer: Brain imaging studies starting to venture into the research of criminal psychopathy[13]
- Structural Brain Abnormalities in Borderline Personality Disorder[14]
- A Cognitive Neuroscience Perspective on Psychopathy[15]

Abnormalities in brain formation, activity, circuitry, and chemistry can create a brain that results in a person who causes inevitable harm to those in a relationship with him, and solidifies the existence of the disorder on a neurological and biological level.

Brain or Mind?

Within the sciences of medicine and psychology, the idea of 'the head' has been sharply divided into the study of the brain versus that of the mind. Neurology looked at the brain as an organ while psychology looked at the mind as a mechanism for the mind's processes. Until the popularity in neuroscience and its integrative approach to brain *and* mind, we lived in a limbo of 'either/or' when talking about what happened inside the head.

Neuroscience helped create a bridge for the rest of us to understand how the brain impacted the mind. The brain, as an organ, does not just regulate our breathing and heart functions. It also regulates our emotions, behavioral impulses, and moral compass, and increases or decreases our ability to be happy and successful in relationships through the necessary emotions of empathy, compassion, and conscience that are generated within it. It impacts core facets of how well, or how poorly, our personality functions relating to our behavior and emotions. It weaves together the aspects of the nurture vs. nature dichotomy, proving on yet another level how the brain, as an organ, is part of how experiences, such as abuse and neglect, or biological aspects, such as genetics, impact the development of our personalities.

In many brain imaging studies, the brain itself is shown to be the culprit in some of the symptoms and behaviors of personality disorders and psychopathy. Abuse and neglect, and its disruption to the brain from emotional, physical, and sexual trauma, can be traced to changes in neuropathways and brain chemistry. This shows that the lack of positive and nurturing experiences leads to neurological changes in the brain that change a person's behaviors and eventually the quality of their relationships.

It also reinforces the theory that some people are indeed born that way. Some of the unusual brain issues including brain size, brain volume, brain chemistry, and brain circuitry are different in personality disorders and psychopathy than those of nonpathological people. Sometimes the pathology is related to genetic and inherited factors, such as those exhibited in families where personality disorders are prevalent and passed down as genetic factors in the brain formation.[16] But in other instances, families without personality disorders also end up with a family member with all the brain abnormalities seen in the brains of people with personality disorders and psychopathy.

Perhaps shocking to the rest of us who are not neuroscientists is that *brain abnormalities could actually generate the symptoms and behaviors that constitute a personality disorder as listed in the DSM.*

The behaviors in these cases are not merely willful behaviors, or only a result of neglect and abuse, or even learned conditioning. They are combinations of biology *and* experience that impair parts of the brain that relate to the most problematic aspects of personality disorder as listed in the DSM5—such as lack of empathy, little or no conscience, impulsive behavior, and the lack of self-functioning.

These behavioral and emotional aspects found in the relational dynamics of Pathological Love Relationships can be traced back not just to traumatic neglectful childhoods of the pathological partner but to identifiable neurological parts of the brain that have formed incorrectly.

Survivor Note:

The developmental 'holes in the soul' that were discussed by theorists decades ago, and which were supposed to be only emotional developmental problems, were also seen in the physical brain as abnormalities that contributed to a person's lack of emotional development.[17]

It will be useful, then, to look at what portions of the brain direct the emotions and behaviors to see what goes wrong in the brains of personality disordered and psychopathic individuals. For ease of understanding, we will look at the psychopathic brain and its derailed functioning, although similar neurological abnormalities have been found in Cluster B disorders as well. With this better understanding, we'll then be able to focus on chapters that will be less scientific and more relational relating to Pathological (and Toxic) Love Relationships.

$\mathcal{N}$euroscience for the Rest of Us

Table 3.1 below helps us understand the function of the brain related to the emotions and behaviors of personality disordered/psychopathic persons. It lists different areas of the brain with both their normal and affected functions as they pertain to emotions and behavior.

(Survivors who are not interested in the brain problems of Cluster B/ psychopaths can drop down to the information after the chart and explanations of the brain regions and continue reading from there.)

In Table 3.1, the Brain of Cluster B and Psychopathy column shows the exhibited symptoms of dysfunction for anticipating the likely impact they would have on relationships. This will also be discussed in more detail when we move into the chapters on relationship dynamics. For now, the goal is to understand that brain regions and their neurological problems also explain why people with Low-Conscience Spectrum disorders do not engage in positive and consistent change, as is hoped for in psychological treatment and in relationships.

Table 3.1
Normal Brain vs. Brain of Cluster B and Psychopathy
© *The Institute* 2010

Area	Normal Brain	Brain of Cluster B and Psychopathy	Research Support
Limbic Region			
Anterior Cingulate	• Responsible for cognitive evaluation/processing of mood and affective regulation. • Regulates mood and pain. • Responsible for prediction (and avoidance) of negative consequences and helps orient the body away from negative stimuli.	• Inappropriate emotional responses. • Lack of fear. • Poor learning from negative consequences.	(Johnson, Hurley, Benkelfat, Herperd, & Taber, 2003) (Kiehl, 2006)
Amygdala	• Responsible for processing emotions and fear learning. • Coordinates physiological responses based on cognitive information (fight or flight).	• Reduced response to fearful or aversive stimuli. • Poor fear conditioning. • Poor moral and emotional reasoning.	(Decety, Skelly, & Kiehl, 2013) (Yang, Raine, Narr, Colletti, & Togo, 2009)

Area	Normal Brain	Brain of Cluster B and Psychopathy	Research Support
Hippo-campus	• Storage of long term memory; helps transition memory to more perma-nent storage. • Assists in predicting pun-ishment or consequences and regulating aggression and impulsivity.	• Missed cues that could help predict punishment.	(Raine et al., 2004)
Corpus Callosum			
Corpus Callosum	• Responsible for commu-nication between the right and left hemisphere of the brain. • Assists with processing information and social connectedness.	• Emotional and inter-personal deficits. • Lower reactivity to stress. • Deficits to insight and self-percep-tion.	(Raine et al., 2003) (Pemment, 2012)
Temporal Lobe			
Anterior Temporal Lobe	• Memory storage area. • Emotion. • Left side – language.	• Failure to understand ab-stract language. • Can't tell the difference between emo-tional words & nuetral words.	(Kiehl, 2006) (Fallon, 2006)

Area	Normal Brain	Brain of Cluster B and Psychopathy	Research Support
Frontal Lobe			
Orbitofrontal Cortex (OFC)	• Responsible for communicating with amygdala and assists with learning and response reversal (learning from your behavior).	• Poor ability to learn from poor decisions.	(J. R. Blair, 2003)
Prefrontal Cortex (PFC)	• Responsible for planning, reasoning, and judgment. • Responsible for assessment and control of appropriate social behaviors.	• Poor inhibition related to social behavior.	(R. J. R. Blair, 2008) (Raine & Yang, 2006) (Koenigs, 2012)
Cerebral Cortex			
Insular Cortex	• Plays a role in emotion, interpersonal experiences, perception, and self-awareness.	• Poor response to pain of others. • Lack of empathy.	(Gu, Liu, Guise, Naidich, & Hof, 2010) (Ly et al., 2012) (Decety et al., 2013)

$\mathcal{N}$eurological Deficits and Impact on the Quality of Relationships

The chart explains that deficits in the structure and processing of the brain directly affect how the Dark Triad thinks, feels, relates, and behaves. These disordered processes of thinking, feeling, relating, and behaving have everything to do with the 'dramatic and erratic' and 'severe and dangerous' DSM-given labels of their Cluster B disorder and how these disorders eventually affect everyone around them through their relationships.

The Limbic Region

The Limbic region of the brain, which includes the anterior cingulate and the amygdala, is responsible for emotional language, communication, and the handling of emotional responses.

Deficits in the Anterior Cingulate

Pathological partners with personality disorders and psychopathy have difficulty expressing emotionally appropriate reactions and responses. They are either over-reactive or under-reactive. While highly identifiable in Borderline Personality Disorder, these traits are also related to the other Cluster B/psychopathy disorders. These variations in emotional responses, of being over or under reactive (sometimes to the same situation) can often feel to others like mood disorders. This weakened area of the brain can then cause them to struggle to understand the emotion and meaning behind others language, which is an element necessary for healthy relationships. The pathological person's limited spectrum of emotions (which will be covered later) forces them to learn adaptive mechanisms so that they *appear* to understand emotional language.

The absence of natural and healthy fear, such as fear of punishment either legally, professionally, or within a relationship, results in the person not altering a behavior since they don't fear getting caught. Behaviors, such as infidelity or swindling, then, can continue without this healthy dose of fear present. This is a direct manifestation of the symptom of 'poor response to learning from punishment,' so that when a survivor partner threatens to leave, or the person is threatened with being fired the lesson that most others learn—not to do that again—does not register. The ability to learn from negative consequences means people can learn to say no and stop repeating behavior. But the absence of this ability means the behavior is likely to continue, and with the lack of fear, thrill-seeking adventures are continually sought.

Deficits in the Amygdala

This similar issue related to healthy fear is also present in the amygdala region of the brain. When a deficit occurs, the person exhibits a reduced response to fearful situations and poor fear conditioning. Some are daredevils, loving excitement and risk taking: driving fast, having multiple relationships, or pursuing other adrenaline producing highs. For others, deficits in the amygdala manifest themselves in repetitious behaviors and little to no impulse control, which deteriorates relationships. The normal fear reaction of fight or flight, where the body responds with anxiety, is diminished in people with these brain deficits. Deficits in the amygdala also result in problems related to moral reasoning—the ability to know the difference between right and wrong, which produces destructive and immoral decisions. The person can neither make the right moral choice nor stop the behavior once the decision has been made.

As mentioned in an earlier chapter, the more *overlaps* in behavior that a person possesses, the stronger the resulting symptom will be. This is true in this issue as well. For instance, many of the symptoms in one brain region are echoed again in another area of the brain, thus increasing the strength of the unwanted behavior. There are very few Cluster B/ psychopaths who haven't wrecked their relationships due to an absence of enough healthy fear. This inconsistent *brake* on their behavior is fueled by the deficit of poor moral and emotional reasoning, and when given an opportunity to act unethically or lie or cheat, their lack of fear coupled with moral and emotional reasoning deficits does not give them a reason to **not** act on those desires.

The amygdala's other function is to regulate impulsivity; it's similar to the anterior cingulate in that way. When the amygdala is short-circuited, it can't catch what might have bypassed other impulse regulatory systems, making impulsivity a real and lasting danger.

Scientists agree that although psychopaths do at times experience fear or anxiety (although at much lower levels than normal people), these emotions don't *influence* their behavior. The stoplight of the specific emotion doesn't cause them to pause in their behavior; their foot doesn't even attempt to step on the brakes.

The Hippocampus

The hippocampus aids in the storage of long-term memory and helps to predict the consequences of behavior and possible ensuing punishment. It also regulates aggression and impulsivity.

Deficits in the Hippocampus

This area of the brain, in normally functioning people, helps to regulate aggression and impulsivity, transfer information to memory for future reference, and identify what to be afraid of. This is yet another area of the brain that, in at least two of its functions, is responsible for the lack of applying brakes on behavior. The inability to regulate aggression and impulsivity and the lack of learning what to be fearful of, are internal mechanisms that normally stop other people from violence, verbal aggression, or behaviors of impulsivity like road rage, drug and/or alcohol abuse, gambling, and infidelity. But these mechanisms are minimally operable in the Dark Triad. Without the ability to transfer bad consequences to memory and/or to identify what to fear, even merely the consequences of behavior, there is little platform from which to create a change in behavior. Those with more damage to the hippocampus seem to miss the cues that could help them predict punishment and then respond by changing their behavior.

Studies by Raine (et.al, 2004) note that some psychopaths showed differing *sizes* and *shapes* of the hippocampus that may reflect an abnormality in the neurological-development process which resulted in emotional regulation problems and not enough fear or concern about getting caught.[18] The inability to regulate aggression and impulsivity contributes significantly to the danger, even lethality, of these impulsive-riddled relationships. The nightly news, with its gruesome stories of a person stabbed multiple times, suggests hippocampus problems—when a person's unregulated aggression and impulsivity meet a lack of fear, crimes of exceptional brutality are the result. While domestic violence organizations tend to lump all batterers together as *abusive*, the study of the hippocampus indicates that all abusers do not possess similar disorders and those with hippocampus deficits become famous for all the wrong reasons.

The Corpus Callosum

The corpus callosum facilitates communication between the right and left hemispheres of the brain. This region of the brain is a bundle of nerve fibers that services the two separate hemispheres of the brain. Its purpose is to process information, produce emotional and social connectedness with others, and regulate the behaviors of 'acting out.'

Deficits in the Corpus Callosum

Normally, the left side of the brain processes information analytically and sequentially, and aids in the understanding and use of language. The right side of the brain processes information and aids in the perception of emotional experiences. In a later chapter, we will discuss why people with deficits in the corpus callosum have such a poor use of the language used to express emotions, called emotional language, which affects their partners' own emotional experiences.

In psychopaths, for instance, according to Raine (et al, 2003), the volume in this area of the brain is 22.6% larger and 6.9% longer than other areas, indicating that bigger is not always better.[19] The rate of information transmitted from one hemisphere to the other is abnormally high, which negatively impacts accurate processing of information. Information that is transmitted at high speeds can miss some emotional cues and cause mistakes in assessing situations. This results in responding before thinking. Many psychopaths, and others with this deficit, appear to have no filter — whatever they think comes out before there is a chance to reflect on whether it will be hurtful to others or cause damage in some other way. This deficit also causes inappropriate reactions to emotional situations. Similar disorders in this brain region are seen in Cluster B disorders, but especially in those with Borderline Personality Disorder and Antisocial Personality Disorder.

The increased size of the corpus callosum produces less remorse, fewer emotions, less emotional reactions and less (authentic) social connectedness to others. The aloofness exhibited by a disordered person is related to an inauthentic connectedness to others; this explains why they can quickly end relationships and move on to others at warp speed.

This region of the brain is also responsible for generating insight. Insight helps with empathy—understanding how others feel when harmed—and helps people be motivated to change unwanted behavior.

The Temporal Lobe

This region of the brain is involved in the retention of visual memories, processing sensory input, comprehending language, and the storing of new memories, emotion, and meaning. It is an area fraught with the possibilities of producing negative repercussions in those whose temporal lobes contain deficits. The anterior temporal lobe, which is housed here, stores memory and manages emotion.

Deficits in the Temporal Lobe

Healthy intimacy is highly connected to the retention of visual memories, such as the moment he dropped to one knee to propose, or the sight of you in your lingerie on your wedding night, or the birth of your children. These visual memories develop and strengthen our perceived connection to another person. When visual memories aren't retained, a person will have difficulty making a connection with others; this deficit feeds the pattern of multiple relationships common to those with this deficit. Likewise, new experiences and feelings, which would fill normal memory banks with images of closeness, the emotions felt during those events, and what the person and those events meant, are not comprehended by someone with anterior lobe deficits. When survivor partners wonder "Didn't our honeymoon mean anything to him?" the answer is, "Not really."

As in the language-affected area of the corpus callosum, this is yet another area in which language and meaning is damaged. Later in the book, we will look at the extent of this impact and what it does to a relationship in which communication is necessary to develop true intimacy.

Emotion is negatively affected in the temporal lobe as well as in other areas of the brain, making it a highly problematic area when other areas of the brain are similarly affected. The symptoms of affected emotion can range from too much emotion, to not enough, to rapid fluctuations between the two. Symptoms can also include an overreaction to a situation while, just a short time later, exhibiting no reaction at all to the same situation.

The causes of emotion—*why* people become angry or hurt or have moral resistance to certain issues— is usually not understood by the pathological partner who has a limited ability to comprehend other people's broad range of emotional experiences. Absent from their stunted internal emotions are empathy, shame, guilt, and remorse, to name a few.

The Frontal Lobe—Prefrontal Cortex and Orbitofrontal Cortex

The frontal lobe includes several brain regions; we will focus on the prefrontal cortex and the orbitofrontal cortex.

Prefrontal Cortex

The prefrontal cortex is responsible for the organization of the behaviors related to planning, reasoning, and judgment. It also regulates social behavior with others and is related to what is called *working memory*—maintaining information about others to guide appropriate behavior.

Deficits in the Prefrontal Cortex

Deficits in this area distort the decision-making processes related to planning, reasoning, and judgment, which become fraught with impulsive reactions from infidelity to criminality. Because the prefrontal cortex also interacts with other negatively affected brain regions, problems can be seen in reduced guilt, shame, empathy, and failure to learn from punishment. Highly impacted is the reduced moral decision making and quick responses to temptation without the necessary input from the reasoning and judgment portions of the brain. The overlap of similar reactions can be seen in the other affected area of the frontal lobe—the orbitofrontal cortex.

Orbitofrontal Cortex

This brain region is responsible for organizing behavior, learning from punishment, motivation, empathy, insight, and impulse control.

Deficits in the Orbitofrontal Cortex

Abnormalities in the area that governs organizing behavior is especially evident in psychopaths and people with Cluster B disorders. Their behavior exhibits all the signs of disorganization due to abnormalities in various brain regions related to impulsivity, the result of which means behavior can escalate from zero to bad within seconds. Couple that with difficulty learning from past behaviors, or low to no fear, and the result is behavior that seems to be all over the place.

On the other hand, what does *not* seem to be disorganized in their behavior are the strategic ways in which they manipulate and their covert stealth in executing very deceptive and elaborate schemes. Perhaps the problems in this area only affect their ability to organize *positive* behavior.

As with other regions of the brain, when the ability to learn from punishment is problematic in multiple brain areas, the symptom is intensified. When operating correctly, this necessary brain function applies the brakes to repeated behavior.

The ambush to the brain region responsible for empathy and insight is the kiss of death to a potential relationship. Empathy is the trait that defines us as conscious human beings and separates us from plankton or amoeba. It allows us to share the experience of being human, and to feel and know what others are experiencing, whether that be joy, sadness, or anger. In many ways, it is the marker of true intimacy—the ability to relate to the emotions and experiences of others. Without that, we are cuddling up to a bit of plankton, or petting a one-celled amoeba.

The result of a lack or absence of insight are similar. Without the gift of insight, there is no ability to sustain, or desire to sustain, positive genuine change in behaviors that harm others. Even the success of counseling is predicated on the ability of a person to have insight regarding how their negative behavior affects others. With the addition of empathy, they can understand why that behavior harms someone and, thus, feel that person's pain. They will genuinely desire to not harm others again and are willing and capable of changing and sustaining their new behavior.

The DSM5 uses empathy and intimacy as a measure of the deficits in people with Cluster B disorders (see Chapter One). This indicates that empathy and intimacy are consistently deficient in all the disorders within personality disorders.

===

Survivor Note:

Although they are viewed as deficient personality traits, neuroscience has shown us that these are more than just deficits created in a personality; they are deficits created in the brain that become apparent in the personality.

===

What are Pervasive and Enduring Disorders?

What gives personality disorders the staying power necessary to make them the serious disorders that they are? Personality disorders are described by the DSM5 as 'pervasive,' which is the factor that every survivor should recognize, understand, and then flee from.

In medical terms, a *pervasive cancer* has spread throughout the body and is called *metastasis*. *Pervasive* in mental health language is the synonym for *permanent* or *metastasized*. The definition means 'to spread throughout.' It means that however the disorder got there, whether through genetics or life experience, it has 'spread' throughout the personality structure impacting all areas.

The DSM5 indicates that personality disorders impair personality functioning and are evident in the pathological personality symptoms (see the symptoms checklist from Chapter One) because they are 'pervasive' across a range of personal and social contexts (i.e., in intimate and social relationships) and affect how the pathological partner - [20]

- Perceives and relates to others
- Thinks about and regards others and himself
- Understands what is happening in the relationship dynamics

In someone with a pervasive personality disorder, then, a long-term outcome of responsive change and the sustaining of it, as well as the potential safety of others in the relationship, is limited at best. Hidden in a sentence of the DSM5 is a whole "aha" moment for survivors when they understand exactly what the DSM5 is warning us about when it says the pathological persons are 'unable' to *consistently* modify their personality.

The seriousness of pervasive personality disorders is best understood by comparing them to the other pervasive disorders identified in the DSM5. Other disorders that are called 'pervasive' fall within the Developmental Disorders that we recognize as developmental disability such as Asperger's Syndrome, Autism Spectrum Disorder, or Intellectual Disabilities.

Another way to understand the difference between pervasive impairments is:

- Autism Spectrum/Intellectual Disabilities disorders are de-

fined by a pervasive impairment in the *cognitive* development of a person.

- Low-Conscience Spectrum disorders are defined by a pervasive impairment in the *personality* development of a person.

Both are called 'pervasive' because they are permanent, and, on some
level, affect the person's functionality across several areas (personal, social, occupational). Because of someone's obvious pervasive disorder,
such as a developmental disability, accommodations are made for the
impairment, which is indeed defined as a *disability*. We then readily adjust our level of expectation equal to their level of disorder. In Autism
Spectrum Disorder or Asperger's Syndrome, once the disorder is recognized, accommodations are made because we understand the permanent nature of the impairment. (Yes, autism symptoms have been known
to improve with some treatments, but the person is not considered to no
longer be autistic.)

Personality disorders are *just as* pervasive according to the DSM but
have flown under the radar of detection because they are not as cognitively obvious as in developmental disorders, or genetically noticeable
as in intellectual disabilities. Nonetheless, they are the *only* other pervasive disorders noted in the DSM, which is significant.

===

Survivor Note:

*People are seriously harmed in relationships with covert personality disorders
because they have no way of adjusting their level of expectation to equal the
manifestation of a hidden, yet serious disorder.*

===

No accommodation for the consideration of inevitable harm is made
for high functioning personality disordered people who are corporate
CEOs since the *pervasiveness* of their disorder is well hidden behind their
ability to be highly functioning in occupational situations. It is behind
closed doors in personal relationships where the pervasiveness of their
personality disorder is seen or experienced by others.

Nonetheless, those in a relationship with a person with autism or a
personality disordered partner are in a relationship with someone who
has **both** a permanent pervasive disorder and who also has an enduring
disorder that will exist for their partner's entire lifetime. But it's peo-

ple with personality disordered partners of the Cluster B and Low-Con-science Spectrum who will be most at risk of the dramatic and erratic and potentially damaging effect of the disorder.

The DSM5 issues a warning of sorts in its description of pervasive personality disorders. 'The pattern in personality disorders is maladaptive and relatively inflexible which leads to disabilities in their social, occupational, or other important pursuits, as the individuals are *unable* to modify their thinking or behavior, *even* in the face of evidence that their approach is not working' (emphasis added).

Survivor Note:

*The DSM5 identifies the problem as disabling in some ways; it does not say that people **will not** modify their thinking or behavior. It says they are **unable** to do so. This is the permanence of the disorder.*

The DSM5 also warns that the impairments in their functioning and personality traits are relatively stable. This means that how a disordered person thinks, feels, relates, and behaves stays relatively the same over the course of their lifetime. Whether a personality disorder is established through genetics or life-experience, the pervasiveness and permanence of the disorder is consistent. While neglect, abuse, and pathological learned conditioning **can be** a contributing factor to pathology and personality, these are usually not the **only** contributing factors to pathological personalities, as we have seen in the theory that biology and genetics plays a part in personality development.

Just as personality disorders, psychopathy, other mental health disorders, and symptoms overlap, the overlap also exists between biology (nature) and experience (nurture). There are usually *both* factors at work in the cases of personality disorders and psychopathy. For instance, some psychopaths and other personality-disordered people have been born to loving and completely normal families, and their own childhoods were not filled with trauma. This does not mean that experience and upbringing have no influence on the formation of pathology. It certainly does, but it is more likely part of a complex combination of social, environmental, genetic, *and* neurological causes.

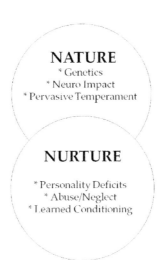

Figure 3.1

Nature/Nurture Overlap © *The Institute* **2015**

Now that you understand what is behind these two theories and what each one represents, it becomes easier to understand how personality disorders are a combination, or an overlap, of conditions related to both theories.

Survivor Work Page Question:

Do you believe that the cause of your pathological partner's personality disorder was related to -

____ Nature (biology, heredity, genetics)

____ Nurture (upbringing, experience, learned conditioning)

____ Neurological abnormalities

____ A combination of these

With the information from the first three chapters and their corresponding worksheets, we will now examine why disorders this extreme are often non-, mis-, or disidentified.

Chapter Three Endnotes

1   Bowlby, J. (1988). A Secure Base: Parent-child Attachment and Healthy Human Development. Basic Books.

2   Armstrong, G. J., & Kelley, S. D. M. (2008). Early Trauma and Subsequent Antisocial Behavior in Adults. Brief Treatment and Crisis Intervention, 8(4), 294–303. https://doi.org/10.1093/brief-treatment/mhn016

3   Moroz, K. (2005). The Effects of Psychological Trauma on Children and Adolescents. https://kuswoyoaji.files.wordpress.com/2014/01/dmh-cafu_psychological_trauma_moroz.pdf

4   Machizawa-Summers, S. (2007). Childhood trauma and parental bonding among Japanese female patients with borderline personality disorder. International Journal of Psychology, 42(4), 265–273; https://onlinelibrary.wiley.com/doi/full/10.1080/00207590601109276#references-section

5,7 Berger, K. (2011). The Developing Person Through the Life Span. Worth Publishers.

6 Bradshaw, J. E. (1988). Healing the Shame that Binds You. Health Communications, Inc.

8   Kendler, K., Aggen, S. H., Czajkowski, N., Roysamb, E., Tambs, K., Torgersen, S., … Reichborn-Kjennerud, T. (2008). The Structure of Genetic and Environmental Risk Factors for DSM-IV Personality Disorders. Archives of General Psychiatry, 65(12), 1438–1446. https://www.ncbi.nlm.nih.gov/pmc/articles/PMC2844885/

9   Reichborn-Kjennerud, T. (2010). The genetic epidemiology of personality disorders. Dialogues in Clinical Neuroscience, 12(1), 103–114; https://www.ncbi.nlm.nih.gov/pmc/articles/PMC3181941/

     Kendler, K., Aggen, S. H., Czajkowski, N., Roysamb, E., Tambs, K., Torgersen, S., … Reichborn-Kjennerud, T. (2008). The Structure of Genetic and Environmental Risk Factors for DSM-IV Personality Disorders. Archives of General Psychiatry, 65(12), 1438–1446. https://www.ncbi.nlm.nih.gov/pmc/articles/PMC2844885/

10   Reichborn-Kjennerud, T. (2010). The genetic epidemiology of personality disorders. Dialogues in Clinical Neuroscience, 12(1), 103–114; https://www.ncbi.nlm.nih.gov/pmc/articles/PMC3181941/

     Kendler, K., Aggen, S. H., Czajkowski, N., Roysamb, E., Tambs, K., Torgersen, S., … Reichborn-Kjennerud, T. (2008). The Structure of Genetic and Environmental Risk Factors for DSM-IV Personality Disorders. Archives of General Psychiatry, 65(12), 1438–1446. https://www.ncbi.nlm.nih.gov/pmc/articles/PMC2844885/

     Berenz, E. C., Amstadter, A. B., Aggen, S. H., Knudsen, G. P., Reichborn-Kjennerud,

T., Gardner, C. O., & Kendler, K. S. (2013). Childhood trauma and personality disorder criterion counts: A co-twin control analysis. Journal of Abnormal Psychology. https://www.ncbi.nlm.nih.gov/pmc/articles/PMC3992260/

1116 Reichborn-Kjennerud, T. (2010). The genetic epidemiology of personality disorders. Dialogues in Clinical Neuroscience, 12(1), 103–114; https://www.ncbi.nlm.nih.gov/pmc/articles/PMC3181941/

12 Raine, A., & Yang, Y. (2006). Neural foundations to moral reasoning and antisocial behavior. Social Cognitive and Affective Neuroscience, 1(3), 203–213. https://doi.org/10.1093/scan/nsl033

13 Abbot, A. (2001). Into the Mind of a Killer. Nature, 410, 296–8. https://www.nature.com/articles/35066717

14 Soloff, P., Nutche, J., Goradia, D., & Diwadkar, V. (2008). Structural brain abnormalities in borderline personality disorder. Psychiatry Research, 164(3), 223–236. https://www.ncbi.nlm.nih.gov/pmc/articles/PMC3286221/
Gunderson, J. G. (2011). Borderline Personality Disorder. The New England Journal of Medicine, 364, 2037–42. https://www.nejm.org/doi/full/10.1056/nejmcp1007358

15 Kiehl, K. A. (2006). A Cognitive Neuroscience Perspective on Psychopathy: Evidence for Paralimbic System Dysfunction. Psychiatry Research, 142(2–3), 107–128. https://doi.org/10.1016/j.psychres.2005.09.013

17 Raine, A., Ishikawa, S. S., Arce, E., Lencz, T., Knuth, K. H., Bihrle, S., … Colletti, P. (2004). Hippocampal structural asymmetry in unsuccessful psychopaths. Biological Psychiatry, 55(2), 185–191. https://doi.org/10.1016/S0006-3223(03)00727-318 Raine, A., Lencz, T., Taylor, K., Hellige, J. B., Bihrle, S., Lacasse, L., … Colletti, P. (2003). Corpus Callosum Abnormalities in Psychopathic Antisocial Individuals. Archives of General Psychiatry, 60(11), 1134. https://doi.org/10.1001/archpsyc.60.11.1134

19 Raine, A., Lencz, T., Taylor, K., Hellige, J. B., Bihrle, S., Lacasse, L., … Colletti, P. (2003). Corpus Callosum Abnormalities in Psychopathic Antisocial Individuals. Archives of General Psychiatry, 60(11), 1134. https://doi.org/10.1001/archpsyc.60.11.1134

20 Alternative DSM-5 Model for Personality Disorders. (2013). FOCUS: The Journal of Lifelong Learning in Psychiatry, XI(2), 189–203. https://focus.psychiatryonline.org/doi/abs/10.1176/appi.focus.11.2.189?journalCode=foc

Chapter Four

Society's Lack of Identification and Its Impact on Everyone— "Who Does That?" Puzzle Piece #1™

Survivor Quick Review

- The personality issues of people with a Cluster B disorder and/or psychopathy have their origins in biology/genetics, environmental/upbringing, neurological issues, or a combination of the three.
- Some of these people suffered abuse and neglect in early childhood, which impaired their development.
- Others possess genetic traits inherited from pathological family members.
- All experience a neurobiological impact in several brain regions, which results in the symptoms of personality disorders and/or psychopathy.

Given the complexity and intensity of Cluster B/psychopathy disorders covered in the previous chapters, it is curious as to why these disorders are not better detected. This mystery of undetected pathology warrants our continued examination of Puzzle Piece #1™.

'Successful' vs. 'Unsuccessful' Disorders

The Preface addressed why professionals often miss the clues of an existing pathological (and toxic) love relationship. The reasons range from a lack of training to the disorder's uncanny ability to hide itself well. Societal systems deal with pathology all the time and yet rarely know it because they identify the behavior (and not the diagnosis) based on the service they themselves provide. These systems see the behaviors as it relates to their own agency's function and label it mostly from their own field-specific evaluation.

The Dark Triad of disorders can fall into two categories. When disorders are outed, either by criminal behavior or by diagnosis, they are deemed 'unsuccessful.' The disorders considered 'successful' are those that fly under the radar; the person has never been arrested and/or has never been diagnosed. Undetected 'successful' Dark Triad disordered people far outnumber those who are detected due to poor diagnosing on our part, and good skill sets on their part. Undetected behavior often operates outside the parameters of law enforcement.

Considering that one person in five has a personality disorder and one in a hundred has no conscience, that's a big swath of pathology flying under the radar and going undetected. Being able to spot pathology in covert behaviors of those who are not overtly criminal, and which is hidden behind career success, is where most professionals fail.

The fact is, most people, including survivors, don't always spot pathology. They may recognize it once it becomes overtly criminal, but people do miss it when it's overtly and externally successful. In fact, pathology evades mental health evaluators, judges, guardians ad litem, court psychologists, and batterer intervention groups, especially when the pathological person is another therapist, a physician, CEO, sports hero, or externally successful in some other way.

Without the overt physical violence or criminality, the covert behaviors of pathology are often missed by the unassuming bystander or family member. High functionality and success can produce an image of surface normalcy. With a low conscience often comes low anxiety, so in business, crime, or relationships, these people look cool, calm, and collected, thus deflecting identification. The more prominent their position in jobs or society, the more likely they are *assumed* to be non-pathological, and, often, the better and longer they can remain covert and successfully hidden. So, the outward success of the pathological person can frequently assist in the successful inward hiding of the disorder.

Many white-collar narcissists and psychopaths are never diagnosed. Some of them have gone on to be Fortune 500 CEOs, brilliant attorneys, chiefs of staff of hospitals or other institutions, decorated military giants and, frighteningly, leaders in government. Their manipulation and charisma are viewed as successful career skills. A little narcissism, or even a dash of psychopathy, is often a bonus in some career fields. While no job application would ever ask about grandiosity as a life skill, the results of career climbing on the backs of others is often viewed as success and is highly revered in the business sector. The seemingly careless risk taking of antisocials and psychopaths comes across as motivation in the boardroom. The kick-butt manager is not viewed as compassionless but as a fiscal bottom-line defender.

Those who have only some of the characteristic traits of a psychopath and are only *almost* psychopathic (such as those executives in a British study who didn't show a strong tendency to social deviance and law breaking), may have just what it takes to charm their way into jobs, and have the conniving, ruthless, and narcissistic personas necessary to work their way to the top—even if it means stepping on others to get there. These high-performing executives are not likely to be serial killers or rapists; instead, the psychopathic behaviors that fuel their rise in their respective organizations are more benign and the colleagues and subordinates who fall prey to them are likely to think of them as backstabbers or bullies, while others may admire them for having what it takes to succeed in a dog-eat-dog world.[2]

Gao and Raine (2010) hypothesize that "successful psychopaths may have superior cognitive empathy (the ability to understand another's perspective) without emotional empathy (the ability to feel empathetic emotions)."[3] If they are cognitively empathic enough for the job, they are not likely to be reprimanded for less than optimal abilities to emotionally empathize.

Overt career success can blind those around them to less obvious deviant and criminal behavior. The Penn State University coach and pedophile Jerry Sandusky, who was convicted of child sexual assault in 2012, flew under the radar for decades largely due to his success on and off the field, sheltered behind a nonprofit agency he created for children. Bernie Madoff was a highly successful investment banker who hid his pathology behind a *Who's Who* circle of high-income clientele who wholeheartedly recommended him to others, keeping his success—and successful hiding—continuing for years. The CEOs of Enron, a respected Fortune 500 Corporation, could never have drained the company's coffers without producing the illusion of overt success. Colonel Russell Williams hid a life of sexual deviancy under his brilliant and lengthy military career until he murdered his wife in 2011. Drew Peterson, long before he became the most hated man on the planet for the murder and suspected murder of his three wives, was a respected law enforcement officer for decades. O.J. Simpson was the most highly regarded football hero of his time before his repeated pattern of violence became his calling card.

The truth is, the covertness of pathology is where we all fall short in spotting those with these disorders. By the nature of the disorders, these people are successful in not only hiding their behaviors, but, once they are spotted, they convincingly relabel their behaviors and motivations, and through gaslighting, they alter how we read them and thus react to them.

In-Your-Face Pathology

Overtly glaring pathology is easier to identify, although usually in retrospect. The public does not always use clinical language to identify disorders, but it normally feels there is something really wrong with the individual(s) when overt pathology strikes. For instance -

- Those who sexually abuse children suffer with co-occurring conditions.
- Mothers who drown their children, like Susan Smith or Andrea Yates, obviously have significant psychopathologies.
- Terrorists who take hostages and administer psychological torture, like the infamous Stockholm Bank Robbery in 1973

(resulting in the term 'Stockholm Syndrome'), are identifiable as probable individuals with Antisocial Personality Disorder, if not Psychopaths.

- Serial killers like Ted Bundy, who raped and killed at least 36 women, leave no doubt that he was the worst-of-the-worst Psychopaths.
- Cult leaders like Jim Jones, who led hundreds to their deaths in 1978, remind us of the power and persuasion of pathology.
- Chronic reoffending domestic violence abusers, like O.J. Simpson and Mike Tyson, convince us that not all domestic violence is treatable, and that the brutality of some abusers increases with each crime.
- White-collar scam artists like Bernie Madoff, who steal millions of dollars from thousands of people, remind us that not all pathology is physically violent—some people do it with panache and a tie.
- The event of twenty children and six teachers shot at Sandy Hook Elementary School by a nineteen-year-old bent on murder has the world wondering, "What kind of pathology *does* that?"

These forms of pathology are recognizable (even if it's after the fact) by most of society, and many would agree that *these* people are significantly disordered and will probably be dangerous to others on some level and for life.

The 'Unsuccessful' and Less Media-Sensationalistic Pathological

We can understand how a successful pathological person can remain successfully hidden for decades if much of his criminality or deviancy is undiscovered. And we can also understand the in-your-face unsuccessful pathological person who is so overtly disordered that even ordinary people can come to realize he is disordered.

But what about the unsuccessful pathological people who do not have glaring behaviors that attract the attention of national media? Ironically, those whose impulse-control problems are just enough to land them within one of our societal or legal systems, but whose problems are not enough to land them on CNN, have a good chance of not being appropriately recognized for the dangerous and severe disorders they possess, despite their poor and risky behaviors. But why is this the case?

Label Soup

The reason that separate societal systems have not cohesively identified by name this cluster of disorders at the center of their workload is that each system has its own view of the *behavior* associated with the pathologically disordered person. Based on that view, each system has its own language for the behavior.

As you review this list of label differences, ask yourself if these different names do not identify the same set of behaviors, thus the same set of disorders.

Law enforcement calls them the *bad guys* (if they are even caught)

Mental health systems call them *patients*

Domestic violence organizations call them *abusers*

Batterer intervention programs call them *perpetrators*

Criminal defense attorneys call them *clients*

Sexual Assault centers call them *rapists* or *sexual offenders*

Financial structures call them *swindlers*

The online world calls them *trolls*

Victims call them *predators*

Children and adolescents call them *bullies* or *cyber bullies*

The swindled call them *con artists*

The judicial system calls them *criminals* (or not, if they are never identified)

Mediators call them *problem personalities*

Child evaluators call them *supervision-necessary cases*

Guardians ad litem call them *the unrecommended child's parent*

Court psychologists call them *the evaluated*

Child Support Services call them *deadbeat parents*

Churches call them *evil* or *unredeemed*

As each system deals with its own view of a specific act the person has committed that falls within their jurisdiction for identification, treatment, or punishment, we overlook the broad category of psychology that these people possibly fall under - Cluster B/psychopathy Disorders. We also miss the larger implication of the disorder, which is the harm to others that the disorder is bound to cause, and how to successfully mitigate it.

Each system dealing with a behavior only sees the person through its own social/legal/law enforcement/judicial/psychological specialty. Yet the systems are likely all talking about the same disorders in action. Looking at the disorder from a system-wide perspective provides a better idea of the disordered person's devastating impact on our society. Without a shared language of the disorders in these various systems, however, the person becomes merely another client, patient, or parolee, and the individual systems that deal with them don't communicate with each other regarding what these behaviors point *to*.

While psychology is not the be-all and end-all of label generators for these disorders, one can't help believing that if all the systems dealing with disorders would get on the same page as to what these disorders consist of, and understood that they all involve the lack of consistent positive change, civil society would become revamped to administer different consequences for those with disorders that have low recovery potential.

We would immediately become better identifiers of dangerous forms of pathology. We would begin to identify across our systems, those who are perpetrating these same recurring behaviors, whether they are successful, or unsuccessful. We must be able to identify the traits that are dangerous to all persons—low (or no) empathy, highly reduced conscience and remorse coupled with low impulse control. Those are the disorders of inevitable harm that destroy our relationships, our systems, and the quality of our lives.

To be able to balance the system-wide impact of pathology, we must begin by -

- Recognizing the label-camouflaged pathology that already exists and overlaps in our systems
- Becoming better able to spot covert forms of pathology before cataclysmic disasters occur
- Creating pathology-specific programs within criminal jus-

tice, family law, law enforcement, mental health, domestic violence, health care, and social services that recognize pathology and its limitations, as well as the needs of survivors in its aftermath

"Sooner or Later, they fool everyone." (Robert Hare, M.D.)

If professionals in various fields miss the detection of covert forms of pathology, it's not reasonable to hold an intimate partner to a higher level of expected detection, but, in fact, that is normally what happens. Most people are not inclined to blame investors who put their faith in criminal hedge fund managers. Instead, they say "Those poor people! They were conned out of their life savings." We empathize with people who become targets of cyber-stalking and have their lives ruined by computer hacking and wonder why the public isn't taught how better to spot these types of people.

But in personal and intimate relationships, survivors are held to a higher level of accountability and are blamed for a level of detection ability that, quite frankly, isn't even possessed by psychology professionals. We don't see survivors as 'conned' like investors, or 'victims' like those in cyber stalking cases. We label them naïve, dependent, drama seekers, violence lovers, etc.

We hold them to a level of knowledge that even the systems that deal with these people daily have not managed to achieve. We expect them to detect behavior that law enforcement is woefully inadequate in identifying. We deride their poor diagnostic skills and maintain that they should have seen pathology that even psychological testing can't often identify. We assume they can uncover personal history that even private investigators miss.

The fact is, as Dr. Robert Hare says of psychopaths, "Sooner or later, they fool everyone." No one is immune to these invisible forms of pervasive and well-hidden disorders. Contrary to popular opinion, the survivors are not gluttons for punishment, or masochists, or willfully in denial. They are perfectly normal, unassuming people to whom those with disorders of the Dark Triad are attracted. While survivors exhibit some unique qualities that are especially appealing to those with these disorders, for the most part, any of us normal people are just as at risk for brushes with a pathological boss, coworker, neighbor, or friend. Because with one in five people with a personality disorder, and one in a hundred with no conscience, the societal deck is stacked against us. And most of us enter these relationships with blinders on.

Detection Reflection Blind Spot[4]

None of us has 'Dark Triad radar' naturally. What has been made abundantly clear is that those with the Dark Triad of disorders have an uncanny ability to reflect detection—personally, professionally, and often criminally. Or, as I often say, "They are sicker than we are smart." A survivor is just out there, being relatively normal, when she appears on the radar of a person with the Dark Triad of personality disorders. She didn't stand on a street corner with a sign stating, "Will work for a relationship with a Narcissist." She may have been fixed up with a "nice successful guy" by a friend, or casually visited the online dating world the Dark Triad frequently haunts. It could have been a guy from the office who was well regarded. Or she could have been innocently having a drink with friends at the neighborhood pub. But, like everyone else, she too wonders how a dangerous Dark Triad personality curled up next to her like a purring cat and, good God, ended up asking "what is this relational slap down that is taking years to get over?"

Public Perception's Blind Spot

When the public is asked if they've ever known a psychopath, most would say they have not - even though they most likely have. Most women don't fear a hook-up with the Dark Triad at happy hour because they, like the public, believe people with real Dark Triad disorders are locked up behind bars. Either that, or their obvious serial-killer weirdness would be easy to detect, or their bank-robber masks and guns would be a sure giveaway. As a result, people don't tend to be on the lookout for people with these disorders entering their lives. The misperceptions about the Dark Triad, and psychopaths, more specifically are that they -

- Are rare. The truth is that one in a hundred without a conscience is certainly not rare, and one in five with a personality disorder is even less rare.

- Are primarily killers, or, at the very least, they are criminals with long-documented histories and are probably wearing a parole ankle bracelet at this very moment.
- Are unable to succeed in either the workforce or in social settings.
- Most likely have some visible physical indication of their illness, such as a tattoo between the eyes like Charles Manson.

With myths such as these, the Dark Triad evades detection simply by being nothing like the public's perception or Hollywood portrayals.

The Myth that Success = Character

Success blinds many people. The stories of blue-collar men working their way through Ivy League schools, crawling their way up the career ladder, and building a life of commitment with a country club membership and two kids in private school, are what we equate with success — that it was hard won, and implies a healthy dash of good character to reach the pinnacle of a career.

These societal assumptions that 'success equals character' miss the fact that there are millions of pathological personalities who destroy people's lives without ever going to jail. They are outwardly successful in positions in law, medicine, the military, business, and politics. Women are not expecting to find the Dark Triad in the pulpit, the penthouse, or the Pentagon. They, like much of the public, believe that success at least *implies* some level of respectable virtue like hard work and diligence, which they, not unreasonably, associate with good character. Yet the swindling Madoff, Peterson the homicidal cop, Simpson the violent professional athlete, and the wife-killing Colonel remind us that outward success does not guarantee character.

Ironically, before personality disorders were so named, they were previously called Character Disorders in the DSM. And who hides their true character better than a person with a disorder of 'social hiding?' The Dark Triad evades detection because the success of those who possess the disorders is mistaken as a sign of good character.

The Myth that Psychopaths are Always Physically Violent

I've never met a man who confessed, on the first date, with eyes lowered and spouting remorsefulness into his coffee, that he had gone to jail three times for beating his girlfriend, had been to Batterer Intervention twice, and failed the classes because he reoffended again. Nope, I don't hear that much.

A prevalent assumption about people with Dark Triad disorders is that they are always violent. A confession of the type mentioned above would send many women (although not all, as we know) out the door with her mace and taser at hand for protection.

There are many ways to destroy lives other than by sheer violence. In a Batterer Invention Group, a psychopath said, as other batterers were sharing their harrowing stories of continued physical abuse towards their mates, "You guys are pathetic! Any criminal can beat a woman. But it takes someone like me to annihilate them without ever lifting a hand."

The weaponry of people with Dark Triad disorders, while chock full of impulse control problems that can lead to violence, is not dependent on just muscle and brawn to destroy a life. In fact, many of the disordered pride themselves on their psychological terrorist maneuvers, which create trauma disorders simply from tactics like gaslighting or coercive control.

Detection fails, even when criminal background checks are completed, to identify previous harm because people with Dark Triad disorders don't always annihilate in the same ways. The absence of apparent violence does not mean that the Dark Triad is not dangerous.

And let's not overlook the other trait of people with Narcissistic Personality Disorder, Antisocial Personality Disorder, or Psychopathy; they are consummate pathological liars. Few are ever going to admit what was never documented in police reports.

The Myth of the Charmer: What's There to Dislike?

Like success and character assumptions that exist regarding charisma, decorum, and polish, few women find men attractive if these men can't string together a compliment, or those who pick their nose in public, or who let the door slam in her face—traits associated with any kind of panache. People with Dark Triad disorders, at least initially during the 'luring' and 'honeymoon' phases, often shine in their ability to be charming and well mannered—the very essence of assumed normalcy and the absence of pathology.

But let's be clear - white collar psychopathy could have written *The Field Guide to Success While Wearing a Mask*, which surely would include how to disarm a potential partner with their charisma. They could have also penned a few other titles, such as *Decorum for Degenerates* or *Dressing for Success as a Cluster B/psychopath.* But these feigned traits of polish and panache doesn't mean there isn't pathology and danger lurking behind the Gucci tie.

In Chapter One we discussed one of the traits of psychopathy—glib and superficial charm. While we might want to skip glibness, charm is on the list of traits of a man who anyone would want to be seen with in public. Society has been raised on fairytales about 'Prince Charming' but not 'Prince Harming.' While not all charm is pathological, it is a noted part of the skill set of people with the Dark Triad disorders; it expertly deflects hidden deficits that a woman will too soon realize. But, in many cases, it isn't soon enough.

Successful psychopaths learn ways of *increasing* their public appeal, from the way they dress to their impeccable manners; this not only assists in attracting partners, it lubricates their ride up the career ladder. In studies of white collar psychopaths, the spit-polished charm seen in Washington, D.C. aristocrats is mirrored in their professional presentation. If their bosses and hedge-fund supporters can't see their disorder, how could their partners? Detection is evaded when the gleaming smile deflects the pathology behind it.

The Ruse of the 'Pitiful Parasite'

Not all people with the Dark Triad of disorders are successful, at least professionally. Not every psychopath or person with a Cluster B is a Wall Street sensation. Some can't string together even dead-end, go-nowhere jobs. While most of us think these are people with no appeal, we don't realize the breadth of human attraction and how people with the saddest of stories can be the most intriguing to some of us.

Many people have daunting levels of what writer/researcher Barbara Oakley calls 'pathological altruism'—an unhealthily high dose of empathy for the perpetual underdog. Unsuccessful and outed Dark Triad personalities command a sizeable share of the dating market with those women who relate, sympathize, and empathize with their stories of woe.

Charities, foundations, and Go Fund Me pages raise millions of dollars capitalizing on the human capacity for empathy. For people with Dark Triad disorders who don't have the resume to carry off overt success, or police records that could surface in a cursory search, there is always that other group of people who understand that sometimes bad things happen to good people. These under performers have a public-relations pitch that would make Mother Teresa cry. Carefully crafted, and with all the angles covered, they present a pieced-together history that makes pure sense to a potential partner who has ample doses of empathy and the heart of a social worker.

Antisocial Personality Disorder (ASPD) is known for its 'parasitic lifestyle' which moves seamlessly from one wallet to the other, from one house to the other, and from one target to the other. Rarely ever consistently self-supporting, his portable life style allows him to glide between supporters who hear his sad story and invest in housing, time, money, or start-up funding for brilliant companies he is going to start. Likewise, people with Borderline Personality Disorder, with their long history of childhood traumas and the need for a little understanding, melt the hearts of not only their partners, but also agencies who pour resources into the rebuilding of a life that they believe just needs a hand up.

Before we judge the survivors too harshly for having fallen for someone who can't hold a job, has lived out of his car, and has an arrest record as long as the Amazon, we'd do well to remember that most social services nonprofits in this country are swindled out of millions of dollars by these people because the agency fails to identify them before they invest large sums of money in their treatment. Private foundations are built on the principles of empathy, but the same people who donate to these foundations are just as likely to help someone they meet. Detection is evaded when the right sad story meets the right empathic ear.

The Myth that All Minds are Alike

Chapter Two discussed the abundance of evidence regarding the not-quite-normal brain wiring of people with personality disorders. In an upcoming chapter, you will learn how those abnormalities create a skill set that benefits the person while he is in a relationship with an undiscerning normal partner. This is a skill set that people without these disorders will never have. As evidenced in the story of the psychopath in the Batterer Invention program, part of what makes the pathological mind so dangerous is the ability to mangle, manipulate, and melt down other people's psyches. Trying to understand *why* a psychopath does these things will be of no use, as we are not endowed with the same motivational drives (what generates the motivation behind our behavior) as those with Dark Triad personality disorders. Years are spent by survivors saying to themselves and to others, "I don't understand why he would do that. What would motivate him?"

We can equate pathology with a medical condition, since the brain of a psychopath is clearly disordered from a neurobiological standpoint. But we don't ask, "Why does cancer destroy blood cells and organs?" since the presence of those conditions *results* in the diagnosis. The same is true in pathology. People do what they do because that's what pathology *does*, and that's how it is identified. One of its symptoms is the deliberate mind-mangling that creates partners who are destroyed and debilitated, and that somehow gives these people pleasure. People without the personality disorders/psychopathy do not feel compelled to do these things to others.

But without the experience of having been harmed by a pathological person in the past, many of us are at the mercy of a power greater than our own ability to recognize it before it's destroyed us. With supersonic speed, people with Dark Triad disorders attach onto others before the disorder is ever recognized. Those of us raised in normal-enough homes lack the psychological discernment to recognize the precision of applied gaslighting, covert coercive control, and the slow, methodical generation of Stockholm Syndrome.

Suited up with charisma, or blanketed in sad stories of woe, once the psychopath is in, the mental reconfiguration of a partner's psyche occurs with frightening rapidity, making it the fastest psychic lobotomy ever performed. Our minds, made up of ordinary genetics and the experiences of normal human interaction, are never a match for the extraordinariness of pathology. And I mean *never*.

One psychopathy expert said that the interns he used with incarcerated psychopaths were rotated regularly to prevent the damage quickly perpetrated by psychopaths who found great joy in evaporating the interns' formerly rational and functioning minds. But survivors don't get to be rotated out of exposure to smiling, smooth-talking psychological terrorists. None of us is born with the skills needed to detect hidden pathology, to our own and to society's peril.

While we have rolled our eyes at people gullible enough to be lulled into cults and wondered how anyone can be recruited into a Jim Jones-type mass suicide, we don't understand or appreciate the skill set of Dark Triad disorders, which gently and lovingly overpowers minds that are never prepared for what these disorders can do to it. While we all believe we are smart enough not to drink the Kool-Aid, we are really all at risk since we are not them and we are psychologically outmatched from the get-go.

Wrapping This All Up—Everyone's Detection Malfunction

What should be clear is that whether we are professionals who encounter the Dark Triad in our jobs, or whether we are a woman simply enjoying a night out with friends and minding our own business, successful and unsuccessful psychopaths will fly under the radar of most people. While the social systems that deal with them regularly seem to be just as clueless as the rest of us, the reasons they remain largely undetected have a lot to do with myths, poor public pathology education, and their extraordinary skill sets. Applying standards of detection to survivors that even professionals don't possess is to blame the victim for society's lack of public pathology education.

Survivor Work Page Question:
My partner had the following qualities mentioned in this chapter, which impacted my ability to see disaster coming: _____

_____

Chapter Four Endnotes

1   Stevens, G. W., Deuling, J. K., & Armenakis, A. A. (2012). Successful Psycho-paths: Are They Unethical Decision-Makers and Why? *Journal of Business Ethics, 105*(2), 139–149. https://doi.org/10.1007/s10551-011-0963-1

2   Board, B., & Fridon, K. (2005). Disordered Personalities at Work. *Psychology, Crime & Law, 11*(1) https://www.tandfonline.com/doi/abs/10.1080/10683160310 001634304

Schouten, R., & Silver, J. (2012). *Almost a Psychopath: Do I (or Does Someone I Know) Have a Problem with Manipulation and Lack of Empathy? (The Almost Effect).* Hazelden.

3   Gao, Y., & Raine, A. (2010). Successful and Unsuccessful Psychopaths: A neu-robiological model. *Behavioral Sciences & the Law, 28*(2), 211–223. https://www.ncbi.nlm.nih.gov/pubmed/20422645

4   Brown, Sandra L., *The Institute* (2016). Blind spots, myths, and ruses: Why people don't spot pathology. Prepared for *Women Who Love Psychopaths. Third Edition.*

Section Two

Puzzle Piece #2™

Dramatic and Erratic Relational Dynamics

Figure 5.1
Puzzle Piece #2™

Chapter Five

The 'Inabilities' of Relationship Building Puzzle Piece #2™

Quick Survivor Review

- Psychopaths and people with Cluster B disorders have innate personality abnormalities that impair their ability to function in a relationship.
- Other people's detection of their disorder may deem them as 'successful' or 'unsuccessful'.
- Society's myths built around different personality traits keep the Dark Triad from being identified.
- Society is poorly trained in public pathology.
- Psychopaths and people with Cluster B disorders 'are sicker than we are smart.'

Our examination of Puzzle Piece #2™—Dramatic and Erratic Relational Dynamics—must first address society's assumption that most people are basically good and, even if there are a few problems in a relationship, these disorders are largely fixable. We will look at why psychopaths and people with Cluster B disorders, once in a relationship, are never going to be able to deliver in the relationship.

The Problem with Assumptions

Mr. Darkness has his bag packed just waiting for the moment he encounters a potential partner. Whether or not the survivor recognizes it, as soon as the relationship begins, he will begin unpacking his personal baggage—a personality disorder chock full of emotional deficits, a brain wired for destruction, issues with empathy and intimacy, conscience and remorse, and a wad of impulsivity.

Before he is out trying to meet her, though, his potential victim is a little behind the eight ball, having no clue of the pathology that lurks in the shadows, or all the elements of true relationship which he will never be able to bring. Like most people, she holds some dangerous and misguided belief about relationships.

All of us have largely unconscious beliefs about the human condition that follows us into relationships, and these become core beliefs from which we operate. So universal are these beliefs with most of society (not just among survivors) that they can blind us to what is right in front of us. So, before we judge the survivor too harshly for being targeted by a psychopath, we need to recognize that she differs very little from the rest of us who believe that anyone can adapt to a new relationship based on sincere desire. If he brings a little emotional baggage with him, well, there are always second chances in life.

Most of us believe that humans occasionally behave badly and are just misguided, but basically have good intentions. With a strong desire to do better, and with the right guidance, we believe they can become good partners.

===

Survivor Note:

Most people don't begin a relationship believing it will be perfect; they begin a relationship believing that whatever is not perfect, can be perfected.

===

This belief system is so prevalent that an entire genre of psychology has been birthed from these ideas. The field of Positive Psychology is 'the scientific study of the strengths that enable individuals and communities to thrive.' The field is founded on the belief that 'people *want* to lead meaningful and fulfilling lives, to cultivate what is best within themselves, and to *enhance* their experiences of love, work, and play.'[1]

This concept of people wanting to lead meaningful lives and cultivate what is best in themselves overlooks the huge deficits within some people to begin this task. This appealing idea of strengths as something that helps others thrive is called a 'strength-based' approach and appears in many fields of psychology, social services, and even school systems. Focusing on someone's strengths (often to the exclusion of their weaknesses) was generated out of the Positive Psychology premise that all human nature is capable of these positive changes.

This field is full of big name believers who use their media platforms to promote these beliefs. Positive Psychology has bled over into a spinoff field called Motivational Psychology. Giants in the field of self-help, such as Tony Robbins, Jack Canfield, and even Oprah Winfrey—none of whom are mental health professionals—believe that 'motivation + desire = results.'

The influential field of Positive Psychology seems to have blinded some clinical professionals, who now gravitate toward this *if you can think it, you can make it happen* application and have forgotten their graduate school training in psychopathology, which identifies who can and who cannot benefit from the Positive Psychology approaches. I jokingly say that we have a new field of psychology called 'Oprah-ology,' whose principles are now espoused by most of society and many mental health professionals.

For all the helpfulness that Positive Psychology brings to relatively *normal* individuals—whose motivations align with wanting meaningful relationships and who have internal strengths from which to draw on and guide them—what is *not* helpful is to apply this theory to everyone.

===

Survivor Note:
A theory created for some but applied to everyone across the board implies that what is wrong with someone can always be reversed simply by desire, and that strengths trump weaknesses even if their biology indicates otherwise.

===

Positive Psychology is an approach for *normal* people although it is rarely presented as such. People who have a conscience, who have empathy, who are capable of intimacy, self-appraisal, and who have the gift and ability of insight, might benefit from this approach. They are people with normal brains who do not possess the neurological problems the Dark Triad have (who by their very natures do not have the biology to pull off Positive Psychology transformations.)

Oops, they forgot to mention that, didn't they?

All theories of psychology are not applicable to *all* populations and this couldn't be truer than in what afflicts the pathology of people with Dark Triad disorders—abnormalities so severe that very few psychological approaches work consistently on them, least of all the *think-it-*

and-the-universe-will-align approach. Strengths-based approaches are for people who *possess* functional internal resources.

The DSM5 Alternative Model discussed in Chapter One outlines the ways in which people with personality disorders/psychopathy lack *normal* strengths. The DSM5 shows us that some people's weaknesses are so profoundly influential that these weaknesses themselves become the personality disorders, dwarfing what non-manipulative strengths a person might possess. Using an approach which does not acknowledge that in these cases, the notion that 'weaknesses trump strengths' is not only counter-productive but invites the result of inevitable harm.

Survivors tell stories of dragging pathological partners to all forms of Positive Psychology sessions, including Positive Psychology-focused marriage counseling, all to no avail. The Dark Triad has been force-fed self-help books and rah-rah motivational lectures and subjected to well-meaning but non-productive marriage counseling marathons. Not only have these attempts been futile, they have prolonged the survivor's commitment in the relationship while she was waiting on his strengths to step up, so he could 'think' the universe into aligning with his positive beliefs.

As we've seen, strength-based focuses cannot be applied unilaterally. There are disorders in which the assessment of weaknesses, as outlined in the DSM 5 Alternative Model, shows us that it's not a person's *strengths* we are concerned with, it's the *absence of strengths* that will be detrimental to everyone around him.

> *Positive Psychology may be a correct theory but not when applied to the wrong population.*

Positive Psychology may be a viable theory, but it's useless in the case of personality disorders. Instead, what would be useful in understanding and identifying which weaknesses are likely to impact a relationship would not be Positive Psychology but something more akin to 'Negative Trait Psychology.' Let's see what that would look like.

Like most of us, survivors believe that we are all similarly motivated in our desire to seek positive change. Survivors also have other reasons for tenaciously holding on to these beliefs, but they begin the relationship much like anyone does—with the belief that 'no one is perfect' and if the pathological partner wants the relationship to succeed, he will abandon his negative behaviors in favor of preserving the relationship. As a society, we are not taught to view these caverns of weakness as clues to impending harm.

To help survivors easily understand those sections in Chapter One regarding what the DSM5 warns about in these *trait weaknesses, The Institute* has broken these traits down into The Three Inabilities—a list of what pathological partners cannot do, or cannot maintain consistently, in their new and continuing relationships.

This simplified list identifies what happens throughout the relationship when a pathological partner's weaknesses overpower his mere verbalization of a willingness to change.

*T*he Three Inabilities[2]

1. The inability to sustain consistent and mounting positive, non-manipulative change.
2. The inability to grow to any significant and authentic emotional, spiritual, or relational depth.
3. The inability to have true empathic insight about how their negative behavior impacts others.

The Three Inabilities© are based on noted deficits in the DSM5 and relate to a pathological partner's issues with his self-identity, self-functioning, empathy, intimacy, and insight. These inabilities comprise the behaviors, thoughts, and actions a partner cannot bring to a relationship. Most Pathological Love Relationship behavior can be attributed to at least one, if not all, of these Inabilities. Survivor partners who understand The Three Inabilities can learn to spot the absences of insight, emotional depth, and sustained positive behavior that has riddled the relationship.

Let's examine these inabilities and how they cause inevitable harm.

Inability 1: The Inability to Sustain Consistent and Mounting Non-Manipulative Positive Change

Why pathological partners cannot sustain consistent non-manipulative positive change:

*   Their neurobiology is deficient.
*   Their goal setting is based on personal gratification and perceived *immediate* needs.

- They fail to be motivated by long-term plans, letting immediate needs direct their behavior.
- Their goals are achieved through manipulation. If the situation changes, then through manipulation, they alter and adapt to it.
- They are risk takers – they have little to no fear response and, therefore, they are not limited by the potential harm to themselves or others.
- They are prone to boredom in relationships and seek to avoid it.

As mentioned previously, biology trumps everything else. At the core of the Dark Triad are deficits that not even Positive Psychology can override. My years at the Personality Disorder Clinic taught me that what lies behind some people's inability to sustain non-manipulative change is not a lack of skill building, like the skills found in Dialectical Behavioral Therapy (DBT), but something more inherent that prevents *maintaining* learned skills—their own biology.

Inability 2: The Inability to Grow to Any Significant and Authentic Emotional, Spiritual, or Relational Depth

Why people with low to no conscience cannot grow to any type of authentic depth:
- They are essentially egocentric and are driven by personal gain.
- Their relationship goals are achieved through exploitation, not connection.
- They are persistently hostile and antagonistic and thus are mistrusting of others.
- Their sense of *self* is lacking, therefore there is little to no self-reflection which limits their ability to relate to others.
- They use an inflation of the *self* to cover up the lack of a real *self*.
- They fear abandonment which limits making deep connections.
- They have heightened emotionality—mood changes happen quickly, and in some cases, the fear of falling apart can worsen the interaction.

Emotional and Self-Shallowness

I don't know many women who are seeking shallow and superficial love mates. But low-conscienced people are nothing if not superficial, which is why we refer to them as 'deep as Formica.' When you meet a low-conscienced person, his charm and egocentricity will likely be the first things you notice. This first meeting reveals the totality of his 'depth.' That moment of kindness, charisma, or generosity is just that—a moment. It's a tool he uses to begin to take control and employ the smoke and mirrors act that will last through the duration of the relationship. But make no mistake, there is nothing beyond this veneer that is attached to something that can grow into emotional or relational depth. The low-conscienced partner's lack of depth is derived from his moment-to-moment needs. His egocentricity and desire to meet his personal needs prevents the connection and depth that naturally form in healthy relationships.

As a normal relationship progresses, depth develops from the shifting between meeting our own needs and meeting others' needs as well. A deep, bonded relationship is characterized by a mutual sense that we are meeting each other's needs willingly and often without much thought. It's natural to think of others and ourselves simultaneously. But people with low-conscience disorders cannot do that, and without a regard for others, no depth of emotion is attained. Any need that the survivor believes has been met by her partner is based on the pathological partner's manipulation to get something else—hardly the mechanism for building true depth in a relationship.

It is why the DSM5 talks about people with this triad of disorders as having 'superficial charm' and a 'lack of emotional depth.' Superficiality is, in fact, a *trait* of the disorder. These people aren't shallow by accident or shallow because they haven't met a survivor partner with sufficient depth to guide them there. They are shallow because it is part of the *disorder*.

A person with a low-conscience disorder views the world with hostility and antagonism. In fact, in personality testing, *antagonism* is what is scored highest by people with Dark Triad disorders. They see the world as a hostile place and seek to tame it through manipulation. The way we see the world (our filter) is based on how we view ourselves, but people with these disorders see others based on who *they* themselves are. Their engrained suspiciousness will always lead to their belief that others are going to 'do unto them' as they have 'done unto others.' They see the world as being about power and control; they believe that *everyone* wants to have control, and if you don't, you're just fooling yourself. Because of this core worldview, they are often hostile and antagonistic in relationships, perceiving that their partner has ulterior motives based on a desire for control, and is out to get them. This skewed worldview makes it impossible to connect emotionally and prevents authentic bonding, leaving the relationship with virtually no depth, which is a necessary component for any healthy relationship.

Emotional, relational, and spiritual depth is created from the development of a meaningful connection. It is also nurtured by a feeling of caring for another person, which leads to insights about that person. But a healthy sense of self is also needed, and this is one of the areas highlighted by the DSM5 as a *pervasive* deficit in the Dark Triad. This lack of self-identity, particularly noted in Narcissism and Borderline conditions, leaves the person with a poor concept of self and often results in distorted self-esteem. A person with Narcissistic Personality Disorder presents as a wildly over-confident larger-than-life personality, while, in truth, he is masking a grossly deflated and non-developed self-identity. This smoke and mirrors trick of projecting a grandiose sense of self hides his actual child-like and abandoned self.

In the film *The Wizard of Oz*, the small, impotent man behind the curtain projects an enormous fear-inducing image of a smoke-spouting head which governs the reality of a whole kingdom and controls people through perceived power and dominance. "I am the great and powerful Oz!", he boasts, convincingly. But it only takes a little dog to pull back the curtain to reveal a tiny, neurotic, and nervous man working in a projection booth. To try to maintain the fiction of this gigantic self-identity, he says, once discovered, "Pay no attention to the man behind the curtain." And so, it is with the Dark Triad who have projected images of the identities they want us to see while none of it really exists.

To possess a 'self' is to know who you are—your essential being that separates you from others and which is needed to be able to gauge who you are, and who you are not, in relation to others. Because people with Dark Triad disorders do not see themselves reflected in others, they remain singular in their view of themselves. They are aware of who they are and of their own needs and wants, but they cannot see other's personal 'selves.' They see people as objects, not as individuals with needs and wants. Without this ability to 'other reflect,' there is no depth of self. Without a self, no relational, spiritual, or emotional depth can exist.

Our relationships, in a sense then, can only be as healthy as our own sense of self. A wounded self-concept results in over-neediness and clinging behavior or aloofness, which impacts a healthy relationship. If a damaged self-concept can harm a relationship, imagine what a virtually nonexistent sense of self can do.

Humans without a strong inner sense of self feel hollow. There is an eternal echo that keeps bouncing off the walls of an empty inner self. The Greek myth of Narcissus, from which we get the word 'narcissism', reflects this sense of emptiness. Narcissus was walking by a river, saw his reflection in the water, and was surprised by its beauty. He became entranced by his own reflection. He couldn't obtain the object of his desire though - which was himself - and he died at the banks of the river from his sorrow. According to the myth, Narcissus is still admiring himself in the underworld, looking forlornly into the waters of the River Styx.[3]

People with shallow self-identities, which is a noted deficiency in the DSM5, don't sense anyone at home inside themselves, so they can either become preoccupied with themselves as did Narcissus, or they can frantically seek out others with whom to fill this internal void. This pattern is often seen in people with Borderline Personality Disorder. This lack of self-identity, coupled with biology, impulse-control problems, and skewed motivational drives, creates an unending compulsion to seek out others to hedge their bets against ever being alone. This fear of abandonment drives them to seek multiple relationships through which to keep the relational pipeline filled.

Fear of abandonment is not only related to their lack of identity. The stress they feel when they are not involved with someone also comes from a fear of the absence of an object to control. Their lack of ability to have emotional intimacy with others is replaced with controlling others, which provides a sense of inner stability—their only internal stabilizer.

==

Survivor Note:

Control is not emotional, spiritual, or relational depth; it is the absence of it.

==

There is a belief that this 'no self' can be therapeutically created, bolstered, or healed to create the self of normalcy, and has been attempted by survivors and therapists alike. The DSM would beg to differ when they remind us that their self-identity issues are not merely an issue of being *unwilling* but *unable*, which has been reinforced by what we know about them through neuroscience.

Inability 3: The Inability to Have True and Empathic Insight Regarding How Negative Behavior Impacts Others

Why people with Dark Triad disorders have no insight into how their negative behavior impacts others:

- They have no empathy or remorse.
- They are antagonistic and callous.
- They are hypersensitive in the belief that they are being slighted.
- They experience a heightened lack of inhibition.

The Biology of Insight

Awareness is different than insight. They are different processes that reflect different depths in understanding. Awareness is shallow like Mr. Formica, whereas insight is deep.

In the chapter on the causes of pathology, insight was discussed as one of the functions *deficient* in the brain issues of the Dark Triad. Hidden in one of the regions of the brain is the operational mechanism for this highly valued function of humanity—insight.

The pervasiveness of personality disorders highlights how debilitating these disorders can be. Insight is *pervasively* absent, whether from brain biology or childhood emotional development, which *underscores what we cannot expect from those with pervasive disorders*. Accommodations are made in Intellectual/Developmental Disability [I/DD]/Autism for how the person's lack of normal ranges in the ability for insight affects their behavior and impacts others, but the same accommodations are not made for people with Dark Triad disorders when their surface functionality masks hidden deficits.

We don't realize that, lurking below the surface of a normal-appearing person, is a deficit so huge that it nearly supersedes what constitutes humanity in us. Healthy relationships cannot be forged with the absence of insight, and this, in turn, also impacts emotional depth, empathy, and sustained positive behavior. Without the fortifying factor of insight, little can be done to motivate change when someone cannot understand the basic violations they have committed. Being *aware* of, or even *agreeing* that an error or uncaring action occurred, is not the same thing as insight. Agreement, in someone with a personality disorder, arises out of a desire to manipulate and change the other person's perception.

Insight, on the other hand, is about *apprehending the true nature of a thing, especially through intuitive understanding, penetrating discernment, and a faculty of seeing into the inner character or underlying truth.*[4] While people with Dark Triad disorders seem to know and understand intuitively how to *manipulate*, they don't have the same ability to make a fearless moral appraisal of their behavior, to "own" their negative behaviors, and to see the other person as harmed by them. Since people are objects to them, they do not experience a sense of any entity separate from themselves. Without empathy, which would generate hearing the survivor partner's feelings, and without the ability to understand how another would feel, the core of what is needed to generate true insight doesn't exist.

In psychology, *insight* is defined as 'an understanding of relationships that sheds light on or helps to solve a problem.' Psychotherapy sees *insight* as 'the recognition of sources of emotional difficulty' and 'the understanding of the motivational forces behind one's actions, thoughts, or behavior.' Insight also includes an element of self-knowledge. From this definition, we can see that what is required to have *true* insight is a recognition and understanding of one's own behaviors and the behaviors of others. Problem solving in a relationship is contingent on this ability; what is lacking in people with personality disorders is the ability to solve problems as they emerge in the relationship.

Notorious in personality disorders/psychopathy are the patterns of blame and projection. The person with a Dark Triad disorder sees all problems in a relationship as being created by his partner with himself as the victim. Even infidelity, money laundering, or stealing is often blamed on a survivor who didn't even have knowledge of his behavior. Not being able to identify the sources of his emotional difficulty always leaves others as the targeted problem; this conveniently precludes any necessity (or ability) for self-change. Likewise, the lack of self-knowledge to understand what motivates *his* own conclusions and behavior leaves the opportunity for insight in the dust.

Survivor Work Question:

My pathological partner displays the following inabilities as described in the lists in this chapter:

_____

$\mathcal{W}$rapping This All Up

'Relationships of Inevitable Harm' occur when we have a level of expectation that is 'not equal to our partner's level of disorder.'

The Three Inabilities© present a clear picture of what pathological partners are unable to do in a relationship. The following chapters cover relationship dynamics and outline the inevitable trajectory of a relationship with someone with a Dark Triad disorder.

Chapter Five Endnotes

1   Positive Psychology Center. (2017). https://ppc.sas.upenn.edu/

2   Brown, Sandra L., *The Institute* (2009). *The Inabilities* in *Women Who Love Psychopaths: Inside the Relationships of Inevitable Harm, Second Edition*. Mask Publishing.

3   Narcissus. *Encyclopedia Britannica*. (2018)

4   Insight. *Dictionary.com Unabridged*. (2018)

Chapter Six

The Trolling and Luring Phase of the Relationship—

Seeking an Opportunity

Puzzle Piece #2™

Quick Survivor Review

- Cluster B/psychopaths have innate personality abnormalities that impair relational functioning.
- These abnormalities are caused by Nature-, Nurture-, and Neuroscience-related reasons and are why Cluster B/psychopaths are unable to grow to any emotional or spiritual depth.
- Cluster B/psychopaths are unable to sustain positive, non-manipulative change.
- Cluster B/psychopaths have no insight into how their behavior affects others.
- The personality abnormalities can be successfully or unsuccessfully hidden and largely overlooked by the societal systems in which they interact.

Continuing with our examination of Puzzle Piece #2™: Dramatic and Erratic Relational Dynamics, the chapters associated with Puzzle Piece #2™ explain the frustrating, drama-filled, erratically charged dynamics of a Pathological and Toxic Love Relationship.

Looking for Love in All the Right Places

All psychopaths need love, right? They aren't going to *not* seek it out just because they have a little psychopathy going on. They are out there on the move, looking for a target—I mean love— just like anyone else. Since there is no Match.com for psychopaths, these people are going to enter the dating stream like anyone else—except they have motivations and techniques that are a little (okay, a lot) different from those of your average dater. Consequently, the dating allure of a psychopath is going to be comprised of camouflage. Since no one wants to date someone overtly disordered, he must be subtler. How Pathological Love Relationships begin, then, are as abnormal as the King of Darkness himself. How could it be otherwise?

PLRs differ from merely normal, bad, codependent, addictive, or sometimes abusive relationships in that the elements that *power* the relationship are based on the pervasive pathology of the partner. This is important to understand because not all bad, codependent, addictive, or abusive relationships have a pathological partner who exponentially changes the relational playing field and creates an outcome of inevitable harm based on what they can never bring to the relationship via their own problematic biology.[1]

The pathology of a partner has everything to do with how the relationship evolves—it begins with luring, endures like a marathon, and crashes and burns in the end, leaving a traumatic aftermath. That's because the elements of pathology, as seen in Puzzle Piece #1™, are carried over and affect Puzzle Piece #2™—The Relationship Dynamics—with pathology as the driving force in the relationship.

S tages of a Pathological Love Relationship[2]

Over the next few chapters, we are going to look at the stages and dynamics of a PLR. These stages and dynamics include:

- The Pre-Relationship Stage—Luring and Trolling
- The Early Relationship Stage—Love Bombing and Twin-ship
- The Mid-Relationship Stage—When the Mask Slips and Why the Relationship Can't Be Repaired
- The End-Relationship Stage—The Many Types of Discarding
- The Post-Relationship Stage—The Boomerang

The Pre-Relationship Stage: Luring and Trolling

Since Darkness is not like other men, he doesn't approach a relationship like other dating partners. But with no history or knowledge of PLRs, his potential partner has no idea that 'love' doesn't happen for him as it does for others. His approach is schematized like a battle plan, and he has trained a long time to acquire his tactical maneuvers. That's because Darkness seeks relationships with his reptilian brain; he hunts partners as a predator would.

Darkness has a detailed idea of whom he prefers and why, and, while anyone will do for a one-night stand, there are others who are sought for the fulfillment of his concept of 'relationship.' Since relationships with Darkness are not successful (they might be long, but they are never healthy or successful), he has perfected his maneuvers via the multiple relationships and countless one-night stands who have flowed in and out of his hookup pipeline. He has worked out how to troll and lure, how to love-bomb while cheating, how to cover his tracks, how to produce Stockholm Syndrome effects in partners, how to hide what he is doing with the cunning of a Special Forces Operative, how to create crazy-making communication that causes his partner to stop trying to communicate, how to create intense and fast-paced relationships before she recognizes his predatory nature, and how to disappear when new victims fill his pipeline.

But that's not exactly the way the survivor thought this attentive, smiling charmer was going to be. That's because Darkness, with all that malfunction going on in his brain tilted towards pleasure and with no brakes on behavior, who lives by the need to dominate, control, and con, *hunts* relationships as opposed to entering them. He begins with his pathology strongly leading the patrol for yet another mate for the ever-growing harem. He uses the techniques he has honed over many other successful conquests to continue trolling for others.

"Trolling" is fishing lingo that means 'to fish by trailing a baited line along behind a boat.' And once there is interest in the bait, and he has a target's attention, Darkness shifts to luring her into the situation he desires.

Both tactics are regularly seen in his cousin, the pedophile.

*P*redatory Tactics

Camouflaged Luring Tactics

As we have seen from Puzzle Piece #1™, the characteristics and symptoms of a Cluster B or psychopath are based in part on control and dominance generated from having no or low conscience. These people are hardwired with a natural motivational drive to manipulate others.

To successfully enter a relationship, someone with a Dark Triad personality disorder must use his skills to bypass his huge deficits (a lack of conscience, empathy, and honesty) and instead, direct the potential partner's attention to the mask—the presentation of his most alluring and appealing (albeit feigned) characteristics.

Psychopaths are often

- Charming (yet superficial)
- Extroverted—talkative and salesman-like
- Ingratiating
- Using their best listening skills for luring someone into a relationship

It should seem obvious that *luring*, or behavior which 'attracts, entices, or allures,' is not normal relationship behavior. While in normal relationships, one attempts to present oneself in one's best light, and there is a conscientious attempt not to represent oneself falsely. Conscience dictates that it's one thing to show your best features and another thing to *manufacture* a whole persona. Those who create personas to attract others are often referred to as 'con men,' because the *motivation* behind the representation is to lure someone into a manufactured situation.

===

Survivor Note:

The act of luring is manipulative and used by the Dark Triad to artificially and deceptively attract and entice potential partners into a relationship by the manipulation and misrepresentation of his personality and by tapping into the partner's own desires, which he quickly learns.

===

Therefore, luring is not only manipulative, it is considered *predatory*. We recognize it best in the case of pedophiles who lure children into their homes through enticements, such as games, a puppy, or attention, preying on the child's *situational vulnerabilities* that they have assessed. This behavior is considered luring because the pedophile is misrepresenting his intentions and manipulating a child's understanding of his motivations.

Strategic luring assesses the vulnerabilities of the target; the predator builds his presentation to match the target's current vulnerability. This is the manufacturing of a persona that someone wouldn't normally select if they knew the predator's true personality, but they were enticed, or *lured*, by fallacy.

While few would disagree that children can be lured, this isn't so readily believed about adults since we don't understand the natural predisposition, or the cultivated skill set of the predatory nature of the Dark Triad. The same skill set of the pedophile is no doubt present in the Cluster B/ psychopath who prefers adults to children.

As discussed in a previous chapter, if we take a broader look at the behavior associated with the terminology, we can see that the *behaviors* of predatory hunting, whether the person is called a pedophile, or a player, or a psychopath, are the same and are generated from the same disorders; they are simply targeting different populations. The same pedophile, player, or psychopath, who houses the same types of disorders associated with Cluster B and/or psychopathy, uses the *same skill set generated out of the same disorders* as defined in the DSM.

While we can understand that pedophiles are dangerous to children because they are convincing, the same disorders of the Dark Triad make them dangerous and convincing to adults.

Survivor Note:

There's been much research and consensus regarding how children can be lured by someone so devious, but there is not much understanding of how the same skill set can be used to lure adults.

We believe that children do not yet have the experience to detect pathology or the red-flag alerts that identify danger. Yet most adults, just like children, lack the experience to detect pathology and identify danger if they haven't *experienced* a predator. When we expect children or adults to have the skills needed to identify predators, we discredit the stealth skills of the camouflaged predator to attract and lure *any* human who has never encountered one, and even some who have. Our court system is an example of professionals who have encountered predators and still do not recognize them.

Therefore, the motives behind luring (dominance, control, coercion, etc.) are no different whether the victim is a child or an adult. The pathological predator hides who he really is, determines what the target wants, and approaches her accordingly. Luring is completely premeditated and is the part of the hunt that sizes up the prey to determine the best approach.

In contrast, healthy relationships do not begin with 'opportunity seeking, vulnerability hunting, or situational luring,' nor do they begin with the result of becoming someone's target. They also do not begin with the survivor needing the skills necessary to assess someone else's pathology. PLRs differ from anything healthy, and partners are targeted and lured precisely because they don't see it coming. Healthy relationships build on a foundation that includes mutual respect, honesty, and non-manipulation. Partners aren't enticed through the wearing of a mask. Healthy relationships are formed from openness and authenticity—showing who you are so you attract someone who genuinely likes the person you are presenting to them.

A survivor, therefore, is not aware of the premeditative approach that hides the core deficits of a socially hiding Mr. Hyde. This person has practiced his approach on many others and perfected his outward Dr. Jekyll presentation, from sparkling smile to decorum to dressing for success. His approach, even as one encounters him innocently drinking his coffee at Starbucks, has been planned and his targets anticipated. PLRs do not begin with the idea of mutual authenticity, or even an 'eyes wide open' approach; they begin with the opposite—-blinders for her and a long-range hunting scope for him.

Into this hunt he brings all the charisma most Cluster B/psychopaths display during the Luring and Honeymoon phases of the relationship. While pedophiles might utilize the offer of playing a game at their house to attract a child, the adult predator begins the luring with his pathology clearly camouflaged and his charm, diplomacy, and attentiveness in full view. Survivors might believe that their meeting was a chance encounter at a pub where she was spending an evening with girlfriends. But Darkness, with his predatory brain, was not out innocently having a drink. He trolls with regularity and with a designed plan and tactics. How he does it and what his tactics are comprise the rest of this chapter.

Unnoticed Tactics

Children are not blamed for not noticing a pedophile. The kids didn't fail to recognize the big 'P' on his chest like the 'S' on Superman's, or his inherent creepiness. Likewise, survivors enter a casual or romantic relationship with Darkness like everyone else does—completely unaware. He doesn't hold up a sign that reads, "I'm a psychopath with no conscience, and I'm going to ambush you."

Instead, full of charisma, the gift of gab, and a highly developed lifetime skill set of 'social hiding,' he comes flying in under everyone's radar. Survivor partners begin by assuming the charisma and charm are who he is—not who he is pretending to be. They come into the relationship unaware of his pathology, and even if there is a little noticed baggage, they believe—as most of us do—that all people can change in relationships.

The Dark Triad, like pedophiles, count on normal people being unaware of them. Beyond not being aware of Darkness' pathology, the impending survivor-victim is ironically not aware that he is, in fact, *very aware of her*. This is the difference between the mindfulness of the predator and that of the prey.

Survivor Note:

These varying levels of 'awareness/nonawareness' form the backdrop for a predatory hunt. That backdrop for the hunt is like how a pedophile becomes aware of a child in whom he is interested, but who is not aware of him.

Predators, whether pedophile or pathological (which is redundant), do their trolling largely unnoticed. No one plans on meeting a predator, whether they were fixed up with the nice guy at the office or met him on the golf course. Trolling behavior that is actively seeking others who seem unaware capitalizes on the element of surprise in the approach. The less *you* are aware, the more *they* are aware.

Targeting Tactics

Children are not blamed for being exactly who or what a pedophile is looking for. No one begins a friendship or relationship looking for lurking psychopathy, and this is happy news for a lurking psychopath or pedophile. Personality typologies have now been studied extensively so that we can understand *what* a predator is looking for, not only in children, but in adult partners, as studied by *The Institute*.[4] Neither children nor adults are responsible for their personality configurations and histories that make them *who* or *what* a predator seeks, just as it is not a gazelle's fault that she's the type of meat preferred by a lion.

The unusual characteristics of the behavior of the Dark Triad are closely linked to predatory hunting. For instance, much of the research regarding psychopathy indicates that the reptilian brain of people with Dark Triad disorders is more developed, making this hunting instinct very pronounced. Any predatory species will do what it is wired to do—prey upon victims. But it is the definition of predatory that gives us the most clues as to how targeted a survivor partner is likely to be.

A behavior that is *predatory* is 'relating to, or characterized by plunder, pillage, robbery, or exploitation' and 'engaging in or living by these activities.' Healthy relationships don't begin with plunder, pillage and robbery! And most relationships are not based on living by these activities as part of a descriptor of what happens throughout a relationship. Relationships that are predatory-based are created from the motivations of exploitation, so the 'hunt' for the availability of this potential is what is foremost for predators, whether they are pedophiles or psychopaths.

Relationships that are characterized by plunder and exploitation are no doubt relationships of impending and inevitable harm. Survivor partners ask, *why me?* The answer to this will be covered in another chapter on the personality traits that predators target. But the more immediate motive for these hunters is related to *opportunity*. Predators hunt for opportunity.

Targeted Opportunities

Predators hunt for opportunity because it is how they are hardwired. Animals don't need to be taught to hunt a specific kind of animal; they know what works and they act accordingly. They then keep repeating the same strategy. Even if Darkness is in his first and only marriage, he has preyed on others for various reasons—one-night stands, serial monogamy, or relationships that furthered his career, social, or financial advancement. With each success he learns more about his targets. By the time he is 30 or 40, he is a well-trained hunting machine. His brain, wired for all this no-brakes behavior, has slowly been cultivating skills that no normal person could spot without having previously experienced it.

In group sessions, psychopaths told me that they saw opportunities in -

- Loss
- Grief
- Loneliness
- Feelings of being overwhelmed
- Emotional vulnerability
- A target's perception of emotional abandonment by someone else

"I can pick them out of a room full of people. There's just a certain look, an underlying current of vulnerability. Then to check out if I'm right I'll ask a few questions and when she begins disclosing at the speed of light about being exhausted or having just lost someone, I know that's the one...the opportunity."
~ a psychopath

This highly honed sixth sense of the predator identifies the best target. This list above is not different from what pedophiles target in children; both psychopaths and pedophiles are predators.

Survivor Note:
What seems shocking to adult women is that relational predators know who is vulnerable and why, much like pedophiles know.

While it is widely believed that we can all be targets for them based on the different reasons they have for targeting—friendships that show status, for a promotion at work, and so on—the romantic partners they target serve different purposes, and so the selection is based on different criteria and usually centers around situational vulnerability and opportunity.

Like a heat-seeking missile, their predatory sixth sense finds vulnerability and sees it as opportunity. I know few survivors who have said, "I was at the top of my game when I met him. I was reveling in my career, my life was great, and I was on top of the world." Predators shop in the vulnerability aisle. While these Cluster B/psychopaths have shown a definitive preference for successful women, what makes those successful women accessible *at that time* is their current situation (or for him, opportunity) that has created vulnerability.

"While they cannot control coincidence, they never pass up opportunity."
~ Jennifer R. Young, L.M.H.C.

Survivor Work Page Question:
The opportunities my pathological partner capitalized on were:

_____

_____

Tactics Involved in Assessing Situational Vulnerabilities[4]

Children are not blamed for pedophiles picking up on their personal or situational vulnerabilities. While the Dark Triad's predatory 'nose' and sixth sense for vulnerability seems to be part of their skill set (just like pedophiles) they also look for the *causes* of a potential partner's situational vulnerabilities, so they can quickly determine what is most needed, adjust the mask for the situation, and lunge.

Survivor partners have said they met their predatory partners in these ways:

- Following the loss of a relationship
- After the death of a loved one
- Following an extended time of caring for aged parents or dying relatives
- After completing an exhausting graduate program
- After having moved and not having met new friends
- After a career change or job loss
- Readjusting to life after becoming an empty nester

These are the situational vulnerabilities that Darkness shops for. His intentions are based on the abnormality of his motivation. Potential partners, whose pain is, to the predator, the scent of opportunity, are just looking for the human condition of loneliness, grief, or exhaustion to be relieved by human contact. Most are not seeking immediate or long-term relationships. They are, instead, seeking just the normal relief from human suffering that happens when people are heard and understood.

While the potential partner's motives are normal, Darkness' are not. His unique sixth sense of others' vulnerability, coupled with his highly developed social hiding skills, allows him to rush in for the kill. The irony, of course, is that the Dark Triad has no real internal equipment to, or capability of, empathizing with his victim's pain. But he does have an incredible ability to capitalize on a situation without ever empathetically relating to it.

While most people show empathy for the situations that brought pain to others, and while empathy may become a connecting point for healthy relationships, the Dark Triad, devoid of the feeling of empathy, uses the survivor's pain predatorily to establish a connection. This connection is not based on *empathy* for her situation but an *opportunity* for himself. For the psychopath, her pain is not a shared life event for him. It is the green light to establish a relationship. The adaptive skill set he learned as a pathological adolescent allows him to quickly become her resident therapist or minister, applying a salve to her wounds through a listening ear, helpfulness, or feigned connection.

As someone suffering from pain, loneliness, and the need for human dialogue, she is not on her highest alert to be able to spot the incoming enemy with his predatory weaponry and skill. She is the sitting gazelle that the jackal has spotted.

Survivor Work Page Question:

The situations that I had just gone through, that were probably capitalized on by the pathological partner, include:

_____

_____

Tactics of Twin-ship and Mutuality

Children are not blamed for a pedophile who pretends to have the same interests that they do. And most relationships, whether friendly or intimate, begin with some form of commonality of which predators are very aware.

Once the opportunity has presented itself through some situational vulnerability, Darkness fashions the specifics of the kill. In the animal kingdom, predators note the specifics of the situation to help identify which animal they are going to target—the animal that is not with their herd, that is alienated from others, one that appears to be hurt or weak, the young, the old, or otherwise vulnerable. Animals who hunt look for the vulnerable members of a herd and then isolate them, a tactic that most survivors say their pathological partners used. For example, they isolated survivors from friends and family by occupying all their time. The specific vulnerability determines the tactics of *how* the prey will be lured in.

The charming and engaging psychopath will encourage the wounded target to participate in life disclosure, leading her through a conversation that reveals the specifics of her vulnerability. *The Institute* calls this 'Assisted Strategic Life Disclosure Tactics.'© *The Institute* 2010 For example, disclosures could include -

- Years in court going through a horrible divorce
- Her cheating boyfriend
- Her special needs child
- Her parent's death
- The overwhelming responsibility of caring for a big house
- Her exhaustion from working a whole year on her thesis while ignoring her social life

Pedophiles look for children who seem like the lost child in their family dynamics—the one who gets less attention, has trouble at school, whose father just left the family, the smaller child who is bullied, or the one who is learning-impaired.

These 'specifics of vulnerability' help the psychopath narrow his approach and create the mirrored reflection of her needs as a billboard advocating for their connection. He becomes everything she has lost, is seeking, or is missing. Or he has the same life experiences which become a point of bonding between them.

Survivor Work Page Question:
The life-disclosing conversations into which I was led included:

_____

_____

T ori

Tori had just gone through the divorce from hell from her therapist husband who used his knowledge of psychology as a weapon against her.

He labeled her with every diagnosis in the DSM, leaving her feeling exhausted from trying to negotiate a divorce with the mastermind of psychological subterfuge. She spent six months selling her house, packing, and moving to another state to escape his psychological brutality. Now settled in, she could exhale—let her hair down while recovering. She wasn't looking for a new mate—Lord no! But a little conversation wouldn't hurt, she thought, as she considered a visit to a local pub in her new town.

She'd spent the day putting the final touches on her latest masterpiece—an oil portrait of the Madonna. Her hands and hair still splattered with paint, she put on some of her most-loved artsy-fartsy bohemian clothes, wrapped some hippie beads around her wrist, pulled on her leather boots and went to the pub for some fun and a glass of wine.

Only moments after she settled down with her wine, she felt eyes on her. From across the room, a brawny looking man with a beard, clad in a checked flannel shirt and jeans, made his way to her. Within moments he was nestled beside her, commenting on her paint-splattered condition, which she explained were remnants of her latest painting success.

"Oh, an artist," thought the psychopath.

"What did you paint?" he inquired.

"The Madonna!" Tori beamed.

"European art," mused the psychopath to himself.

"I love the Renaissance period, don't you?" he purred, despite having never seen art except in magazines.

Tori, off and running, explained that so great is her love of Renaissance art that she went to Europe to see it in person.

"Travel," thinks the psychopath. Proudly, but a bit shyly due to having never left the town he was born in, he proclaimed, "I spent my youth backpacking across Europe."

"Oh, I love Italy!" offered Tori.

The psychopath made a mental note to himself, "Italy." He went on to state, "That was one of my favorite spots while I was in Europe. I spent months there. What were your favorite cities?' he inquired, for clues about where to lead her next.

"Tuscany, Assisi, and Rome", Tori responded.

"Wow! Those were some of the cities I spent time in. I want to continue this conversation, but I need to use the restroom. Be right back." Off to the restroom and on his smart phone, he looked up some of the great artistic spots of Tuscany, Assisi, and Rome. Reciting them to himself so he remembers, he went back to Tori.

"Yes, in Tuscany I loved the old peasant farmhouses and sunflower fields, and in Assisi the centuries-old cathedrals, and in Rome" . . . he trailed off, smiling, noticing a cross around her neck.

"And the religious history in Europe is so mystical!" he offered, knowing not one religious fact nor ever having set foot in a church.

"Yes, I prayed in all those cathedrals!" Tori confessed.

"Amazing! My father was a minister here in these mountains for years," he added. (His father was the town drunk and panhandled for a living.)

And so, within minutes, he had become a total reflection of all of Tori's loves and value systems, creating a totally seamless connection from her history and heart to his invented reflection.

"I feel like we have lived the same lives!" exclaimed Tori.

"Bingo!" the psychopath makes a giant mark on his mental score card.

Reflective Relationship Tactics

As their relationship progressed, each subsequent detail of Tori's history and values that he mined through a guided-life review produced more opportunities for him to mirror her life and concerns.

- Her abusive husband (his wife was abusive, he claimed)
- The daughter she was raising by herself (he was raising his daughter by himself, he claimed)
- Her love of nature (they went hiking in the forest, which he despised)
- Her love of trivia committed to memory (he read encyclopedias to keep up with her)
- Her love of Italian food because she was Italian (he claimed to love Italian food despite finding it too spicy)

Survivor partners often speak of how these predators mined their history and mirrored it back to them, creating a type of *reflective relationship©* that they had never experienced before. While opposites attract, many have not had the experience of meeting their twin and falling into a relationship with him. The dynamics this creates is quite different from when opposites attract, and time is spent learning to like new things. The sensation of kinship through mutual interests and experiences creates a different kind of relationship, full of bells and whistles that create what is perceived as a tight bond of 'twin-ship'©. For survivor partners with healthy self-knowledge and self-acceptance, this shared reflection of all their likes and values feels like a gift, unmatched in other relationships. If you like yourself enough, why wouldn't you welcome someone just like you into your life?

Survivor Work Page Question:
The ways in which he mirrored my life included:

_____

_____

Wrapping This All Up: The Perfect Concoction

Pathology that is unnoticed and combined with predatory hunting techniques that accurately assess vulnerabilities turns any potential partner into a gazelle in the headlights. Just as in pedophilia, once a target is tagged for her vulnerabilities, Darkness begins his quick assessment of her needs, desires, and current weaknesses and mirrors back to her the very familiar reflection of her own life, interests, and values.

Feigning twin-ship and mutuality, while increasing the rapid speed of connection to avoid detection, the predator engages his partner in a whirlwind romance that would leave any prey panting. All these dynamics are simmering in the beaker of their relationship, a chemistry heated by the intensity of the disorder—an unfair advantage that works to a predator's advantage *every time*.

While most of society understands and empathizes with a child's inability to counter the luring pathology of the pedophile, what makes pedophilia successful is the same bundle of pathology exhibited by the Dark Triad—masking their intentions while utilizing tactics of coercion a child has never experienced. Adults are no less at risk when our own normal psychological makeup renders our skill set no match for the stealthy luring approach of pathology.

Let's look at what's lurking in the next phases of this relationship made, not in heaven, but in holy hell.

Chapter Six Endnotes

1   Brown, Sandra L., *The Institute* (2007). Consistent relational patterns in Cluster B/Psychopathic disordered partners: Case studies of qualitative research. Agency raw data. Report prepared for outcome study for *The Institute*.

2   Brown, Sandra L., *The Institute* (2007). Pre, early, mid, late and post relational dynamics of Cluster B/Psychopathic partners: A grounded theory outcome. Prepared for *The Institute's Therapist Training Program and Manual: Treating the Aftermath of Pathological Love Relationships.*

Chapter Seven

The Early Phase of the Relationship—Love Bombing, Twin-ship, and Trance Puzzle Piece #2™

Quick Survivor Review

Regarding the trolling and luring tactics, the potential partner is unaware of the predatory strategies that are being used:

- The attempts to suggest 'Twin-ship' and Mutuality
- Assessments of Situational Vulnerabilities
- Strategic encouragement of Life Disclosure

Why This Happens

I have noticed that there is a tendency by survivor bloggers on this topic to grossly simplify what constitutes the early relationship. While these writers can identify some of the behaviors that Darkness perpetrates, what is missing is an analysis of the complexity of what is happening to the survivor that she carries as symptoms well into the aftermath stage, which can become a roadblock in treatment and recovery. And since this book is ultimately about not just *what* happens but *why* it happens, understanding what is happening internally to the survivor in the early relationship is paramount.

The goal in this chapter is to describe some of the predatory tactics used by Darkness, but more importantly, to explain *why* those tactics work well into the future and create the desperate sense of attachment and feelings of having met their soul mate that survivors are noted to exhibit in Pathological Love and Toxic Relationships. Later in the book, we will look at how the hocus pocus examined in this chapter is highly related to survivors' number one aftermath symptom: cognitive dissonance.

*P*redatory Tactics (continued)[1]

Darkness has baited the hook, has started trolling, and has gotten a nibble. He has approached someone, engaged in conversation, led her through techniques designed to elicit optimum disclosure, then reflected back to her what she was looking for, and thus, has created twin-ship. He has identified enough situational vulnerabilities to act as a billboard for what she is seeking, then has matched her situational vulnerabilities with his own sad stories to elicit empathy (there's no use dating someone who won't willingly empathize with him). He now has enough intel to go to work.

In healthy relationships, getting to know someone can take months to a year or more. But Darkness, with all his classwork at *The Preparatory School for Psychopaths*, can do this in an amazingly short period of time. Skills normally associated with con men who, through a short conversation, can lead people through rapid disclosure have the same skill set as all predators.

Like a pick-pocket who can bump into someone and remove their wallet in a second and without their noticing, Darkness too has fleeced his partner of what he needs to continue his pursuit. Not all survivors even realize they over-disclosed, believing that they've simply engaged in conversation and shared life histories. Maybe Darkness has acquired her phone number, email, or names of her friends so he can pursue her directly or through others. He might know her weekly patterns and set up an 'accidental' encounter where she gets her daily coffee or haunt the pub until he runs into her. Whatever was fleeced will be used for the next contact with her as he moves from trolling and luring into establishing the beginnings of a relationship.

*T*ori

During Tori's brief but illustrious sharing with Darkness, she talked with him about her daily schedule and the breaks she took while painting. After painting in the beautiful morning light, she'd take a nice long walk to unwind in the afternoon, on a specific trail in the forest; this, she mentioned, was her pattern. Darkness had lived in the area his entire life and had never walked that trail. But with a trail map in hand, he planted himself on that trail in the afternoon, with rations and a newspaper, as he waited for her.

Here she came, bounding down the trail with her dog.

"Oh my God! This must be fate!" he gushed. "I love this trail! But I read in the paper they had some robberies and sexual assaults out here. You really shouldn't be here alone. I can't let you be at risk, and that poodle probably can't do much. Let me at least walk behind you," he gallantly offered, "so you can finish your walk. I won't bother you if you prefer to walk by yourself."

As the walk proceeded, he trolled for more information. Tori gladly shared more of her life's story with him, and with what he was learning, he lured her further. He invited her for coffee, but she said she always goes to the grocery store after her walks and today was no exception as she is out of food.

So, a few days later, instead of running into her on the trail again, which might be too obvious, he planned it so he would run into her at the grocery store, which he had noticed when she turned into the store after their walk.

"We have to stop meeting like this!" he blushed.

After some chitchat at the meat counter, he picked up two delicious rib eyes, offering to cook her dinner after her long day of painting — and he's in. In three encounters, he is invited — or rather, allowed — to her home.

The evening, full of more strategically elicited life disclosure, gave him many more 'ops' for approach in the future. As he grilled the steaks, he scanned her yard, noticing that it needed mowing, the gutters were full, and the house itself could use a little touching up.

(Duly noted. Offer to help.)

Sipping wine by candlelight, he led the conversation with his own feigned history, telling stories of his abusive ex-wife and his poor orphaned daughter. Tori responded with her own similar story.

As the night drew to a close he said, "I know how hard it is to be a single mom. I couldn't help but notice those full gutters. They're going to cause water problems soon if they aren't cleaned. I insist on being a boy scout here. I'll bring my ladder — how's 4 p.m. tomorrow?"

The next afternoon he arrived with a ladder, a bottle of wine, flowers, and some chicken for the grill.

Pacing Tactics: Immediacy and Control[2]

Children are not blamed for how quickly a pedophile moves into their lives and takes control, but in PLRs, the survivors are often held responsible.

PLRs are known for the warp speed at which the predator moves into establishing twin-ship and feelings of mutuality. Survivors are swept into the relationship, driven with the pedal-to-the-metal by Darkness. The needs of the Dark Triad include immediacy and control, while the survivor partner is clearly unable to keep up. Overflowing with charisma and a motivational drive jacked up for the thrill of a new relationship, the Dark Triad's pursuit is unrelenting.

Predators understand the power of overwhelming attention. In a PLR this is called *love bombing* — the recipient is overcome with the whirling emotions of too much attention and passion far too soon, which becomes ungrounding and disorienting. The pacing of the relationship creates what survivors have called a vortex that emotionally pulls them in quickly, as they are overwhelmed by the speed of the developing relationship and the hot swirl of emotion, partly masked in twin-ship. Relationships birthed in this way don't allow the survivor to notice red flags that present themselves or reflect on whether immediate twin-ship connections are authentic. There's too much contact too soon; combined with the inability to check out Darkness' supposed history, the relationship is ripe for future lack of inspection as well.

But then, that was the plan all along.

In contrast, normal relationships build slowly, a steady stream of moments spent over time that allow partners to sense and know each other, to think about and compare shared stories and life experiences. With the absence of these normal dynamics, any target lacks the ability to assess the incoming predator.

Love bombing carries over into the Early Phase of the relationship and can be pulled out of the bag of tricks during the mid-relationship phase, or whenever the partner threatens to leave. And once established, it can be a frequently used tool in Darkness' repertoire.

Survivor Work Page Question:
The pacing of this relationship was: _____

*T*ori

Darkness is a wealth of incredible help. A daily routine of house repair begins with him arriving at about 4 p.m., staying through dinner and then later and later each night, as wine and stories flow. Her house has never looked so good!

Each night, as they sit on the couch with their bottle of wine and Tori discloses more and more of her life being gently, but continually, prodded by him, she feels like she has never bared her soul to someone like this before. She thinks he should consider being a counselor—such great listening skills and highly empathetic. He has great insights for her new life as a single mom and is spiritually attuned. He's just so much, well, like her!

With eyes lowered and looking shamefully into his wine, he bares his soul too—the beatings, the alcoholic father, the unfaithful wife. He's never told anyone this before, but he feels, well, like they are soul mates and that she 'gets it.' He is amazed that he couldn't tell a therapist his life story, but he can tell her so easily.

Evenings that ended at 9 p.m. during gutter cleaning last week are now ending at 11 p.m., and then 1 a.m. He calls multiple times a day to check in to see how her artwork is going, what she needs from the store, and with details of a great concert happening over the weekend. He texts daily interesting facts about Renaissance painters (that he looked up on the Internet) that he calls her 'motivational quotes' and calls every morning with a deeply emotional wish for her to have a great day, which exudes depth and connection—like that of a marriage.

Each day, as he invites himself over, he brings a gift—a book on Renaissance Art, a tour book on Italy, a romantic card. Tori's once-bohemian schedule of painting whenever she got up, painting as long as she wanted, walks in the forest, and late nights of more painting, has changed.

She receives a wake-up call in the morning at 9 a.m. (when she used to sleep until 10:30), a text by mid-morning in the center of her painting time, a phone call by late morning to see how the (interrupted) day and painting is going, more artist-fact texts through the day, another call by afternoon to see what she needs from the store and what house projects she has in mind, followed by his arrival almost every day at 4 p.m., with dinner and evenings lasting into the wee hours filled with wine and life stories. Darkness has taken control of her former life.

Where did her life go? In a matter of a couple of weeks, it has become a whirlwind of Darkness. But why is she so exhausted?

Intensity Tactics[3]

Children are not blamed for how intensely the pedophile pretends to care about them, but survivors consistently are. In emotions, *intensity* is noted as 'a high degree of emotional excitement, a depth of feeling.' People with personality disorders can recreate their own excitement-seeking nature in others. What they lack in emotional breadth they make up for in intensity, partly because many have a degree of charisma that bolsters the level of their excitement seeking.

And excitement is contagious, isn't it? Sporting events or concerts are known for the mutual vibe that is produced. It's what is often the most fun about these events—being part of the collective high energy of others. This is exactly the type of contagious energy and emotional excitement that is brought to the new relationship. It's why people say, "His excitement was electrifying", or "His energy was palpable." This intensity sometimes seems to be the factor related to all the fast-paced activity of the new relationship. The sheer pacing of this relationship that continues 24/7 can initially feel exhilarating; from daily date nights to 50 texts a day. Everything seems intense—contact, emotions, and activities.

Stories from survivors have led *The Institute* to examine and develop a theory about these early relationship dynamics. *The Intensity of Attachment*© is the term most used by these women and describes an unusual, intense, quickly established, and with an unshakeable depth of connection that is misinterpreted as soul mate status.

Those with personality disorders/psychopathy are noted for this intense presentation to others as well, not just intimate partners. Bosses, coworkers, friends, and neighbors note this same intense focus when something is desired from them. But in potential intimate relationships, intensity has all the confused earmarks of this false soul mate status. Characterized by the relentless reinforcement of invented twin-ship and mutuality and continual pursuit, the relationship becomes intense and immediate 24 hours a day, 7 days a week.

Survivor Note:

From the moment of meeting the target, constant contact is the hallmark and modus operandi of a pathological while pursuing a PLR.

Most women tell stories of relationships that were created quickly and, within days or weeks, had evolved into dating exclusively, living together, or married—all of which were often a departure from their normal relationship patterns. Unsure of what overcame their normal sense of caution, women were swept into these relational whirlwinds at warp speed that were driven by an intensity they had never experienced before.

But unexamined intensity has many layers and is created from several different sources, not just from emotional excitement. We don't always gravitate to intensity simply because it is part of a collective energy. Sometimes, intensity's unidentified source has its root in deeper problems such as pathology, especially in PLRs.

My utter burnout managing the personality disorder clinic stemmed from many sources, one being the intensity of working with the cluster of disorders called 'dramatic and erratic.' Drama has all the constitutional elements of intensity. I don't know a person alive who doesn't agree that Borderlines, Narcissists, Antisocials, and Psychopaths aren't intense to experience. While Borderlines and Narcissists may have more recognizable emotional intensity in the dramatic and erratic ups and downs of their emotions and relationships, Antisocials and Psychopaths also share an intensity in their self-presentation, even though it's sometimes better hidden than in those with BPD and NPD. While we may not always be able to put our finger on *why* Antisocials and Psychopaths are intense, because their lives are well hidden, that vibe is still there; they throb with some sort of mysterious unnamable energy that feels like you could cut it with a knife.

It took years for me to figure out that the intensity I experienced in sessions with them, even without the dramatic and erratic stories of their latest antics, was in fact, *me* experiencing the disorder *itself*. The disorders labeled as 'dramatic and erratic' are chock full of emotional deficits contained in a brain wired for outrageousness, amped up by unregulated excitement seeking, and, for some, eye-batting charm. Normalcy, in all its flat-lined predictability, pales to the vibrating intensity of that much disorder packed into one human being. Sixty hours per week of person after person with these disorders was wreaking havoc on my own nervous system. Feeling the intensity of the disorder contained in my twelve-by-twelve office was like being slowly electrocuted, one session at a time.

What *The Institute* finds as a factor in the early phases of the relationship is the intensity of the disorder itself, which is *mistaken* for soul mate status and perceived deep intimacy. And while nothing could be further from the truth, that this much intensity is indeed what intimacy is all about or 'he's just that into me,' the survivor partner remains unaware of the manipulation and experiences the throbbing intensity as excitement.

Survivor Work Page Question:
There was a high degree of intensity in our relationship, exhibited by the following examples: _____

_____

$\mathcal{M}$anufacturing Intensity: The State of the Trance[4]

Intensity, far from what should be considered true intimacy, can be artificially manufactured to quicken the sensation of bonding, attachment, intrigue, and sexual response.

Children are not blamed for the ways pedophiles use cult-like programming to manufacture reactions in artificial emotional environments, but survivors often are.

In the harrowing book *The Game*, author Neil Strauss talks about the time he spent living and studying with a pick-up artist named Mystery (of course that would be his name!) who taught others his sleight-of-hand ability to quickly pick up women while leading them into entrancement—a type of trancelike state unnoticed by the victim—to acquire sexual access to them, often within minutes.[5]

Sounds pretty hocus pocus, except Strauss will tell you that it worked more often than it didn't. The love bombing, immediacy and control, and the intensity of the pacing led women into their uncharacteristic behavior of quickly responding to the suggestion of sleeping with a tall, hook-nosed, stringy-haired pick-up artist who dressed ridiculously in a *Cat-in-the-Hat* hat simply to prove the point that it isn't about how he looked, it's about how entrancement *works*.

Luring and early relationship development is all about weaving together intense experience elements that draw people in and overcome normal sensibilities (like sleeping with an unattractive stranger wearing a Dr. Seuss hat). These tactics create seemingly natural scenarios that induce a slight state of trance, which taps into what is called 'state-dependent learning.'

State-dependent learning refers to the specific ways and settings in which we learn behavior and reactions.[6] When someone experiences intensity, love bombing, and fast-paced intimacy causing a slight trance state, this can influence how she behaves later. Learned behavior in trance states can be tapped into by Darkness and intensified further with each usage.

Love bombing, fast-paced intimacy, and the intensity of over-disclosing are states of being that are easily recreated and repeated once the pattern is set.[7] Add to it survivors, whose personality traits include a level of suggestibility (covered later in the book), and you have the ingredients for establishing a pattern that can be repeated and whose victim has been trained to respond.

Most predators, without the benefit of psychology training in state-dependent learning, know these tactics naturally. Psychopaths and pedophiles also intrinsically understand these principles. Children or adults can be led into natural trances that create the opening for the experience which will become a pattern. Some of these gurus explained these principles and created an entire industry now called Seduction Techniques, a multi-million-dollar field crowded with hundreds of teachers. Students learn the power of trance, suggestibility, mirroring, parroting (covered later), love bombing, and intensity as evidenced by some of the topics they teach -

- Pacing for profound rapport
- Mirroring her
- Maximum speed seduction
- Personality trait exploitation
- Covert hypnotic commands
- Sleight-of-Mouth expressions
- Subliminal arousal techniques
- Sensual domination
- Allure

These topics illustrate that the tactics used by psychopathic partners to control their victims—mirroring, twin-ship, intensity—are now considered *techniques.* They stress the following elements:

- That the pace or speed increases the probability of seduction
- That there are personality traits more amenable to these

techniques (which we will discuss in our chapters on Super Traits of the personality)

- That hypnosis or trance states can set commands which work through state-dependent learning and that become part of the relationship dynamics
- That the words used are purposeful and not random
- That, through trance, a predator can increase sexual arousal, bypass a survivor's normal sexual patterns, and dominate the experience through overcoming her natural aversion to quick sexual or relationship development

The reason these tactics work is that the trance state is a natural state of mind involving the way the mind tunes in and tunes out. Its success is also related to what happens with, and to, information while the person is in these states of 'tuning.'

For instance, survivors are often shocked at how quickly they responded to Darkness and how their normal sensibilities, later described in the chapter on Super Traits, were reactively different in this situation than in other non-pathological relationships. Consequently, they fear their ability to read others in the future because they now realize what should have been obvious was not picked up, no matter how blatant the behavior. While some of this disconnect is related to personality traits that cause them to be more suggestible than those without these traits (discussed later in the book), trance states that are established early in the relationship have set the groundwork for *capitalizing* on suggestibility. Since Mystery's techniques have worked on a wide variety of women, personality alone is not the determining factor as to why these techniques work. Hypnosis, as a form of trance inducement, works on nearly everyone.

The true mystery about how Mystery, the pick-up artist, and Darkness can work so quickly has everything to do with what they are tapping into during the trolling, luring, or early relationship phase.

Survivor Work Page Question:

I experienced similar 'Seduction Techniques' being applied to me, which included:

_____

Tuning Out and Hyper Focusing

It seems paradoxical to say that both 'tuning out' and 'tuning in or hyper focusing' exist during the luring phase and/or early relationship development, yet pedophiles use this technique all the time. We will start with the tuning out process that most of us know: 'highway hypnosis.'

People experience this phenomenon as they get sleepy watching the double-yellow lines on the highway. Before long, you have arrived at your exit and you don't remember the last few miles of driving. While driving, your mind was tuning out. By the time you tuned back in, things had happened—time had elapsed, you were back into awareness, and at your destination. For a few minutes, though, you were in a *trance*—an altered state of consciousness that causes *slow reactivity.*

Many accidents (and let's call a PLR an accident) occur when potential partners are tuning out due to the constant repetition and intensity of the predator's pursuit, and things they would normally notice and react to are not as clear and sharp as when they are not in an altered state, like the shadow out of the corner of their eye that ends up being a deer that jumps into their path which results in totaling their car. Or the stories that don't quite add up during Darkness' luring but are missed, as the survivor is not operating on full consciousness. Just like information is missed about how many exits one has driven past, the information about storylines not adding up, the excess charm, and the overly intense pursuit are often missed when tuning out.

Time is also experienced differently when one is tuned out. Survivors like Tori are often shocked at how much time was spent with Darkness when their entire schedule had been gobbled up, yet they were unaware of precisely how that happened and that it didn't seem like they had been together as long as they had. Or they are stunned that the relationship really happened as quickly as it did; they had no awareness of being in a tuned-out trance. They often cannot explain where their former life, interests, hobbies, and friends went. While outsiders might want to label this as being love struck or being just so into him, trance states are directly responsible for how someone is tuned out during these periods where their normal reactions and conscious decision making is interrupted. Repeat that scenario over months or even longer and you have a person being manipulated by the techniques like those used by Mystery.

154

If it didn't work, it wouldn't be a multi-million-dollar industry.

Although trance is associated with the tuning out process, it is also associated with hyper-focused attention, which is how hypnotists use it in formal hypnosis (and how Darkness also uses it). The only difference between trance and formal hypnosis is that *formal hypnosis* is a 'guided focused and controlled trance.' That's why the hypnotist says, "Stare into my eyes—" because leading someone into staring (or for Darkness, love gazing) forces attention on the person about to control the subject.

Survivor Note:

Hypnosis and trance both involve the ability to heavily focus on one thing while blocking out other things.

This is an example of how tuning out trance states and hyper-focusing trance states can be piggy-backed for greater impact. When a partner is highly focused on Darkness' storytelling (and who is a better storyteller than Darkness?), she may miss the nuances that belie contradictory information, the body language that doesn't match the narrative, or the reactions of others who are not entranced by his theatrics. She might have missed him texting late at night, making secretive phone calls, or giving explanations that didn't add up. This focused attention on a single thing (the pathological partner) is essentially a trance state.

So, before we argue that this is too much hocus pocus to be what is actually happening, we need to remember that this state is not radically different from 'flow states' experienced by top athletes, musicians, and artists who describe it as "when you're completely involved in the process of creating something new and you don't have enough attention left over to monitor how your body feels—the fact that you're hungry or tired or to listen to your mind chatter."[8] In other words, the person is so intent on achieving a specific goal that they lose track of everything else. They further describe being in the flow state as being 'completely involved, focused, and concentrated—there's a sense of ecstasy of being outside of everyday reality, a loss of a sense of self. Worries and concerns drift away, and time is lost while you just focus on the present moment and whatever's producing this state becomes its own reward.'

Hyper-focused trance states produce a loss of awareness of time just like the tuning-out trance state does. When people are rapt and focusing on each other like in the love-bombing stage of luring or in the early relationship, they lose track of time. The psychopath, who has abundant energy to maintain intensity, can easily use that intensity to encourage hyper focus. The enormous amount of time he is spending with his partner allows him to get her to hyper focus on him. In the early romantic stages of a relationship, all the gazing into each other's eyes that's done is fertile ground for the trance-induction technique. As she tunes out her former life and interests, and hyper focuses, with guidance from Darkness, on the new relationship, her altered consciousness is missing important clues about the shadows that are just beyond the corner of her eye, like the deer about to jump into the path of the oncoming car.

But as noted in the description of the flow state, the trance state can feel so utterly focused as to be calming, even ecstatic, which is often described by the survivors as "being so enraptured" in ways they may have never felt before.

===

Survivor Note:

This enjoyable state becomes its own reward and is what is craved and missed when the relationship deteriorates. The survivor feels as if she is in withdrawal; these flow/trance states become like an addiction.

===

Trance states can also create a high tolerance for emotional and physical pain, which is why they are used medically in pain management. Pain can be tuned out, squelched, or numbed by trance states (and flow states), and emotions, injury, and even bodily exhaustion can be discounted, allowing survivors to stay in unimaginable circumstances, such as Pathological Love Relationships.

Survivor Work Page Question:
I experienced the following examples of tuning out and/or hyper focusing: _____

_____

Trance, State-Dependent Learning, and Their Impact on the Relationship[9]

State-dependent learning, mentioned previously, concerns how what is learned in a trance/flow state influences the way someone behaves later on. The patterns established in the early relationship will continue long after the relationship ends. They will also appear in aftermath trauma symptoms, because the love-bombing and manipulative language used in the early relationship embeds in the survivor certain perceptions of Darkness and corresponding emotional and sexual responses.

The romantic language and professions of love in early relationships are perceived differently when someone is in a trance state. When the psychopath speaks in metaphor and symbol (for instance, "I have you locked in my heart"), these symbols are stored as strong subconscious messages and images. An internal image of being locked and unable to escape can be created in the subconscious mind under the guise of love and being 'in his heart.' But as we know, love should never be related to being trapped. The early relationship is full of love imagery that is not only intense but is intensely *creating* a hostage type of attachment below the surface of consciousness.

That's why the psychopath's messages have such staying power and emotional strength long after his partner discovers his true nature. Therapists who try to rationally discuss the woman's perceptions of her partner quickly encounter these roadblocks in the survivor's emotional memories, which are related to the symbols introduced in a period of state-dependent learning.

Trance also produces subconscious perceptual biases. If the psychopath is telling his partner wonderful things and she feels euphoric with him, she tends to associate those wonderful and euphoric things *with* the memory of him, even after he's turned into a monster in the next stage of the relationship. While in the trance, a woman tends to cement what she felt and/or learned in that state. That's why it's so difficult for women to believe he's a liar, swindler, or cheater because she learned all those other wonderful things about him *in* a euphoric trance state that has been embedded in her memory *before* she learned of the other side of his Jekyll/Hyde personality.

In the early stages of a relationship, what is being built in state-dependent learning periods are the associations of intensity, bondedness, symbols associated with the love language, and the emotional rewards of being in a euphoric state. These learning states create perceptual biases and lead the woman to believe that their bond is unbreakable. This belief will overpower rationality, reality, or facts in the future when his behavior is at odds with the embedded results of state-dependent learning.

Even after the relationship ends and the survivor is knee deep in traumatic aftermath symptoms, if you ask her which memory produces a stronger feeling—the memory of being intensely bonded to him or the memory of his cheating—she will say, "the memory of the bonding."

The Psychopath's Hypnotic Stare

The psychopath's stare has its own allure and may be effective in inducing a trance state. Many women, before they knew their partner was a psychopath, thought it was sexy or intense. There really is something extra powerful to the psychopath's stare. Dr. Reid Melloy, in his book *Violent Attachments,* says that both women and men have noted the psychopath's unusual and unnerving stare. He refers to the stare as a 'relentless gaze that seems to preclude the psychopath's destruction of his victim or target.'[10] It is also often referred to as 'The Reptilian Gaze' because of its primitive predatory look.

Dr. Robert Hare referred to the gaze of psychopaths as "intense eye contact and piercing eyes" and even suggested that people should avoid having consistent eye contact with them. Other writers refer to it as a "laser-beam stare" or an "empty hypnotic look."[11] Women in our practice have labeled the gaze as -

- Intense
- Sensual
- Disturbing
- Intrusive

They have said,

- "He stared me down in the bar until I couldn't stand it anymore."
- "He looked at me like I was the most delicious thing!"
- "He looked right through me like he could see everything in me. I didn't know what that was. I never had that experience before, and I'll never forget it."
- "I thought he could have eaten me alive."

Eye gazing, as trance induction, means that the words that follow the induction are fused into a victim's mind with much more intensity. Eye-to-eye locks, in which the psychopath strokes her face and leads her into a slight trance state saying things like, "You are the most giving woman; you have given me what no one else has. I know that you will always give to me this way and that we will be together forever. I know you would never hurt me, or leave me, or lie to me, or cheat." These "set commands" are the hypnotic handcuffs that keep her attached to him long after she wants to leave.

Women have reported that certain phrases play repetitiously in their minds long after the psychopathic partner is gone. These trance states and state-dependent learning build off each other, increasing the strength of the message, lasting past the early phase of the relationship, and play havoc during the end of the relationship when they feel addicted or held hostage to a feeling state and don't know why.

Wrapping This All Up: More Than Sleight of Hand

Darkness, like Mystery, brings more than just wrong motives to the early relationship. He brings covert strategies steeped in psychology—his ability to extract strategic life disclosures, rapid seduction techniques, the ability to alter a victim's state of consciousness, and the use of state-dependent learning. This creates a level of hostage-type attachment that is strongly connected to the emotions generated during love bombing.

For a survivor, it means she continually lives in a replay state of the honeymoon phase of the relationship. No matter what happens from that moment forward, what is most internally experienced and/or what guides decision-making are the euphoric feelings and identification of the psychopath as soul mate that was created in this early phase. It is a false high that keeps on giving and blocks her ability to recognize any cautionary red flags. Even after she is discarded, survivors often talk about this replay state, citing the feelings induced during love bombing despite all the instances of his infidelity or other behavior. They cite the addictive quality of those feelings which replay in their minds far more frequently than any of Darkness' bad behavior.

But, alas, there are still more changes ahead in the next phase of relationship.

*T*ori

"You won't believe it. I know it's too soon . . . I know it's only been six weeks. . . but he gave me a ring!" Tori says breathlessly over the phone.

"WHAT? That's crazy!" screams her friend. "Have you met his daughter? His family? What do you know about this guy?"

"I will soon—he promises. His daughter is touring Europe right now. I know everything about him—his childhood, his plans for the future— all of it," Tori offers. "He wants to move in, save money, and get married in a couple of months. I know it's fast, but we really are soul mates. We're two peas in a pod!"

"He could be homeless. You don't know! Have you seen his house?" her friend demands.

"He drove me past the outside of it. But he just sold it and put his stuff in storage and is staying with a friend. It was very nice."

"Did you look it up on the county records? You don't know he owned it," her friend challenges.

"Really? He's gonna show me something he never owned? Is that what you think?" Tori fumes.

"Well, come by my house. I wanna see that ring. You know I used to be a jeweler. Let's see what he got you!" her friend offers.

The following week, an examination of Tori's ring reveals the stone is cubic zirconia, and it's been worn a great deal in the past but has recently been cleaned and buffed to remove wear on the band.

Chapter Seven Endnotes

1   Brown, Sandra L., *The Institute* (2015). Atypical trauma presentation in pathological love relationship survivors. An interagency report; also prepared for *The Institute's Therapist Training Program and Manual: Treating the Aftermath of Pathological Love Relationships.*

2   Brown, Sandra L., *The Institute* (2007). Consistent relational patterns in Cluster B/Psychopathic disordered partners: Case studies of qualitative research. Agency raw data. Report prepared for outcome study for *The Institute.*

3   Brown, Sandra L. and Leedom, Liane J. (2008). *Women Who Love Psychopaths: Inside the Relationships of Inevitable Harm.* First Edition. Health and Well-Being Publications, LLC.

4   Brown, Sandra L. (2009). *Women Who Love Psychopaths: Inside the Relationships of Inevitable Harm with Narcissists, Sociopaths, & Psychopaths.* Second Edition. Mask Publishing.

5   Strauss, N. (2005). *The Game: Penetrating the Secret Society of Pick Up Artists.* Harper Collins.

6   Degun-Mather, M. (2006). The Nature of Dissociation and the Long-Term Consequences of Child Abuse. In *Hypnosis, Dissociation and Survivors of Child Abuse: Understanding and Treatment* (1st ed., p. 62). Wiley.

7   Brown, Sandra L., *The Institute* (2009). Trance states influence early relational luring in Pathological Love Relationships. Agency raw data included in parts of *Women Who Love Psychopaths. Second Edition.*

8   Fabrega, M. (n.d.). How to Enter the Flow State. https://daringtolivefully.com/how-to-enter-the-flow-state

9   Brown, Sandra L., *The Institute* (2009). Trance states influence early relational luring in Pathological Love Relationships. Agency raw data included in parts of *Women Who Love Psychopaths. Second Edition.*

10   Meloy, R. (1997). *Violent Attachments* (2nd Edition). Jason Aaronson, Inc.

11   Birch, A. (2015). Psychopathy: Is it in their eyes? http://psychopathsandlove.com/psychopathy-and-the-eyes/

Chapter Eight

The Mid-Phase of the Relationship— When the Mask Slips
Puzzle Piece #2™

Quick Survivor Review

- The relationship was controlled through immediacy and rapid pacing.
- Intensity was misread by the survivor as intimacy.
- Tuning out and hyper focusing were utilized to produce trance states.
- Seduction techniques were employed.
- State-Dependent Learning occurred, which produced constant memories of the emotions elicited by love bombing, even in the future when his pathological behavior became evident.

Continuing with the examination of Puzzle Piece #2™—Dramatic and Erratic Relational Dynamics, is a discussion of the abrupt changes in the relationship as she heads into the mid-phase of the drama-filled experience.

Until Now

In the animal kingdom, a predator's speed overcomes the prey's ability to think and make rational decisions to protect itself. The isolated animal runs in a zig-zag pattern which clouds its ability to make the correct next decision. Eventually exhausted and unable to examine options for survival, it succumbs and surrenders to the animal that is faster, smarter, and has a more developed skill set for plunder.

Surrendering to the Pathological Love Relationship in its early stages is not like getting eaten by a lion. It is like succumbing to a symphony of sensory euphoria. Unaware of her vulnerability, she has been wined and dined, delighted with unusual and copious amounts of attentive listening, and her brain has been swimming in an elixir of endorphin producing chemicals like oxytocin that result in a sense of incredible well-being. She has been overcome by the feeling of twin-ship and mutuality, of an eternity of time spent together, and has been doused with compliments. If this isn't Prince Charming, happily ever after, or having found her soul mate, she doesn't know what is.

Now she is headed into the next phase of the relationship which will feel very different than the trolling and luring of the early phase. In fact, the differences she will feel in this mid-phase of the relationship will give rise to most of the symptoms she will experience throughout the rest of the relationship and well into her future.[1] Sometimes these phases are a quick overlap with not much of a demarcation between the early and mid-phases, depending on the length of the overall relationship. Other times, each phase can be much longer and with a more pronounced demarcation.

An example of this is when the love bombing of the early phase is carried over or used intermittently in the mid-phase. For some, the love bombing continues well into the mid-phase with attention, sex, and perhaps luxurious gifts, trips, and plans for the future, especially when the survivor is becoming suspicious or investigatory. But for others, love bombing that was part of the luring and early relationship phases seems to vanish in the mid-phase, which rapidly descends into the discarding phase.

Whether the mid-phase is short or long, whether it overlaps with the luring and early relationship behaviors of twin-ship, mutuality, or love bombing, what the mid-phase exhibits in all relationships is the issue of *revelation*. This is the phase when something is revealed that conflicts with what the survivor thought she knew about her partner. It is when his mask slips, and she sees, learns, or feels something notably *different*.

The most common reason she feels something different is that Darkness is not wired for monogamy. The brain regions responsible for impulse control and his motivational drives that seek excitement lead to trolling for other relationships.

$\mathcal{H}$is Relational Timelines—It's Sure Crowded in This Relationship

Children are not blamed for not getting out sooner when it's discovered that they've been part of a pedophile's ring and they learn that the pedophile has contact with other children. That's because what is known about pedophiles is that their skills have enabled them to establish a relationship bond with a child before other children are introduced into the mix.[2]

While it appears that Darkness has what he wanted with a new relationship established at warp speed, it is far from the monogamous union that survivors think it will be. Up until now, it has been, for her, a tornado of passion, deep and honest sharing, and the joy of twin-ship. But, brewing beneath Darkness' outward professions of love are those motivational drives that just don't do well with the boringness of consistency—especially a single, consistent partner.

With a brain wired for seeking excitement, motivated by avoiding boredom, fearing abandonment, and hungering for some new manipulation, Darkness can never be tied to just one relationship. Once a survivor partner is vetted and ensconced in the relationship, the Dark Triad is out trolling for new material to fill up the pipeline in case this relationship becomes too demanding, too boring, or too wise.

Darkness' hard-wired predatory sixth sense never shuts off. After someone has committed herself to him, his in-person time with her may begin to dwindle (although texting and calling continues) as he begins the hunt anew. He trolls wherever he is. While getting his coffee, he is testing the waters with the barista by maintaining eye contact. When having lunch, he sees how chatty the waitress is and if she'll take his business card. At work, he is flirting with a coworker. While having beers with the guys, he is chatting up women he meets, and combing the place looking for others who have potential. Then there is his online life—dating sites, forums, chat rooms, and sex sites that are regular haunts for the 'go-go-now' brain and which offer the potential for unlimited access.

Darkness is employing all his skills, all the time, in various phases of relationship—from mere luring or trolling new recruits for shown interest; to early relationship contact by texting, phoning, and going online;

to the mid-relationship, where he is dating/sleeping with others; and in multiple relationships that are simultaneously or sequentially ending, due to wisdom on her part or boredom on his; and lastly, in the post-relationship phase, which we will discuss later.

Juggling these many relationships in their various phases of development would do in a normal man. That much expended energy, and even name remembering, are not for the faint of heart. But Darkness comes naturally wired for all of it—his go-go-now brain, lack of guilt, conscience and remorse, his gift of gab, ability to date at warp speed, and being driven by the need for excitement and his thrill-seeking behaviors all spells infidelity as the thrill of each new opportunity for manipulation precisely meets his needs.

There are those pathological partners who are indeed monogamous, although it is rare. This monogamy can be influenced by the public image that they want to portray, especially in religious communities. A pathological partner who wants to be seen as above board, without fault, and staunchly religious, may opt out of physical romances to protect his image. This doesn't mean, though, that online porn or sex chat forums aren't being utilized.

For most Dark Triad personalities, there will generally be others entering and exiting their relational pipeline. The survivor's sense of closeness to her pathological partner is directly proportional to the activity in the pipeline—when there are fewer people in the pipeline, he can give her more attention. When she feels he is being aloof, he's working on new recruits— trolling, luring, and developing early relationships.

$\mathcal{T}$he Relationship Cycle[3,4,5]

The survivor usually senses or becomes aware of the insertions of new recruits into Darkness' pipeline by mid-relationship, although this doesn't mean that is when the activity began. Some survivors can, in retrospect, identify the probable insertion of others even in the very beginning of their own relationships, but with love bombing dominating the luring and early phases, and the corresponding trance and state-dependent learning that was experienced, many survivors don't *tune in* to Darkness' distraction and aloofness until the mid-relationship phase.

While we are limited by a two-dimensional drawing to show all the different stages and phases of Darkness' relationship cycle, each stage shows the multiple people overlapping on the relational timeline. The diagram below presents a simple representation of the stages. For example, if you imagine this circle superimposed on itself multiple times, you'll have an idea of what it would look like to have five people in pre-stages, six in the early stages, three in the middle stages, five in ending stages, and four in post-relationship interactions, all occurring at the same time.

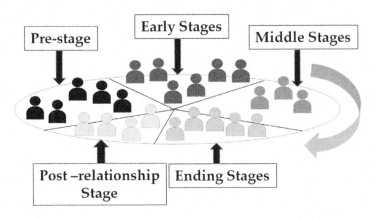

Figure 8.1
Stages and Phases of Darkness' Relationship Cycle © 2007

Survivor Work Page Question:
I identify with the relational timeline cycle and experienced the following phases of the timeline:

_____

Noticing

Survivors may notice distraction or aloofness as new recruits enter the pipeline and Darkness' time and interest are pulled in other directions. Survivors describe subtle, or not-so-subtle, shifts demonstrated by these factors -

- How much time he is around
- The lack of love bombing
- The beginning of criticism and disinterest

- More time spent texting or calling others
- Leaving the room, coming home later or not at all
- More time on the computer
- Fewer compliments, less sex
- Storylines of where he has been don't add up
- Texts from others she doesn't recognize
- Receipts for places she hasn't been

Survivor Work Page Question:

I became suspicious of his behavior when: _____

_____

$\mathcal{T}$he Face Behind the Mask [6]

mask[7]

noun

a covering for all or part of the face, worn as a disguise, or to amuse or terrify other people.

synonyms: disguise, false face

Finding, or perhaps truly seeing, the mask for the first time is like pulling a thread on a sweater and watching it unravel. What precipitates a survivor seeing the mask is her noticing the changes in Darkness' emotional distance, which causes her to look closer. For some survivors, this could be a few weeks or months into the relationship, while for others it could be decades.

Survivors might have caught a glimpse of a text, overheard part of a phone call, saw a dating site web page left open on his computer, or have contracted an STD. They could have given money to a new business venture only to find that the business never existed. They might have discovered undisclosed criminal behavior or a swath of unclaimed children. They could find out that his MBA was ordered from the back of a magazine or that he doesn't have the house he pointed out to her and, instead, still lives with his mother. Perhaps she was contacted by previous girlfriends or wives and finds out he wasn't married just once before but four times.

How that thread on the sweater comes to unravel is not the point. But some fact becomes known to her that conflicts with what she thought she knew so deeply about him generated from state dependent learning, which raises in her a different level of awareness and concern. Although it will be a long time until she reconciles the reality with the fantasy, something has piqued her curiosity, and that begins the questioning that may take months, or even years, to answer.

Noticing vs. Reacting

While her curiosity and suspicion have been aroused from the distancing and movement she notices in the relationship, the reaction and action steps of her disengagement could be months or years off. Blocking these steps are all the effects of the entrancement techniques used in the luring in the early and mid-relationship phases. The suggestions repeated during the unrecognized trance have cemented the connection that will be felt throughout the relationship, including when the sweater begins to unravel, and long afterward. The constant references to building closeness and a future together leave a survivor sure of the relationship in ways she has never been before. In opposition to this learned acceptance are whatever clues or facts she has found out about his true identity or behavior.

This conflict between facts and feelings, resulting from what happens in state-dependent learning, creates what's called *cognitive dissonance* — 'a debilitating condition of immobility that prevents the survivor partner from developing and maintaining one clear perception of Darkness as the man behind the mask with a hidden life.'[8,9]

Mid-relationship dynamics are filled with the cognitive dissonant reactions of ping-ponging between 'he loves me/he loves me not,' and 'I'm leaving/I'm staying.' Family and friends who watch these shifts of emotion are driven to the same distraction as the survivor. The objective view, of both the survivor and others witnessing it, is that the facts of the various discoveries should be enough to warrant action-oriented steps toward ending the relationship.

What is unseen and unknown, though, is that the emotions developed and learned in that trance-like state have created the sensation of gorilla-glue bonding that is stronger than randomly emerging facts of infidelity or other hidden life events. It is in this inescapable subconscious holding pattern that the victim is caught throughout the mid-phase of the relationship, and for which she will be judged by those around her.

Cognitive dissonance prevents action because it produces the need for constant and infinite review and verification—the sufferer believes that more intel will solve the conflict. Survivors are driven to the investigation of hidden life events for more and more proof of disloyalty, lies, and infidelity to squelch the growing conflict between facts vs. feelings. But more information does not negate the emotions learned in the trance state—at least not in the early time of the mid-relationship.[10] Instead, it uses up precious internal emotional resources as the partner spends months, or years doing the following -

- Monitoring his texts
- Breaking into his computer
- Following him or hiring a private investigator
- Contacting new women in the pipeline
- Putting key loggers on his computer to find out what sites he is visiting
- Checking his credit card bills to see where he has been

Each fact revealed produces spiraling depression, anxiety, and more cognitive dissonance as he may continue to express love, affection, or plans for the future. Survivors describe their "emotional temperature" as varying wildly from moment-to-moment, being dependent on what is discovered that day, or through his nightly interactions with them.

It takes enormous amounts of time and energy to keep the investigation going which creates an increasing inability to *act* on what is found. Cognitive dissonance sounds incredibly irrational to others: "If I find out ONE MORE TIME that he's cheated, that's it!" or "I don't believe that woman who called me. Of course, she's making it up!"

Paradoxically, it feels just as irrational to survivors themselves, who wonder where their previous line in the sand regarding acceptable behavior in a relationship *went*. More uncovered events simply lead to being more frozen until a survivor becomes completely unrecognizable to herself.

Survivor Work Page Question:
My behaviors of trying to investigate his hidden life included:

_____

Confronting the Mask

While cognitive dissonance and state-dependent learning are likely to have slowed her reaction time, at some point survivors bring their newly found information to Darkness. It could be suspicions or facts, events, or documentation. It could even be caught in the act factuality. Darkness, with all his training in profound rapport techniques, has an explanation for every event, which amounts to gaslighting. He will usually respond to most confrontations with these examples -

- Denial
- Plausible explanations supported by his accomplices
- Gaslighting — deflecting by acting as if something is wrong with his partner (i.e., mental illness, some kind of breakdown, paranoia, a reaction to stress, etc.)
- Increased attention, sex, professed plans for the future

Each go-round of confrontation that he responds to with denial or gaslighting adds to her growing cognitive dissonance as she ponders plausible explanations, considers her profound state-dependent feelings of bondedness, is persuaded to believe *she* is the problem, and wonders how she can get back to the feelings she once had that were created by the love bombing. Her goal is to fix what is wrong.

$\mathcal{W}$rapping This All Up

What makes PLRs different than normal or merely bad relationships are the unusual relationship dynamics not found in healthy relationships. While early or mid-phases of normal dating might not lapse quickly into exclusivity and might include the casual dating of several people until the parties settle on the right one, the pathological partners in a PLR continue casual dating of *everyone* while stating they are exclusive with someone — but, in truth, are not.

In pop culture we call these people 'players,' but in our chapter about "who does that" we noted that what society *calls* these disorders hardly defines their true pathology. Many players would fall into the Dark Triad. Relationships that are implied to be exclusive but include many other hidden partners are relationships of manipulation that we sometimes label Serial Monogamy. The person is monogamous for the one hour they are with a date or partner, but then they engage in repeated "monogamous hours" with lots of other people, too. This is hardly the monogamy most women are seeking.

Sooner or later, every relationship is challenged by the need to climb out of the love nest and make a real relationship not based on endorphins and sweat, but based on emotional depth, consistent behavior, and insight about others. While Darkness' charm and sexual skill might be good honeymoon and early-phase elements, the relationship will quickly deteriorate when these other elements don't, and can't, surface.

The next chapter examines those elements that Darkness inherently cannot bring to a relationship, even as the survivor tries desperately to understand the problems and to address them. Besides the defense mechanisms of denial and gaslighting, the Dark Triad brings a boatload of his own issues to the mid-phase of the relationship. What begins to occur, as the survivor attempts to problem solve their relationship, will add gasoline to the burning symptoms of cognitive dissonance producing significant aftermath trauma.

 Tori

"So, the ring was fake—that doesn't mean his intentions aren't sincere—it just means he doesn't have any money!"

"Are you sure? What else is fake?" her friend demands. "What about that house he just sold? Let's look that up at the town hall's deed registry."

"I'm not starting a relationship with suspicion," Tori says defensively.

"And where has he been lately? He was like super glue in the beginning, and now he's hardly ever around. Don't you find that odd, especially if you're going to get married?"

"I hear from him all day long. He calls, he texts—he's just been busy with a project, which is why he's not here as much."

Her friend presses, "How's the relationship?"

"He's distracted by this project—that's all! Stop making this into something it isn't. I'm not a suspicious person."

"Maybe you should be," she suggests.

Darkness was busy. He had multiple women in his relational pipeline, all requiring attention. Some he was trolling, some he was luring, and then there were those he was drawing into a relationship with the same entrancement techniques he'd used on Tori.

But her friend's suggestions had planted a seed of doubt in Tori. She had become suspicious, and as Darkness' schedule began to change, she sneaked into his phone and computer for a little peek. She *had* noticed those swings between closeness and aloofness; the places he said he'd gone to that he'd never been; the claims that he had money, but didn't; jobs he said he'd had, that he didn't; his family who she'd never met; his college degree that he couldn't find; his friend's house where he stayed that he wouldn't take her to…

Tori decided it was time for a chat to get answers to the mounting inconsistencies. Their early phases of relationship were built on intense mutual sharing, so, surely, they'd be able to work through these miscommunications. What she had come to know about him was that he was just like her—full of sharing and the need for compatible communication. Maybe they had strayed recently in their communication, but it had been the bedrock of how their relationship was created, and it would be there when they needed it most—she just knew it.

Chapter Eight Endnotes

1,6 Brown, Sandra L., *The Institute* (2007). Pre, early, mid, late and post relational dynamics of cluster b/psychopathic partners: A grounded theory outcome. Prepared for *The Institute's Therapist Training Program and Manual: Treating the Aftermath of Pathological Love Relationships.*

2 Brown, Sandra L. and Young, Jennifer R., *The Institute* (2015). Predatory tactics in Pathological Love Relationships. Prepared for *The Institute's Therapist Training Program and Manual: Treating the Aftermath of Pathological Love Relationships.*

3 Brown, Sandra L., *The Institute* (2007). Consistent relational patterns in cluster b/psychopathic disordered partners: Case studies of qualitative research. Agency raw data. Report prepared for outcome study for *The Institute.*

4,9 Brown, Sandra L. and Leedom, Liane J. (2008). *Women Who Love Psychopaths: Inside the Relationships of Inevitable Harm.* First Edition. Health and Well-Being Publications, LLC.

5 Brown, Sandra L. (2009). *Women Who Love Psychopaths: Inside the Relationships of Inevitable Harm with Narcissists, Sociopaths, & Psychopaths.* Mask Publishing.

7 Merriam-Webster. (2018, March 17) *Mask.*

8,10 Brown, Sandra L., *The Institute* (2007). Cognitive dissonance perceived as traumatic in Pathological Love Relationships. Raw data from a study; also, in *Women Who Love Psychopaths: Inside the Relationships of Inevitable Harm with Narcissists, Sociopaths & Psychopaths. Second Edition* (2009). Mask Publishing.

Chapter Nine

Communication and The Building Blocks of a Relationship Puzzle Piece #2™

Quick Survivor Review

- During the relationship, Darkness is establishing other re-lationships which are at various stages.
- Survivors begin noticing changes in his behavior, includ-ing distraction and aloofness.
- What a survivor notices is contradictory to Darkness' deni-al, resulting in cognitive dissonance.

Continuing on with Puzzle Piece #2™, further into the mid-phase of the relationship is the profound display of what the DSM has warned about all along—the deficits that will never be overcome.

*P*aradise Lost

There's trouble in paradise now! A bundle of uncompleted emo-tional development combined with a short-circuited brain has arrived, completely undetected, on the victim's doorstep, and, with a Gucci suit and charming demeanor, has invited her into a relationship of inevitable harm. But Darkness has noticed, in this mid-phase, that she notices his movement both toward and away from her, and that needs some explain-ing. The love-bombing stage flooded her brain with oxytocin, producing an extreme feeling of well-being, and his seduction techniques bonded her to him at rapid speed. But now that she feels that all is not well in the relationship, she will be met with difficulties not soon overcome.

If there is a point at which these relationships of inevitable harm are going to fail, it is when she encounters issues that require more than charm and smooth talking to explain. While it may take time for these perceived inconsistencies to reveal what is truly behind the relationship, this chapter will help identify *why* he will doom the relationship to failure—because of his inability to communicate and to problem solve. And there are plenty of problems to address.

$\mathcal{T}$he Intercourse Problem

Problems begin when the survivor is sensing betrayal and feels the relationship failing, she wants to work at repairing, or at least stabilizing, the relationship. But, in order to fix something, you need the right tools. So, let's talk about the tool of intercourse—no, not the hot sweaty, best-sex-you-ever-had kind of intercourse that is often associated with the Dark Triad—the real intercourse—communication.

The word *intercourse* means 'the interchange of thoughts and feelings.'[1] It is the building block of all true intimacy and one of the areas that the DSM5 notes as *deficient* in people with personality disorders.

What makes these disorders so soul destroying to others is related to what they *cannot* do or bring to a relationship—self-functioning, consistent self-identity, empathy, and intimacy.[2] These deficiencies, then, provide a schematic for what is going to go wrong in the relationship. The disorder defined as 'dramatic and erratic', and previously, as 'severe and dangerous' warns us about the Dark Triad's poor prospects for building a healthy or successful relationship.

Relationship counseling involves teaching partners how to build a healthy relationship. When building a house, the first thing that's done is to create footings upon which the foundation will sit. In a relationship the footings are the intercourse which is communication and the foundation of a relationship. Communication is what creates, or destroys, relationships, and it is why it is the focus of relationship counseling, because it is through communication where emotional safety is birthed. It is, after all, how we come to know someone—through sharing our feelings, experiences, histories, hopes, dreams, and thoughts. Poor communication produces poor relationships. But why?

While communication can happen on many levels, such as body language and innuendo, its primary form is in what we *say*. Our use of language, and the meaning behind our words, helps create intimacy. Mixed messages—when what we say and what we do are not in sync—produce a shaky foundation upon which the crooked structure of the relationship will be built.

The Dark Triad brings to the task of relationship building all the skewed and hidden deficits identified in the DSM5. The very foundation from which everything else will be built—understanding, emotional safety, and true and abiding intimacy—is cracked beneath the structure that is built upon it. Once the next level of building begins, one might never notice that the foundation underneath it was defective all along.

Biology

On the one hand, the Dark Triad appears to be the Master Communicator, at least initially—an uncanny creator of relationships through entrancing storylines, humor, intensity, and charisma. And up until his new partner notices that something is not quite right, the Master Communicator seems very invested in creating a dialogue between them. But later, communication patterns become mazes that end in utter frustration, with parallel meanings and misconstrued language. These communication problems can't be solved by her because what is wrong with his biology which influences his communication trumps everything.

Normal communication includes the use of both abstract and concrete concepts. Our ability to communicate successfully is predicated on the ability to move fluidly between understanding when a person is talking either abstractly or concretely and to understand the differences. This inability to understand the difference between abstract and concrete concepts is a unique deficit in personality disorders and psychopathy.

Language and the meaning behind it is created in the brain—yep, one of the Dark Triad's affected regions of the brain seen in Chapter Two. He is both biologically challenged from converting language into its proper meaning, while also motivated to control, con, and manipulate, which damages the very foundation that communication is trying to build.

Abstract Language[3]

Abstract language, used by normal people but challenging for the Dark Triad, consists of intangible concepts without a physical form.

It names qualities like love, commitment, honor, and fidelity—words without concrete meaning to Darkness—and so he lacks an understanding of the behaviors associated with these concepts. As we know, the word 'love' can be a noun, but in a relationship, we want it to be a verb. There are actions associated with the word *love*.

Survivor Note:

Impairments in knowing what constitutes the building blocks of a relationship result in the inability to authentically communicate intimately, or to exhibit the consistent positive behaviors that are seen, for instance, in love.

All normal language uses both abstract and concrete words effortlessly. Most of us have never been challenged with having to utilize only one communication pattern except with children or perhaps the intellectually disabled. In our repertoire of language in relationships, we haven't had to change our basic format of communicating. But in Pathological Love Relationships, a survivors' entire use of the human language has had to change, causing feelings of inadequacy about *their own* ability to communicate since half of their language has become of no service to the relationship. The survivor must learn to communicate with language that has been vastly limited in order to have *any* chance whatsoever of talking apples-to-apples with his communication challenges.

While the beginning of the relationship is not likely to reveal his communication deficiencies or highlight the improbability of him ever effectively communicating abstract ideas, like love and fidelity, the survivor will eventually notice traces of problems he has with abstract language -

- He has a blank look on his face when she uses words he does not understand.
- When responding back to her about the context of a word, he uses the context incorrectly.
- He changes the discussion when an abstract word comes up that he doesn't want to discuss.
- Abstract words and their meaning are declared off limits for future discussions.
- Abstract words are demeaned and labeled 'stupid' to avoid discussion.

Agreeing on the surface with the implied meaning behind words like love, fidelity, and commitment can't produce real intimacy when these words aren't truly comprehended, especially when the non-understood words are replaced with the closest concepts Darkness has for them. When 'love' is replaced with 'compliance' or when 'monogamy' is replaced with 'serial monogamy,' the elements of what builds a real relationship don't even exist.

Abstract problems become more noticeable as the relationship continues, and the inevitable discussions about love, fidelity, trust, and commitment arise when the survivor notices the ebb and flow of someone else entering the stream of their relationship.

Survivor Note:

The DSM5 noted one of the Dark Triad's deficits as intimacy because intimacy can never be acquired without true communication.

Survivor Work Page Question:
My pathological partner showed signs of not understanding abstract language through:

_____

Concrete Language[4]

On the other hand, the Dark Triad is more adept at concrete language—the ability to describe things as they seem on the surface. Concrete language is often associated with words related to our senses—hot, cold, soft, hard, etc.

Concrete language is the language most used by and with children. But unlike people with personality disorders, normal children who don't have the neurological problems seen in the Dark Triad eventually deepen their language skills as they age and as the brain regions responsible for translating language into meaning develop. This is not necessarily so with personality disorders and psychopathy. Some of the research about language and issues with meaning were covered in Chapter Two which provided a basis for our understanding that the language center is a flawed area of the brain.

Normal adult communication patterns are dependent on using *both* concrete and abstract words, but in PLRs, there's difficulty in understanding the Dark Triad's responses. A survivor partner may say, "My heart hurts from all this!" (explaining the deep emotional wounding she is feeling from the recent infidelity). A common answer from Darkness might be, "Are you having chest pain? Do you need to go to the doctor?" A survivor partner might feel he is clueless to the pain he caused (and he probably is) and is wounded on yet another level by not being able to communicate her abstract feelings about their current problem. Multiply this scenario by years and you have a deteriorated relationship with a frustrated survivor who shuts down and no longer tries to communicate—which Darkness is sure to use against her.

While concrete, focused communication by Darkness can only create a deep-as-Formica relationship, he does have the skill sets to try to overcome his lack of abstract language and the damage it is doing to the relationship. When the wrong emotional word is used or not responded to, he will reach into his repertoire of romantic language to deflect his hidden language deficiencies.

Table 9.1

What the Psychopath is Bad and Good At © *The Institute* **2008**

He's Bad At	He's Good At
Abstract language	Concrete language
Unmoved by some emotional concepts.	Smooth talking and hiding communication problems.
Devious motivation for communication.	Semantically changing the meaning of words.
Language is contradictory.	Mimicking and parroting words and/or gestures back to her.
Lack of emotional processing related to empathy, conscience, remorse, fear, sadness, and disgust.	Having a predatory sixth sense for loneliness, grief, vulnerability.
Avoidance of communication he doesn't want to have.	Nonverbal cues like body language, eye lingo, and gestures/movements.

Clearly IQ is not the issue. Many of the Dark Triad have large enough IQs, hence their many career successes. Their deer-in-the-headlights reaction is related to their brain's inability to understand the necessary abstract language of normal relationships. While they may pretend to understand—sometimes to manipulate and even find enjoyment in their partner's frustration in trying to communicate with them and sometimes to hide—the result of not being able to relate on a conceptual level to what love, fidelity, truth, or trust *mean* is the foundation upon which she will be forced to try to build, or repair, a relationship of inevitable harm. These abstract concepts, to which the pathological partner cannot relate, include -[5]

- commitment
- compassion
- consensual
- courage
- democracy
- empathy
- future
- healthy
- humanity
- faith

- identification
- interpretation
- justice
- kind
- lessons
- liberty
- love
- loyalty
- morals
- mutuality

- peace
- poverty
- principles
- real
- reality
- sensing
- sentimental
- solutions
- tension
- tolerance

Survivor Work Page Question:
My pathological partner did not understand the concepts of:

_____

_____

But the problems with language don't end there.

Semantics

Semantics is 'the interpretation of a word or sentence; the meaning behind, and in, language.'[6] Not only does Darkness not understand the concepts behind abstract words, he uses words in ways that don't *match* their normal interpretations. Viewing this in light of the brain issues outlined in Chapter Two, we can better understand why Darkness interprets the word 'love,' when used by the survivor, as 'compliance.' Given that he doesn't understand the full meaning of the word, confusion and frustration is likely to happen. He will engage in what the survivor experiences as twisting words and finding conversational loopholes when she uses the word 'love' and Darkness takes it to mean 'compliance.' The inability to communicate and get on the same page about what certain words mean creates enormous discord in this exercise of intercourse.

Most people know and use the same words and understand the meaning of those words. But with The Dark Triad -

- She talks apples and he hears oranges.
- She talks apples and he tries to make an apple an orange.
- She talks apples and he says apples aren't even apples.

Her language is not his language. When she asks, "Do you love me?" it's important to understand what Darkness' *meaning* and *interpretation* of the word love *is*. Given his problem with abstract concepts, just what is love to Darkness? Multiply this meaning/concept misinterpretation by millions of sentences and you have a relationship existing in schizophrenic hell.

Possible misinterpretations, meanings, and concepts of abstract language in a relationship and what they might possibly mean to The Dark Triad are -

Table 9.2
Normal Person's Language vs. Psychopath's Language
© *The Institute* **2007**

Normal Person's Language	Psychopath's Language
Love	Her compliance
Trust	Paranoia
Communication	Opportunity
Bonding	Attachment
I need you	I want you
Lying	This is my truth
Stealing	Borrowing
Cheating	Equalizing the playing field
Monogamy	Monogamy in the moment
Future	Right now
Morals	To each their own
Interpretation	How the psychopath views/sees it

Normal Person's Language	Psychopath's Language
Problems	Her hassling him
Humanity	Suckers
Courage	The absence of fear
Sentimental	Unsafely soft
Faith	Not fact

Research into the language of the Dark Triad has found that language, meaning, and semantic problems are generated in the vault of the language centers in the brain.[7] These semantic gymnastics, referred to in the lexicon of the Pathological Love Relationship as 'word salad', have their genesis not only in the brain issues covered in Chapter Two but are also associated with the word twisting and conversational loopholes used to *avoid* the traditional use of words so Darkness can convert and subvert language to support his views and manipulative desires. This means that his language deficits are not *merely* brain generated—some portions of this communication mayhem are *willfully* sought, driven by the need for coercive control of the communication process.

For instance, he may -

- Not answer questions, or he may answer with something unrelated
- Redirect the question to her
- Twist one word in a sentence into a fight
- Reference other discussions
- Use phrases that distract her, so she must ask him to clarify, thus getting off track of the original discussion
- Use gaslighting to warp her reality
- Project his behavior onto her
- Go into long storytelling to deflect the original discussion
- Use a word to express an idea when the normal use of that word means something completely different

While these tactics are not all related to semantics, they are ways that the manipulation of communication, language, meaning, and interpretation are all used *against* the survivor due to Darkness' pathology, which is driven by antagonism.

In healthy relationships, communication is used to *enhance* the quality of a relationship. It isn't driven by personality deficits, a need to dominate communication, or manipulate it to punish a person for trying to communicate.

Sam Vaknin, a self-proclaimed narcissist who writes extensively about the interior motives of the Dark Triad, wrote in his book *Malignant Narcissism* about the pathological use of language.

===

"Language is a weapon of self-defense. It's used to fend off, hide and evade, avoid, disguise, shift semantics, say nothing in length, use evasive syntax, disguise the source of information, talk 'at' others and lecture, use his own private language, emphasize his conspiracy theories, rumors and phobias. Language is not to communicate but to obscure; not to share but to abstain; to agree without appearing to do so. Language is a weapon, an asset, a piece of lethal property, a mistress to be gang-raped. Language is a lover, composition but not content."

===

This confession about the ways Darkness *uses* communication highlights the deficits warned about by the DSM5 in haunting brilliance. In Vaknin's description of intercourse, we see all the deliberate markings of communication sabotage—it's *purposely* established for fending off, hiding and evading, avoiding, and disguising. Whether the brain's problems with language are being underscored by sheer willful arrogance or for dominance and control is hardly the point. What's important to recognize is that *this* is the level of the skill sets brought to the relationship in which a survivor partner will attempt meaningful and problem-solving dialogue in the mid-relationship phase.

Survivor Work Page Question:
My pathological partner played with semantics in the following ways:

_____

_____

But there are still more problems in this discourse on intercourse…

Contradictory Language

Darkness will say one thing and completely contradict what he said in the previous sentence with just as much passion and conviction. Trying to follow these ping-pong contradictions of passionately held, yet totally opposite, formations of thought give women mental whiplash. A survivor's own brain, limited by *her* absence of pathology, can't possibly comprehend, much less track, these wildly disparaging thoughts from both ends of the opinion spectrum. The result is total disorientation.

As a therapist at the personality disorder clinic, I too came home dizzy and disoriented from sincerely trying to follow and understand these wildly divergent statements uttered in single sentences. After I lamented to my clinical supervisor that my brain hurt, and I couldn't form complete sentences, she wisely asked, "Sandy, are you going in there—in their inner world—trying to understand and follow their thoughts and reasoning?"

Research evidence suggests that what is called 'bilateral language processes' are characteristic of psychopaths. These processes produce a tendency for psychopaths to make contradictory statements because each brain hemisphere is trying to run the language show, so what's produced is speech that is poorly integrated.[8] But the confused survivor doesn't know that.

Survivors who are trying to keep up with distortions in meaning and language, purposeful word twisting and dodging of the meaning of words, and contradictions in sentences, get their brains delivered to them as scrambled eggs. Their entire communication pattern is challenged as their normal brains try to understand stealth pathology.

> **Survivor Work Page Question:**
> My pathological partner expressed contradictory statements like:
> _____
> _____

But unfortunately, intercourse-run-amok is not over just yet...

Experiencing Emotion

Converting language into meaning, interpreting language, and confronting contradictory language are not the only communication obstacles in a PLR. Darkness' *experiencing* of the emotion associated with a word or concept is also a neurological deficit found in the brain, as discussed in Chapter Two.

Feeling understood in communication is what builds trust and emotional safety. But a survivor *feeling* understood assumes that Darkness is also *feeling* or at least *understanding* what the survivor feels. This is empathy—the ability to understand how others feel and the ability to experience a wide range of emotions.

It is why the DSM5 notes that the lack of empathy and the resulting lack of intimacy are detrimental key factors in personality disorders. The inability to empathize is the *coitus interruptus* of true intimacy. We cannot create emotionally safe, successful relationships, or solve problems in our relationships with people who are deficient in empathy. Word association tests done with psychopaths reveal that some emotional words register as neutral words to them. "I am devastated by your cheating" equates emotionally with them as "Will you pass the butter?"

What is at the heart of psychopathy, then, is a limited spectrum of emotions. People with psychopathy have emotions that are simply not experienced or are experienced in a distorted way that's not equal to normal people's experience. Some of these emotions are totally absent in disorders like psychopathy, or in such low volume in disorders like BPD, NPD, and ASPD as to be harmful to their intimate partners.

Survivor Note:

Not enough of an emotion—not just the meaning of it but the experiencing of it—crumbles the foundation of relationships.

As humans, we enjoy a wide range of emotions that enhance our experience with others. These include joy and even sadness. The other necessary emotions of guilt and remorse help to curb our behaviors and increase the quality of our relationships by stopping behaviors that harm our loved ones.

Whether the impact of the lack of a full emotional spectrum of emotions in personality disorders and psychopathy is the result of interrupted emotional development or problems with the brain regions that regulate these emotions, the result is that Darkness does not experience what other people do, and to that degree, it causes inevitable harm in relationships when the foundation of creating intimacy is already severely impaired.

Necessary to not only relationship building but also to the experience of what it means to be human is the experience of learning from, and adapting our emotions to, our intimate partners. As a relationship partner, the Dark Triad has no concept of authentic love through abiding bonding and connectedness, no experience with empathy, and a lack of guilt and remorse that produces healthy conscience.

Without the range of normal emotions, without the ability to learn from experience, without the skills to understand language and meaning, the psychopath must learn skills of adaptation to walk amongst us while hiding these deficits to lure a partner and eventually create a relationship with her.

Survivor Note:

In this way, empathy is a necessary emotion to enact conscience and conscience is necessary to regulate bad behavior.

That's why Darkness appears unmoved by some emotional concepts related to the problems of abstract language. His partner may be pouring out her heart while Darkness seems unmoved by her pain (except in the luring and honeymoon phases, in which his emotions are feigned). It doesn't make sense to her how Darkness, who uses language like a well-honed tool, is equally challenged with the same problem that he otherwise seems to wield so deftly.

Just as with white-collar psychopaths, who are noted for having a form of 'cognitive empathy' but not 'emotional empathy,' these two forms of unrelated empathy can cause a survivor to think that emotional and relational empathy exists. However, even the feigned display of emotional empathy, which may not be true empathy at all, is part of how he has adapted skillfully to feign human interaction.

The deficits he has in both understanding abstract language and experiencing emotion have likely been with him since adolescence, if not earlier, since personality disorders and psychopathy, as noted in the DSM5, are formed by adolescence or early adulthood. Personality disorders create problems in social, relational, and occupational functioning and, from Darkness' perspective, need fixing on a superficial level for him to appear to be more normal than he can ever be.

Every human has a skill set. People on the Low-Conscience Spectrum of disorders also possess their own unique skill sets for adaptation, or social hiding—being able to blend in with average people. Darkness creates an external image of himself, with behaviors to match, that on the surface are compatible with the rest of society's behavior, and he learns to say and do things he can't truly comprehend. This is the ability of Darkness to appear to relate well while understanding poorly. His skill set for appearing to be normal is, as Cleckley termed it, *the ability to wear the mask of sanity.*

However, the ability to *consistently* use appropriate speech, demonstrate appropriate emotion, and behave within normal parameters is what Darkness cannot do and is what makes these attempts at mimicry pathological in the sense that the inconsistency in thinking, feeling, relating, and behaving defines what a personality disorder *is.*

The inability to consistently maintain these normal human expressions is when his mask slips—when the survivor discovers that the problems that exist in their relationship have everything to do with what her partner says and what he experiences, as well as his inability to understand certain concepts in language. While Darkness' skill set includes the ability to lure, attract, and woo in the early phases, his mask slips when a survivor partner realizes that his language, his ascribed meaning to that language, and his emotion is a mask.

Speaking well but relating poorly is eventually recognized by all survivors, and the language he employed to appear to be like her is just a false front cardboard cutout that hides the soon-revealed lack of meaning behind both language and emotion. The parroting of phrases identified as important to her, the presumption of understanding what she means, and the mimicking of emotion are a skill set created for social hiding.

Survivor Work Page Question:
My pathological partner did not seem to experience the following emotions: _____

_____

Mimicking and Parroting

This adaptive skill set of The Dark Triad, which is developed early in life and honed to perfection in adulthood, is predicated on the need to 'hide in public.' The very recognition that psychopaths need to hide elements of their personalities causes every survivor partner I have ever treated to ask, "Does he know he's disordered?"

There is an ocean of distance between 'awareness' and 'insight.' As detailed in Chapter Two, the brains of people with personality disorders have been impaired in the areas of empathy and insight. An *awareness* of their problems can seem to come with all the bells and whistles of *insight* when it really isn't insight at all.

Let me tell you a story about a young, developing Dark Triad and how he learned to become "aware" of his issues. This story was relayed to me by a psychopathic client.

Pete the Pathological had an older sibling, Nick the Normal, who was not laden with the problems of no empathy, lack of insight, or a limited range of emotional experiences. He was simply normal—with his wide range of emotions, he could imagine how others felt in bad situations and he had genuine love for others.

One day the boys came home from school. Their mom was sitting on the couch crying, with a black eye, saying that their father had beaten her, packed his things, and left. She was beside herself, wondering how they would be able to live, how they would earn money, and what would happen to all of them. Nick the Normal went to his mother and hugged her. He got ice for her eye, and then he sat down with her to help problem solve the situation. He would get a paper route and make money, or maybe they could move in with Grandma and Grandpa, or maybe their church would help them. Pete the Pathological stood off to the side just watching in an uncaring and bored way, while thinking to himself, "Good! I always hated that bastard. Glad he's gone." He didn't approach his mother or even comment on her injuries. He offered no emotion or solutions, proceeded to pick lint off his pants and thought about whether this opportunity would give him time to slip away to play baseball.

The mother instructed the boys to go outside so she could pull herself together. As soon as they were outside, Nick the Normal lit into Pete the Pathological. "What is WRONG with you? She was bruised and bleeding, and you just stood there like a stump. You didn't say one thing to comfort her! You didn't offer to help find work. You didn't do anything." And POW, Nick the Normal punched Pete the Pathological right in the face.

Pete told me in therapy that it was at that moment he recognized he didn't feel what he should feel, like others did. He learned a powerful lesson with that punch—that if you don't act like others, there are consequences. He said he replayed that scene with his mother over and over in his mind, noting what Nick the Normal did. Walking himself through the scene, he noted that when someone does this, you are supposed to do what Nick the Normal had done. If someone is injured, you should say, "Are you okay?" even if you don't care if they are okay. If someone is crying, you should pat their hand and say, "There, there—it will be ok" even if you don't feel like it. If they are bruised, you get ice. If they are afraid, you say something to make them less afraid. If tears are on their face, that means they are upset. If their voice is shrill, it means they are scared.

Pete the Pathological learned that he did not have the natural reactions to other's pain that his brother did. It wasn't a problem for him, but it was apparently a problem for others. A way of avoiding the pain of a punch or punishment was to learn what was socially expected when people displayed emotions that he didn't experience.

Pete the Pathological said he practiced certain phrases, inflecting different tonality in his voice to match Nick's. He even stood in the mirror to imitate the emotions that *should* appear on his face *as if* he were experiencing that emotion.

Pete learned early the necessity of the *social hiding* that Dr. Robert Hare says is a key skill set of psychopaths but that I also believe are skill sets of Cluster B disorders. They become private investigators of sorts, learning how to appear more normal to fit in and to avoid the problems brought about by not experiencing humanity as others do. While they become amateur psychologists studying what consists of normal emotions in social and relational situations, as we have seen, this is not the same thing as truly *experiencing* actual emotion, which is necessary for empathy and intimacy.

Mirror, *noun*, a reflective surface[9]

Mimic, *verb*, to copy or exaggerate (as in manners of gestures), often by way of mockery[10]

Mimic, *noun*, actor, impersonator, mime, performer, play actor[11]
Parrot, *verb*, to imitate someone else's words without understanding them[12]

These skills are based on Darkness' awareness that there are parts of themselves that are different from those of other people. Some even accidently confess to these differences, while others avoid ever noting them.

While Darkness may have difficulty processing specific feelings, he does learn how the survivor partner uses words and what her perceptions are of the meaning of words, and parrots them back to her even if he does not understand their meaning or significance. Mirroring involves copying someone else while communicating with them, and while the Dark Triad may have problems experiencing emotions, he can certainly use *his partner's* emotions to mirror the emotion back to her. He can copy her postures and gestures, the tone of her voice, her body language, breathing rhythms, even her choice of words, implying they are on the same page, which increases the sense of mutual communication, especially in the luring stages when he is most motivated to do so. Tori's story is full of examples of her partner's mimicking and parroting back her experiences and emotions.

In normal communication, mirroring is natural, but the Dark Triad's use of it is learned and contrived and is used as a mechanism for social hiding. This can become apparent in situations like problem solving when the survivor wonders about betrayal and his responses to her questions are her own words fed back to her which doesn't constitute natural problem solving at all.

An African Grey parrot can learn phrases—he can be taught to recite Einstein's *Theory of Relativity*. If you were in the other room and didn't know he was a parrot, he would sound like he knows his subject matter; however, he obviously couldn't answer questions about the subject because the parrot does not have total comprehension of his topic. When it comes to emotions and language, neither does Darkness.

Survivor Note:

Repeating is not comprehension, and awareness is not insight.

Awareness is the knowledge of a fact or situation. Darkness is certainly aware that he's different, whether he confesses it or not. But insight is the ability to develop an accurate and deep intuitive understanding of a person or thing. The ocean between knowledge of a fact and an accurate deep intuitive understanding is why the DSM5 highlights this lack of insight as a major factor in personality disorders. It is precisely this accurate lack of deep understanding about how their behavior affects others that bars any hope of consistent change in their behavior.

While the pathological partner may act as if he is aware that there is a problem in the relationship, insight would force him to accept responsibility, not blame others, and change himself for the benefit of the relationship. The difference between facts/awareness and deep intuitive understanding/insight is immense. Darkness may be aware that they argue all the time—she harasses him and asks him to do things he doesn't want to do. All of these things stack up to an *awareness* of problems, but his perception is that the problems are all about her. *She's* the problem.

Insight would allow him to deeply understand the ways in which his behavior hurt her, would empathize with the pain he caused, would motivate him to consistently attempt to change, and to take responsibility for causing her pain. Insight is based on *accurate* perception. Both neurologically and emotionally, Darkness is not wired for this.

Survivor Work Page Question:
My pathological partner mimicked and parroted me in the following ways:

_____

_____

*W*rapping This All Up

The Three Inabilities©, discussed in an earlier chapter, have a profound impact on communication in a relationship. Language, meaning, and communication add to what creates emotional depth. When we refer to the pathological partner as being deep as Formica, we're referring to his inability to bring to the relationship the needed elements of communication, including his ability to empathize. Likewise, the inability to have insight into how behavior affects others is intimately connected to the ability to understand what someone is communicating back to us.

It is only when communication is successful that the ability to sustain change becomes part of our motivation to improve relational health. For this reason, The Three Inabilities© become the foundation upon which pathological partners build a relationship, and survivors will undoubtedly become victims while trying to communicate with them.

While communication has the potential to solve problems in relationships, Darkness has ways of distorting it that will prevent it from ever being the resource it could be. In fact, the distortions he employs will produce even more trauma in the survivor. This lack of emotional development, a brain not wired in many ways for even the most generic forms of communication, the dwarfed emotional maturity that omits critical and necessary emotions, and the Polly-wants-a-cracker types of parroting that is presented as his attempt at true intercourse, are what he brings to this task of problem solving in relationships.

So, while the survivor is vibrating with a sense about the ebb and flow of the relationship connection, and as she whips out the thing that every couple uses to solve problems—communication—she is met with yet another baffling exchange which creates more cognitive dissonance.

The 'Oz-man behind the curtain' who was believed to be the Master Communicator in the love bombing early phases is totally deficient in the ability to understand his partner's words about love and fidelity. He seems to have his own private language regarding what those concepts mean. His sentences don't match the love-bombing behavior, and he doesn't seem to understand the pain she is describing. What he does have, however, is an ability to manipulate language, a way to hide the facts and sidestep her questions, and a method of distorting her reality in his attempts to convince her that she is paranoid. Whether these gaslighting effects are contrived to fend off, avoid, and evade, or they are natural acts of his biological defects, the outcome is the same.

There are two very different sides to Darkness—the slick-tongued love bomber and the emotional imbecile whose only motivation in that moment is to be who she wants him to be to ward off conflict. With years of skill building under his belt, he spins a story that is plausible enough to keep the relationship securely in the middle-relationship phase.

But the seed planted by the display of both sides—Jekyll and Hyde—has created another layer of cognitive dissonance. Now swirling around in her head are questions about holding two differing belief systems about him—is he *more* Jekyll or *more* Hyde—and her notion of, "What's wrong with me? Why don't I know the answer?"

Those questions will remain as the relationship continues, and the survivor will be met with more relationship issues that will produce more pain and more questions.

Survivor Work Page Question:
I was impacted by my partner's conflicting behavior as evidenced by:

_____

_____

Chapter Nine Endnotes

1   intercourse. (2018, March 18). http://www.dictionary.com/browse/intercourse

2   Brown, Sandra L. The Institute (2007) Pre, Early, Mid, Late & Post Relationships Dynamics of Cluster B/Psychopathic Partners: A Grounded Theory Outcome. Prepared for The Institute Therapist Training Manual 'Treating the Aftermath of Pathological Love Relationships.

3-5 Brown, Sandra L. (2010). Women Who Love Psychopaths: Inside the Relationships of Inevitable Harm. Second Edition. Mask Publishing.

6   semantics. (2018, March 18). http://www.dictionary.com/browse/semantics

7   Intrator, J., Hare, R., Stridke, P., Brichtswein, K., Dorfman, D., Harpur, T., ... Machac, J. (1997). A Brain Imaging (Single Photon Emission computerized tomography) study of semantic and affective processing in psychopaths. Biological Psychiatry, 42(2), 96–103. https://www.ncbi.nlm.nih.gov/pubmed/9209726

8   Yeschke, C. (2004). Interrogation: Achieving Confessions Using Permissible Persuasion. Charles C. Thomas.

9   mirror. http://www.dictionary.com/browse/mirror?s=t

10   mimic. https://www.thefreedictionary.com/mimics

11   mimic. https://www.thefreedictionary.com/mimics

12   parrot. https://www.collinsdictionary.com/us/dictionary/english/parrot

Chapter Ten

Crazy-Making Communication and The Event Cycle Puzzle Piece #2™

Continuing with our discussion about the Dramatic and Erratic Relational Dynamics is a further examination of the actual dynamics while communicating.

Quick Survivor Review

- Darkness is impaired in his abstract language usage; he understands and uses primarily concrete language.
- His misuse of words causes both semantic differences and language that contradicts itself from one sentence to the next.
- People with personality disorders and psychopathy experience emotions differently and so try to express *normal* emotions through mimicking and parroting.

*T*he Three Step Tango

An unusual dynamic occurred when I was attempting therapy sessions with people with Dark Triad disorders. Not only was my brain twisted into knots when trying to follow their sentences, but I frequently found myself being lambasted for persecuting them, or else they were begging me to rescue them from their situation. I often felt victimized by their accusations, but in their next sentence, they presented as if *they* were the victims. Then just as suddenly, they were persecuting me, followed by another 90-degree turn, immediately followed by trying to rescue me from some perceived and projected situation.

It was a swirling, messy tango of role-swapping—the client as victim/persecutor/rescuer and me on the opposite end of whatever position from which they were communicating. When they were the victim, I was the persecutor. When they were the persecutor, I was the victim. When they were the victim, they wanted me to rescue them, and when I didn't, I was immediately the persecutor. It was a three-step rapid-fire process of manipulation they used to get me in the position they wanted which would produce the desired result.

Head swirling, I again crawled back to my very wise clinical supervisor who taught me about the very static communication patterns of Cluster Bs and psychopaths. It's referred to as the Karpman Triangle[1], or, more descriptively, the 'crazy-making communication patterns.'

Darkness, with his communication limitations, creates a backed-into-the-corner communication process that forces normally highly communicative people to interact using his disordered patterns. These patterns are static—stuck in either rescuer, persecutor, or victim mode—and upon which all interactions are based. He perceives that he and the survivor are always in one of those roles.

The highly antagonistic personality of Darkness, combined with the deficits of self-identity and self-functioning, cause Darkness to see himself as a victim—continually persecuted. Perceived persecution can be something as benign as being asked a question by his partner. Because his communication perceptions are limited to his either being victim, persecutor, or rescuer, and his perception of *her* being either victim, persecutor, or rescuer, there is no neutral ground from which to discuss a current issue. He will always be in one of those roles, which will force the survivor to be in one of the other roles—none of which fosters healthy, much less normal, communication patterns.

As shown in Figure 10.1 below, each partner moves around the triangle, taking on different roles as an interchange progresses. Darkness is the victim while the survivor is forced into the role of rescuing him or persecuting him. He may later shift and take on the role of the rescuer or persecutor. When one role shifts, it forces the other person into one of the two remaining roles. Each shift causes the other person to also shift.

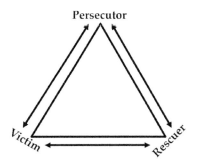

Figure 10.1
The Karpman Triangle
Victim/Rescuer/Persecutor Triangle

To make matters worse, these roles can shift moment to moment or sentence to sentence. The same argument covering the same topic only moments before, or a day later, can result in totally different roles taken on by each partner.

Survivor Note:

The lack of consistency and lack of resolution reached each time a topic is approached creates not only frustration but more traumatic cognitive dissonance as the survivor partner is trapped within the dysfunctional patterns of The Karpman Triangle.

It's not unlike the Bermuda Triangle, where partners enter the vast, murky waters of vanishing communication, and resolution never appears. But this crazy-making communication found in the Karpman Triangle is not normal communication. The survivor may be a communications director or a teacher, and nowhere else in her life does she communicate in this way, because at her work, manipulated roles do not hold healthy communication hostage as a means by which to control the outcome of a discussion. In her day-to-day life, she communicates effectively and without drama. But as soon as the phone rings and he is on the line, communication reenters the Triangle, because this is the only way Darkness communicates. She is bound by the limits and roles of the Triangle and even when she attempts to communicate normally, using her conversational career skill set, the process still pulls her in and she is quickly thrust into the role of rescuer/persecutor/victim.

Being trapped in the Triangle, she concludes there is something wrong with her that makes her unable to communicate without arguing, without great confusion, and without experiencing the utter frustration of being placed in roles she doesn't recognize. The traumatic reaction of cognitive dissonance is enhanced as she recognizes, "I am a good communicator, but I communicate poorly with him." The allegations she has likely heard from him—that the problems in the relationship are her fault—are reinforced by her inability to understand the consistent patterns of Darkness' communication.

I, too, experienced the hair-pulling frustration of trying to utter just a simple sentence in therapy without it getting twisted into something akin to a witch hunt. "So how was your week?" could elicit the reply, "Why would you ask that? Why would you assume I had a bad week? Is it because you think I'm a horrible person that I'd have a horrible week?"

Or "You look good today" would lead to "So you think I looked bad last week? That's because I'm having a horrible life. Of course, I look bad. If you had my life, you'd look like this too!"

But ever-changing role positions on the Triangle are not the only challenges. All those deficits listed in the DSM and all those communication problems mentioned previously are backdrops to what happens in dialogue. In the three-step tango around the Triangle, the partner must dodge Darkness' other communication problems[2] -

- Impulsivity—talking before thinking
- Triangulating—turning other people against her
- Asserting that he knows everything therefore she can't contribute any new information to the conversation
- Lying
- Drama
- Manipulation
- His juvenile decision-making skills
- Changing subjects to avoid continuing the conversation
- Meaning/language differences
- Blaming
- His immature emotional age
- His not taking responsibility for his behavior/choices

- Gaslighting to warp her reality
- Projecting his behavior on others

A dialogue about his suspected cheating could shift sentence to sentence from him being a victim to a rescuer to a persecutor. A survivor must also deal with the lies in each sentence—the blaming, the gaslighting, and the projecting. *In each sentence.*

Additionally, each sentence can get bogged down in problems of abstract language or his not being able to express appropriate emotion. The survivor might have to stop after each sentence to deal with semantics or to gauge whether he is faking an understanding of the issue and just mimicking and parroting. Survivors often forget what the point of the argument was because "who can keep up with what the point was in dynamics like these?"

Most normal people understand that communication is the bedrock of problem resolution—that when you have a problem you talk it out. What is supposed to be mutual problem-solving turns into a game of brain volleyball as the pathological partner uses manipulation to avoid the issue, increase the impact of cognitive dissonance, and keep anything from being resolved.

Operant Learning and Classical Conditioning

Each go-round resulting from a woman's noticing that something is not right, and her corresponding attempts at communicating with her partner, teaches her something. In her professional life, problems are solved by communication. But in a Pathological Love Relationship she is taught that what she knows in her work life about communication is not applicable in this scenario. So, while she is driven by the extreme investment she has in this relationship and her desire to believe in the validity of this twin-ship, she is met with a learning curve to which she cannot apply her own communication skill set to resolve. What she encounters are highly developed techniques, like those used in cults, which corral her beliefs and change her behaviors.

Operant learning is a kind of learning in which[3] -

- the power of a behavior (i.e., attempting to communicate)
- is changed (i.e., no longer attempts to communicate)

- by the ramifications that follow the behavior (mind mangling and cognitive dissonance caused by the communication).

In Operant Learning, consequences can be either positive or negative. When a partner tries to communicate but ends up in the Karpman Triangle where gaslighting and blaming abound, she learns that she'll receive a negative consequence, either directly or indirectly, from her attempt. She learns that the process goes nowhere, that he gets angry and it makes the problem worse, or that she'll be severely confused, which will take days to get over.

Operant learning consequences can also reward what Darkness perceives as the right behavior. When she suspects cheating but does not confront him, she is rewarded for exhibiting the right behavior as perceived by Darkness. Perhaps he spends more time with her, dangles a few more carrots (offers to get married, moves in, etc.), but in some way, he is rewarding her for leaving him alone.

Through these processes of reward and punishment, people's behavior is controlled and changed. Cults also control large groups of people by rewarding or punishing behavior. Thus, eventually, Darkness no longer needs to engage in unwanted relationship dynamics since the outcome is already known to the survivor partner, who learns not to go there, or she will suffer the consequences of emotional and cognitive turmoil. It becomes not worth it to her to suffer for days by being emotionally upset and suffer more cognitive dissonance by thinking through the conversation and wondering, "Is he really that clueless? Maybe *I* am clueless." The pain of cognitive dissonance and the need to avoid these rhetorical questions that are never answered becomes the driving force behind avoiding conversations about the relationship.

While we can understand how Operant Learning can occur with behavior modification in children (i.e., if you do that, then you go in time out), *The Institute* believes that the impact on survivors is driven by what has become their number one symptom of trauma—cognitive dissonance.[4] Learning how to be in a PLR becomes reinforced by her need to avoid the emotional pain of cognitive dissonance. Learning to pick her battles teaches her that, to have less pain, she must stay away from situations that produce it.

Surely communicating, confronting, or trying to problem solve are the top issues in the Pandora's Box of a PLR—when opened she is punished, and, worst of all, her level of discomfort created by these two conflicting ideas is ignited like a raging forest fire. How survivors end up applying "therapeutic ignoring" is a response to Operant Learning and the need to avoid the increasingly unbearable emotional pain.

But survivors are also taught to accept unacceptable relationships through Classical Conditioning reinforcement as well. The widely known example of Classical Conditioning is that of Pavlov's experiment resulting in a dog salivating merely from hearing a bell being rung. The dog learned to relate the bell with what was going to come—food. Likewise, survivors learn what is to come from a look, a tone, or even a sense that her partner is cheating, and without anything else happening, the mere look, tone, or feeling can produce anxiety, rapid heartbeat, and cognitive dissonance.[5] Being trapped by both Operant Learning and Classical Conditioning, she always seems to be experiencing cognitive dissonance any way she turns.

This combo-pack of control techniques has been used by cults and oppressive dictatorships for centuries because it is highly effective. In healthy relationships, conditioning is learned, but it's learned from respect, love, and emotional safety. One learns that she can trust someone because healthy behaviors are reinforced and rewarded. In PLRs, Operant Learning and Classical Conditioning result in manipulation, perceived harm, and eventual avoidance of the impending impact of cognitive turmoil. While the survivor partner believes that she is simply initiating communication to save her relationship, she is being conditioned not to communicate at all.

Survivor Work Page Question:
The Operant Learning and Classical Conditioning techniques that were used on me included:

_____

_____

$\mathcal{P}$ersuasive Reasoning, Coercion, and Subterfuge

While Operant Learning and Classical Conditioning can produce compliance in a partner who is trying to avoid added emotional pain,

Darkness' skill set includes *additional* highly effective methods, many of which are used by cults and other Snakes in Suits types.[6]

Compliance is the act of 'conforming; a tendency to yield to others and cooperate.'[7] Stephen Covey, author of *Seven Habits of Highly Effective People,* noted that successful (and normal) people employ compliance (also known as 'agreeableness') in their dealings with others as opposed to being demanding and oppositional (like Darkness).[8] These traits are what make the survivors successful at their jobs as CEOs, professors, and accountants, for instance. It was also a trait in the women we saw at the clinic, which led us to conduct personality testing with them. While agreeableness can be helpful in normal interactions and produce a win-win for all parties, in Pathological Love Relationships, even good traits are used as weapons against survivors to induce compliance.[9] This is where Darkness knows exactly how to milk more compliance out of anyone who exhibits even a little agreeableness or compliance.

Whether Darkness was naturally endowed with salesmanship abilities or he learned this skill as a budding young psychopath, he has developed a concoction type of manipulative behavior that other non-pathological people don't seem to have. His charm and ability to draw others in is used to produce the desired result of *compliance.*

Compliance is produced in three ways -

- Persuasive reasoning
- Coercion
- Subterfuge

Persuasive Reasoning

If Operant or Classical learning is not effective, Darkness can always fall back on persuasive reasoning—what appears on the surface to be an "open exchange" eventually becomes a covert form of changing someone's mind.[10]

"How could I be cheating if I am with you every night?"

"If I were cheating, would I be planning a future with you? Would we be buying a house together?"

Seemingly open dialogue that is dipped in rhetorical questions sends a survivor, now conditioned to avoid further emotional pain, deeper into the woods of believing what she's told. Darkness comes prewired with an absence of fear or anxiety, which means this reasoning will be doubly persuasive. Cool as a cucumber, he's different from those who are nervous and don't make eye contact when they are trying to manipulate others.

The pacing of relationships in PLRs is so rapid that it produces excitement, although exhaustion, reduced sleep, and a brain bathed in the euphoria-producing oxytocin. Research indicates that a normal person's ability to fend off persistent persuaders is reduced when one is rushed, stressed, or tired—certainly the condition of most survivors.[11] People who are in healthy and meaningful relationships, and who sense that they are being authentically supported and not manipulated, are much less likely to be victims of persuaders.

Strengthening the power of persuasion is the status and power of the persuader. The survivor's belief that Darkness is successful, if his status is one of a well-known doctor, attorney, or community figure, increases his power of persuasion. Many survivors have been persuaded into participating in activities or situations that violated their own beliefs, values, and morals, creating an even deeper layer of cognitive dissonance. Their perception of themselves was altered as their behavior fell under the control of persuasion. This was no doubt influenced by the relative status and power of Darkness as the persuader.

An additional unfair tactic used to induce compliance, sometimes in conjunction with other tactics, is coercion.

Coercion

Coercion is 'the practice of persuading someone to do something by using force or threats.'[12] There's a fine line between persuasive reasoning and coercion. While reasoning may start off civilly with the intention of manipulation, it will quickly lapse into threats and intimidation if the survivor is not persuaded. But coercion can also occur via innuendo— hinting at, without overtly stating, what may be the result if a survivor's compliance does not align with Darkness' skewed reasoning. For people with Dark Triad disorders who are violent, this is an extension of violence. With those who are not physically violent, coercion can take the form of psychological violence.

When challenged by the many factors covered over the last few chapters, communication completely breaks down when physical or psychological violence is introduced into the relationship dynamics. The pathological partner's prey-driven sense is heightened by the fear he senses when he threatens to impact a survivor's career, to reveal embarrassing secrets to her family, or to be violent, and she is forced into behaviors in which she would otherwise not engage. Taking medication from a hospital for his addiction, skimming funds from the coffers at her workplace for his insatiable financial appetite, performing a sex act that she is uncomfortable with—all these actions create the taste for blood in Darkness that will not be otherwise satisfied. Once coercion has been introduced into the relationship, it becomes a lasting and preferred form of communication for the Dark Triad and it will increase the survivor's cognitive dissonance and impact her for years to come.[13]

But it is rarely used alone and is often combined with the next tactic.

Subterfuge

Subterfuge is defined as 'deceit used to achieve one's goals.'[14] Essentially, all PLRs are based in subterfuge—from their beginnings with emotions and feelings mimicked and parroted, to the onset of persuasive reasoning and coercion. Since it's all a mask, it is all deceit and subterfuge. The pop psychology word for this is 'gaslighting' taken from the 1944 movie *Gas Light* (a must see for all survivor partners).

In the movie, the main character, Gregory, does everything in his power to isolate his wife, Paula, from other people. Gregory allows her neither to go out nor to have visitors, implying that he is doing so for her own good because her nerves have been acting up which is causing her to become a kleptomaniac and also to imagine things that are not real. On the one occasion when Gregory does take her out to a musical gathering at a friend's house, he shows Paula his watch chain, from which his watch has mysteriously disappeared. When Gregory finds it in her handbag, Paula becomes distraught and he takes her home. Paula begins to believe she should not go out in public. Then a picture disappears from the walls of the house and Gregory says that she took it, but Paula has no recollection of having done so. Paula also hears footsteps coming from above her in the sealed attic and sees the gaslights dim and brighten for no apparent reason. Gregory suggests that these are all figments of Paula's imagination.

The appeal of subterfuge to Darkness, whose motivational drives center around power and dominance, is the ability to control another person's reality and, therefore, everything about her. *Everything.* Gaslighting is not only psychological dominance—it is 'reality shifting' for the sake of taking down a competent woman for sheer enjoyment and entertainment. These once competent prosecutors, teachers, and radiologists have now been reduced to disabled patients, stuck in fetal positions in their own beds, suffering from what they perceive as 'breaks with reality,' known in psychology as psychosis.

They weren't psychotic, they were gaslighted! Using our own normal psychology as a reference will not aid us in understanding the entertainment that the Dark Triad derives from using this technique—and with amazing frequency.

Subterfuge in one patient's life consisted of her supposedly having heard his conversations on the phone with hedge fund broker giants like T. Bone Pickings, with Darkness planning to move her into a million-dollar home, only to find out none of it was real—not Mr. Pickings, nor the money, nor his supposed career. She ended up in a single-wide trailer when the scam was over.

A doctor who allowed her flim-flam psychopath to run her practice lost her license when he purposely over-billed insurance and Medicare and then skimmed the overage off the top. Darkness then told her, "I always wanted to take down a doctor."

Given Darkness' mask, subterfuge is his main communication technique. His skills at stealthily hiding reality aid in the believability of the reality he is creating for her eyes only. Telling her there is "no one else" when her intuition is telling her otherwise creates paranoia about her own mental health when his version of the altered reality is presented with such assurance. And, as you have guessed, this twisting of reality increases the cognitive dissonance she is experiencing day by day in her life with Darkness.

Before we jump to judge survivors as 'naive' or who 'should have seen it coming,' cults in America have taught us a lot about how indoctrination can happen to many *normal* people. Unfortunately, the stories about those who fell prey to the cults label the victims as disordered without understanding how Operant Learning and Classical Conditioning, persuasive reasoning, coercion, and subterfuge turn any normal person into a compliant near-robot. Let's not forget Charles Manson and his influence over previously normal middle-class young women whom he sent out on a murderous rampage. Or the Symbionese Liberation Army that kidnapped Patty Hearst in 1974 and controlled her behavior so that she assisted in a bank robbery and didn't want to return home, being told the FBI would shoot her. The Rev. Jim Jones, leader of a religious sect, convinced 912 people to commit mass suicide in a Guyana jungle. That's a large group to persuade to accompany you to literal death.

While these are the extremes of cults, the techniques are the same. The only difference is in what the victims were led to do. If we were to ask, "Who does that?" we would have to conclude that Manson, the SLA, and Jim Jones were likely psychopaths. And survivors of PLRs are exposed to the same techniques that these psychopaths used on their followers. While the outcomes in these cults were murder, bank robbery, and mass suicide, the outcomes (to a lesser degree) in survivors are the results of the same techniques that worked so well for cult leaders. They are based on communication techniques that alter a person's behavior through Operant Learning, Classical Conditioning, persuasion, coercion, and subterfuge.

Survivor Work Page Question:
My relationship had elements of Operant Learning, Classical Conditioning, persuasion, coercion, or subterfuge, as evidenced by

_____

_____

While the crazy-making communication patterns of The Karpman Triangle are challenging enough, they are superimposed on the *other* skill sets that Darkness brings to this task of working out problems as they arise in the middle phase of a relationship. Figure 10.2 below shows the added dimensions to the roles of victim/rescuer/persecutor. Unfortunately, there are still more dynamics that are going to impact her relationship and increase her cognitive dissonance.

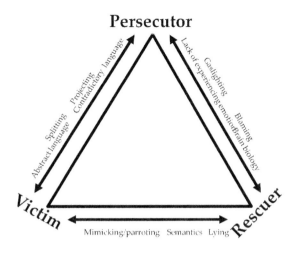

Persecutor

Splitting   Abstract language   Projecting   Contradictory language

Gaslighting   Lack of experiencing emotion   Blaming   Brain biology

Victim

Rescuer

Mimicking/parroting   Semantics   Lying

Figure 10.2
The Karpman Triangle
Victim/Rescuer/Persecutor Triangle, *The Institute* © 2012

$\mathcal{T}$he Event Cycle

While the Karpman Triangle is tied to the *roles* Darkness and the survivor partner play in this process of trying to communicate, it is also tied to the *events* that they are communicating *about* and what Darkness does—behaviorally—to manipulate the events. Let's take a look.

The DSM5 has called Cluster B/psychopaths 'dramatic and erratic,' which refers not only to their emotional state but their behavior as well. Driven by the motivational drives of power and dominance, the manipulation of communication, and the joy of gaslighting, Darkness knows how to keep the dynamics as confusing as possible in the middle phase of the relationship.

A mystery to survivors is oftentimes the bizarre behavior that Darkness exhibits when problems surface. Based on what she has been noticing in their relationship, she has begun a dialogue with Darkness about her suspicions—since he's been gone a lot, he seems distracted and aloof, and/or she has found suspicious texts. She's then thrown into the dialogue patterns of the crazy-making Karpman Triangle. While she is trying to wiggle outside of the Triangle and communicate like she normally does professionally, she is met with the other defenses of gaslighting, projecting, lying, blaming, etc. Also introduced into the conversation are the dramatic and erratic behaviors of dodging around the conversation, displaying inconsistent behaviors which sometimes involve coercion, subterfuge, and/or persuasion.

It goes something like this:

When the survivor mentions newly-found texts he's written to other women <or insert any relational problem they are having>, Darkness responds by:

Raging. . . and when that doesn't work he immediately...

Accuses her of having someone else . . . and when that doesn't work he immediately...

Carrot-dangles (talks about getting married, buying a house) . . . and when that doesn't work he immediately...

Threatens to kill himself . . . and when that doesn't work he immediately...

Tells the truth (just to confuse her) . . . and when that doesn't work he immediately...

Threatens to tell others, to get her fired from her job . . . and when that doesn't work he immediately...

Agrees that he has a problem and she's the only person who 'gets him' . . . and when that doesn't work he immediately...

Says the relationship is over . . .and when that doesn't work he immediately...

Agrees to go to counseling . . .and when that doesn't work he immediately...

Says he will just find someone else (he already has!) . . .and when that doesn't work he immediately...

Confesses he didn't want to worry her but he's really sick (usually terminally ill) . . . and when that doesn't work he immediately...

Shows interest in going to church and finding God . . . and so on.

While this is a list showing the blazing confusion in the ping-ponging dialogue regarding an event, let's look at it as a chart that gives a *visual* display of what a line of conversation is like:

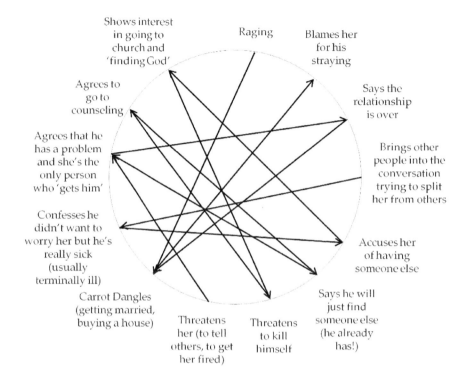

Figure 10.3
The Event Cycle © *The Institute* 2010

This ping-ponging can last through a few of these scenarios, or it can run the entire gamut of behaviors, depending on the length of the dialogue. It's certainly manipulative on Darkness' part, but survivors often think the behavior is more related to conditions like Bipolar Disorder or addiction. Although the pathological partner might also have those conditions, it is part of the dramatic and erratic presentation encompassing persuasion, coercion, and subterfuge, which is another form of dominance. The movement on the diagram is no doubt similar to the emotionally erratic behavior a survivor experiences as they follow Darkness around the cycle in his dramatic displays.

Wrapping This All Up

The impact to the survivor is a case of whiplash in need of a full neck brace for recovery. Ranging between feigned kindness and conciliatory behaviors, to threats and violence, the two sides of Darkness can easily be viewed as a Dr. Jekyll/ Mr. Hyde dichotomy. While it may have taken getting to the middle relationship phase to see such blatant displays of the two sides of him, the survivor has now seen the disorder behind the mask. And who wouldn't fear that? Operant Learning and Classical Conditioning will teach her how to avoid one side while reaping the supposed benefits of the other side, all the while desperately trying to figure out what is going on, and how to stay in, or leave, the relationship.

Survivors have a lot of information to process—the unusual brain functioning, the problems with language and meaning, the lack of experiencing emotion, the charming and persuasive side, the contradictory language, the inability to sustain change or have insight, the horror of The Karpman Triangle, and the rapid jumping around the Event Cycle—none of which they were ever exposed to in order to understand what this relational nightmare is (or how to repair a relationship she is extremely bonded to). Given that psychopathology is one of the most complicated fields in psychology, how can we expect her to understand enough, at that stage, to exit?

Tori

Tori decided that the best way to understand the mishap with the engagement ring was to talk to her partner about it. Maybe he was swindled when he bought the ring and he was the victim of an unethical jeweler. She was sure it could be worked out with a little dialogue.

"The ring looks beautiful on your hand!" he beamed.

"Yes, it does. Can we talk about it a moment?" she asked.

Darkness glanced at the ring and then, as he grabbed his keys, hurriedly uttered, "Sure! You know I saved MONTHS for that beauty. Had to cut back on some of my expenses but it was worth it, don't you think? Anyway, let's talk later tonight—I gotta get to work."

"It will only take a moment—can't you give me five minutes?" she begged.

"Why would you WANT to get me in trouble at work? Is it worth getting me fired over?" He was fuming now. "You obviously don't like it, or you wouldn't want to discuss it. You have no idea what I went through to get it—the things I sacrificed and did without. I know it's not as good as what your former husband gave you. Well, I'm sorry if it's not good enough. That's what this is about, isn't it—it's not up to your hoity-toity standards. I'll never be able to give you the standard of living he did, so maybe I shouldn't even try. You should just go back to the moneybags, as clearly that's what you're all about! I can't believe you're rejecting my ring." He reached over and grabbed the ring off her hand, slamming the door behind him as he made his exit.

Meanwhile, Tori stood, mouth gaping, wondering, "What was that?"

"Did you ask him about the ring?" her friend inquired later.

"I tried. He accused me of trying to get him fired, of comparing it to my last ring, of being a gold digger and rejecting his ring. He thinks he can't provide the way my ex did. I felt like I victimized him for asking to talk about it. I never got to ask him about it—and he tore the ring off my hand!"

Chapter Ten Endnotes

1   Karpman, S. B. (2014). *A Game Free Life*. Drama Triangle Publications.

2   Brown, Sandra L. (2009). *Women Who Love Psychopaths: Inside the Relationships of Inevitable Harm with Narcissists, Sociopaths, & Psychopaths*. Mask Publishing.

3   *Operant Conditioning*. (2018). https://simplypsychology.org/operant-conditioning.html

4, 5   Brown, Sandra L., *The Institute* (2007). Cognitive dissonance perceived as traumatic in Pathological Love Relationships. Raw data from a study; also, in *Women Who Love Psychopaths: Inside the Relationships of Inevitable Harm with Narcissists, Sociopaths & Psychopaths. Second Edition* (2009). Mask Publishing.

6   Babiak, P., & Hare, R. D. (2006). Snakes in suits: When psychopaths go to work. *Applied Psychology, 44*, 171–188. https://doi.org/10.1111/j.1464-0597.1995.tb01073.x

7   *compliance*. http://www.dictionary.om/browse/compliance

8   Covey, S. R. (1990). *Seven Habits of Highly Successful People*. Free Press.

9   Brown, Sandra L., *The Institute* (2007). Consistent relational patterns in cluster b/psychopathic disordered partners: Case studies of qualitative research. Agency raw data. Report prepared for outcome study for *The Institute*.

10, 11 Serin, R., Lloyd, C., Hanby, L., & Shturman, M. (2013). What and Who Might Enhance Offender Compliance: Situating Responsibility. In P. Ugwudike & P. Raynor (Eds.), *What Works in Offender Compliance* (p. 101). New York: Palgrave MacMillian.

12   *coercion*. www.OxfordDictionaries.com

13   Miklosovic, Jessica C. (2010) "Cognitive dissonance: effects of perceived choice on attitude change," *Modern Psychological Studies*: Vol. 15: No. 2, Article 3. https://scholar.utc.edu/mps/vol15/iss2/3

        Wicklund, R.A.; Brehm, J. W. (1976). *Perspectives on Cognitive Dissonance*. New Jersey: Lawrence Erlbaum Associates Publishers

14   *subterfuge*.www.OxfordDictionaries.com

Chapter Eleven

The End Phase—The 'D&D' Processes Puzzle Piece #2™

Continuing with Puzzle Piece #2™ is what happens in the next stage of the relationship as it ends, which will be no less dramatic and erratic than how it has been all along.

Quick Survivor Review

- Personality/psychopathy disorders are noted to communicate largely through the Crazy-Making Triangle.
- Interactions within the Triangle become more treacherous when other tactics are also used during communication.
- Survivors are trained to respond to Darkness' communication patterns through a process of Operant Learning and Classical Conditioning, persuasive reasoning, coercion, and subterfuge.
- Normal communication patterns are further frustrated by what happens in the Event Cycle.

The Inevitable End

Where did the silver-tongued love bomber go? How did the survivor go from dripping in oxytocin love juice to this brain-twisting relationship? "Wasn't I just in a relationship with my soulmate? But I loathe this man!"

The pathological partner's relationship timeline has moved from the pre/luring stage, past the love bombing of the early phase, through the middle phase chock full of communication disasters and dramatic and erratic behavior that ping-pongs around the Event Cycle. It is now headed for The End.[1]

By now, Darkness has a lot of opportunities in the pipeline in varying pre-relationship, early, and mid-stages. He is probably also active in other hidden behavior—swindling, drug dealing, or time on the town. This reduces Darkness' motivation to work too hard on his current, secure relationship when others are available. And as we have seen, the mid-stage gets complicated when his mask is torn off, revealing the bundle of pathology that he truly is. All survivors in the mid-stage begin to complicate Darkness' life by expecting the high of the early stage to continue, even though they have inklings that others have entered the pipeline. They are also beginning to identify communication issues and erratic behaviors. This causes stress to Darkness, who must now work at a task he's not good at—communication—when charm, sex, and talking his way out of a situation will no longer hold the relationship. What he *is* good at are pre- and early-stage courtship, and mimicking and parroting in those new relationships that have become his priority.

*T*he Jekyll and Hyde Split

Once a survivor has seen Darkness' duality through his Jekyll/Hyde split, her need to understand it is kicked into high gear. She has spent months, or years, trying to understand the two very different sides of Darkness, and the end phase will culminate in a heightened recognition of the dichotomous experiences she has had with him.

The word *dichotomy* means 'a division or contrast between two things that are, or are represented as, being opposed or entirely different.'[2] This entirely different personality representation is what is implied when we say someone has a Jekyll/Hyde persona, notably present in personality disorders and psychopathy. These dual sides of one person are indicative of the dichotomous, or entirely different emotional *experiences* and *relationships* the survivor will experience with both sides of Jekyll and Hyde.[3]

Most of us (unless we were raised with pathological family members) have not been exposed to these extreme splits or entirely different sides in others so it's difficult for us to understand them. But it is this extreme split in Darkness's behavior that requires the survivor to develop two different skill sets to be in a relationship with two very different sides of Darkness. She has a skill set for Jekyll, responding to all the feigned

214

love and support, and a separate skill set for the maniacal Hyde with his impulsivity, communication issues, manipulations, and infidelity problems. She must constantly shift gears, skill sets, and coping strategies based on which side of him walks through the door.

This ping-ponging back and forth between two skill sets and coping strategies results in the Jekyll girlfriend and the Hyde girlfriend. There are her different moods, conversations, histories, hopes, and fears that come with each side of Darkness. There are different approaches she must use, or topics to avoid, with each of his sides. In a very Operant Learning and Classical Conditioning sense, she is trained in responding to both sides of Darkness and must rapidly shift and adapt to whichever side is present.[4]

While we have touched on cognitive dissonance as an originating source of trauma by having to hold two differing belief systems (He's Jekyll/ He's Hyde), *The Institute* believes it is from having to respond to two sides of Darkness, that creates the foundation for cognitive dissonance that is then enflamed throughout the relationship and produces traumatic aftermath.[5] The dichotomous sides of Darkness create dissonance (or the lack of harmony) in the survivor.

In healthy relationships, a person's core self-stability creates the ability to know what to expect in a relationship. In Pathological Love Relationships, the inconsistency of Darkness' core self-instability (being both Jekyll and Hyde) is what causes cognitive dissonance in the survivor in the middle phase of the relationship and is extremely heightened in the end phase.[6] With every appearance of the charmer, she hopes that side is there to stay, but she is only to be met soon after with the other antagonistic side.

Darkness' rapid shift between personas creates the survivor's constant internal emotional movement between feelings of love and disgust, or trust and distrust that become the consistent symptoms of cognitive dissonance. Women say they feel bipolar in their ups and downs, moment to moment, jumping between "I love him" one moment to "I loathe him" the next. She is unable to hold one consistent view of him, of herself, or the relationship which is experienced as 'relational insanity.' She expresses this as the inability to stay on the same page with herself about who he is or what he does. By mid-relationship she has experienced this hundreds of times, especially during disputes with him when the mask drops, and he is trying one moment to woo her back with charm, and the next minute manipulating her with rage, coercion, and subterfuge—and it's all happening in one conversation.

Survivors have entirely different experiences with, and emotions about, both sides of Darkness.[7] Some of these experiences and emotions are generated from the silver-tongued love bomber while others are created in the middle and end phases of the relationships when the mask slips and the confusion from relational insanity begins. The following is a list of dichotomous and paradoxical emotions or experiences that are now fully active in the end phase of the relationship.

*T*he Relationship Dichotomies and Paradoxes©[8]

She feels extreme bonding . . .	. . . and yet expects probable abandonment.
She feels extremely protected by him . . .	. . . and yet extremely exposed and at risk because of him.
She trusts him deeply . . .	. . and yet red flags of distrust are building.
She is worshipped as a sexual Madonna . . .	. . . and yet often treated like a whore.
She feels an intense amount of love towards him. . .	. . . and yet loathes him at the same time.
She thinks he is the most exciting person she has ever met . . .	. . . and yet she is exhausted by him.
She senses his child-like vulnerability and woundedness . . .	. . . yet his adult mystique and hidden life are very intriguing.
She hears him say he supports her . . .	. . . yet she watches him sabotage her.
She's had the most fun with him . . .	. . . and yet in the midst of the fun, he will often rage.
She thinks he is a wonderful soulmate . . .	. . . and at the same time the sickest person on the planet.

He acts as her rescuer . . .	. . . and yet he is her tormenter.
He can be very calculating in what he does. . .	. . . and yet be very impulsive.
He is frequently hypersexual. . .	. . . and yet he is often nonsexual and refuses her sexually.
He idealizes her . . .	. . . and yet will totally devalue her.
He is super-connected to her, inhaling her exhaled air. . .	. . . and yet totally aloof.
He acts as if he totally understands her . . .	. . . and yet is clueless about her feelings and motives.
He is the kindest of people. . .	. . . and yet can be the most sadistic.
He is overly generous . . .	. . . and yet incredibly cheap and selfish.
He is attractively macho. . .	. . . and yet wimpy and needy.

This list of relationship dichotomies and paradoxes is typical of PLRs but represents nothing a survivor is likely to have experienced before. The intensity of emotions listed on both sides of the chart exist simultaneously, affecting her rapidly changing relationship dynamics. Let's look at a few of these dichotomies and paradoxes to see their destructive power.[9]

The Dichotomy of Bonding vs. Abandonment

The survivor feels as if she has bonded with Darkness more closely than with anyone else in her life. This feeling was generated with the assistance of what she experienced in the 'state-dependent learning' phase and was accompanied by the chemical gush of oxytocin. Darkness, too, has mirrored back this incredible sense of soulmate status, yet he himself has not experienced any feelings related to bonding. But when the mask slipped, and the bait-and-switch began, she became aware that at any moment she could be abandoned or left behind in the relationship. While she once felt he was the one with whom she was most bonded, and the one who would spend a life time with her, she simultaneously believes that she has never been more at risk of being dumped, cheated on, abandoned, or emotionally devastated.

"Our intimacy and intense emotions exploded rather than evolved. He seemed to want and need so much from me. But it was a smoke screen—he could also be gone in a flash."

"He would draw me in and then push me away with various methods. I was constantly perplexed about why it seemed that he wanted a relationship with me on some levels but not on others. He was committed at times but not entirely. I've never been so confused about how someone really felt about me."

Darkness is likely to gaslight her by telling her that she's crazy and the relationship is the same as it has always been, making her question her own perception. Or he may tell her that something she has done, such as questioning him or challenging him, has caused him to want to abandon the relationship. This attaching and rejecting builds internal stress, constantly ping-ponging back and forth like in the old game of pulling petals off a daisy while aligning each one with "he loves me, he loves me not."

"The intensity—the changeability—how one minute it could all seem good and normal, and I would forget the craziness, and then suddenly the tables turned and the monster I was living with reappeared."

The Dichotomy of Idealizing vs Devaluing

The survivor has never felt such adulation before. Darkness has told her he sees her as "the most incredible person—brilliant, loving, sexy." His idealizing of her has sped up the sensation of attachment that Mystery called 'profound rapport building.' Yet by mid-relationship he is devaluing her, which increases his sense of power over the relationship. This leaves her feeling that she needs to do something to get him to feel how he previously felt about her. An enormous amount of emotional energy can be spent trying to figure out *how* to shift the relationship back to the previous dynamics in which the good side of the psychopath was experienced.

The Dichotomy of Perceived Protection vs Created Dependency

A survivor in a PLR never feels more protected than in the beginning stages of the relationship. He may have even talked about the protective feeling he has toward her. Since pathological people are extroverted and dominant, they do tend to project a sense of being the protector. But, while the survivor may be cuddling up to his supposed super powers of keeping harm away from her, her suspicions are growing. In many ways she has never felt more exposed, at risk, or in a strange state of neediness. And she's right. Protection by a psychopath is an illusion. Her exposure to disease, financial ruin, emotional devastation, and his impulsive behavior is at its highest point.

"I wanted the security of a relationship, a father for my children. I was invested in an illusion. He wasn't any of that—although he always pretended to protect me."

The Dichotomy of the Pursued Madonna vs the Alleged Whore

The experience of Darkness' heightened sexuality draws her in through the deepening emotional powers of the sexual connection. He is highly sensual, and she is intensely pursued sexually. Darkness is likely to describe their sexual relationship as unique or deep and meaningful, or simply great sex. Whichever way the psychopath spins the lingo, she most assuredly feels special and pursued as the archetypal Madonna.

But eventually, to humiliate her, the treatment of her as the Madonna will be dropped, and he will begin to treat her as merely a sexual object to be reviled—a whore. The dichotomy of having experienced this intense sexual bonding with him and then being debased (as a whore or simply as a sex partner) sets up pursuit/rejection dynamics in their sex life. Many women speak of feeling humiliated to have to beg for sex, not merely to have the sexual experience but to try to emotionally reconnect with their partner and have him experience the bonding that she thought the relationship was based on.

"I don't know what it was that we had. I used to think I knew. I thought he was as connected as I was. In the beginning, he couldn't get enough of me. But halfway through the relationship, he withheld sex and acted as if I was repugnant. He called me horrible sexual names . . . he even used the 'c' word. How could I have dropped that low in his eyes?"

Darkness will often accuse their partners of infidelity, so they can label them as whores and reject them. Or they will introduce a survivor to deviant sexual practices and then tell them no one else will ever want them because of their participation in them. Or they will compare them to their previous sex partners to coerce them into more unwanted sexual acts, so the cycle repeats itself.

"I am repulsed by my own sexual behavior. I allowed so many things that were against who I am as a person—my own personal values. I will never be the same sexually . . . I feel so dirty and violated. Of course, that's what he wanted all along. He reminds me of every horrible sexual act I performed and how normal men would think I was a whore. Since I'm so disgusting, he thinks I should just stay with him—since we are alike and understand each other sexually."

The Dichotomy of Trust vs Distrust

Darkness spent a lot of time in the luring phase establishing trust with his partner. He may have told her stories about his own trustworthiness or performed trustworthy actions to cement her trust in him early on. This became the basis by which he could constantly refer to himself as trustworthy while doing everything that proves he was untrustworthy.

"Half of being a con man is the challenge. When I score, I get more kick out of that than anything—to score and get the trust is the biggest kick of my whole life."

---

*"I opened the door and saw him in bed with another woman. By the end of the evening, I wasn't sure I had seen it at all! He didn't convince me that it meant nothing—he convinced me it **didn't happen** and there was no one in the bed with him! It took me forever to learn to trust my own perceptions. When you think you are going crazy, it's easy to rely on someone else's version of reality. I now see that it wasn't the issue of reality—it was the issue of truth and trust and that I was so conflicted as to whether I trusted or distrusted him."*

The Dichotomy of Excitement vs Exhaustion

When the survivor began the relationship, it was highlighted by the most excitement she ever experienced in a relationship, but, over time, the excitement of the intensity of the relationship causes extreme emotional exhaustion. The adrenaline rush the survivor used to have is beginning to burn itself out. The drama, the highs and lows, the daily power struggles, the weekly uncovering of some new lie, and the constant fear of the relationship ending are producing a bone-weary fatigue.

"I kept thinking—if this is the most exciting man I have ever been with, why am I so exhausted in every way—emotionally, physically and even financially? If this is so much fun, why do I feel like THIS?"

The Dichotomy of His Child-like Vulnerability vs His Adult Mystique

Darkness invested a lot in portraying himself to his victim as wounded. Psychopaths have no problem simultaneously playing both dominant and doomed personas. He most likely acted as if his hidden pain was disclosed only to her. She was the only one who understood him or with whom he felt safe enough to share his pain.

Women say that he had a "child-like quality to him" or that he seemed vulnerable or emotionally wounded. This wounded quality, combined with Darkness' air of aloofness, creates a confusing mystique. Women define him as different, unique, and eccentric. Some find him electrifying. Some women mistake the sense of his hidden life for mystique.

A conflict exists for a partner when she gets an inkling that she should leave yet feels as if she is abandoning a wounded child who needs her. She also wants to stay because he is so baffling that she wants to figure out him or the relationship before she exits.

===

"Was he a child or a man? Was he a power-hungry psycho or a knee-clinging toddler? I don't know—he was both. I couldn't put my finger on what it was in him that pulled from both sides of me—the part that saw him as powerful and mysterious, and yet the part that saw him as damaged and in need of me."

===

The Dichotomy of Loving vs. Loathing

The survivor feels the magnetic pull into an emotional vortex from which she can't free herself. She mistakes intensity for love and passion for bonding. It doesn't take Darkness long to test the depths of her love (and tolerance) and to figure out he has a lot of wiggle room to manipulate her in the relationship.

As a woman begins to see the other side of Darkness' mask, she recognizes his lies and inconsistencies. She loathes his lies, his deviancy, his disorder, and she may loathe herself for loving him, even amidst everything she finds out.

===

"I felt insane most of the time. I had never loved anyone like I loved him. It's to the point now that I cringe when I am around him. I used to feel sorry for how sick he obviously is. Now I feel repulsed, but in a flash, I can be right back in the memory of how good it was, and a second later, I'm cringing."

===

Survivor Work Page Question:
I recognize the dichotomies I felt exhibited in (list dichotomies from above): _____

$\mathcal{T}$he 'D&D' Processes

It is from these dichotomous and paradoxical emotions and experiences that the survivor will enter the end phase of the relationship. Already confused about the dual sides of Darkness and her emotions in reaction to both sides of him, she will be met with an equally confusing end of the relationship precisely when she is the most unclear about him.

With the pipeline well stocked, Darkness does not need the hassle of The Inquisition that he gets from the survivor. By the end of the middle relationship phase, Darkness has done his best to manipulate her through all stages of the Karpman Triangle and the Event Cycle with him utilizing persuasion and subterfuge, and, if that didn't work, coercion. He's had a few problems along the way with some communication hiccups that were less than effective on his part. So, in his warped logic, he's given it his best shot.

In PLRs, the end phase of the relationship in the jargon of the lexicon is referred to as 'the Devaluing and Discarding' process or the 'D&D'. But, by now, his partner has already been on the receiving end of the devaluing -

- Implying that her suspicions and/or concerns are a sign of her mental illness
- Reducing her to a sex object
- Picking apart her appearance
- Suggesting she is needy and dependent
- Implying that it's no wonder she had problems in her previous relationships—no one really wanted her

The months leading up to the formal D&D are already paved with his manipulative intentions, which lay the groundwork for his exit. But D&D could just as easily stand for 'Damaged & Destroyed' as Darkness exits stage left.

Survivors are plagued with feelings along the lines of "If only I hadn't _____, then the relationship wouldn't have ended." There are no books titled *Happily Ever After with a Psychopath*. Hard-wired into his biology and motivational drives is the never-ending thirst for a new supply that will occur no matter what she did or did not do.

Reeling from rejection by the love bomber, survivors feel a panic they never experienced in the ending stages of normal relationships. While there is always a period of grief and regret in normal relationships, the PLR is full of video replays of the dichotomies—"I love him/ I loathe him," and "It was the most intense relationship I ever had/I am so exhausted." The dichotomies flood the mind with unanswerable questions, which create neuropathways in the brain resulting in what's clinically known as rumination. This is no ordinary rumination like the occasional memory that brings a twinge and a smile—it is **obsessive** rumination that causes professional women to come crawling to therapists on their hands and knees, begging for relief.

The months or years that the relationship continued brought the ensuing cognitive dissonance that slowly created brain changes and the ping-ponging, called in the lexicon Monkey Mind. The slow erosion of her cognitive functioning was not merely an emotional impact—it was a biological brain impact that changed her ability to control her once-rational mind. The totality of the aftermath symptoms will be covered in a later chapter, but the point here is to realize that the end of a PLR is not merely a 'bad breakup.' Long-term exposure to pathology brings with it real cognitive consequences.[9] Cognitive dissonance is evident in a survivor partner's assertion that "I still want the relationship/even though I know he's a psychopath."

Crippled by the unsolvable and paradoxical thoughts of Monkey Mind and stalked by flashbacks and ruminations (often of the good memories), the professionally successful survivor is rendered inoperable—her mental faculties have flatlined.

$\mathcal{D}$arkness' Exit Strategies

At the end phase of the PLR, Darkness usually employs one of three exit strategies -

- The Devalue & Discard process
- The Disappear & Discard process
- The Dating & Disappear process

Devaluing and Discarding

After weeks/months/years/decades of the devaluing process, Darkness may strike his final blow and end the relationship, or perhaps the latest infidelity/lying/manipulation causes the survivor to end the relationship.

In healthy relationships, partners, although brokenhearted, mutually conclude that it is in their best interest to end it. While there may have been some heated dialogue in the final moments, most partners come to a point of eventually wishing the other partner well and moving on. But in PLRs, Darkness does not possess the ability to problem solve or communicate, and certainly the end of the relationship requires communication skills. With his pipeline full, his motivation for a humane ending does not exist, nor is he biologically wired for empathy or insight that would be used in a humane breakup.

In healthy relationships, something called *closure* occurs— 'the act of bringing something to a conclusion.' Through discussion of the good and the bad, partners have their last say about what harmed them, and while their differences may not be resolved, each has spoken their piece and has felt heard. They leave with their questions answered, their hearts poured out, and their consciences cleared.

Breakup counseling is often sought when closure is not attained, and most of the focus of counseling is trying to simulate closure in an artificial way, even without actual closure. In PLRs, given Darkness' deficits, there is never closure. There is no admission of guilt, no teary confessions, no validation of her suspicions with an honest disclosure of "yes, I found someone else," no questions answered, no apologies made. It ends with all the questions that existed the day before still going unanswered. While normal people are wired with the need for humane closure to bring a relationship to a conclusion, to ritualize the end of something, and to make space in a spiritual sense for a new beginning, what a survivor perceives as a need to move on will never be met. What she is left with is blame, projection, memories of coercion, labels of mental illness, a lack of answers, personal degradation, and a mind full of ruminations.

The final conversation is riddled with all the communication deficits Darkness possesses, making the last dialogue a far cry from anything that resembles closure. And with this torturous baggage deposited at her feet, he simply leaves. Even survivors who can identify an end from a blowup or a specific declaration are never given closure, just a demarcation that he is gone (although probably not for long, which will be discussed in the section on post-relationship dynamics).

Disappearing and Discarding

For some people with Dark Triad disorders, the weeks/months/years of devaluing culminates in the Great Disappearing Houdini act. Some members of the Dark Triad utilize devaluing for a time and then, without a demarcation, vanish. The survivor does not have the opportunity to request closure (not knowing she wouldn't get it anyway). She is left not knowing any of the circumstances surrounding the end of the relationship. Some pathological partners vanish into the beds of those in the pipeline a few blocks over, while others pack up and leave the state or even the country. He changes phone numbers, email, social media, even jobs—and the slate is wiped clean for the new life with whomever is next.

Survivors have enlisted the police, FBI, and private investigators, fearing the worst, only for their partners to be located a few blocks away. Sometimes they're as far away as another country. A better, more enticing offer, a new means of financial support, or the scent of new material has been dangled in front of Darkness' face and he is gone.

Some survivors never pick up the trail of where he disappeared to. They are left wondering if he was offed by someone he owed money to or abducted by aliens, without even a hint of closure to be had.

But some disappear in another way with yet another form of D&D.

Dating and Disappearing

Some of the Dark Triad leave without even entering the devaluing phase, and there's no clue of their imminent departure. Amid what the survivor perceives as the relationship proceeding as normal, Darkness simply never returns. All the earmarks of Devaluing and Discarding aren't applicable—he simply vanishes.

In this version of D&D—Dating & Disappearing—no forewarning by devaluing gives any clue to the impending disappearance. Instead, Darkness decides to skip the degrading communication, without the male anatomy to own up to his departure. He simply leaves her believing he will be home for dinner and never returns.

Not a 'Bad Breakup'

All three forms of D&D are clear representations that PLRs are not like normal breakups. Most women don't need to engage the FBI to find out their relationship is over and that he isn't missing—that he's curled up in someone else's bed. Most endings don't include breakups based on disappearances. These earmarks of PLRs are tied to the poor bonding ability, lack of empathy, and the go-go-now brain that's motivated by new supply in the pipeline.

While it would be apparent to most people that, if you ever did this to a woman, you should, in fact, move to a different country, because if she or her daddy found you, there would be hell to pay. But Darkness, with no conscience, doesn't read the situation the same way. He hasn't given it any more thought than the day he planned it. So, months or years down the road, abandoning the relationship is no longer even a lingering memory, which means one day he'll be looking through his phone, sees her number in the speed dial, and thinks he'll call and see how she's doing.

$\mathcal{P}$ost Relationship Dynamics—Here Comes the Boomerang[10]

Darkness feels no guilt about devaluing, discarding, or disappearing, and so the survivor partner becomes just another phone number in the pipeline. This is why the Relationship Cycle© is designed in a circle. Those who are discarded and in the post-relationship stage are eventually *recycled* by Darkness into the pre-relationship stage as 'a potential' when the pipeline thins out.

While the relationship might have been fraught with violence and arrests, or whether she turned him in for embezzlement or drug dealing resulting in jail time, it's all water under the bridge for Darkness. Driven **not** by rational brain processes but by that big old motivational drive, he gets nervous when the pipeline gets thin.

Nowhere in her previous experiences of breakups did she learn the three different D&D processes, nor would it be reasonable for a rational person to think that someone who did *that* would have the gall to return as if nothing happened—but then, she never *really* understood Darkness to begin with.

Without the knowledge of this emotional boomerang, she is still vulnerable and, therefore, still an opportunity for him. Mr. Opportunity may wait for a moment that presents itself for a natural contact—her child is graduating from high school, a parent dies, he reads in the paper about her promotion, or a mutual friend gets married—a natural event that would prompt a normal person to make contact. Or he may try to demonstrate that he does, in fact, still have sentimental thoughts about her on her birthday, Christmas, New Year's, or their anniversary. These casual out of the blue contacts are not initiated as supportive gestures.

They are *calculated* inquiries into her availability to reenter the pipeline in the pre-relationship phase.

In 30 years, I've never seen Darkness **not** reach out to a former partner after the relationship ended. More often than not, these contacts were misread by the survivor as innocent. As we know, the Dark Triad are predators who hunt by planning and finding opportunity, so it is not innocent or coincidental.

Time predisposes the survivor to believe he is long gone when he has merely slipped off the radar—temporarily. The longer the time with no contact, the more the survivor believes he is happily ever after somewhere else. She may have heard rumors that he is married and has children now or has a stunning line of multiple girlfriends. I've seen predators go as long as 10 *years* without contact, only to reappear when they see an opportune time to test the waters.

It is this surprise attack that creates danger for the gazelle again. Darkness now has an advantage he didn't have before in that he knows her weaknesses, her history, and what to mimic and parrot that will lower her defenses. It's far less prep time for Darkness to deal with these repeats in the pipeline.

It's for this reason that *The Institute* always stresses to our clients to be vigilant about contact from Darkness and that casual contact is anything *but* casual—it's premeditated. We haven't had a client yet who believed she would hear from her partner again and the worse it had ended with him, the more she believed he would be crazy to contact her—only to find that the day rolled around when he did! But this isn't about what is rational, it is about what Darkness *is*.

In every interaction we have with survivors about his contacting her again, they argue with us—adamantly, angrily, that he will *never, ever* contact her because of how she handled "the last time he contacted her, a few months ago"—and the time before that, too. Oh, wait—he already contacted you? Yes, but only to say he was sorry for how he handled things. Yes, but only to say he ran into so-and-so. Yes, but only to wish my child a happy birthday. Yes, but only because he was drunk…

How she handles the eventual contact will have everything to do with whether she falls prey to him again. As a sinister amateur psychologist, Darkness is best at reading opportunity. When she answers his call five years later to "give him a piece of her mind" and proceeds to ream him, Darkness is grinning because even anger or hate is attention, and what he perceives as the flip side of love. Rubbing his hands together, his go-go-now brain says, "She wants me. I just have to be contrite." *Any* contact is a green light for him to resume the pursuit.

Survivor Work Page Question:
Which D&D process did you experience ?

ori

Tori was mesmerized at the events that led up to the ring being torn off her hand. But her friend—not so much. It didn't ring true for her, so she began a little digging, starting with the house he claimed to own. A quick search of real estate records showed that he never owned that house. His steady job of 25 years at a plant with a pension didn't turn out to be real either. His claims of having been in Europe or in the Special Ops in the Army were just fiction. In fact, by the time her friend was done investigating, none of what he had claimed was true. The fake ring was the loose thread on a sweater that, when pulled, unraveled the whole thing.

Tori's head was swimming in the haze of the love bombing that had made her feel so close to him. Her *desire* for that story to be true versus the reality of the facts produced the mind-mangle of cognitive dissonance. And where had Darkness vanished to?

Wanting some closure, Tori called Darkness. The litany of the uncovered facts when shared with him got a response with the accusation that she was crazy and incapable of a normal relationship. He was worried about her mental health—he hadn't realized how deranged she was, or he never would have dated her. Plausible explanations were given for every falsehood that was uncovered, from the house he didn't own to his supposed time in Special Ops and how she had not acquired the correct information. He verbalized that he felt compassion for her obvious mental illness but later raged at her for her accusations. Tori began to doubt her friend's investigation, not Darkness' explanation of it. Head spinning, she felt she had made a horrible mistake after all, since there were answers to every allegation.

Tori asked if they could meet in person to talk it out, but Darkness, aloof and disinterested, created in her an even stronger longing to understand. But her calls and texts went unanswered. It had only been two weeks since the ring was ripped off her hand. Surely, he was in pain too over this abrupt misunderstanding.

She went out to dinner with her friend to talk more about her feelings about the puzzling facts of the investigation. Her friend was sure that once she laid it out again for her, Tori would see the relationship for what it was—the false presentation of every fact he ever claimed. As they strolled into the restaurant, there sat Darkness, cuddled up in a booth with a new woman, sliding the cubic zirconia ring onto her finger while gazing into her eyes.

Wrapping It All Up

PLRs don't resemble normal relationships—not in the beginning with all the luring and predatory hunting, not in the early phase with the love bombing and the mask, not in the middle phase with the communication problems and his warped motivational drives, and not in the end with the variety of D&D processes. With all this abnormality of not just the relationship dynamics but with Darkness himself, any normal person is going to be harmed.

But what *The Institute* has found is that there is a *type* of person who is going to be unusually harmed due to what she brings to this relationship of inevitable harm, and it is precisely this type of person that Darkness targets. Let's personally meet this type of personality.

Chapter Eleven Endnotes

1, 7, 10 Brown, Sandra L. *The Institute* (2007). Pre, Early, Mid, Late & Post Relationship Dynamics of Cluster B/psychopathic Partners: A Grounded Theory Outcome. Prepared for *The Institute Therapist Training Manual.*

2   *dichotomy.* http://www.dictionary.com/browse/dichotomy

3, 5, 6, 8   Brown, Sandra L. *The Institute* (2007). Pathological Dichotomous Behavior and Its Impact to Relationship Dynamics Study. Study prepared for *Women Who Love Psychopaths, First Edition.*

4   Brown, Sandra L. (2010). *Women Who Love Psychopaths: Inside the Relationships of Inevitable Harm.* Second Edition. Mask Publishing.

9   Brown, Sandra L., *The Institute* (2006). Survivor symptom survey. Agency raw data.

Section Three

Puzzle Piece #3™

A Survivor-Partner with Super Traits

**A Partner
with Super Traits**

**Figure 12.1
Puzzle Piece #3™**

Chapter Twelve

The Super Traits of the Survivor Partner: Agreeableness and Cooperativeness—The Relationship Investment Traits
Puzzle Piece #3™

To continue understanding the components of a Pathological Love Relationship, we look at the next piece of the puzzle. So far, we have looked at Puzzle Piece #1™—A Partner with a Cluster B/psychopathy Disorder and its connection to personality disorders and their causes. Puzzle Piece #2™ centered around the Dramatic and Erratic Relational Dynamics and dealt with language and meaning issues, the relational timeline, the Karpman Triangle, the Event Cycle, and phases of the relationship.

Now we add the third Puzzle Piece: A Partner with Super Traits. PLRs are not random; Darkness is a predator who *seeks*, and just what he is seeking is relevant to understanding the victims who will become entangled with him and why.

Quick Survivor Review

- Pathological Love Relationships are known for their dichotomies ("I love him/I loathe him").
- The End Phase of the relationship is defined by one of the three D&D processes.
- Pathological Love Relationships have a Post-Relationship phase, which begins with a camouflaged request for reengagement after the relationship ends.

Our Unnoticed Personality

Personality seems to be one of those factors in ourselves that slides

233

under our radar of copious concern unless we struggle with something huge like paralyzing shyness. Like the color of our eyes or that beauty mark on our face, it just *is*. Since our birth we've lived with our personality, so it doesn't warrant a constant checking in with it like something that fluctuates such as our horoscope or mood.

We probably all have friends who have a larger than life personality—for instance if they are extroverted, they command a room, they are loud, and they say what they think. Most of my friends are always sort of surprised when their own personality is described to them. Many have commented, "I haven't thought about it that way. I don't see myself like that." Our personalities are just that static consistent way we have always been and, unless we have been written up at work or have identified some disaster that our personality contributed to in a life event, we are all pretty oblivious.

To top it off, few people have had their personalities assessed or tested to receive clinical feedback that might alert them to areas that are over or under the bell curve of what is optimally normal. The closest most people come to understanding that personalities can have problems is after an encounter with Darkness. And most people who come to understand problem personalities like Darkness' identify the 'too low' of certain traits like not enough empathy, conscience, or remorse. Most of personality research has been focused on the low end of the personality spectrum—those with *too little* of a certain personality trait. Those on the 'low-conscience spectrum,' discussed in Chapters One and Two, have been on the radar of personality researchers for decades. Not enough empathy, compassion, agreeableness, and cooperativeness is what constitutes pathology—personality disorders, psychopathy, and other forms of various pathologies that harm others.

In contrast, very few people identify the 'too much' of personality as problematic. It seems to have taken decades to look at the other end of the spectrum of *too much* of certain personality traits like empathy, compassion, or tolerance. Some of this is related to the marketing efforts of gurus who imply that most of us *need more* empathy, compassion, and tolerance, as offered through their books, webinars, and meditations. According to them, just about everyone is too low in these traits and by having more, we will change the energy complexion of the world, usher in world peace, and heal the planet. Some neuropsychologists equate higher happiness with higher levels of empathy, compassion, and tolerance, which they suggest creates a less conflict-filled existence with the person and the world. I think our survivors would take issue with that claim.

My dialogue with one of the empathy neuropsychologists centered around the fact that those with *too much* empathy, compassion, and tolerance did not encounter the lasting happiness that he claimed these traits produced in others, but rather led to misery, since an overabundance of empathy and acceptance is bound to be a problem when activated with the wrong people. The psychologist had never heard of too much empathy. This widespread appeal from gurus about the *necessity of more* empathy and tolerance implies that not all our personalities come with an equal measure of traits. And that much is true.

But the understanding and research on the "too much" of traits, like empathy (called *hyper empathy*), has been around a short time compared to the nearly ancient research on the 'not enough' traits exhibited in Darkness. Gurus imply nearly everyone needs more empathy. But what about those people who are already over the bell curve—has anyone really found out what too much of a good thing like empathy and tolerance can do?

Writer/researcher Barbara Oakley captured my attention with her book *Cold-Blooded Kindness*[1] which examined how hyper empathy can look like other psychological issues when it is feigned and used for evil. Then her groundbreaking book *Pathological Altruism*[2] looked at not just feigned hyper empathy but *real* hyper empathy, which, when taken to extremes, can cause harm in the person's life and even the lives of others.

It has been *The Institute's* long-standing interest to understand what is behind these unrecognized elevated personality traits in a world that keeps screaming that we need more of them, oblivious of their sometimes-detrimental effects. And with Darkness' skill set of being able to use anything good as a weapon against others, understanding these "too much" of a good thing traits warranted our investigation and our explanation.

Survivor Note:

Not all personality trait elevations are problematic in all situations.

Our personality traits normally remain unexamined because most of them don't cause problems except in certain situations with certain people. Most people only realize that some of their personality traits are out of range if they encountered problems, like in a PLR, and were tested and informed of it.

$\mathcal{A}$greeableness and Cooperation: The Relationship Investment Traits

So, what are the traits that are over the bell curve that put survivors at risk?

The traits of the survivors that were shown to be significantly elevated in our research using both the 2007 Temperament Character Inventory[3] (The TCI) and the 2014 Five Factor Form/Five Factor Model Rating Form[4] (The FFF/M) were described in different terms but they measured similar traits. What the Five Factor Form/Model described as 'agreeableness,' the TCI described as 'cooperativeness.'

Both elevated personality traits (agreeableness and cooperativeness) are connected to what *The Institute* calls *relationship investment* traits. *The Institute* views relationship investment traits as those traits naturally occurring in a personality that promote a person's deep interest in others. This trait is 'other-person oriented,' meaning that someone who possesses this trait can keep others in mind as they interact. These people are described as warm, sociable, likable, friendly, and tolerant of others. They possess greater than normal patience, are generous toward the disadvantaged, are peacemakers, and are forgiving. It is the *amount* of agreeableness that predicts how well a person will adapt to adversities and how well they can roll with what life has dealt them.

Survivor Note:

Survivors' ability to adapt to known or unknown pathology is an innate tendency in their personality. It is not a conscious decision to people please but rather a naturally occurring element of their personality.

There have been many misguided assumptions as to why highly successful women invest in relationships that turn out to cause inevitable harm. These assumptions are precisely why survivors have been wrongfully labeled as dependent and codependent.[5] Without the understanding that the survivor's personality influences the course of her interactions, factors such as abuse, trauma, learned helplessness, PTSD, relationship addiction, and various forms of dependency, are *assumed* to be the culprits. *The Institute* believes there is a better explanation.

Understanding Investment

A Return on Investment (ROI) is a banking term associated with whether what you initially contribute will pay off in the end. A return is a measurement of the gain or loss generated on an investment related to what was invested in it. Relationship investment can be generated from the naturally occurring traits of personality and temperament and not *just* driven by deliberate thought processes and conscious choice.

Therefore, our personalities can *predispose* us to be enthusiastic and trusting investors if our traits and personality wiring are on the higher end of trait elevations in agreeableness. Within PLRs, Darkness capitalizes on the person's natural predisposition to invest without knowing what they are investing in. Survivors have a naturally occurring elevated trait that already categorizes relationships as important investment vehicles. While some people may prefer stocks and bonds, these trait-elevated survivors find relationships to be a significant source of what produces happiness in their lives.

This can be seen in the rich and deep relationships in which they've been involved and have maintained over their lifetimes—still having relationships that they've invested in from childhood, high school, college, and even former employment positions. No doubt this relationship investment trait has created a rewarding life of happy relationships with others. People with these traits care deeply about the quality of their relationships and their return on investment. In past relationships, the investment has paid rich dividends in the enhancement of the quality of their lives.

Until Darkness…

What is the unrealized trait that elevates someone's relationship investment status, creating a natural tendency to find meaning, happiness, and life contentment in relationship?

The answer lies in the trait and the facets called 'agreeableness.'

The Traits of the Five Factor Form/Five Factor Model Rating Form of Agreeableness

One of the main elevated personality traits in the Five Factor Form is 'agreeableness.' It is an over-arching trait that includes several facets:

- Trust
- Straightforwardness
- A Giving Nature
- Cooperation
- Humbleness
- Empathy

The scores on these facets determine if a person has low, normal, high-normal, or high Agreeableness. Survivors of PLRs consistently scored in the 'high-normal' category which is beyond the bell curve of the safety net of the 'normal' range for this trait.

Let's break down the facets by using their *additional* descriptors to get a bigger picture of what these facets comprise.

Table 12.1
Traits and Additional Descriptors

Trait	Additional Descriptors
Trust	Trusting of others and trustworthy, optimistic about human nature, sees others through who she is.
Straightforwardness	Up front, honest, confiding.
A Giving Nature	Altruistic, sacrificial nature in relationships, considerate, willing to compromise her interests for the sake of others, sentimental.
Cooperation	Prone to assisting rather than attacking, motivated by social harmony, reciprocal in relationships, helpful, values getting along with others, avoids conflict, sociable, motivated by helping, sharing, donating, volunteering.
Humbleness	Modest in her portrayal of herself, gentle, well-tempered, warm, approachable, likeable.
Empathy	Tender-minded, kind, generous, compassionate, peacemaker, forgiving.
Loyal*	Allegiance to others, faithfulness, committed to obligations.

Trait	Additional Descriptors
Tolerance*	Tolerant of differing opinions and behaviors.

(* Added by *The Institute*)

$\mathcal{T}$he Temperament Character Inventory Trait of Cooperativeness

The TCI, the *other* testing instrument used in earlier research in 2007, uses the word 'cooperativeness' to describe the traits similar to agreeableness. Cloninger, the creator of the TCI, described cooperative individuals as 'socially tolerant, empathic, helpful, and compassionate' as opposed to those traits in the pathology of Darkness— 'intolerant, callous, unhelpful, and vengeful.' He described cooperative persons as "facilitative people who showed unconditional acceptance of others, empathy with other's feelings, and willingness to help without a desire for selfish domination." Most importantly, he regarded high cooperativeness as a sign of psychological maturity and of advanced moral development.

The trait of TCI labeled 'cooperativeness', which is similar to agreeableness, included the following facets:

- Tolerance
- Friendliness
- Compassion
- Supportiveness
- Guided by moral principles

As we can see, the Five Factor Form and the TCI measured similar traits using different terms. On each instrument, the survivors tested in the 'high-normal' range of these traits.

Let's examine the newest research performed with the Five Factor Form and take a closer look at how stellar traits in high-normal abundance could harm the survivor.

Agreeableness and Cooperativeness[6] and How They Operate

The two lists of the traits of agreeableness and cooperativeness and their corresponding similar facets capture the personality of a highly relationship-invested survivor whose combination of traits creates a relationship in which she is tolerant, compassionate, empathic, optimistic about human nature (and unfortunately, his inability to change), trusting of others, trustworthy herself, loyal (even in the face of betrayal), helpful in facilitating a cooperative style in relationships (even a PLR), and tending to see others through who she is.

Despite the dangers of being too tolerant of bad behavior or empathetic in the face of betrayal, people with high agreeableness (cooperativeness) traits are often considered 'transformational leaders' in their ability to lead others to consensus and moral decisions. Leaders like Gandhi, Mandela, and Martin Luther King, Jr. who had high agreeableness, motivated and mobilized people who seemed un-transformable, through the power of their own personalities. And as those stellar leaders believed that people could be transformed through leadership, the survivor too likely felt that a slightly rebellious Darkness could be transformed through her example of cooperation and tolerance. After all, it was Gandhi's, Mandela's, and King's *personalities* that were active in their leadership (not merely their beliefs) that changed others.

People with high-normal agreeableness carry with them strong personalities and, through tolerance and kindness, are capable of investments into potential outcomes that could be a win-win for themselves and others. However, these facets of agreeableness only seem to be detrimental to the survivor whose psychopathic partner *uses* these traits for coercive control. Let's look closer at some of the facets to see how they can be exploited by someone with a personality disorder.

Specific Facets [7]

Trusting and Trustworthy: The survivor is optimistic about human nature, and sees others through who she is, or as she sees herself

Of all the facets of 'agreeableness,' *The Institute* believes this one little facet may be at the center of how Darkness flies under the radar of detection (along with his natural ability to hide well).

Not only is the survivor trusting and trustworthy, her natural tendency is to see others through who she is, or as she sees herself. When we look at her characteristics, it indicates she comes tweaked with all the delicate and sensitive traits of being 'other-oriented'. Since her relationships outside of a PLR are likely to have been successful, nothing is on her radar that would signal an adverse condition in which she must think/feel/relate/behave *differently,* which means that nothing makes her instinctively alert to potential danger and to act differently by not trusting others or seeing others as she sees herself.

Her natural reaction to others is to think they are similarly motivated by agreeableness and cooperativeness. This *predisposition* of seeing others as she sees herself is also related to her optimism about human nature. Her belief system is a filter through which she sees the world, and so she believes people are more like her than not. And if problems arise, she has the natural gift of team and relationship building that has always worked in the past to smooth out problems. Optimism about humanity and the ability to lead others to transformation is obviously paramount as a trait in transformational leaders.

Before the PLR, the survivor, in some ways, unconsciously projects her own traits on others, assuming they are similar. Since she is trustworthy and sees others similarly, she believes most people are trustworthy. When they are indeed different or antagonistic, she is *predisposed* to believe in their ability to change. Survivors often say that what bothers them the most is why they instinctively believe others are capable of change without stopping to question that belief. That's because this is no more a learned behavior in them than it was in Mandela or King.

If we go back to the banking analogy, trust (aside from merely the emotional component) is a relationship in which one party gives another the right to hold the other party's assets.[8] Assets in a relationship can be fidelity, love, commitment, monogamy, and yes, trust. These are gifts or highly prized values of a successful intimate relationship. They are more valuable than other traits such as kindness or an even temper. Essentially, trust is the cement that holds relationships together, which is why the loss of trust is often a deal breaker. When someone has lost trust, the relationship is bound to end. But trust in the survivor has undoubtedly been influenced by some of her other facets (listed later in this chapter), showing us that facets in the list are connected to other facets.

Facets seem to impact other similar facets, compensating for when one facet in a belief system is challenged. This helps to somewhat correct the cognitive dissonance that one facet may be creating. So, when trust is breached, optimism—or seeing others through who she is—seems to provide a correcting (although false) view of the situation that temporarily reduces cognitive dissonance. These facets, working in tandem, seem to impact the facet of trust.

But all trust is not created equally or operates the same in all people. Survivors operate out of 'blind trust,' without proof or demonstrated reliability. Trust is hijacked and impacted by seeing others through who they are, optimism about human nature, and the motivation of social harmony. In this way, trust becomes blinded.

Other people with normal levels of agreeableness would operate out of *conditional* trust—trust that has been earned over time when expectations are met as promised. Survivors who have low levels of suspicion and high-normal levels of trust believe that conditional trust is rude and, moreover, if demanded, something that would disrupt the social harmony of their relationship. Never having had their blind trust challenged or abused it does not occur to them to operate from conditional trust. Non-survivors, or those who employ conditional trust, operate in ways which provide self-protection. They wait for others to prove they're deserving of trust and don't assume they are simply reflections of themselves. They don't merely turn over their trust card to others they just met and give them *carte blanche* without the person having earned trust.

But brushing up against Darkness' untrustworthiness, a survivor's other facets simply accommodate what she has discovered.

- The value she places on social harmony moves her toward wanting resolution in the relationship.
- Her optimism allows her to believe that change can happen.
- Her kindness, tenderheartedness, and sentimentality allow her to focus on what has been good in the relationship and what is worth redeeming while approaching the relationship with gentleness and not as a raving madwoman.

Further into the PLR, as Darkness reveals the repeating nature of his pathology, she will always be challenged either to accept the reality of his pathology or go with her natural and hard-wired inclination to be optimistic that he can change. This facet produces significant trauma in survivors when their filter is forever glossed over with the film of pathology. They wonder, "Who does that? Who purposefully hurts others?" Their worldview is tainted in a way that violates their core beliefs when their sanguine trait of optimism is tainted by the pervasiveness and permanence of pathology.

The Neurological Aspects of Trust

There is another reason why survivors are so trusting. As we have seen in an earlier chapter, our personalities are not just some static mechanisms unrelated to the brain as an organ. Personality seems to be generated, in part, in the neurobiological framework of the brain.

Studies about trust have shown that the act of trusting someone is connected to elevated levels of a hormone in the brain called *oxytocin*. Oxytocin is the bonding hormone that's released after childbirth and also during sex, which produces what is called 'the cuddling effect'—a sense of emotional well-being and bondedness with others. But birth and sex are not the only events in which it is produced—it is created when we engage *in the act of trust*.

Research studies indicate that it literally feels good to trust. As the level of oxytocin rises, people are more likely to *reciprocate* trust. The stronger the reciprocated trust, the more the oxytocin levels rise, and the well-being sensation is greater.[9]

Oxytocin occurs in people who have received a trust signal from someone else which normally occurs during social interactions. When oxytocin is increased in the brain, the person also feels more *trustworthy*. A survivor's elevated trust is kicked into high gear when Darkness shares his deepest secrets with her which he claims to have "never told anyone before." Her sense that he trusts *her* increases her oxytocin along with increasing *her* sense of bondedness and trust toward *him*.

Survivors who had blind trust to begin with are further accelerated in trust when the hormones in their brain encourage even more trust through the good-feeling hormone of oxytocin.

Cycle of Trust

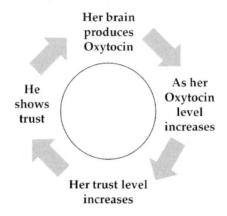

Figure 12.1
Cycle of Trust © *The Institute* **2009**

Straightforwardness: Up front, Honest, Confiding

Agreeableness, with its orientation toward cooperation with others, still carries with it the facets of being straightforward and up front. These are not opposing personality traits but rather reflect a survivor's ability to be diligent in her communicating style. No doubt these skills have assisted her in her career success as a doctor, CEO, teacher, or nonprofit administrator. These traits in abundance, however, may have contributed to Darkness' ability to easily extract her core values and history in the early phases of the relationship and to mimic and parrot them back, creating her perceived soulmate status. She is no-nonsense, and if you ask her something, she will give you what you are seeking (at least before she comes to fear the communication nightmares of the Karpman Triangle).

In the PLR, this straightforward approach combined with a *predisposition* to trust makes it easy for Darkness to manipulate her. This strong facet may be what is noted in survivors as 'over-disclosure'—her premature open-book style disclosure that gives Darkness her every core value, hope, and dream served up on a silver platter. With no reason not to be who she is, she is an open book and, unfortunately, a mine of information for those looking to manipulate. Darkness, with his predatory nature, no doubt fires up the backhoe and starts digging.

A Giving Nature: Altruistic, Considerate, Compromises for Others, Sentimental

Altruism, with all its facets of being unselfish and even sacrificial for the well-being of others, has rarely been studied for the problems it could produce when people possess it in high-normal or high quantities.[10] In Barbara Oakley's book *Pathological Altruism*, leading neuroscientists investigate the complexity of this trait and explain how too much altruism in a person can be harmful and can benefit malevolent types like Darkness who seek to capitalize on it. Survivors are good examples of how the benevolent trait of altruism can be used against them. Personality is not a light switch that can be turned on and off at will—altruism cannot be permanently willed into the off position. Instead, personality is like a river, naturally flowing in a particular direction following a specific path, making it problematic when it is too high and overflowing into areas it shouldn't and sometimes causing grave damage.

Agreeableness is also related to being kind, considerate, and tender-hearted—sometimes to the point of being sentimental. As problems arise and a survivor replays a memory of her relationship, what stands out is that **one** Christmas which was harmonious, or that **one** time when he was kind and romantic, not the **many** times when he was caught lying or was emotionally abusive. These traits create a type of memory time warp, which I refer to as Positive Memory Intrusion[11], in which what is focused on (the positive experiences in the relationship) are most connected to her *own* personality traits, creating a stronger memory than the negative memories. Add to this the love-bombing encased in State Dependent Learning and trance states and you have a predisposition both naturally occurring in the personality and also enhanced in trance. Because of this, her tenderheartedness will return her, again and again, to the potential she once saw in her partner.

Survivors are kind and considerate so emotional street-fighting with Darkness is not in their natural problem-solving repertoire. While domestic violence professionals link these traits to battered women's syndrome or learned helplessness connected to relational dynamics, they don't recognize that sometimes they stem from a naturally occurring *personality* facet.

Cooperation: Assists rather than atacks, is motivated by social harmony, is reciprocal in relationships, gives through helping/sharing/donating/volunteering

Another facet of agreeableness is a person's helpful and cooperative nature. High-normal facets of helpfulness in survivors means that they are likely to jump in quickly to aid Darkness when he parades his tales of woe—his depression from a divorce, the need for an attorney to get his children back, his search for a therapist to deal with his childhood trauma. To Darkness, this helpful response early in the relationship is a green light. He sees these early responses to his approach as confirmation of her future and continued helpfulness; he knows that even in the mid-relationship phase, she'll always be seeking ways to assist as the relationship deteriorates.

Not only are survivors relationship-oriented and invested, they highly value social harmony in their relationships and will go the extra mile to make their relationship investment pay off in harmonious ways. This creates some of the longevity in the relationship—as problems emerge with Darkness, she will further invest in the relationship by reducing conflict and elevating harmony in whatever way she can. As relationship problems manifest, she will always be *predisposed* and motivated toward helping the relationship recover. She will largely refrain from attacking and will work toward conflict resolution—repeatedly. While others, whose personalities do not register so high for social harmony, would perceive the relationship as 'too high maintenance,' her line in the sand is considerably farther away than theirs.

Included in agreeableness is naturally occurring behavior related to helping, sharing, giving, and volunteering. While truly valuable in her professional career, these traits, called 'pro-social behavior,' propel her into an unending *predisposition* to assist Darkness and mend the relationship. Pro-social behavior is normally generated from empathy and concern for the welfare and rights of others and so is connected to the personality facets of empathy and cooperativeness. Pro-sociability benefits society—many nonprofit organizations depend on our pro-sociability to feed the poor, rescue animals, and help the needy.

People with high-normal pro-social behaviors are *predisposed* to react to cues of need or distress and will do so without thought for whether it is safe or even prudent to do so because personality is comprised of our natural *tendencies*. Naturally occurring pro-social behavior in a personality initiates actions of helping, sharing, volunteering, and assisting. The survivor, chock-full of kindness, empathy, and helpfulness, has an automatic reaction to becoming engaged in pro-social *actions* and not just emotion.

Disengaging from a *predisposition* of pro-social behavior is difficult and hard to approach therapeutically. While work is often done with survivors concerning boundaries, what therapists fail to realize is that her actions are not boundary violations generated from a conscious need to make others happy, as in codependency, but rather they are unconscious and personality-driven and so are less likely to be conscious. In the PLR, no matter the ongoing problems with Darkness, the survivor's initial reaction will always be to jump in with both feet to give, help, assist, volunteer, and share, to benefit *her* bottom line, which is social harmony.

Humbleness: A modest self-portrayal of herself—gentle and well-tempered

Humbleness is often a misunderstood facet. There is a societal assumption that humble people are passive or weak. But certain philosophies and religions see humbleness as a sign of restrained power and leadership. Viewed in this way, humbleness entails an accurate assessment of one's own limits and a proper appraisal of one's strengths and weaknesses which can quietly operate as power.

Humble people tend to focus on investments in others, much like some of the other facets of agreeableness and cooperation. It's not that people who are humble think little of themselves, it's that they tend to think a lot about others and put their investment in others to serve a greater good. They lack self-absorption and aren't arrogant or prideful, so they are free to invest in the betterment of others.[12] Unlike Darkness in all his ego and grandiosity, survivors have an 'other-oriented' approach, putting others first and seeking their own needs second.

Humbleness is often a sign of a person being well-tempered and easily approachable making it a form of 'soft strength.' As we have seen in other facets, humbleness is affiliated with cooperation as the humble are more likely to assist others and are more charitable and generous to others in need. And who could be needier than Darkness with his formidable issues and deficits?

The humble are warm and engaging when approached and, prior to becoming involved in a PLR, they have had no reason to suspect ill motives because, as we saw in previous facets, they tend to see others through who they are—such as humble, kind, and gentle. A survivor's well-temperedness will steady the relationship and keep it forging ahead, at least until communication problems arise, and when the confusion and cognitive dissonance produced in Karpman Triangle and the Event Cycle become her undoing.

Empathetic: Tender-minded, kind, generous, compassionate

The facet of empathy is the most readily identifiable, the most studied, and the most focused on in survivors than any of the other facets. This is the facet that's at the core of the gorilla-glue that holds survivors in PLRs. It is their empathy for their partners that can be heard in their stories of inevitable harm in which they state, "He acts like this because he was abused as a child. He was so neglected and beaten. I can only imagine what he lived through."

Empathy is the ability to identify with the thoughts and feelings of others. It holds relationships together as we can relate and experience, to some degree, the emotional and inner world of others. It is also associated with emotional intelligence—through experiencing how others feel, we can compassionately address the struggles of another.

For many people who have normal amounts of empathy, the sight of a homeless person brings twinges of pain, if not survivor guilt, for being so fortunate ourselves. Our empathy allows us to imagine what their life is like and we may dig into our pockets to help. But for those with high-normal agreeableness, a one-time donation is not likely to satisfy the need to address a societal crisis like homelessness or animal cruelty. For issues they care deeply about, they are motivated not to merely help out but to *solve* the core problem. This certainly includes the ongoing issues with Darkness and their relationship.

As we have been taught not to judge someone else until we have walked in their shoes, survivors are not only quick *not* to judge, but they can be in the other's shoes in a split second, imagining the pain and turmoil, which is well supported by their personality facets of helpfulness, supportiveness, and resourcefulness. A survivor's empathy, no doubt, is woven inextricably with her other personality facets, and as she encounters the turbulent waters of the PLR, she will deeply empathize with Darkness' feigned distress and will see it through the lens of her own personality. Even after Darkness' mask is torn off and his behavior is revealed, she will still struggle with not being helpful enough to address what she perceives (wrongly) is causing him to ruin their relationship.

Her strong empathy is what allows Darkness to sow such destruction and, for this reason, survivors are often labeled 'empaths.' Perhaps you have seen articles floating around on the Internet about *Empaths and Toxic Relationships* which imply that a survivor is likely an empath because of this *single* facet elevation. While I will discuss this in a later chapter, we can see from the research that empathy is *only one* of *several* elevated facets, creating the type of personality configuration that is targeted by a pathological predator. It is dangerous for survivors to believe that empathy is the **only** facet that is causing them to be a future target. Survivors need to understand the complete picture of *all* the elevated traits and facets in order to guard themselves.

Loyalty

The Institute has recognized the fierce loyalty in survivors. Not merely patriotic, hand-over-the-heart gestures, this loyalty has its roots in an investment in the relationship that has produced allegiance, faithfulness, and homage. Loyalty in this case is also associated with dependability, reliability and trustworthiness.

Writer Josiah Royce defined *loyalty* as 'the basic moral principle from which all other principles can be derived. It is the willing and practical devotion to a person or cause, not a casual interest but a *wholehearted* commitment.'[13] (emphasis added)

This noble facet is not just a mere part of a personality package— it is a *virtue*. Virtue is no slacker; it's associated with moral excellence, goodness, and righteousness and implies that the virtuous conduct in their lives is based on moral and ethical principles. Virtues are traits that show exemplary character and, in certain religions, are seen as pathways to heavenly-like characters as noted in Catholic catechism. The modern-day virtue of loyalty is seen in those whose lives are lived, not by whim and chance, but by the application of moral and ethical principles.

Imagine a survivor full of this virtue who finds herself involved with someone who is immoral and unethical. Guided not by knee-jerk reactions to his many betrayals but by loyalty, abetted and supported by her other personality facet trait of trust, she will not be persuaded to find someone else, out him to others, or turn him into the Feds despite what she discovers and despite the many others who are entering and exiting his pipeline.

Tolerance

In the TCI, tolerance was listed as one of the facets of cooperation. While not listed in the Five Factor Form, *The Institute* has discussed it as a facet because of its repercussions in a PLR.

Tolerance is defined as 'a fair, objective, and permissive attitude toward the opinions, beliefs, and practices that differ from one's own; and the act or capacity for enduring.'[14] It is easy to see how this skill set would be a useful career aid in avoiding entanglements and dealing with conflicting opinions. But in PLRs, where tolerance is shifted into high gear out of necessity, it is often misread as learned helplessness and associated with those from abusive backgrounds and a history of violence.

Tolerance, in its gentility, allows a partner to easily accept differing opinions and practices, including Darkness' reoccurring radical behavior. With optimism, even behavior she does not like in Darkness can be tolerated until he changes. Tolerance will be tested, stretched, and expanded as the mid-relationship dynamics challenge her ability to remain tolerant while empathizing or waiting on the promised changes.

It seems to suggest the question, "When does a personality facet become a coping mechanism?" The herculean tolerance of survivors appears to be a skill set that is over used for the purpose of adaptation to something that can't be changed in Darkness. At the point in the mid-relationship phase where the survivor realizes his betrayals/lying/coercive control, she must adopt a coping strategy until she can make the decision to disengage.

There are two general types of coping styles—emotion-focused and problem-focused.[15] A problem-focused coping style consists of any coping behavior that aims to solve a specific problem or eliminate a certain stressor. It is applied when an individual perceives the problem as solvable and the situation as changeable.

On the other hand, an emotion-focused style is applied when the individual believes that the situation cannot be modified. Most of these strategies consist of thinking processes that reduce emotional distress and include avoidance, downgrading the problem, finding positive points in difficult situations, alcohol consumption, crying, or talking with a friend. These emotion-focused strategies don't lead to positive psychological or physical results, but the individual will have a better feeling about the situation. Since problem-based coping strategies result in better physical and mental health, they directly reduce the source of stress.

But since the survivor may not yet be at the problem-solving phase of eliminating the stressor of Darkness, she is left with emotion-focused strategies while needing to increase the use of her tolerance *as* a coping mechanism. At some point, tolerance changes from a personality facet into a form of coping. Tolerance for not just going the extra mile but, for a full-blown marathon, is noticed and judged by her family, friends, and unknowing therapists who mistake it for other issues.

Wrapping This All Up

The Five Factor Agreeableness and/or the TCI Cooperativeness traits of the survivor aid Darkness in capitalizing on the approachable, trusting, and optimistic nature of the survivor. As a personality-disordered predator, Darkness more than likely *seeks* exactly the types of traits that blind these women to his approach.

These traits are notably responsible for women being targeted and ending up in a Pathological Love Relationship. Darkness can fly under her radar based almost solely on her relationship investment traits and facets. Once he's in, the fact that she sees others as she sees herself, her tolerance, and her value of social harmony above all will easily carry the relationship, even when reality intrudes.

These highly prized traits that create durable and enduring skills in nonpathological interactions become weapons turned back against the survivor by Darkness, who can use even a woman's own gentleness against her.

Chapter Twelve Endnotes

1   Oakley, Barbara (2011). Cold-Blooded Kindness: Neuroquirks of a Codependent Killer, or Just Give Me a Shot at Loving You, Dear, and Other Reflections on Helping That Hurts. Penguin Random House Publisher Services.

2   Oakley, Barbara (2011). Pathological Altruism. Oxford University Press.

3   Cloninger, R., Przybeck, T., Svrakic, D., & Wedel, R. (1994). TCI-Guide to Its Development and Use. Center for Psychobiology of Personality, Washington University, (July). https://www.worldcat.org/title/temperament-and-character-inventory-tci-a-guide-to-its-development-and-use/oclc/32133789

4, 7   Widiger, T. A. (2004). Five Factor Model Rating Form. https://onlinelibrary.wiley.com/doi/abs/10.1111/j.1467-6494.1992.tb00970.x
Widiger, T. A. (2009). Five Factor Form. http://journals.sagepub.com/doi/abs/10.1177/1073191113517260?url_ver=Z39.88-2003&rfr_id=ori%3Arid%3Acrossref.org&rfr_dat=cr_pub%3Dpubmed&

5   Brown, Sandra L., Young, Jennifer R., The Institute (2016). Misidentification of Super Traits in Pathological Love Relationships—Stop Calling it Codependency. Prepared for Women Who Love Psychopaths. Third Edition; and The Institute's Therapist Training Program and Manual: Treating the Aftermath of Pathological Love Relationships.

6   Brown, Sandra L. and Young, Jennifer R., The Institute (2014). Five Factor Form/Five Factor Model Rating Form: Traits of agreeableness and conscientiousness in pathological love relationship dynamics. An interagency report; also prepared for The Institute's Therapist Training Program and Manual: Treating the Aftermath of Pathological Love Relationships.

8   trust. https://www.investopedia.com/terms/t/trust.asp

9   Zak, P. J. (2008). The Neurobiology of Trust. Scientific American, (June), 88–93. https://doi.org/10.1038/scientificamerican0608-88.html

10   Batson, D. C., & Powell, A. A. (1978). Altruism and Prosocial Behavior. In T. Millon & M. J. Lerner (Eds.), Handbook of Psychology: Personality and Social Psychology (Vol. 5, p. 691). John Wiley and Sons, Inc. https://doi.org/10.1002/0471264385.wei0519

11   Brown, Sandra L., The Institute (2008). Positive memory intrusion and cognitive dissonance in Pathological Love Relationships. Case studies of qualitative research.

12   Austin, M. (2012). Humbleness (Humility). https://www.psychologytoday.

com/us/blog/ethics-everyone/201206/humility

13 Royce, J. (1995). The Philosophy of Loyalty. (J. J. Macdermott, Ed.). Vanderbilt University Press.

14 tolerance. http://www.dictionary.com/browse/tolerance

15 Sharif, F., Parsnia, A., Mani, A., Vosoghi, M., & Setoodeh, G. (2014). Comparison of personality traits, coping styles, and psychiatric disorders in adult suicidal and non-suicidal individuals. International Journal of Community Based Nursing and Midwifery, 2(3), 148–156. https://www.ncbi.nlm.nih.gov/pmc/articles/PMC4201200/

Chapter Thirteen

The Personality Traits of Survivor Partners: Conscientiousness and Self-Directedness—The Integrity-Oriented Life Traits Puzzle Piece #3™

Continuing with Puzzle Piece #3™ we look at additional trait elevations related to The Super Traits of survivors.

Quick Survivor Review

- The Five Factor identified elevations in the trait of agreeableness.
- The Temperament and Character Inventory (TCI) identified elevations in the similar trait of cooperativeness.
- The trait of agreeableness/cooperativeness is called the 'Relationship Investment Trait.'
- These trait elevations are instrumental in *who* is targeted — because of trait elevations she is more likely to quickly enter into a Pathological Love Relationship.

*I*ntegrity-Oriented Life Traits: The Traits of Conscientiousness and Self-Directedness

Both the 2007 TCI and the 2014 Five Factor Form/Five Factor Model Rating Form research studies identified an *additional* trait elevation of conscientiousness and self-directedness that aids Darkness' ability to keep her in the relationship making disengagement difficult. Again, these are different terms used by each assessment model that measured similar traits. The Five Factor Form/Five Factor Model Rating Form described this trait as 'conscientiousness'[1] while the TCI described it as 'self-directedness.'[2] Both of these elevated personality traits identified from the three assessments used in research are connected to what *The Institute* calls *the integrity-oriented life traits*.

The issue as to why strong, independent women have difficulty disengaging from relationships of inevitable harm has also been the topic of much misguided assumption, just as the trait of agreeableness has been. Survivors are judged for both 'not seeing it coming' due to their high-normal agreeableness, and for 'not disengaging sooner,' due to their high-normal conscientiousness.[3]

Conscientiousness is the trait that makes us careful, allows us to perform tasks well, and helps with being organized and efficient. High-normal conscientious people have good self-control, are more plan oriented than spontaneous, and are dependable. They are not highly reactive, but rather think things through before acting, and abhor making mistakes in their careers or personal lives. High-normal Cs are neat, systematic, and deliberate, especially in matters regarding life decisions. These are traits usually possessed by people who are known to have good character, are hard-workers, reliable, perhaps prone to be workaholics and slightly perfectionistic as they hold themselves to high standards of excellence.

For instance, they are part of a dream team for employers—endowed with industriousness and a great work ethic, these are the people who make companies into cash cows for the lucky owner. They are role models in a company, causing others to work even harder to be able to compete with them and they tend to consistently outperform their colleagues (at least until they are taken down by a PLR).

So strong is this trait of conscientiousness that it can help academic advisors predict with good certainty which students will be academically successful. Our survivors are not only academically successful, they are successful outside of academics, climbing their respective career ladders with admirable success. However, persistence, a term often associated with conscientiousness, pays off in successful dividends when it's applied to a goal such as medical school, *but* when applied to a PLR, persistently trying to make the relationship work creates a reoccurring cycle of inevitable harm.[4]

$\mathcal{U}$nderstanding What Motivates the Integrity-Driven Life

The word *conscientious* contains the root word *conscience*, which immediately separates the survivor from Darkness by his own lack of conscience. The dictionary describes *conscientiousness* as 'governed by, or conforming to, the dictates of conscience.'[5] Conscience regulates behavior, and it is this trait that's connected to impulse control that we read about in Chapters One and Two. Darkness, as we have seen, has low or no conscience and high impulse-control *problems*—from lying to infidelity to embezzlement to road rage.

If Darkness, with poor impulse control, is at the low end of the spectrum of conscientiousness, then the survivor is on the higher end. Darkness (with his low conscience and high impulsivity) has out-of-control emotional and behavioral impulsiveness that are not regulated by his conscience or anything else for that matter. But where a high-normal amount of the trait is represented in the survivor, there is another issue—*so much* conscience and *so little* impulsivity which hampers her ability to quickly leave a situation no matter how dangerous, or apparent, it becomes.[6] While it would seem odd that conscientious people wouldn't be alert to the nuances of behavior—including in Darkness—it is this trait of having fewer impulsive reactions which can be the handcuffs that keep her in the relationship far past the time when rationality would indicate a cut-off.

We've all heard of Catholic Guilt, for instance. (I'm not picking on Catholics; I just remember the term.) The term was coined to describe the high amount of 'taught' conscientiousness that stressed the importance of self-control—to be careful not to put oneself in tempting situations, to be vigilant about things that could lead one astray. Guilt is easily produced in highly conscientious people because they (a) have a conscience, (b) have a moral compass, (c) know the difference between right and wrong and when they erred, (d) have a desire to follow their beliefs and values.

The psychology field hasn't given enough consideration to the effect of a naturally occurring high-normal conscientiousness level outside of religious behavior. We haven't given much thought to its ability to **keep** people in dangerous and debilitating situations. Or have we merely thought about conscience that is *taught,* as in religion, and not understood its possibly different and dangerous effects when it is naturally, but excessively, occurring in the personality?

A high-normal amount of conscience produces high standards of self-behavioral excellence. Conscientiousness is what develops our internal moral compass that we come to trust and value. It helps us differentiate what is important in life and keeps our behavior aligned to it. It provides a big picture view of what purpose our life has and what we value within it. This could be family, relationships, monogamy, honesty, authenticity, religious beliefs, or work ethics to name a few. In fact, conscientiousness is best viewed as 'life ethics'—a conscientious life lived by the core principles of emotional, moral, and integrity-driven ethics.

People who are driven by life ethics are also deeply impacted when they fail to live by those ethics. Guilt and shame are the predominant emotions experienced when one fails. The survivors also have relationship investment (agreeableness) traits that place such an *excessively* high value on successful outcomes in relationships that they are more likely to suffer even *more* impact when the relationship fails.[7]

People who have high levels of conscientiousness suffer *greater* feelings of guilt, shame, failure, and cognitive dissonance regarding their part in an experience than those who have lower levels of conscientiousness.[8] This explains in part why survivors have such serious cognitive dissonance, which will be discussed in a later chapter. Conscientiousness carries with it more than just guilt. It has facets that shape this package of both high conscience and low reactivity/impulsiveness that freezes people in situations that would have been better off had they left earlier.

Traits of the Five Factor Form/Five Factor Model of Conscientiousness

• Efficient
• Organized
• Dependable
• Achievement-Striving
• Self-Disciplined
• Deliberate

These facets comprise the overall trait of conscientiousness, and scores on these facets determine if a person has low, normal, high-normal, or high conscientiousness. In our studies, survivors consistently scored in the 'high-normal' range. Let's break down the facet descriptors to get a bigger picture of what they represent.[9]

Table 13.1
Facet of the Trait and Descriptors

Facet of the Trait	Descriptors
Efficient	Competent, slightly perfectionistic, resourceful
Organized	Methodical, ordered
Dependable	Reliable, takes obligations and commitments seriously
Achieve-ment-Striving	Ambitious, prone to workaholism, resourceful, efficient, aims to fulfill outside expectations, sets lofty goals, expends great effort—often to the detriment of other pursuits
Self-Disciplined	Devoted, controlled, not impulsive
Deliberate	Cautious, reflective, careful, persevering, diligent

Let's see how the Temperament Character Inventory (TCI) describes these facets of conscientiousness.

$\mathcal{T}$CI Traits

In the TCI assessment used in 2007, Cloninger identified conscientiousness similarly as *self-directedness,* as it relates to self-determination. It is the ability to 'regulate and adapt behavior to the demands of a situation to achieve personally chosen goals and values' (like relationship success). Often referred to as *willpower,* it is driven by goals that are purposeful and not merely by reactive impulses.[10]

Self-directed people see the big picture of what they are trying to achieve and are committed and diligent in their effort to make that happen. When problems emerge in the mid-phase of the relationship, they aren't impulsive and reactive—they don't cut and run. Unlike Darkness who is highly impulsive, survivors are not—while in a PLR they will not impulsively leave without applying all their resources to try to improve it.[11] While dependency is often assumed to be the reason for not leaving, their slow disengagement stems from a personality trait.[12]

Survivors with high self-directedness (and conscientiousness) tend to take responsibility for their actions and are resourceful in solving problems. Since part of a personality disorder is an *inability* to take responsibility for actions, Darkness is amenable to having her take full responsibility for the problems they are encountering. This fuels her desire to dig in deeper, become more resourceful, and find solutions. In some ways, it appears that the pathological partner's low trait of self-directedness engages with the survivor's high-level trait of self-directedness to bring a perceived balance to those things that are impacted in the relationship by his deficits.[13]

Conscientiousness and Self-Directedness: How They Operate[14]

The Five Factor[14] and the TCI both explain this trait and facets almost identically. Even the wording of the self-directedness facets in the TCI is like that of the Five Factor Form:

- Responsibleness
- Purposefulness
- Resourcefulness
- Self-Acceptance
- Congruent/Enlightened Second Nature

The combined facets of conscientiousness and self-directedness are traits of what *The Institute* refers to as the 'integrity-oriented life.' While we call the agreeableness trait the 'relationship investment trait,' the conscientiousness trait is related to a life guided by goals, beliefs, values, and the steady application of all necessary resources to meet those goals.

Right off the bat we can see that this trait and its facets are all about a conscious observance of one's own behavior—of doing the right thing— which implies that these survivors have a high degree of self-control. They are rule compliant and like to know exactly what the rules *are*. For instance, in relationships—are we monogamous or casually dating? Survivors with this trait follow conventional forms of integrity—no lying, stealing, cheating, or violence. They are responsive to authority and don't necessarily like bucking the system like Darkness does. Because of this high degree of integrity, high-normal Cs are less likely to divorce or have affairs, they tend to argue less, and they elicit less criticism from others because they play by the rules.

Living by the rules has normally produced good life outcomes, but any failure, including the PLR, produces stronger reactions to failure in those who hold themselves to exacting standards of excellence and positive outcomes.[15]

Conscientiousness is a *patterned* form of self-control, not merely emanating from a religious upbringing or a lecturing father. Rather, it is a deeply engrained pattern of personality. People with these high-level traits have clarity on issues of morality and right and wrong. They live their lives by principles as opposed to opportunities. This self-control and self-discipline apply not just to their vocation—it comprises the core of a well-developed life *of conscious behavior*. Let's examine the sub-facets of this trait and see what characteristics they represent.

Specific Facets[16]

Because facets are related to the over-arching trait, like conscientiousness, you will notice that facets are similar to each other. The descriptions and explanations have many overlapping qualities which are repeated throughout the explanations. As tempting as it is to remove the descriptions that sound alike, they are left in, so the reader can see the similarities that *reinforce* the *predisposition* to the behavior within the trait.

Efficient, Competent

This facet emphasizes the ability to perform successfully in all areas of life, working in a productive and organized way. Efficiency—preventing the wasteful use of resources—is also a focus. These are characteristics of someone working toward maximizing productivity (like communication) while minimizing poor outcomes (such as relational failure). High-normal Cs are not used to failure since they exhibit such high competence in solving most problems.

As the relationship problems emerge, a high-normal C will naturally use all available resources to maximize the probability of a positive outcome and will be almost intolerant to accepting lesser, more unproductive outcomes.[17] This work toward good outcomes is not necessarily based on fear of losing the relationship. The survivor naturally works this hard on *all* problems areas. Her efficiency will aid in finding solutions to perceived relationship chaos, or perhaps this facet will help her competently engage in surveillance behavior to find out what Darkness has been doing. Since failure is not an outcome often experienced or well tolerated, her investment in good outcomes will keep her forging ahead indefinitely.[18]

Organized, Methodical, Ordered

These characteristics value simplicity over chaos, especially in relationships. Ironically, survivors are in relationships with people that possess disorganized and chaotic personalities. Her skill sets are geared toward trying to reduce the chaos so evident in relationships during the mid-phase and end-phase when everything is unraveling faster than it can be knit back together. The roller coaster of the *crisis du jour* while being trapped in the crazy-making patterns outlined in the Karpman Triangle and The Event Cycle, keeps a survivor working at warp speed to bring the relationship to a more organized and simpler functionality.[19]

Dependable, Reliable, Takes Obligations Seriously

Dependability is the quality of being counted on and relied upon. No doubt during the luring and love-bombing phases of the relationship, the survivor learned Darkness' feigned woeful history and heard that she was the only dependable person in his life. Conscientious people take those types of obligations and roles in other's lives seriously and will work diligently to never disappoint. But in the PLR, the hurdle of meeting Darkness' every need will constantly be raised higher, producing the failure she fears most.[20]

These characteristics are also evident in people who take responsibility for the management of their lives. They recognize they are responsible for the outcomes of their own choices and feel the freedom to choose their own direction in life. This high level of responsibility keeps their moral compass pointed in the right direction and their behavior is always above board. They don't consider blaming others for choices they have made. They live by their own values and beliefs and own the choices they make based on those values and beliefs.

But in a PLR, where Darkness is wired to never take responsibility for his actions and choices, the survivor may overcompensate, taking more responsibility for parts of the relationship over which she has no control—from his infidelity to his tax evasion.[21] After the relationship ends, she will hold herself to exacting levels of responsibility for having entered and stayed in the relationship which will contribute heavily to her traumatic aftermath symptoms of self-loathing.

Achievement-Oriented Striving, Ambitious, Resourceful, Aims to Fulfill Outside Expectations

These facets indicate a strong motivation to achieve or succeed. Remember that the trait of agreeableness is thrown into her elevated personality makeup too, so what often motivates survivors in their personal lives is the quality of their *relationships*. They gain gratification from achieving success despite the difficulty. It's not that they go looking for difficulty, it's that their personality is well suited to achieving the best possible outcome no matter how hard it gets. Achievement-oriented strivers are different than those less-motivated people who simply try to avoid overt failure like Darkness does. Those with ambition invest intense effort over the long haul in the pursuit of their goals, and conscientiousness is all about goals.[22]

The facet of resourcefulness is related to the ability to 'deal skillfully and promptly with new situations and difficulties.' Those high in resourcefulness are proactive, competent, and innovative with an ability to problem solve and find avenues for resolution—they rarely lack ideas for how to solve problems, which makes them the good career leaders they are. Difficulties are perceived merely as challenges. As discussed in the chapters on relationship dynamics, Darkness does not have authentic problem-solving skills. He relies on manipulation, gaslighting, and coercion. Her resourcefulness will have her finding him new job skills, a therapist, self-help books, and a 12-Step group, all which produce the reassurance to her that they are getting there. When those solutions prove ineffective, she will dig deeper to find another avenue with more resources. She optimistically believes in the power of her own resourcefulness to support a lagging relationship—it's aided her well in her life and career so far, so why wouldn't it work in her relationship?[23]

Aiming to fulfill outside expectations has Darkness' name written all over it. Being achievement oriented, all outside expectations to her are merely a hurdle to jump, a goal to exceed, and an opportunity to invest in the relationship. But Darkness will always be raising the bar for her to work harder. Her goals will never be met since his goal is to see (through his manipulation and coercion) that she never achieves that which she values. Her inability to achieve will become a factor in her aftermath symptoms.[24]

Self-Disciplined, Non-impulsive

Facets of conscientiousness essentially highlight a survivor's pattern to live by her values and core beliefs. These are based on standards of excellence that guide her conscious behavior, including behavior in relationships. Survivors with this characteristic do not give up quickly, believing that the *principle* of the relationship is more important than its *setbacks*.[25]

High-normal Cs often have *lofty goals that can lead to burnout,* and this isn't just a career hazard. The goal of turning a psychopath into a soccer dad will most certainly lead to burnout (as well as the mind twisting produced by cognitive dissonance). Her investment in the turnaround of undetected pathology, even with all her resourcefulness, will no doubt lead to a second hazard—*devoting undue effort to a cause and to the detriment of other pursuits.* While conscientious people can turn into workaholics, in a PLR this undue effort is focused on recapturing the essence of the early phases of the relationship and of creating meaningful communication with the pathological partner in an attempt to problem solve. The survivor's intense focus on repairing the relationship leaves the rest of her life, which was once well rounded, devoid of anything she once enjoyed.[26]

Most survivor partners ask, "What happened to my life? Where did my hobbies go? Where are my friends?" The reason that a survivor's life becomes the exact size and shape of Darkness' life has to do with her consistent attempts at salvaging the relationship at the expense of her former life. While high-normal conscientiousness has benefits in the realm of integrity, it can be used in a maladaptive way, resulting in setting lofty goals within the PLR that can never be achieved. This results in burnout caused by expending boundless energy in trying to change a psychopath—to the detriment of herself.[27]

Reflective

People with high levels of conscientiousness have an ability to be reflective, think deeply, and be introspective. They think about deeper existential issues like meaning, purpose, and direction. Remember Mr. Deep as Formica? Survivors are the antithesis of Darkness—they are seekers of steady and consistent direction for their lives and can delay their own gratification to achieve those goals.

As the relationship declines, the survivor partner is focused on the core values of her life, not just the blip on the radar of his inconsistent behavior. Her long-term goals regarding a meaningful relationship are pinned to her mind like a post to her social media page, and they guide her choices and provide her with purposefulness, as well as tolerance, to ride out the storm.[28]

Self-Acceptance

This facet includes self-confidence and a realistic appraisal of both her strengths and limitations. Unlike Darkness, who is blanketed in his narcissism and grandiosity, the survivor possesses a balanced recognition of both sides of *her* personality and abilities. Along with her straightforwardness, she does not feel the need to be something or someone she is not.

She is not naturally crippled by the self-doubt and self-esteem that characterizes the sufferers of codependency and addictions©. She does not come into the PLR with a predisposition, genetic or otherwise, to self-esteem issues which have plagued her entire life. Most survivors are not riddled with early childhood issues or adult traumas that created poor self-concepts. This is proven through this high-normal ranking in the facet of self-acceptance.

This strong core no doubt appears quickly on Darkness' radar, as more than one psychopath has proclaimed, "I've always wanted to take down a strong woman." While Darkness will prey on anyone for what he needs in the moment and would not likely turn away a codependent lover, those he finds most interesting to toy with and bat around are those who challenge his ability to do significant damage to their self-confidence.[29]

Along with the agreeableness trait's facet of empathy, self-acceptance in a partner is also sought by Darkness for the promise of being entertained well into the future. This will also be a source of significant cognitive dissonance when she wonders, "Where did my self-esteem go?"

Her value system does not include -

- Lying (which violates her belief in straightforwardness)
- Fighting (which violates her belief in social harmony)
- Cheating (which violates her belief in loyalty)
- Aloofness/neediness (which contradicts her self-acceptance)
- Stealing/drug dealing/embezzlement (which violates her conscientiousness)

This deep ability to trust her own nature (called *second nature*)—to always choose the right path as opposed to the alluring path, to choose those things that she values, and to say no to those things that don't stack up to her values—is why the manipulation employed by the pathological partner creates such a devastating and traumatic blow to her self-concept because she has violated all those beliefs.[30]

The PLR will take her down a road full of potholes through gaslighting, explosions of subterfuge, the humiliation of his pipeline, and the disorientation of communication. It will strike her at her strongest personality characteristic of self-acceptance—the knowledge of herself as someone who previously lived by her values.

Combining Traits of Agreeableness and Conscientiousness—A Double-Edged Sword

The high-normal trait elevations of agreeableness and conscientiousness in survivors are a double-edged sword. On one hand, they have gifted her with deep care and investment tools for producing relationships with quality, which come first in her life. They have bestowed her with tolerance, trust, integrity, and perseverance to keep working at a relationship she values. Her desire for relationship quality, coupled with the tenacity to keep working at it, are what high-normal As and Cs bring to the table.

On the other hand, high-normal amounts of A and C have their crosses to bear, bringing with them the optimism about human nature even when Darkness' pathology comes to light. Blind trust and relationship investment ushers her into the center of a PLR before she has time to question or inquire more. And the self-discipline, low reactivity, and dependability *keep* her engaged in inevitable harm due to her being achievement and goal oriented.

High-normal trait elevations with normal nonpathological persons present few problems for survivors with high A and C. It is her relative normalcy with elevated A and C in the hands of predatorial and coercive Darkness where these elevations are going to be exploited.

Survivor Note:

Relative Normalcy + Pathology = Inevitable Harm

Agreeableness then, is the trait by which Darkness draws her in, and conscientiousness is the trait by which he retains her.

Wrapping It All Up

Darkness' own authentic abnormal personality stripped of his mask, his love bombing, and rapid-seduction techniques, is absolutely nothing that is a match for a survivor with Super Traits. Without his predatory tactics of luring, without his ability to use state-dependent learning techniques, without his sleight-of-hand trance-inducing tricks, he is nothing. He has always been the tiny, impotent, illusionary man behind the curtain. Everything about him, from his mis-wired brain to his skewed drives of coercion and control, is the antithesis of a relationship-invested and integrity-oriented survivor.

What I hope is abundantly clear is that Super Traits are a group of personality tendencies that make for a beautiful person. The traits are those any normal man would feel blessed to have in his partner. The traits of a kind, compassionate, and integrity-oriented person have only been problematic in the hands of antagonistic, manipulative, and juvenile Darkness.

Super Traits aren't the problem. It is personality disorders/psychopathy that dismantle normal psyches into piles of ashes. It is personality disorders that the DSM cites as 'unable to sustain positive nonmanipulative change' generated from neurological deficits that result in the inability to be empathetic or intimate. If Super Traits are present in a normal relationship, there's more than enough to provide the fertile ground from which love can grow and be sustained.

The study of personality trait deficiencies and elevations and their influences on both ends of relationship dynamics has been a long time coming. The theory of Super Traits addresses many of the questions I've had during my time working in the field. I believe that, long after I am retired, using these principles of personality Super Trait combinations as risk factors will become the guiding force in prevention, intervention, and treatment for people in PLRs.

But more importantly, it is my hope that most survivors will discover answers in our findings. How and why women of such quality end up in PLRs is better understood now that personality science has addressed these issues in a more thorough manner than pop psychology or past theories of learned behavior or codependency have.

So, let's understand why survivors still aren't more universally recognized.

Chapter Thirteen Endnotes

1, 9, 14, 16   Widiger, T. A. (2004). Five Factor Model Rating Form. https://onlineli-brary.wiley.com/doi/abs/10.1111/j.1467-6494.1992.tb00970.x

2, 10   Cloninger, R., Przybeck, T., Svrakic, D., & Wedel, R. (1994). TCI-Guide to Its Development and Use. *Center for Psychobiology of Personality, Washington University*, (July). https://www.worldcat.org/title/temperament-and-character-in-ventory-tci-a-guide-to-its-development-and-use/oclc/32133789

3, 4   Brown, Sandra L. and Young, Jennifer R., *The Institute* (2014). Five Factor Form/Five Factor Model Rating Form traits of agreeableness and conscientiousness in pathological love relationship dynamics. An interagency report; also prepared for *The Institute's Therapist Training Program and Manual: Treating the Aftermath of Pathological Love Relationships.*

5   *conscientious.* https://www.merriam-webster.com/dictionary/conscientious.

6, 7, 11, 13, 15, 17-30 Brown, Sandra L. and Young, Jennifer R., *The Institute* (2014). Five Factor Form/Five Factor Model Rating Form traits of agreeableness and conscientiousness in pathological love relationship dynamics. An interagency report; also prepared for *The Institute's Therapist Training Program and Manual: Treating the Aftermath of Pathological Love Relationships.*

8   Fayard, J., Roberts, B., Robins, R., & Watson, D. (2012). Uncovering the Affective Core Conscientiousness: The Role of Self-Conscious Emotions. *Journal of Personality, 80*(1), 1–32. https://doi.org/10.1111/j.1467-6494.2011.00720.x_

12   Brown, Sandra L., and Young, Jennifer R., *The Institute* (2016). Misidentification of Super Traits in Pathological Love Relationships—Stop Calling it Codependency. Prepared for *Women Who Love Psychopaths. Third Edition;* and *The Institute's Therapist Training Program and Manual: Treating the Aftermath of Pathological Love Relationships.*

Chapter Fourteen

The Nonidentification, Misidentification, and Disidentification of Super Traits Puzzle Piece #3™

This chapter is connected to Puzzle Piece #3™—A Partner with Super Traits—and will look at what is behind the misdiagnosis of the survivor's Super Traits, and why.

Quick Survivor Review

- The Five Factor Form identified elevations in the trait of conscientiousness.
- The Temperament Character Inventory identified elevation in a similar trait of self-directedness.
- The trait of conscientiousness/self-directedness is called 'The Integrity-Oriented Life' trait.
- These trait elevations are instrumental in how long a survivor is in a PLR and because of this trait elevation she is more likely to work at the problems of the relationship.

Super Traits Nonidentification, Misidentification, and Disidentification: What Super Traits Are Not

It's not easy to challenge previous belief systems, especially in psychology. The field of neuroscience surely had their bump in the road challenging the belief system about the *nurture theory* of personality disorders that had been around since the late 19th century when they presented their very *nature*-oriented theory.

Eventually, a field grows because someone begins to look at a staunchly held theory and thinks outside the box, researches it, tests it, and speaks what he or she found. *The Institute* is often referred to as a pioneer in the PLR field because we have studied and challenged old theories like learned conditioning and codependency as they both relate to PLRs, which I will be discussing in this chapter.[1] I understand that these new ways of looking at well-loved and believed theories rattle the mainstays of pop psychology assumptions about codependency just as neuroscience findings rattled personality disorder theories.

The practice of what I call Oprah-ology, with its pop-psychology terminology applied to survivors of PLRs, flies in the face of real psychology with not much science behind it (when pop-psychology ideas are elevated above real psychology). Part of *The Institute*'s success comes from the fact that survivor partners *recognize themselves* in our explanation of Super Traits. There is a sigh of relief, a big "Yessss" to the explanation of the rationale behind their personality trait elevations. They feel someone gets it, they feel understood, and they don't walk away from our theories, heading for even more cognitive dissonance that would come from trying to apply the wrong terminology to themselves.

We've heard hundreds of stories from survivors who have bounced from therapists to websites to survivor blogs, looking for something *other than* pop-psychology labels that don't fit. These are not treatment-resistant survivors who are fearful of, or avoiding, help. By their own constellation of Super Traits, they are serious about their recovery and are genuinely looking for help. With all that high-normal conscientiousness they are packing, they are very aware that all the faux-therapeutic mish-mosh they are being labeled with is a far cry from what is really going on with them.

At play in the therapeutic mish-mosh are the issues of nonidentification, misidentification, and disidentification. As described in the Preface and Introduction, many aspects of Pathological Love Relationships, ranging from the partner's pathology to the relationship dynamics, have been unidentified — until now. When aspects are nonidentified, *clues are missed completely* whether they relate to the partner's pathology, unique relational dynamics, or the aftermath trauma. The survivor's Super Traits can also be nonidentified — those unique personality factors that contribute to not only a woman being targeted but also complicate the difficulty of disengagement. *The Institute*'s catch phrase, "You can't treat what you don't recognize," is applicable and so survivors spend additional years seeking help from someone or something that can rightly identify their Super Traits.

Beyond nonidentification, most aspects of PLRs are misidentified—incorrectly identified as a bad breakup, or as only a domestic violence-related relationship, or as one in which the pathological partner is just a bad guy. But misidentification of the survivor's own personality aspects has *drastic* consequences for a survivor, who is dependent on the identification of her own issues to receive the appropriate intervention, prevention, and treatment. The misidentification of the survivor's elevated Super Traits contributes not only to the wrong treatment being offered, but a misunderstanding of her *motivations* while in the PLR.[2]

Disidentification is the most drastic issue of all. It involves *the elimination of the identity or characteristic qualities* of someone. While the entire PLR is often disidentified and collapsed down to fit the stereotypical categorical form of an abusive relationship, the higher risk to the survivor is the disidentification that happens when her own *identity* and Super Trait *characteristic* qualities are replaced with diagnostic or pop-psychology conditions that don't apply.[3]

What are these?

Codependency and Generalized Dysfunction

Everyone has a pet peeve. Me too. Nothing makes my blood pressure rise faster than when I read articles about codependent survivors of Cluster B and Psychopaths, implying that the wide-reaching personality constellation is primarily due to a nonclinical condition. I tend to expect this from survivor bloggers who are not mental health professionals and who are reaching into their glossary of pop-psychology terminology that they know their readership is familiar with. It's another thing to read it from mental health professionals who are using Oprah-ology instead of clinical foundations. So, let's sort this out.

Codependency is often associated, correctly or not, with other 12-step programs, assuming that other 12-step groups are an outgrowth of the widely respected Alcoholics Anonymous. Who doesn't respect A.A.? God bless Alcoholics Anonymous and Al-Anon, which have restored sanity to millions through their 12-step approach.

Like any successful approach, the 12-step approach has been widely adapted and used by other organizations for different problem areas, utilizing their own version of the steps such as what is seen in Codependents Anonymous—The Twelve Promises. Some of the other organizations utilizing a 12-step approach have found less successful application in their treatment than the original 12 steps, because some organizations believe you can 12 step anything whether it is a true emotional or medical condition like addiction, or whether it is an undefined condition like codependency.

Before the term 'codependency' existed, there was Al-Anon that used a similar version of the original 12 steps created by A.A. (formed in 1951) for the family and relatives of alcoholics who had their own problems from reactions to a loved one's drinking. In 1978, Adult Children of Alcoholics was formed for recovery of adults who were impacted by growing up in an alcoholic home. Ala-teen was a similar version of Al-Anon but for teens who were still under the same roof or being parented by an alcoholic.

In the 1980s came the Codependent Anonymous meetings which were created (not by A.A.) to address issues related to growing up in dysfunctional families, whether with an alcoholic or addict, or any other kind of dysfunction. Codependent Anonymous states it 'does not endeavor to define codependence but has a list of characteristics of codependents that involve various behavior patterns.'[4] The inability to *define* codependency is telling.

The codependency movement was made hugely popular by Melody Beattie, a survivor of this undefined, but very broad condition herself and author of the best-selling book *Codependent No More*. But the undefined condition is not a proven clinical diagnosis like alcoholism and addiction. Codependency suffers from the same public relations problem that narcissism seems to be suffering from lately—being an over-used term that seems to apply to just about anyone and anything that can be broadly described as dysfunctional.

Melody Beattie describes the characteristics of codependency -[5]

- Caretaking
- Low self-worth
- Repression of feelings
- Obsessing over things

- Attempting to control
- Denial
- Dependency
- Poor communication
- Weak (personal) boundaries
- Lack of trust of self and others
- Anger
- Sexual problems

Beattie's renowned list of characteristics is anecdotal and was not then, nor is it now, connected to a diagnosis found in the DSM. The characteristics are survivor-based in that her experience as a recovering survivor of this broad-based condition informed her conclusions. Codependency is a broad category of symptoms that can be applied to a broad category of sufferers, but the *reason* for acquiring these symptoms might not always be codependency.

Today, there are 12-step groups (or other words like 'promises') created by different founders for a myriad of conditions such as overeating, self-injury, sexual and relationship issues, and for the condition of codependency which was created according to Codependents Anonymous for 'all forms of dysfunction.'

The term codependency, and the symptoms associated with it eventually crept into the family dynamics and domestic violence lexicon, co-mingling with the similar ideas of learned behavior and learned helplessness from dysfunction. This nonclinical concept of codependency became part of the fabric of family counseling and provided a useful catch-all for a collection of symptoms, and is why many survivors have been labeled with codependency by the therapists from whom they sought help.

However, the main-stream psychological community, which operates on research and diagnostic criteria, could find no real evidence to support or adopt this concept. That didn't stop the Oprah-ologists, who somewhere along the line had replaced mainstream psychology for its more "pop" versions and, thus, adopted this catch-all concept. Comprehensive textbooks on psychiatry today include no references to codependency—nor does the DSM5.

Because of the broad definition of codependency, and its wide acceptance and application growing broader with each passing year, the lack of a cohesive definition has made it hard to evaluate it through research so that it could be quantified and find its way into psychiatry textbooks or the DSM. It's telling that the theory of codependency has been around since the 1980s and still has not been validated by the scholarly psychology field.

The closest alignment of codependency with anything resembling diagnostic criteria is the category of Dependent Personality Disorder in the DSM. This will be addressed later in this chapter.

So, while I don't mind some forms of pop psychology, and I am a big fan of Oprah, I don't feel that the use of pop psychology is adequate when we are trying to understand what is at the heart of people being targeted by the sickest forms of psychopathology. After all, if *The Institute* simply accepted the codependency label and tried treating survivors for it or sent them off by the truckloads to 12-step groups, we might very well get them killed by not addressing the true issues that contribute to their problems and to their being targeted.

Rationale

The reason we feel codependency is not applicable to approximately 75 percent of survivors lies in our repeated research conducted on Super Traits and the relational dynamics of PLRs. Codependency in its broadness gives plenty of room for just about anyone to fall somewhere within its range of symptoms. However, using our three personality testing instruments, those traits at the heart of survivors' issues were revealed to be completely *opposite* from those traits that define codependency.

First, let's look at both the agreeableness/cooperative traits compared to codependency to see why many of the symptoms of codependency **do not match** the Super Traits of the survivor partners' naturally occurring, predisposition, or hard-wired personalities. We will look at how codependency *could* be perceived to be similar and then discuss the differences. (Only the traits that are applicable to codependency are listed. Other traits are covered in the next list.)

Table 14.1
The Institute's Comparison Chart of
Super Traits vs. Codependency Traits
The Institute© 2016

Agreeable/Cooperative Super Trait Descriptors	Codependency Symptom Descriptors
Reciprocal in relationships (given in return)	Caretaking, dependent
Willing to help without desire for selfish domination; concern for social harmony	Attempting to control
Straightforward, upfront	Poor communication, repression of feelings
Trusting and trustworthy	Lack of trust of self and others
Well-tempered, gentle	Anger
Tolerant	Unmoderated feelings (intense, vacillating)

As we can see from the list, the personality traits the survivor was born with, which are operating before and during most of the PLR, are not representative of a codependent *style* of relationship behavior. In fact, the Super Traits appear to be the *opposite* of the symptoms of codependency. *How* situational codependent behaviors and reactions are generated is discussed later in the chapter.

Now let's look at the conscientiousness/self-directed Super Traits compared to codependency. (Only those that are applicable to codependency are listed).

Table 14.2
Conscientiousness/Self-Directed Super Traits
Compared to Codependency
The Institute © 2016

Conscientiousness/Self-Directedness Super Trait Descriptors	Codependency Symptom Descriptors

Self-confident	Caretaking (people pleasing)
Thoughtful to others	Attempting to control
Purposeful, goal-directed behavior	Poor communication
Controlled impulses	Anger/unmoderated feelings (vacillating)
Self-accepting	Low self-esteem
Resourceful, persevering	Can't meet one's own needs

Conscientiousness traits, like agreeableness traits, are not reflected in codependent behavior, but clearly something is setting off the bells and whistles of *perceived* codependency. Let's see which traits are being misread by both the public and professionals alike.

So Why the Confusion?

The facet descriptors of agreeableness and cooperation that are often misattributed to codependency are those related to empathy, tolerance, optimism about human nature, loyalty, and trust.[6] Because the survivor's agreeableness/cooperation traits are in the high-normal range, they are indeed notable and are very noticeable in the PLR dynamics, which is what a counselor may be picking up on.

At first glance, empathy, tolerance, and some perceived survivor Pollyanna-ishness regarding trust and loyalty can smack of codependency or even dependency. But for this "theory" (and I am using that word loosely as it applies to codependency) to be true, it matters *how* and *where* behavior is formed.

Treatment for Pathological Love Relationships is a relatively new genre of counseling and focus. Research on survivors' trait elevations did not exist until *The Institute* began studying PLRs and later conducted our further research with Purdue University. What **did** exist were old theories that were applied to the PLR concept using the only relationship categories available at the time—dysfunctional, abusive/domestic violence, addicted, and so on.

These relationship categories are connected to the psychology field's own respective theories about the roots of relationship problems. Marriage and Family counseling models, and treatment for domestic violence, addictions, sex/relationship addictions, and early childhood trauma, all have their theoretical reasons for both Darkness' behavior and the behavior of his survivor as it relates to each of these theories.

Like the Nurture vs. Nature debate discussed in Chapter Two, these relationship-related treatment approaches theorize that early childhood issues are at the *root* of why relationships later became dysfunctional. What has been missing are the factors of PLRs, which include both the survivor's personality trait elevations and the pathological personality of *someone else.*[7]

Previous theories looked at behavior as generating from the *family* environment and not from the naturally occurring, predisposition, or hard-wired aspects of *personality* such as in the personality disorder of Darkness or the Super Trait personality elevations of the survivors. The theorists believed that relationship dynamics were created not by hard-wired personality traits but by *family environments.* There had not been much research conducted regarding how *personality* impacts relationship dynamics—only how an *environment* impacts relationship dynamics. Looking at family or environmental impact did not take into account the biological, hard-wired predisposition of personality and its contribution to relationships, as detailed in the Alternative Model of the DSM5. Therefore, the behavior in PLRs was seen through the lens of the Nurture Theory—what happened early on that made someone display dysfunctional *behavior.*[8] The family system does have a powerful impact on establishing belief systems that turn into behavior. In fact, trauma resulting from the family system can eventually lead to changes in behavior which makes the issue of Nurture Theory very important. But even though these behaviors are deeply ingrained over many years of reinforcement, they are learned and can be unlearned.

Theorists who study PLRs look at behavior not only as the external manifestation of family and environmental impact, they *also* see behavior as generated from hard-wired or naturally occurring personality.[9] *This view is completely different from that of looking only at the external manifestation of dysfunctional behavior.*

The character trait of codependency is believed to generate from these external factors—experiences living with an alcoholic or dysfunctional family, or a violent environment. Likewise, for example, the batterer who *learned* his violence from the controlling behavior of others, or the victim who developed *learned* helplessness or codependent behavior. These explanations are based on external influences.

Survivors and therapists not familiar with the concept of personality and behavior *assume* that what is behind perceived codependency in the survivors is related to dysfunctional families, addictions, abuse, and trauma. What *The Institute* did not believe that the PLR dynamics and the survivor's alleged codependency could be largely explained by early family problems or trauma, especially if those problems *did not exist*.

Trauma, for all its debilitating aspects, is treatable. And while survivors suffered significant trauma from the PLR, after the trauma was treated, these unusual displays of personality trait elevations were *still* present. Likewise, treatment for the condition of codependency did not mitigate the problem. That is because it was hard-wired, predisposition, or naturally occurring personality and not learned helplessness/codependency that put the survivor at risk for a PLR.[10]

Additionally, it was widely assumed by most therapists that survivors were victims of early childhood trauma or violence, yet *The Institute* found that this assumption was largely erroneous among survivors. While *some* of the survivors had dysfunctional families, came from alcoholic homes, had pathological parents, or suffered abuse, the overwhelming majority did *not*. To be certain of this we added another survey (The Adverse Childhood Experience Scale) to the research that asked about early childhood experiences. The clear majority of survivors reported that they did **not** have trauma, alcoholic homes, pathological parents, or dysfunctional families in their backgrounds but, instead, came from rather normal upbringings. So, the assumption that their alleged codependency was generated from the messages and trauma of a dysfunctional past was not true for most women.[11]

So, If It Wasn't the Family Environment, What Was It?

The Nature Theory taught us that we are born with certain personality features (for good or for bad) that are innate, hard-wired or naturally occurring. In personality disorders, some features are more engrained than others, and neuro-genetics and abnormalities can reinforce these proclivities. These types of proclivities, especially those associated with personality disorders, resist attempts to be unlearned—it's like trying to unlearn your brown eyes.

- If you have a Nurture issue, you have the opportunity for relearning.
- If you have a Nature issue, you have less relearning opportunity because the characteristic is an intrinsic part of you.

All the wishing for blue eyes isn't going to change your brown eyes.

- Codependency is a Nurture issue—a learned behavior.
- Super traits are a Nature issue—innate, naturally occurring, a predisposition, or hard-wired.

The difference is night and day. For knowledgeable therapists, this should impact what they are treating and why, *because how the problems were formed is key in determining how they should be treated.*

The same proclivities of the hard-wired personality disorder are the same proclivities of the naturally occurring Super Traits. Super Traits are not at the level of a *disorder*, and these personality traits can be positive and pleasant in the right partner's hands. But they still must be dealt with for what they are, which is not codependency.

Many therapists and survivor bloggers, then, are trying to get survivors to unlearn or relearn behaviors that they assume were generated from some issue with their family or past experiences. They have not realized these are not Nurture issues —they are related to hard-wired or naturally occurring personality traits out of which one cannot be 12 stepped. If you were born with it and its part of your personality, you didn't learn it, and, thus, it's a whole different ball game.

All this misinformation can be very dangerous when the following occur -

- There's no new language for a new concept.
- Old concepts aren't applicable.
- We begin with assumptions that *all* symptoms are generated out of the *same* histories.

Survivors and therapists grab the only known explanation and language and apply it to this situation when it is just not applicable. This means that treatment is **not** going to be effective and that the survivor is going to remain at risk in future relationships. The survivor will be treated for codependency, but therapeutic work with a *personality trait* requires a vastly different approach.

*D*isidentification

You know the adage, "If it walks like a duck, looks like a duck, and sounds like a duck, it must be a duck." And we all believe that, right? We've heard what we thought was a quack and we instantly thought, "Must be a duck." But despite widespread belief, most species of ducks do not quack. Ducks make a wide range of calls ranging from whistles to cooing to yodels and grunts. The Muscovy ducks on my pond don't quack at all—they make a sound like a dove, which is like a coo or a purr. Until I heard the Muscovy, I, too, thought (erroneously) that all ducks quacked.

Well, the same thing has happened with codependency.[12]

- We see a trait like cooperation and we declare it the 'duck' of caretaking.
- We see tolerance and declare it the 'duck' of dependency.
- We begin with assumptions that all behavior that seems alike is generated from the same source.
- So, if it quacks like codependency then it must be codependency, and we are going to treat it by sending it to a Codependents Anonymous meeting.

But just like a quack, we can make assumptions that are based on the wrong facts.

What Creates Codependency?

Let's start at the beginning. At the root of the codependency theory is the symptom of poor self-esteem. Much of the other behaviors listed above about codependency and catalogued by Melody Beattie stem from poor self-esteem, and this is what is largely focused on when treating codependency—or a return to loving oneself. A poor self-concept and people pleasing as symptoms of codependency are learned behaviors and originate in a dysfunctional/alcoholic/traumatic family or relational system.

All low self-esteem is not produced by dysfunctional family systems or only in early childhood. Sometimes it comes from other sources, sometimes later in life, situationally, and sometimes only briefly.

The aftermath of the PLR results in acute, *but situational*, symptoms of low self-esteem generated not always from a historical dysfunctional family or early childhood abuse but from the pathology of an antagonistic and coercive partner.[13] *Situational* low self-esteem from a PLR is not a long-term issue of the poor self-esteem that is often seen in codependency, which produces the symptoms of dependency and caretaking, weak boundaries, difficulty with reality, and poor communication.[14]

In most cases in a PLR, low self-esteem is *situational* and generated as a byproduct of the relationship dynamics and from the damage by someone else's psychopathology. It is not a lifelong battle stemming from a family system. While personal/intimate relationships with pathology are likely to be more damaging than a casual relationship with Darkness, it still doesn't explain why, for instance bosses, friends, and neighbors are *also* harmed by Darkness, which can result in their own situational self-esteem issues generated from Darkness' malicious gossip, gaslighting, or a rash tongue lashing. It is statistically impossible that most of the people Darkness has abused (be it boss or friend) are *all* codependent because of dysfunctional families or trauma and as evidence by a loss of self-esteem due to harm by Darkness. That's ridiculous. Pathology harms everyone, codependent or not.

While aftermath symptoms on the surface can reflect self-concept damage such as problems with reality testing, boundary issues, fluctuating emotions, and lack of trust (the codependency list)—these symptoms were not always created from early childhood or dysfunctional families and were not always a historically long-learned pattern of relational relating.

These symptoms are in fact, the *opposite* of what a woman's core personality has been since childhood, which is why she experiences so much cognitive dissonance about who she has become. The symptoms that appear to be related to a learned pattern of interaction are not representative of her personality constellation.[15]

The Super Trait of cooperation (agreeableness) that survivor partners have, when it falls within the high-normal range, is not based on poor self-esteem. That means there is a wide chasm between *facilitating* cooperation amongst others in the cooperation/agreeableness trait and the *people pleasing* of codependency. The quack of cooperation is not codependency.

Survivor Note:

If you don't have the root symptom of long term (pre-PLR) low self-esteem from which the rest of the codependency traits are created, you probably don't have codependency.

Codependency also does not correspond to the high-normal conscientiousness (self-directedness) traits of survivors, which are goal and value driven. Survivors are more proficient at reaching goals than their peers, are self-disciplined, upfront, and persevering.[16] In thinking about the occupations of most of our clients, it is their conscientiousness that has raised them to the top of their careers. I don't know that I have met a *codependent* judge, nor do I believe that one could rise to the top to become a judge if she were crippled with codependency, which often affects careers. There is no doubt that Codependents Anonymous would disagree, though.

Likewise, *persevering* as a personality facet of conscientiousness is not the same as the *persistent* people pleasing of codependency.[17] Aspects associated with codependency such as difficulty with boundaries or owning one's own reality are crippling, *lifelong* belief systems that would not result in achieving the emotional rigors of judge-ship or that of an attorney, or CEO of a Fortune 500 company. Those crippling belief systems would have impacted other areas of the survivor's life—not just the portion of their life in a PLR—and would have resulted in a poorer quality of relational and occupational life. In contrast, these survivors had relational success in other areas of their lives outside of the PLR. I would remind the reader who might want to hold a PLR against the survivor that absolutely **no one** enjoys relational success in a PLR because it's impossible. So, the quack of perseverance is not codependency.

Misidentification

While some of the traits are *dis*identified, others are *mis*identified. Difficulty in *acknowledging and meeting one's own needs and wants,* noted in codependency, only become an issue in the PLR when gaslighting, cognitive dissonance, and trauma are impacting the neurological and executive functioning of the brain.[18] Prior to the aftermath of the PLR, survivors didn't struggle in meeting their own needs. A *situational* crisis with a resulting neurological impact is not the same thing as a lifelong struggle with knowing how to meet one's ongoing needs, as in codependency.[19]

Difficulty in maintaining *functional boundaries,* as seen in codependency, is at odds with a survivor's personality trait of cooperation (agreeableness) and conscientiousness.[20] It is the skills of cooperation, not codependency, that make the balanced leadership noted in Super Traits. Boundary issues in PLRs happen because psychopathology is manipulative and coercive and violates everyone's boundaries no matter what their personality constellation. Pathology trumps normalcy *every time*. Weak boundaries would be evident in areas of a person's life other than the PLR and would have impeded vocational success. Equating successful gaslighting or coercion as a boundary problem is akin to viewing gastrointestinal issues as a universal sign of colon cancer.

Difficulty in *expressing one's reality in a moderate fashion,* a trait of codependency, is at odds with a survivor's high-normal trait of conscientiousness, which (until the PLR) produces level headed and stable people.

'Hyper empathy, tolerance, and optimism about human nature' are mislabeled as symptoms of codependency, but as the following comparison chart (Table 14.3) suggests, they are not related to the core issues of codependency, which stem from poor self-esteem and become behavioral and relational adaptations.

In medicine, any existing symptom could be related to multiple causes in multiple organs or systems. To find the correct diagnosis is to find the *origin* of the symptom. For a group of traits to be considered codependency, they should be *originating out of* low self-esteem and not the personality constellation.[21] Let's look at the misidentified traits of codependency and see if they can be better accounted for by being created out of the situational relational dynamics of the PLR, as opposed to the long-term, nonexistent history of many of the survivors.

Table 14.3
The Institute's Comparison Charts
Survivor Codependency-Like Symptoms Generated from PLRs
The Institute © 2016

Codependency Symptom as a Situational Reaction of the Survivor	Relational Dynamics of a PLR and the Symptoms of Cognitive Dissonance and Trauma
Low self-esteem	Produced from devaluing, discarding, infidelity, blaming, pathological lying.
Poor functional boundaries	Produced from threats, coercion, manipulation, violence, gaslighting.
Difficulty owning one's reality	Produced from gaslighting, his hidden life, his pathological lying, multiple hidden relationships, the effects of the Karpman Triangle and the Event Cycle, and from the results of the developed cognitive dissonance and trauma reactions.
Difficulty meeting one's own needs	Produced from coercion, manipulation, threats, and from the results of the developed cognitive dissonance, trauma.
Repression of feelings	Produced from coercion, manipulation, threats, the effects of the Karpman Triangle and the Event Cycle, and from the results of the developed cognitive dissonance, trauma.
Obsessing	Produced from coercion, threats, the effects of the Karpman Triangle and the Event Cycle, resulting in neurological impact which includes the symptoms of intrusive thoughts, cognitive dissonance, trauma.
Attempting to control	Produced from coercion, his hidden life, the effects of the Karpman Triangle and Event Cycle, pathological lying, and from the results of the developed cognitive dissonance, trauma.

Codependency Symptom as a Situational Reaction of the Survivor	Relational Dynamics of a PLR and the Symptoms of Cognitive Dissonance and Trauma
Denial	Produced from his hidden life, pathological lying, the effects of the Karpman Triangle, and from the results of the developed cognitive dissonance and trauma.
Poor communication	Produced by the effects of the Karpman Triangle, the Event Cycle, and his pathological lying.
Lack of trust of self and others	Produced by his pathological lying and hidden life and from the results of the developed cognitive dissonance and trauma.
Anger	Devaluing, discarding, hidden life, pathological lying, infidelity, coercion.

Not only are the symptoms of codependency **not** the survivor partner's original personality traits, they are only manifested *situationally* in the PLR. The root cause is not the survivor's symptoms of codependency but is instead a *manifestation* of the relationship dynamics of a PLR in which the very nature of pathology can be traced by the reactions that are produced in others, which are cognitive dissonance and traumatic reactions.[22]

This is a far cry from long-term codependency generated in early childhood, and, in fact, these reactions are also seen in those who attempt interactions with Darkness, e.g. bosses, employees, friends, and families who do not have early childhood issues. It is not that these symptoms are *only* produced in intimate relationships (in which of course they are heightened and more intense), it's that pathological people elicit similar reactions in many of their interactions with others -

- Communication problems generated from interactions stuck in the Karpman Triangle
- Situational reactions generated from the effects of the Event Cycle
- Trust-related reactions because of coercion, pathological lying

- Repression of feelings based on the antagonistic personality of pathology
- Boundary violations due to pathology's need for dominance and control ©

Instead of labeling the victims of pathological partners as somehow disordered, we need to be aware that pathology IS a disorder, and the powerful personality of pathology railroads everyone.

The important takeaway is, therefore, that situational behaviors are not necessarily systemic behaviors from childhood.

==

Survivor Note:

*What should be clear is that traits which are misidentified and disidentified end up being **non**identified, meaning that clues are missed completely. Various reactions to pathology are assumed to be generated from early childhood experiences replaying themselves out in the PLR, even if the survivor says they don't exist.*

This is diagnosis at its worst.

==

The Institute's Situational Behaviors of PLRs As Non-Systemic
The Institute © 2016

- It is incorrect to believe that survivors suffer from lifelong patterns of poor self-esteem when the research shows that most have strong core self-concepts which were briefly (and naturally) impacted by cognitive dissonance-producing and coercive Darkness.
- It is incorrect to believe that survivors suffer from lifelong patterns of difficulty with boundaries and controlling behavior when research shows that most have a cooperative-reciprocal style found in stellar leadership qualities which were briefly (and naturally) impacted by the railroading and manipulation of Darkness.
- It is incorrect to believe that survivors suffer from lifelong patterns of difficulty ascertaining their own reality when research shows most are noted as having psychological maturity and good mental health which was briefly (and naturally) impacted by gaslighting, pathological lying,

and accomplices who helped hide the pathological part-ner's true nature.

- It is incorrect to believe that survivors suffer from life-long patterns of not being able to meet their own needs when research shows that most are noted as having life-long patterns of achievement, both personal and profes-sional, driven by stable goals and values; these patterns of achievement were briefly (and naturally) impacted by the neurological changes in the brain caused by Darkness' psychopathology and the trauma he inflicted.
- It is incorrect to believe that survivors suffer from lifelong patterns of repression of feelings when research shows that most are straightforward, upfront, and open about who they are and what they need; this was briefly (and natural-ly) impacted by the neurological abnormalities of Darkness causing communication problems, and the effects outlined in the Karpman Triangle and the Event Cycle.
- It is incorrect to believe that survivors suffer from lifelong patterns of anger and unregulated emotions when research shows that most have good impulse control and are tender, kind, and humble; these qualities were briefly (and natu-rally) impacted by the survivor's neurological changes cre-ated from the impulse-driven, problem-riddled Darkness, full of aggression and anxiety-producing antagonism.
- It is incorrect to believe that survivors suffer from lifelong patterns of a lack of trust of themselves and others when research shows that most have high-normal levels of trust, tend to see others through who they are, and are optimistic about human nature; this trust was impacted briefly (and naturally) by the gaslighting, betraying, and pathological lying of Darkness.
- Lastly, it is incorrect to believe that survivors suffer from lifelong patterns of caretaking when research shows that most are reciprocal in relationships and are motivated by social harmony and assisting rather than attacking; this was impacted briefly (and naturally) by the masked rela-

tionship of the PLR and Darkness' lack of assuming responsibility for his own problems. The survivor's history of relationships outside of the PLR shows healthy and balanced relationships that were indeed reciprocal before the PLR.

A Correct View

Looking at whether codependency is applicable is like looking at what constitutes a personality disorder discussed in Chapter One. What is looked for is the *enduring pattern of behavior* that is characteristic over a lifetime, not in a single stress-filled, gaslighted relationship. What was the survivor like before the PLR? What were her behaviors and her motivations in other relationships? While we know by her personality that she would always be a cooperative facilitator, did she fall into patterns that were connected to caretaking, as opposed to caregiving? Her role in caregiving is highly likely, given her personality traits, but it is in the PLR where aspects of anxiety, heightened dysfunctional resourcefulness, and a lack of self-care become *situationally*, but not permanently, problematic. If these aspects *were* permanently problematic, *The Institute* would not have seen such positive results in recovery.

The relational dynamics of a PLR do change lifelong, personality-driven, and naturally endowed behavior through the natural effects of psychopathology on a primarily normally functioning individual. While high-normal rankings in the Super Traits place a woman at risk for being a target of Darkness and produce enough impact to increase problems in disengagement and traumatic aftermath not seen in those who ranked in the normal range, the high-normal ranking is still *not* equivalent with codependency or even dependency.

$\mathcal{W}$hat About the Others?

What about the other percentage of survivors who did not test with high-normal agreeableness (cooperativeness) and conscientiousness (self-directedness)?

It is not that codependency does not exist in *some* survivors; it's that the percentages are much smaller than therapists assume they are and treat them as such. Clearly, most of our survivors do not test as codependent. Entire books, websites, and articles that are written *as if* most of the survivors are codependent is clinically inaccurate according to our three research assessments.

The three conclusive testing instruments, with 600 survivors tested, showed that the overwhelming majority of survivor partners did *not* test high on the aspects in the testing instrument related to behaviors associated with dependency.[23]

The testing instruments were set up on a continuum which included low, normal, high-normal, and high traits. Both ends of the continuum (low or high) denote pathology. People too low in certain traits produce the symptoms seen in some personality disorders. For instance, some personality disorders such as Cluster B/psychopathy are often associated with the *opposite* traits of our survivor partners. Some high traits on the test also indicate personality disorders. While the survivors are high-normal in agreeableness and conscientiousness, Cluster B/psychopathy personality disorders rank low in these traits. Traits in which the survivors tested low, people with Cluster B/psychopathy personality disorders tested high.

Only a small percentage of the survivor population tested high in some traits associated with what would produce codependency-like traits of lifelong low self-esteem. These survivor-partner minorities *did* have histories of abuse, dysfunctional families, early childhood trauma, pathological parenting, or alcoholic homes.[24] While this is not a guarantee that survivors who had those situations all had traits of low self-esteem, it is more likely in that minority sub-group than others who did not have it.

The minority are discernible from our true Super Trait survivor group, as they acknowledge *lifelong* battles with self-esteem, boundaries, trust, speaking up for themselves, historical anxiety, and perhaps a history of Complex Post Traumatic Stress Disorder.[25] In free form comments, they didn't say, "What happened to my self-esteem? I never had problems before!" Instead they said, "I've always had issues with self-esteem and this just made it worse." This minority has widespread boundary issues, more difficulty applying the techniques of recovery, and slower progress in symptom management, as they are always drawn back to early childhood or family issues that are unresolved, and which distract them from the task of PLR recovery.

Survivors who are in the minority have longer recoveries because early childhood and dysfunctional family issues *are* at the core of lifelong problems and are *not* situational symptoms of a PLR. They are the minority who *do* need recovery from dysfunctional family issues while simultaneously or prior to, recovering from the PLR. They have multiple issues to deal with that have complicated their risk factors for another PLR and for the length of recovery.

What should be emphasized is that the *overwhelming majority* of survivors from a PLR do not have the trait markers of dependency or symptoms of codependency, as evidenced by our 600-person research sample and 30 years in this field. This means that, by far, most of the survivors are high-normal in agreeableness and conscientiousness, and that treating for codependency is going to miss the mark in most of the cases.

This is also why there has been such widespread frustration among survivors when they go to a therapist who assumes they are typical abuse survivors, have learned helplessness, or that their partners' violence stems from his own family dynamics (even when the family dynamics **do not** exist) and not from a personality disorder (that **does** exist). Therapy is focused on resolving the pathological partner's family history or the survivor's low self-esteem, which is assumed to be chronic (as in codependency) and not situational (as in a PLR).

She is sent to codependency groups where she finds most of the material not applicable to her. Family sessions go nowhere as her partner's display of hard-wired behavior is not modified by therapy. She did not have self-esteem issues prior to a PLR, her family was pretty normal, she didn't experience abuse in early childhood, her only boundary issues are in the PLR and not with others, she hadn't had a problem with her reality until the gaslighting started, she didn't obsess until the changes in her neurological condition caused intrusive thoughts, her personality traits of agreeableness/cooperativeness mean she isn't a controlling person (which is assumed in codependency), and she trusts both in herself and others with a lack of trust only occurring during the PLR.[26]

None of it fits, but there she sits for a year in a codependency group getting more and more frustrated because none of this seems applicable to her. She wonders if she is just in denial. Meanwhile the therapist probably *does* think she is in denial, or treatment resistant, as she is not conforming or responding to the treatment set out to heal her nonexistent codependency.

Dependent Personality Disorder

The closest true diagnostic disorder in the DSM related to codependency is Dependent Personality Disorder (DPD). It is not an *exact* match for codependency, as codependency is outwardly focused on caring excessively for (i.e., controlling) *others* and Dependent Personality Disorder is outwardly focused on having others care for *them*.

DPD is described as a pervasive and excessive need to be taken care of that leads to submissive and clinging behavior and fears of separation, beginning by early adulthood and present in a variety of contexts, as indicated by five (or more) of the following -[27]

- The person has difficulty making everyday decisions without an excessive amount of advice and reassurance from others.
- The person needs others to assume responsibility for most major areas of his or her life.
- The person has difficulty expressing disagreement with others because of fear of loss of support or approval. (Not included in this are realistic fears of retribution, for instance in domestic violence situations).
- The person has difficulty initiating projects or doing things on his or her own (because of a lack of self-confidence in judgment or abilities rather than a lack of motivation or energy).
- The person goes to excessive lengths to obtain nurturing and support from others, to the point of volunteering to do things that are unpleasant.
- The person feels uncomfortable or helpless when alone because of exaggerated fears of being unable to care for himself or herself.
- When a close relationship ends, the person urgently seeks another relationship as a source of care and support.
- The person is unrealistically preoccupied with fears of being left to take care of himself or herself.

As far less than an exact match, DPD is often a secondary misidentification and disidentification of a survivor's Super Traits. First, we will look at the traits of DPD (as they somewhat align to codependency), then we will compare those traits to Super Traits to see if we are talking about the same kind of behavior.

Table 14.4
The Institute's Chart of DPD Compared to Super Traits©
The Institute © 2016

Dependent Personality Disorder Trait	Super Traits of Agreeableness/ Cooperativeness/ Conscientiousness/ Self-Directedness
Difficulty making decisions	Goal directed, team leader approach
Wants others to assume responsibility for his/her life	Resourceful, reciprocal, self-confident
Difficulty disagreeing	Straightforward, upfront
Difficulty initiating projects	Resourceful, aims for achievement, persevering
Goes to excessive lengths to obtain nurturing/support	Motivated toward assisting, thoughtful to others, supportive to others
Feels helpless	Self-confident, purposeful
Immediately after a relationship ends, urgently seeks other relationship	Self-determined
Fears caring for self	Persevering, Resourceful, Goal-Directed

The core feature of the **Dependent Personality Disorder (DPD)** is a strong need to be taken care of by other people. This need, and the associated fear of losing the support of others, often leads people with DPD to behave in a clingy manner and to submit to the desires of other people. To avoid conflict, they may have great difficulty standing up for themselves. They find it difficult to express disagreement or make independent decisions and are challenged to begin a task when nobody is available to assist them.

Being alone is extremely hard for them and when someone with DPD finds that a relationship they depend on has ended, they will immediately seek another source of support. DPD will typically have major impacts on most areas of an individual's functioning. Particularly in

American culture, there are societal expectations for adults to exhibit independence, decisiveness, confidence, and self-reliance. An individual who does not meet these expectations will have difficulty functioning in occupational, academic, and interpersonal settings. Individuals with DPD may continue to reside with their parents past their twenties, may be unemployed, and may not learn how to drive a car, or continue or complete their education.

While PLRs produce *situational* behaviors that are seen in DPD, the long-term behaviors associated with it, which are necessary to make the diagnosis of a personality disorder, are not present in the survivor.[28] Their core personality traits of high-normal agreeableness and high-normal conscientiousness are not aligned with DPD and the survivor' high-normal traits of conscientiousness and leadership-like traits do not match the traits of DPD.

Borderline Personality Disorder (BPD)

Survivors are also often misidentified as having BPD. Behind the misdiagnosis is the emotional upheaval and intensity of emotions experienced from the PLR and are often symptoms of untreated trauma, specifically PTSD. As described above in DPD, while PLRs produce *situational* behavior that is also seen in Borderline Personality Disorder, the long-term behavior associated with it necessary to make the diagnosis of a personality disorder, is not present in survivors. Their core personality traits of high-normal agreeableness and high-normal conscientiousness are not aligned with BPD. Their seemingly similar symptoms are a situational manifestation from the emotional turbulence of a PLR and/or untreated trauma©. The traits of BPD are -[29]

- Frantic efforts to avoid real or imagined abandonment
- A pattern of intense and unstable relationships with family, friends, and loved ones, often swinging from extreme closeness and love (idealization) to extreme dislike or anger (devaluation)
- A distorted and unstable self-image or sense of self
- Impulsive and often dangerous behaviors, such as spending sprees, unsafe sex, substance abuse, reckless driving, and binge eating

- Recurring suicidal behaviors or threats, or self-harming behavior such as cutting
- Intense and highly changeable moods, with each episode lasting from a few hours to a few days
- Chronic feelings of emptiness
- Inappropriate, intense anger or problems controlling anger
- Having stress-related paranoid thoughts
- Having severe dissociative symptoms, such as feeling cut off from oneself, observing oneself from outside the body, or losing touch with reality

Empaths and Highly Sensitive People

So, to make diagnosing even *more* confusing, survivors are often told they are, or perceive themselves as empaths and/or Highly Sensitive People, referred to as HSP. The reason survivors assume they are empaths has to do with the intensity in which they feel other's emotions. Sometimes survivors say they were always this way and their high reactivity to other's emotions caused them to be labeled by therapists as codependent, DPD, or BPD. Disliking those labels, they conclude they must be an empath. Other survivors feel they became that way through the PLR, which would most likely have been *generated* out of trauma. So, let's sort this out.

Hyper Empathy

I see lots of articles with titles like *Empaths and Psychopaths*. While there has been a plethora of research on empathy, especially the low empathy seen in psychopaths, true research on hyper empathy is not so abundant. What seems to have replaced true *personality research* on hyper empathy is a general explanation of what makes one an empath. While hyper empathy is not a complete explanation for the existence of empaths or HSPs (which are different than empaths), I believe just the word empath leads people to believe that survivors, with their high level of empathy, are empaths. However, having high-normal empathy does not necessarily constitute one as an empath the way that empath coaches define it.

Like codependency, the word 'empath' covers a broad category of traits and there is a wide description of it without much definitive research. The concept of empaths is a product of both pop psychology, some neuroscience, and new age, metaphysical, or energy-related fields. In my curiosity, I have taken some training to better understand the concept of empaths.

Metaphysical/Paranormal

The word 'empath' has become popular of late and has replaced some of the other words that were once associated with the concept of empaths in the metaphysical or paranormal fields—like mediums (who might also have additional gifts or skill sets). The defining line between these gifts can become overlapping as some may be empaths who feel the feelings and sensations of others, while another gift might be knowing the future, while others might know the past. For some reason in some circles, people who used to call themselves 'mediums' now call themselves 'empaths'.

Myers-Briggs 'INFJ'

Some of the chatter about empaths suggests they often become counselors since half the challenge of treatment is being able to "understand the feelings of others" in order to help. Likewise, the Myers-Briggs Test (a personality-type assessment tool) which places individuals into one of 16 personality *types*, found those with the typology of the INFJ (Introversion, Intuition, Feeling, Judging) are also highly connected to those that make the best counselors and are also highly connected to what they call 'the empath-type personality' despite that they make up less than one percent of the population. This would make empaths rare in the Myers-Briggs focus.

The Myers-Briggs empath personality, which is defined as their INFJ personality, appears to be similar to our Super Traits found in the Five Factor Form we utilized. I, myself, identify as an INFJ. INFJs are known to be born with a sense of idealism and morality, are natural diplomats, warm and sensitive, decisive and strong-willed, not dreamers but doers, and they find helping others as their purpose in life, fight tirelessly for ideas, work to create balance, and like to create movements to right the wrongs of society.[30]

Sound familiar? It should—these are almost identical to both agreeableness and conscientiousness. We did a short Myers-Briggs assessment of our survivors because I found bloggers saying, "all survivors are INFJs." However, not all of the survivors we tested are an INFJ. They had varying mixtures of the 16 personality types of the Myers-Briggs test although most of them included some overlapping similarities under the N (intuition) and the F (feeling) in the INFJ personality type, which we feel captures the essence of the high-normal empathy in survivors—the trait most recognized by others in them or recognized by themselves.

*E*mpaths & Empathy

Beyond the personality-type assessments that are available in the psychology field, like the Myers-Briggs, is how empaths are described by others who treat or help empaths. Empaths are defined as 'having the ability to apprehend the mental or emotional state of another individual.' They are described as 'feeling everything sometimes as an extreme, are less likely to intellectualize feelings, utilize intuition as a filter through which they experience the world, naturally giving, good listeners, world-class nurturers, know what others are feeling even without speaking to them, and other people's negativity feels assaultive and exhausting to them'.[31]

The trait of empathy that empaths have is defined as 'the ability to understand and share the feelings of another.' The word *empath* then, is taken from the word *empathy* and implied to have an even *greater* ability to understand, share the feelings of, and be affected by other people's emotional states. The definitions of both are almost identical. According to those who treat or help empaths, they also have stress reactions to other people's emotions and are prone to developing eating disorders and possible addictions as a way of managing the sensitivity to other people's emotions.

I've seen nonclinical quizzes comprised of a mere seven questions all the way to those with 32 questions and containing a scale by which the very broad and generic quiz tries to rank empaths. But these have not produced any useful quantified assessments to utilize. Some PhDs and MDs have websites that highlight studies about empaths and HSPs, but I think we are still a long way from getting more diverse research behind it to fully explain this elevated trait.

Energy Sensitivity

Then there is what other's call the "woo-woo" theories about empaths who don't tend to believe in anything that isn't a psychological science. The metaphysical or energy field notes empaths as 'being wide open in their energy portals' which allows everyone else's 'energy' to trespass without permission. In their view, empaths, being more sensitive and wider open, must learn how to regulate their own valves for allowing trespassing energy to bombard them. These workers focus on what is felt by the empath from the energy of another person as opposed to only the emotions of the other person—because energy can contain more than just emotion.

Neuroscience

Then there is the neuroscience understanding, again bridging the gap between the mind and the brain, that describes how what is happening in the brain amplifies what the empath is perceiving in the mind and emotions. Empaths are thought to have hyper mirror neurons which pick up on the emotions of others and then empathize with them. If their partner is sad, they feel their sadness. There is also brain chemistry sensitivity known as 'dopamine sensitivity' which increases the sense of pleasure. Neuroscience contemplates whether empaths need less dopamine in order to feel happy. They can be overstimulated by dopamine and, therefore, tend to enjoy their time alone (which might explain the exhaustion they experience during love bombing). Then there is a neurological condition called 'synesthesia' where people can feel the emotions or sensations of others in their own body. And, lastly, there is the theory about empaths and their sensitivity to electromagnetic fields as described by the description of the energy field workers. They can be sensitive to changes in others' energy and even the electromagnetic fields of Earth and the Sun.

While neuroscience has provided some clues as to aspects of how empathy works in mirror neurons between people and perhaps some brain chemistry and neurological quirkiness, it might be a leap to assign the trait of hyper empathy to a full category of being, since the survivors are far more complex than *one* facet of hyper empathy.

Is being an empath the totality of what survivors experience in their Super Traits? Where is the rest of it? The trust, cooperation, loyalty, tolerance, efficiency, dependability, deliberate-ness, self-discipline, perseverance, competence, and striving for achievement that coexist *with* that facet of empathy? Have survivor trait elevation problems been more than just empathy?

I think the survivors would say yes.

Just to test it out, we used one of the broad and generic empathy quizzes that are on the Internet on our own survivors. The percentage was upwards of 90 percent of participants who found themselves to be empaths according to this quiz, which would be expected since this characteristic is tied to the issue of empathy which is elevated in their trait of agreeableness.[32]

For *The Institute*, this only tells us that survivors have elevated empathy. It tells us nothing about *the rest of* the facets of agreeableness/cooperation and absolutely nothing about survivors' elevated trait of conscientiousness, or in other words, the rest of what is elevated in them.

To add *even more* confusion for survivors, some empaths are also HSPs according to empath experts who have highly sensitive nervous systems that are activated by bright lights, noise, strong colors and odors, and are easily stimulated by commotion. We tested that too. (What is confusing is that this is the same sensitivity that persons on the autism spectrum have. We are not suggesting that survivors are autistic, but we are pointing to how these quizzes are so generic that they even confuse us.)

We gave one of the broad and generic HSP Quizzes to our survivors, and many were scored as being HSPs, especially those who had experienced trauma/PTSD in which their fight/flight systems were still revved up.[33] While it doesn't appear that all HSPs have had trauma according to websites on HSP, our quiz takers obviously did (coming out of a PLR), so it was hard to differentiate if they were HSPs *before* the trauma.

So, while survivors are likely empaths because of elevated agreeableness/cooperation, and while they may test as HSPs, especially following trauma, working with them as empaths or for HSP sensitivity is bypassing the *rest* of their personality elevations and missing other facets that work in tandem with their personality system that places them at risk in future relationships.[34]

Wrapping This All Up

Sadly, lots of nonidentification, misidentification, and disidentification has negatively impacted the survivor's recovery. In defense of my field, until our research there was no information about personality trait elevations in PLRs from which to correctly identify a survivor's Super Traits outside of codependency, empaths, or HSPs, and then correct the therapeutic approach accordingly. Survivors have had to endure not only labels they instinctively knew were incorrect but the pain of not getting appropriate treatment because of identification issues. The most disturbing part is that the prevention they needed to ward off more PLRs was not occurring when the use of pop-psychology nontheories led survivors down a path that will never lead to recovery.

On a positive note—that was then, and this is now. Now is a promising time because there is a new view, a new understanding, a new model for working toward recovery. Specialized education, trauma-informed approaches, and trait-specific techniques exist and are being expanded upon continually as we learn more. The field is ripe for more research on Super Traits and how elevated traits impact relational dynamics, aftermath symptoms, recovery, and future risk.

While this research and knowledge is relatively new, which means not many therapists have been trained in this knowledge and in our approach, *The Institute* is working to change that. Survivors can grab hold of hope because *The Institute* is working on the following for survivors:

- To add additional depth to pathology-informed educational practices, understanding the relational dynamics, trauma-informed aftermath symptom management techniques, and Super Trait specific education, *The Institute* offers an affordable year-long online course, *The Living Recovery Program*™™, to reach as many people as possible and to assist survivors in self-help measures that work for their *specific* trauma and personalities. Survivors can utilize self-help measures or add this for additional support while getting other services from trained therapists or *The Institute*.
- *The Institute* continues to offer a wide variety of psycho-educational products for Pathological Love Relationships recovery through the website.
- *The Institute* continues to offer trained mental health professionals our Model of Care approach for survivor partner treatment. By 2019, the program will be offered online through our university-type platform so that we can reach more therapists.
- *The Institute* has spearheaded the first national association

for this unique counseling genre for mental health professionals in a field-specific approach, utilizing a specialized relational theory, and a collaboratively created approach for treatment from some of the best clinicians and theorists in the field. The new *Association for NPD/Psychopathy Survivor Treatment, Research & Education,* will lead this emerging field in treatment approaches and continued research and can be found at www.survivortreatment.com.

- Soon we will be adding a similar educational training program for survivor bloggers, offering corrective field-specific knowledge based on a recognized theory and recovery approach that will bring cohesion to the information on the Internet.

- Through the association we will continue to support research on Super Traits and PLR theory development and enhance our Model of Care Approach for the mental health field.

The dawn is breaking in the field and this new genre of counseling psychology and understanding. This should provide hope to survivors that the misidentification, nonidentification, and disidentification they have lived with will soon be replaced with real knowledge and research. Gone will be guessing and pop-psychology approaches that don't work—they will be replaced with a sound understanding that we hope will permeate all recovery approaches, from survivor bloggers to therapists.

Chapter Fourteen Endnotes

1-3, 6-10, 12-21, 25, 26 28, 34 Brown, Sandra L., and Young, Jennifer R., *The Institute* (2016). Misidentification of Super Traits in Pathological Love Relationships—Stop Calling it Codependency. Prepared for *Women Who Love Psychopaths. Third Edition*; and *The Institute's Therapist Training Program and Manual: Treating the Aftermath of Pathological Love Relationships.*

4   What is Codependency http://www.norcalcoda.org/am-i-codependent/

5   Beattie, Melody (1987). *Codependent No More*: *How to Stop Controlling Others and Start Caring for Yourself.* Harper Collins Publisher.

11, 23, 24, 32 Brown, Sandra L. and Young, Jennifer R., *The Institute* and Purdue University (2014). Outcomes of Research: Personality descriptors of women who have been in relationships with antagonistic men with borderline, narcissistic, antisocial, and psychopathic disorders. Raw data from a 600-person research.

22 Brown, Sandra L., *The Institute* (2007). Cognitive dissonance perceived as traumatic in Pathological Love Relationships. Raw data from a study; also, in *Women Who Love Psychopaths: Inside the Relationships of Inevitable Harm with Narcissists, Sociopaths & Psychopaths. Second Edition* (2009). Mask Publishing.

27 Porter, D. (2018). Dependent Personality Disorder https://www.theravive.com/therapedia/dependent-personality-disorder-dsm--5-301.6-(f60.7)

29   Borderline Personality Disorder. (2018) https://www.nimh.nih.gov/health/topics/borderline-personality-disorder/index.shtml

30   INFJ Personality "The Advocate". (2011-2018). https://www.16personalities.com/infj-personality

31   Orloff, J. (2018). How to Know If You are an Empath. https://drjudithorloff.com/how-to-know-if-youre-an-empath/

https://drjudithorloff.com/quizzes/empath-self-assessment-test/

33   HSP Surveys. (2018) Retrieved from The Highly Sensitive Person: http://hsperson.com/test/highly-sensitive-test/

Section Four

Puzzle Piece #4™
Extreme Aftermath Symptoms

Figure 15.1
Puzzle Piece #4™

Chapter Fifteen

Aftermath and Trauma Puzzle Piece #4™

Puzzle Piece #4™—Extreme Aftermath Symptoms—is the fourth element of the Pathological Love Relationship Puzzle. Together, the four puzzle pieces comprise a Pathological Love Relationship. And now, as we look at this last identifier, we will be discovering why a personality-disordered partner + a dramatic and erratic relationship + a survivor partner with misidentified Super Traits ends up with Extreme Aftermath Symptoms.

Quick Survivor Review

- Super Traited persons are often non-, mis-, and dis-identified
- The Super Trait identification problems often are misattributed to labels of codependency or other forms of generalized dysfunction
- Super Trait identification problems are often misattributed to diagnoses of Dependent Personality Disorder and/or Borderline Personality Disorder
- Super Traits are often assumed to be Empaths or Highly Sensitive Persons

---

Aftermath

noun

Something that results or follows from an event, especially one of a disastrous or unfortunate nature; a consequence

---

The disastrous consequence of a PLR is the set of consistent traumatic symptoms seen in survivors. Relationships that are merely bad or dysfunctional are differentiated from PLRs by their lack of the qualifying experiences outlined in Puzzle Pieces #1-4™ which include the conse-quences of the relationship, or the traumatic aftermath covered in Puzzle Piece #4™. These symptoms are noteworthy because all relationships and their breakups don't produce aftermath symptoms. Normal break-ups, although painful, don't leave victims curled up in fetal positions and on disability—but relationships with Darkness do.

The aftermath, from which survivors are desperately seeking recov-ery, is what this book is about for all the reasons listed in the Preface and Introduction of the book. Earlier chapters have addressed why survivors' experiences have had identification problems including, just as important-ly, the identification problems of their trauma. While that would seem to be a relatively easy, cut-and-dried diagnosis for a therapist, it isn't always.

The counseling center I managed many years ago was a dual-focused treatment center, mainly serving people with personality disorders who also had trauma, until we began working exclusively with survivor part-ners. While my binary training in psychopathology and trauma was ex-tensive, it still didn't prepare me for the type and amount of trauma that I would need to address while working with the survivors.

Frankly, that surprised me because some of our personality-disordered clients had suffered some catastrophic trauma. The worst of the worst trauma was Dissociative Identity Disorder (DID), formerly called Multi-ple Personality Disorder (made famous by classic movies such as *The Three Faces of Eve*), depicting the mind-splitting aspects of the disorder. Work-ing with DID patients who had personality disorders, horrendous early childhood trauma, and other internal personalities for which they had no conscious knowledge, required that I undergo years of clinical supervision and specialized case consulting to adequately treat these clients' trauma. Having to deal with their hard-wired personality disorder issues *and* se-vere trauma required specialization in two fields. My ongoing training in trauma treatment was key to treating the most extreme responses of Com-plex Post Traumatic Stress Disorder (C-PTSD) and DID. Little did I know then that my background in treating extreme trauma would prove to be extremely useful later while treating survivor partners.

Thank goodness I had that background. Exposure to someone else's psychopathology produces trauma in various forms in almost everyone, from DID patients, who were horrifically abused as children, to survivors of PLRs and the effects on them from their partner's psychopathology. My experience in trauma treatment helped me to understand the survivor's trauma in unique ways which would have otherwise been easy to misinterpret. It has also been misinterpreted by others trying to treat them or family trying to understand what happened to them.

What has given me extreme concern is that PLR survivors have intense trauma symptoms without much understanding of it themselves, or by the clinical community. In our experience, 90% of survivors have *some* form of trauma-like symptoms and 50-75% of them have full blown PTSD or C-PTSD. Survivors cannot heal if they are not getting treated for the trauma they have. Many survivors do not even realize they have trauma except to the extent that their aftermath symptoms are not getting better and they aren't even sure what the term 'aftermath' means. To date, their choices have largely been to make do with a website here and another survivor's tell-all book there, without much real understanding of their unique trauma or how to get well other than to simply "go no contact." To understand the unique aspects of trauma in a PLR, let's start by understanding trauma in general and then see how PLR trauma is both similar and, at the same time, different.

*I*s It 'Aftermath' or is it Trauma?

'Aftermath' is a term that has become chiefly used when discussing the particularly distressing symptoms of survivors from PLRs. Since much of what is written about the aftermath is written by survivors themselves, these symptoms can be defined in ways that are broad and wide-reaching. They can be common symptoms not much different than those imposed by bad or dysfunctional relationships, or aftermath symptoms can be very specific to trauma symptoms but never noted as such. Survivors can have a hard time defining just what the lexicon word of 'aftermath' means when it has been wrongly conceptualized as 'any symptom I have after a PLR.'

Because "the aftermath" has been largely defined by survivor bloggers, many survivors seem unsure exactly what this bundle of symptoms is related to, which is unfortunate because, to recite *The Institute's* catch-phrase, "You can't heal from what you don't identify." So, let's be clear—aftermath symptoms have their roots in traumatic reactions.[1] In fact, many aftermath symptoms are really *trauma* symptoms that are often unidentified, and are sometimes described using the same terminology as is used for PTSD—and sometimes not, if being described by other survivors. Whether they carry the exact terminology or not, however, many of the *symptoms* are indicative of trauma reactions.

Survivor partners can have symptoms ranging from mild trauma reactions to severe Post Traumatic Stress Disorder (PTSD) and Complex Post Traumatic Stress Disorder (C-PTSD). In our experience, we have found that 90% of survivor partners will have some form of trauma-like symptoms including, but not limited to, PTSD and C-PTSD.[2] This *aftermath*, experienced by most survivors, is a significant trauma disorder, and is one in need of treatment from clinical providers.

Unfortunately, many survivors' trauma is assumed to be not trauma at all—or somehow less impactful, as many services for these survivors are being provided by other survivors as 'coaches' who are not trained in Trauma Informed Care. This indicates to *The Institute* that survivors' trauma is likely not identified as such, or is viewed somehow as less impactful than, say, a war vet's PTSD, since coaches are not trained in Trauma Informed Care but think the survivors' trauma is within their helpful reach. If the aftermath were truly noted as the likely trauma that it is, the survivor would be sent to a trauma therapist. Vets with PTSD aren't sent to coaches, they are sent to trauma therapists because their symptoms are recognized as trauma. This means much of what is really a survivor's trauma is still being colloquialized behind the term 'aftermath.'

What Constitutes Trauma?

Over the last 25 years, trauma disorders have become a specialization practice. Trauma can be produced by a variety of situations, such as -

- Early childhood adversity—child physical and sexual abuse, resulting in residual trauma, or adult traumas like domestic violence and sexual assault.
- Mass tragedies such as 9/11, or school shootings, or serious accidents—car accidents or plane crashes.
- Unthinkable tragedies—the murder of a loved one, the disappearance of one's child, or a child with a terminal illness.

Trauma Timeframes

Types of trauma are measured by the length of time the person has experienced symptoms -

- Symptoms that last only a few days constitute a Traumatic Reaction.
- Symptoms that last up to a month indicate an Acute Stress Disorder. These are the same symptoms as PTSD, but they resolve faster, so the disorder does not develop into the stages of PTSD.
- Symptoms that last longer than one to three months indicate PTSD.
- Symptoms that last longer than that and have been associated with long-term traumas (like years in a domestic violence situation, a concentration camp, a sex trafficking ring, or a PLR) may indicate Complex PTSD, which is a more chronic form of PTSD and requires longer treatment.

$\mathcal{D}$iagnosing PTSD

Survivor Note:

To be formally diagnosed with PTSD, one must be assessed by a mental health professional. This information is for educational purposes only. If you think you may have PTSD, consult a mental health professional.

Survivors may fill out the following work pages and follow up with a mental health professional for more information about their trauma symptoms. The symptoms on the work sheet below are what a professional would be considering, to determine if PTSD existed or would use similar criteria for another type of trauma disorder if your symptoms did not appear to match PTSD.

To be diagnosed with PTSD[3], an adult must have **all** of the following symptoms, and they must have lasted for at least one month:

- At least one re-experiencing symptom
- At least one avoidance symptom
- At least two arousal and reactivity symptoms

- At least two cognition and mood symptoms

Re-experiencing Symptoms Include:

- Flashbacks—reliving the trauma over and over, with the presence of physical symptoms like a racing heart or sweating
- Nightmares of the event
- Frightening thoughts about the event

Re-experiencing symptoms may cause problems in a person's everyday routine. The symptoms can start from the person's own thoughts and feelings; words, objects, or situations that are reminders of the event can also trigger re-experiencing symptoms.

Survivor Work Page Question:
I had _____ number of re-experiencing symptoms.

Avoidance Symptoms Include:

- Staying away from places, events, or objects that are reminders of the traumatic experience
- Avoiding thoughts or feelings related to the traumatic event

Things that remind a person of the traumatic event can trigger avoidance symptoms. These symptoms may cause a person to change his or her personal routine. For example, after a bad car accident, a person who usually drove before the accident may avoid driving or riding in a car after the accident.

Survivor Work Page Question:
I had _____ number of avoidance symptoms.

Arousal and Reactivity Symptoms Include:

- Being easily startled
- Feeling tense or on edge
- Having difficulty sleeping
- Having angry outbursts

Arousal symptoms (often called hyper-vigilance) are usually constant instead of being triggered only by things that remind them of the traumatic event. These consistent symptoms can make the person feel stressed and angry. This may make it hard to go about daily activities such as sleeping, eating, or concentrating.

Survivor Work Page Question:
I had _____ number of arousal and reactivity symptoms.

Cognition and Mood Symptoms Include:

- Trouble remembering key features of the traumatic event
- Negative thoughts about oneself or the world
- Distorted feelings like guilt or blame
- Loss of interest in enjoyable activities

Survivor Work Page Questions:
I had _____ number of cognition and mood symptoms.
Did you potentially meet the criteria for PTSD? _____

From this list, we can see that most survivors will have experienced at a minimum some *traumatic reactions* even if they did not have enough symptoms as outlined above to be assigned a diagnosis of PTSD. But over half to three quarters of survivors will have more than just a traumatic reaction.

$\mathcal{T}$he Traumatic Stress Continuum

Most survivors will have had symptoms consistent with *some* form of trauma. A few traumatic reactions that dissipate in a few days would be considered a lesser traumatic reaction. Multiple traumatic reactions that do not dissipate would be on the higher end of PTSD or C-PTSD. Because the length of time that someone has trauma symptoms can vary, the effects are evaluated on a continuum from low to high.

Low End ➡ High End

TraumaticReactions → Acute Stress Disorder → PTSD → CPTSD → DID

Figure 15.2
Traumatic Stress Continuum

Most survivors seek education or support when their reactions and symptoms have not dissipated; these then begin developing into chronic forms of stress-related disorders which need to be addressed by a professional who is skilled in trauma-informed care.

$\mathcal{W}$hy Trauma Is Non-, Mis-, and Dis-Identified

What is universally frustrating to survivors is not being able to figure out what is wrong with them so that they can heal. Darkness' pathology has likely been hidden, the dramatic and erratic relationship dynamics not recognized for their psyche-destroying powers, her Super Traits assumed to be some form of dependency/codependency, and now, her trauma will face some challenges, too, in being properly diagnosed. Some of the problems of her trauma identification stem from how her trauma looks to counselors, how the DSM identifies trauma, and some of it from how she describes her experiences and symptoms. Let's sort this out so survivors can understand why their trauma symptoms have identification problems and how to be a better advocate for themselves and their symptoms.

Survivor Created Non- and Mis-identification—The Lexicon of the PLR Community

By far the biggest problem is that survivors often don't know they have a trauma disorder, so they don't seek counseling with the right kind of therapist—a trauma therapist—or they don't seek counseling at all.

While the word 'aftermath' is a specific term that is now unique to PLRs, this isn't the only term that seems to have stuck—an entire language for events, relationship processes, actions, and symptoms related to PLRs has been developed. It's not an especially helpful language other than its community-bonding aspects—being based in a current, catchy and vague vernacular that, for good or ill, has become a common language for survivors and which has manifested into a community lexicon used to discuss and explain PLRs, as we have done in this book.

While it is helpful to survivors to feel that they have found a community experience specific to their experience with a PLR, the way in which this community sometimes treats all aspects of a PLR as a collectively 'normalized' experience may mislead some survivors into overlooking their *specific* traumatic reactions which are not merely part of a normalized experience in the PLR community.

Survivor Note:

If survivors had known they were having trauma reactions and not merely a shared normalized experience, they might have sought qualified help for a true trauma disorder.

Many survivors have full-blown PTSD which they misidentify as a normal reaction to a PLR (which it is), while missing that it is *also* a trauma reaction. Survivors have spent years in online venues believing their participation in social media groups and their growing understanding of these symptoms, that are common to everyone else in the group, were bringing them closer to recovery, all the while not recognizing these shared 'normal-for-them' experiences indicated true trauma that needed treatment.

If survivors don't recognize their symptoms as a trauma disorder, they are not likely to seek trauma treatment. After perhaps years on social media or in online support groups, their symptoms are still present and relatively untreated, and quite possibly worse than ever before. Trauma can worsen with time and from the lack of treatment, which is why some of the survivors we have treated after years on social media PLR-oriented groups have heightened symptoms both from the length of time with untreated trauma and from some unique aspects of worsening trauma that often occurs in online non-trauma informed care group participation, which we will discuss.

Survivors who eventually figured out that their symptoms are, in fact, trauma reactions, are faced with problems in having that trauma recognized by those from whom they seek help. Here's why…

Therapist Translation Problems

If a survivor is fortunate enough to ascertain that words such as 'trig-

311

gering' mean more than an experience normalized by her online community and may, instead, be trauma, she is met with more problems her community lexicon will bring to the *therapist*. Instead of the survivor describing her symptoms in a traditional way, therapists are met with the private language of PLRs that does not always match their understanding or experience of trauma symptoms or even relationship dynamics. A list of the words often used by the survivor to describe the experiences in a PLR to a therapist are -

- Luring
- Pipeline (multiple relationships simultaneously)
- Baiting
- Triangulation (crazy-making)
- Fauxpology or 'non-apology' apology (a false apology)
- Flying monkeys (accomplices of the pathological partner who help hide his actual life, and/or inflict additional harm)
- Gaslighting
- Grooming (isolating to control)
- Ghosting (ending the relationship by disappearing)
- Getting hoovered (getting sucked back into the relationship through false promises of change)
- Love bombing
- Masking (covering motivations by mirroring and parroting)
- Mirroring
- Narc speak (pathological communication style)
- Parroting
- Event cycle
- Projection
- Proxy recruitment (use of accomplices to harm the survivor)
- Scapegoating
- Supply (ego gratification from exploiting others)
- Target (partner)
- Trauma bonding
- Vetting (process of bonding followed by searching for next target)
- Word salad (the communication manipulation used)
- Devalue & Discard or D&D (devaluing the survivor so the

pathological can break up without closure, then discarding her like yesterday's garbage)

PLRs, as a fairly new genre of counseling, means that therapists are still learning about the relational dynamics, trauma, and needed treatment. The unique lexicon of PLRs often interferes with the understanding by therapists of the trauma or relationships when survivors have difficulty identifying their experience outside of PLR-speak that has become so second nature in PLR groups.

Unrecognized trauma in survivors is associated with not only the 'clubby' language used in describing the relationship, but by other factors within the psychology field that allow survivors to fly under the radar and not be identified as trauma survivors. So, while the therapist is likely to be confused by the terms in the PLR lexicon, the therapist heads to the DSM to see if the survivor's symptoms match the DSM for trauma and finds more confusion.

Psychology Field Identification Problems

The psychology field contributes to the problem of survivors flying under the radar of diagnosis. It begins with how the DSM defines what trauma *is* and *what must be present in the experience to diagnose it*. Survivors are often the educators of therapists not trained in PLRs and need to advocate for their own symptoms.

An explanation of why an accurate diagnosis doesn't often happen follows...

Trauma is Created by Abnormal Life Events

We at *The Institute* believe that there is more to trauma than physical harm, witnessing violence, or death. We believe that trauma results from events outside of our normal experiences. That means someone must recognize that the survivor's experience was, indeed, outside of one's *everyday experiences* and therefore could be perceived by the victim as traumatic. Survivors themselves may have learned to normalize Darkness' pathology and may or may not yet be able to verbalize these 'outside of normal' experiences. Unless survivor partners had previous PLRs or pathological family members, they may not even know their intimate experiences with Darkness' pathology are indeed *outside the normal ex-*

periences of most people. A relationship with a dangerous psychopath is an abnormal life event but the survivor might be more cognizant of her symptoms than the abnormality of what she lived through.

Therapists too must *also* recognize the survivor's experience as outside normal experiences and not merely a dysfunctional relationship from which to begin looking deeper for the trauma that could occur as the abnormal event that the PLR was. It is, after all, not every day someone is exposed to a partner without a conscience. However, while we at *The Institute* believe that trauma is created by abnormal life events, the DSM to which the therapist will refer, defines *which* life events create trauma. A therapist using the DSM will not see a PLR listed as one of those events. *This is the first hurdle that both survivor and therapist must jump through in moving toward an accurate diagnosis.*

Trauma is Created from Extreme Fear and Powerlessness

At *The Institute* we believe these abnormal experiences will also produce *fear and powerlessness* which can cause trauma. As we have shown in prior chapters, the unknown and not previously experienced PLR dynamics, can, and do, instill fear and powerlessness, especially when one has realized that the biological makeup of Darkness tends towards violence, even if he may not have been violent *yet*.

While therapists are adept at looking for fear and powerlessness in relationships, it is often connected to acts of violence or dominance and not that of covert psychological subterfuge, coercion, and gaslighting that is often well-hidden under the survivors' not yet detected symptom of cognitive dissonance. Survivors whose relationships were more the subterfuge of gaslighting than violence might have more problems with therapists imaging fear and powerlessness created from subterfuge. Cognitive dissonance that often causes survivors to detail the intrusive thoughts of the *positive* experiences can throw a curve ball to a therapist looking for fear and powerlessness in *violence*.[4] *This is the next hurdle that a survivor's therapist must clear to see the trauma that is often hidden.*

Trauma is Only Recognized as Coming from Certain Types of Experiences

While the survivor may have had events outside of normal experiences, she may also be feeling fearfulness and powerlessness that is camouflaged under cognitive dissonance. The DSM distinguishes for the therapist what *types* of experiences are expected to produce PTSD, which include exposure to -

- Death
- Threatened death
- Threatened serious injury
- Actual or threatened sexual violence

Well, well…isn't *that* convenient for the subterfuge used by Darkness? Look at that wide swath of missed PLR experiences you could drive a Mack truck through! Only death or threatened death, serious injuries and sexual violence made the cut from what would be considered severe *enough* to cause trauma. Any survivor of a PLR knows this is not the case.

While the PLR dynamics are indeed different from everyday experiences, and while they have produced fear and powerlessness, they may not be the *types* of experiences that make a therapist take note of possible PTSD if one of the four types of experiences are absent and their primary symptoms are created more from subterfuge than violence. *This is another diagnosing hurdle both survivor and therapist must clear.*

Psychological Abuse is not Recognized as Trauma

To make diagnosing matters harder, what is notably absent in criteria for PTSD is the aspect of psychological abuse, as opposed to only threatened or actual physical or sexual violence. Considering that the DSM Alternative Model of Personality Disorders (Chapter One) took great care to *include* relational deficits in empathy and interpersonal functioning that will likely *cause* psychological abuse to others (and for some, that abuse will result in PTSD), the criteria for PTSD is *silent* on psychological abuse as a type of experience that leads to PTSD.

This seems ridiculous considering that we know what a lack of empathy produces—a lack of conscience which is associated with sadistic behavior that includes psychological sadism. However, there is a wide range of Darkness' behaviors that fall more into the psychological terrorism category than the category of physical violence. This means that if the types of violence-oriented experiences listed above are not present, (which they aren't in psychological abuse), PTSD is not always diagnosed.

Just because the survivor's experience doesn't match the criteria in the DSM doesn't mean she wasn't *traumatized*. Survivors often have all the symptoms of PTSD without being given the diagnosis of it, which is unfortunate. PLRs produce symptoms in survivors *exactly like* traumatic reactions and PTSD because the experiences were *traumatic to* the survivor. A psyche does not fail to have a traumatic reaction simply because a particular situation is not defined in the DSM. Many survivors have all the symptoms of PTSD, stemming from psychological terrorism, whether PTSD was diagnosed or not.

As we can see, the factors of a survivor's

- unrecognized abnormal life event,
- fear and powerlessness camouflaged by cognitive dissonance,
- trauma that may not meet the type of violence criteria,
- and psychological abuse as an unrecognized factor in PTSD diagnosis,

leaves a wide swath for her to be unidentified as a trauma patient. Survivors who have a trauma disorder and are instead treated for a relationship problem, codependency, or merely boundary issues, remain an untreated trauma survivor.

There are other factors as well that can impact not getting properly diagnosed.

Survivors Diagnosing Their Partners

It may seem odd that we spent the first few chapters helping a survivor form a reasonable assumption about the disorder(s) their partner may have, only to tell them therapists hate for them to suggest Darkness' disorder. The reasons that have been highlighted throughout this book about why personality disorders are highly debated in the clinical community, and why survivors are often unidentified as having been in a PLR by the psychology field, captures some of this dilemma.

Survivors who quickly identify Darkness as a psychopath or narcissist early in the therapy process run the risk of therapists not seeing those symptoms of a personality disorder in Darkness at that time to agree with his symptoms, why the events she experienced are outside one's normal experiences, that there was fear and powerlessness even without

316

the dreaded violence or sexual harm, and that the survivor truly has trauma symptoms. Survivors who are too upfront with their knowledge, based on resources like blogs and social media, make a therapist think that the over-stretched and over-used catch all term of 'narcissism' or 'psychopath' is like the over-used word of codependency. The survivor can lose immediate credibility in not only describing her trauma symptoms but as a person insightful about her own history. The survivor's overuse of the PLR community lexicon in early treatment can make her seem very invested in this identity of herself that she has found online.

===

Survivor Note:

It is more effective for survivors to use the behavioral terms that match Darkness' personality disorders and the symptom terms that match her trauma to avoid diagnosing him or herself. It is likely in later sessions that therapists might flush out more questions that will lead to some assumptions about Darkness' possible disorders. Explaining the dichotomous nature of the relationship outside of the PLR lexicon language can help a therapist understand aberrant relationship dynamics. As some survivors may end up being the therapist's educator, pacing when one reveals these bits of information is required to prevent rejection of the material being introduced.

===

PLR Symptoms Can Look Different

Perhaps what is most problematic for survivors getting treated for their trauma is that the trauma from PLRs can have slightly different symptoms in what we call 'its presentation.' Sometimes survivors do have histories of being victims of violence that make therapists *consider* PTSD as a diagnosis. But when survivors begin to tell therapists what their symptoms are, especially related to cognitive dissonance, PTSD as a result of being a victim of violence no longer makes sense.[5] How a survivor describes the symptoms that are manifesting in their day to day lives and the problems they are having with the symptoms indicates, in a therapist's mind, something completely different than what was first thought to be the issue.

That's because PLRs result in a unique presentation of PTSD symptoms. I call them the 'fingerprint' or unusual 'markings' of 'PLR PTSD.' For example, a therapist looking for the PTSD re-experiencing symptom of horrible violent flashbacks might miss the unique fingerprint of a PLR which includes re-experiencing flashbacks of *positive* memories and perhaps even more frequently than negative memories, or fluctuating between the negative and the positive memories.[6] Not hearing survivors mention predominantly negative memories and hearing mostly positive memories can cause a therapist to miss the re-experiencing symptom and assume the problem lies elsewhere. The therapist may be accustomed to assault victims who have one clear view of their assailant as violent and clearly at fault, but the therapist is not familiar with addressing cognitive dissonance in a PLR survivor who may recall her experiences with feelings of both loving and loathing, and trust and distrust, created by state-dependent learning.[7] This is a very different presentation to the therapist unfamiliar with PLRs.

These unique fingerprints of PLR trauma make the survivor's presentation *atypical* in both storyline and symptoms.[8] While the similar features of trauma reactions may indeed be present, their *presentation* can be slightly different, or atypical. This is likely to throw a curve-ball to a therapist who's trying to determine if a survivor has PTSD. Let's see why.

Table 15.2

The Institute's **Typical and Atypical PTSD/PLR Reactions Chart**
The Institute © 2015

Typical PTSD Reactions	Atypical PTSD/PLR Reactions
Re-experiencing	
Flashbacks of the *traumatic* event.	Flashbacks of the *positive events* which cause pain and longing in the remembering.
Trauma replay which, like flashbacks, replays themes (even if not the exact same event) of *helplessness, fear, horror.*	Trauma replay which, like flashbacks, replays themes of the early relationship of love-bombing or *positive* experiences.
Constant ruminating about the *negative* events.	Constant ruminating about the *positive* events or feelings, as well as negative thoughts or events, often explained in the same memory.

Typical PTSD Reactions	Atypical PTSD/PLR Reactions
Nightmares of the *negative* events.	Nightmares of the events; however, they are often of the *positive* memories which are experienced by her as intrusive and nightmares but are considered by the therapist as only dreams and not nightmares.
Avoidance	
Avoiding people, places, and things that remind them of the *negative* events.	Avoiding people, places, and things that remind them of both *negative and positive* events to avoid more cognitive dissonance symptoms.
Avoidance of *discussing* the events.	Validation-seeking through *chronic story telling* as a symptom of trauma replay and a symptom of cognitive dissonance.
Cognition and Mood	
Difficulty remembering key *negative* events.	Strongly held *positive* memories planted by state-dependent learning and trance.
Troubling thoughts of the *traumatic* event.	Thoughts of both *good* **and** *bad* events.
Difficulty remembering key events of the *traumatic* event.	Difficulty remembering a traumatic event while state-dependent learning has resulted in intensely remembering *good* events.
Negative thoughts about oneself or the world.	Negative thoughts about oneself or the world, not only generated from trauma (if applicable) *but also generated by cognitive dissonance* which is counseled differently.
Distorted feelings of guilt or blame.	*Distorted* feelings *generated from* cognitive dissonance.
Loss of interest in enjoyable activities *caused by depression.*	Loss of interest *caused by trying to avoid cognitive dissonance.*

The atypical symptoms in this list *are* traumatic reactions—they're simply not typical in their presentation as traditional PTSD symptoms. Survivors find the symptoms on the right side of the list to be *just as* or even *more* traumatic than traditional PTSD symptoms. But as we can see, the symptoms listed on the right are not always produced by violence or what the clinical community would consider traumatic experiences. They are primarily reactions produced by cognitive dissonance—having two simultaneous experiences and relationships with Darkness.

While this list looks merely at the atypical PTSD symptoms, there are *more* aftermath symptoms that are unique to PLRs.

*T*raumatic, But Not from Trauma

In the list above, you see that many of the symptoms of PTSD in the left column are generated out of trauma. But the similar, yet different, symptoms of trauma in a PLR, are generated out of *not just* the traumatic experience but by a unique and quirky symptom seen universally in all PLRs— *cognitive dissonance*—which is an additional component of PLR trauma.[9]

In fact, cognitive dissonance is so universal it is the hallmark symptom in all PLRs. If a survivor does not have cognitive dissonance, they were probably not in a true PLR. In 30 years, I haven't seen a PLR survivor who did **not** have it, which is what made me take note and study this aspect in depth.

So, it seems odd to say that there is a symptom like cognitive dissonance that is *traumatic* to a survivor but not necessarily created by recognized events that are known to create trauma. Much like the loophole in the DSM about unrecognized psychological abuse and how survivors can exhibit PTSD symptoms from psychological trauma, even if the DSM does not recognize it as traumatic to the patient, so can cognitive dissonance be traumatic to a survivor even when the DSM does not recognize it.[10] Over the years of our research studies, cognitive dissonance has remained as the number one symptom listed by survivors as *traumatic to them.*

Cognitive dissonance, which will be explained in more detail in the next chapter, is a typical symptom in all PLRs, and is produced by exposure to -

- someone else's pathology
- the low-conscience of Darkness and his related gaslighting behavior
- his Jekyll/Hyde personality
- the impact from the crazy-making communication
- knowledge of other people in the pipeline
- the after effects of The Event Cycle
- the survivor's necessity of simultaneously experiencing

two differing personalities in the same person (e.g., Jekyll
and Hyde)

This consistent exposure to someone else's pathology and the simultaneous relationships with both sides of Darkness produce the symptoms
of cognitive dissonance in all survivors and is produced regardless of
whether violence existed in the relationship. The therapist who may miss
a survivor's PTSD because, either her abuse was psychological terrorism,
violence did not exist and so it is not recognized as a form of PTSD, and/or
her symptoms of PTSD are atypical in their presentation, is the same therapist who may also not recognize a trauma-like symptom that is not created from traditional trauma but rather is created by cognitive dissonance.

The right side of the previous list showed all the ways that PLRs present differently from PTSD. The consistent symptom of the trauma-like
reaction on the right side of the column is cognitive dissonance which
produces conflicting feelings and thoughts associated with both sides
of Darkness' Jekyll and Hyde personality. While a survivor may or may
not have all the negative symptoms found in traditional PTSD, she does
have the atypical reactions of conflicting positive feelings and memories creating the inconsistency in her thinking, feelings, and behavior—a
symptom of cognitive dissonance.

This explains why survivors have such unrelenting aftermath. It is bad
enough for someone to have one form of PTSD in which she must deal
with the barrage of negative flashbacks, thoughts, nightmares, avoidance, and feelings. It is another thing to be tortured with *two* versions
of this type of traumatic reaction, reliving both good and bad memories
and feelings simultaneously.[11]

The survivor's second set of atypical PTSD symptoms is not created from traditional traumatic exposure to life-threatening events. It is
created from the memory of love-bombing and the early relationship
dynamics and those emotions and memories imprinted from state dependent learning, making the positive memories predominant when she
is re-experiencing them.[12]

A therapist who has never experienced treating a PLR would not
only fail to recognize the atypical PTSD symptoms, but also would be
hard pressed to understand why a survivor is tortured even *more* from
these positive memories than the bad ones.

In normal breakups, positive memories are remembered fondly, but in PLRs, the intrusiveness of the memories is *as* traumatic as the negative memories. Survivors find that the most distressing part of their symptoms is, by far, not the negative memories of overt violence (if it existed), but the barrage of positive memories which blocks their ability to hold on to negative events as a way of distancing from the relationship. Having to process negative and positive memories simultaneously, which overloads the mind with not one, but two traumatic experiences, causes survivors to beg for relief from the positive memories and the resulting craving for the relationship. While the positive memories wouldn't seem to be a part of traumatic memories, they are in fact, *very* traumatic to survivors.

In all my years of doing this work, I have not found one survivor who didn't have cognitive dissonance. It is not only the most severe reaction and most problematic to them, it is also the most consistent symptom, the most time-consuming trauma symptom to treat, and the most misidentified by therapists.

Other Trauma Symptoms

If a survivor or therapist does not realize that a trauma disorder exists, they may also miss other trauma-related symptoms — physical, sexual, spiritual reactions and self-perceptual injuries. Most survivors have stress-related physical health problems ranging from fatigue to startling amounts of autoimmune disorders. Some have the physical symptoms of PTSD such as an elevated startle reflex, while others have the accumulated stress reactions of other medical disorders, or both.

Sexual symptoms can mimic addiction-like symptoms, producing an 'acting out' sexual behavior not aligned with a survivor's high-normal conscientious behavior.[13]

Spiritual symptoms are often devastating, producing a loss of connection with one's Higher Power, along with feelings of meaninglessness and hopelessness that severely impact a survivor's recovery.

Self-Perceptual Injuries©, which are the most disorienting of all, are 'not knowing oneself as they used to be' — a radical change in how survivors perceive their emotions, beliefs, values, behavior, and former stability with a fear that, even if the trauma is healed, their core identities as strong people are gone. Survivors describe it as 'soul trauma.' Self-perceptual injuries are a result of cognitive dissonance and are a consistent symptom in PLR PTSD.[14] One survivor stated, "Cognitive dissonance IS my trauma—it is so disorienting, bouncing from bad to good memories, that I no longer recognize myself or my mind."

PTSD victims from non-PLRs may also have some of these symptoms—it is not unusual for crime victims with PTSD, for instance, to have physical, sexual or spiritual symptoms. However, if a PLR survivor is not identified as having PTSD/traumatic reactions, the symptoms of physical, sexual, spiritual, and self-perceptual impact are likely to be missed. Why would therapists look any further if they have already determined their clients don't meet PTSD criteria?

Hidden Re-experiencing in PLRs

Our exploration and documentation over the years about why PTSD appears differently in survivors of PLRs, often interfering with a trauma diagnosis, would not be complete without discussing the odd and seemingly irrational behavior associated with it. Typical of traditional PTSD is the symptom of re-experiencing that causes flashbacks and nightmares.

But flashbacks in PLRs include -[15]

- Reliving the positive events, including symptoms of craving the relationship, experiencing a deep desire to reunite, or sexual arousal.
- Positive flashbacks occur more frequently than negative, or when negative flashbacks occur, positive flashbacks occur simultaneously.
- Dreams of the honeymoon or love-bombing phase causing them to be perceived as dreams, and not the nightmares that they are which produce distress.
- Unwanted thoughts of the endearing, charismatic, or even wounded side of Darkness.

Re-experiencing happens in both traditional and PLR-related PTSD. The thing all survivors want most is to stop thinking about both the negative and positive events, yet the brain keeps playing them in a never-ending video loop.

Atypical re-experiencing is often missed by therapists because a PLR in a sense involves two relationships—one with Jekyll and one with

Hyde. The re-experiencing, then, involves both good AND bad memories, revealing a "persistent cognitive dissonance" and reaffirming that the trauma is still there. Therapists who only recognize the flashbacks of the bad memories don't pick up on what we call 'positive memory intrusion,' which is the re-experiencing of positive memories. Instead these memories are assumed by therapists to be related to codependency or dependency, or that the survivor is in denial about the badness of Darkness. The therapist can easily miss the intrusive and unwanted nature of these positive thoughts and memories.

Re-experiencing is just that—the survivor is still suffering from cognitive dissonance and is replaying or re-experiencing confusing positive memories. This continual replaying of these memories creates even more trauma, while simultaneously strengthening the rumination loop in the neuro-pathways of the brain. No one wants this.

The Harm of Re-experiencing

Survivors don't understand the hidden ways in which re-experiencing surfaces, and how they unknowingly—and often with help from therapists, bloggers, or coaches—have been making this symptom, and the accompanying brain circuitry problem, much, much worse. (Exactly what has happened to her brain from the PLR will be covered in another chapter.)

Traumatic replay and/or re-experiencing is the continual regurgitation of a traumatic part of a memory—again and again. Because of cognitive dissonance, *both* good and bad memories are replayed as the survivor struggles to answer the question, "Is he good or is he bad?"

In PLR-related PTSD, re-experiencing includes a compulsive need to talk about, figure out, understand, explain, or get support for the issues of a PLR.[16] These are symptoms of cognitive dissonance dysfunctionality. As a strongly driven internal need, it feels intuitive that the survivor *must* need to do this, or why else would she feel like this 50 times a day? She thinks maybe it is the natural course of the trauma trying to resolve itself.

Re-experiencing is the traumatized brain ruminating. Thoughts get stuck in the neuro-pathways that were created by the trauma, creating a sort of feedback loop in which the same memories follow along the neuro-pathways strengthening them. Over time, brain circuitry and the resulting brain chemistry change (which produce depression and anxiety) causes these brain changes to become the likely path a thought takes. It is why PTSD is referred to as 'autonomic,' because it becomes an automated process of thinking and responding.

There isn't a survivor alive who would knowingly create stronger and more debilitating re-experiencing symptoms. Their stated goal in treatment is always to *reduce* these symptoms and reclaim their sanity. They would never knowingly cooperate with their demanding brain to create *more* trauma and more symptoms—but that is, in fact, exactly what most survivors do.

Re-experiencing has a natural proclivity to worsen trauma and is in part how we know someone has trauma through this symptom. But survivors have likely contributed to the worsening of their symptoms, albeit unknowingly. That's because re-experiencing feels compulsively strong—almost as if it has a life of its own and continues to bombard the survivor with good and bad memories producing what feels like the need to talk about it, to process it, to explain it in its entirety to others, or to read bucket loads of books to understand it. The survivor feels that she is being pro-active in trying to reduce her trauma by not simply ignoring it and working with what is coming up.

Re-experiencing contributes to the over-active and exhausted 'brain on fire.' It is utterly counter-intuitive to survivors that the most effective way to cool the brain's ruminating is to NOT cooperate with it in re-experiencing unless she is in a trauma-reducing counseling session that uses trauma-reducing techniques. While survivors may not immediately be able to manage the flashbacks of good/bad memories, **it is the actions of constant reliving through talking and reading about it that produces a type of unhealthy cooperation with it and triggers the feedback-like loop for more ruminations**.

If someone had a friend who was sexually assaulted, and she began re-experiencing it, saying exactly what happened, detail for detail, again and again, most people would do something to pull her out of it—splash cold water in her face, bring her back to the here and now, tell her it wasn't happening now, and that she was having a debilitating flashback. She may want to compulsively tell the details of what he said, then what he did next, then what she said, then how she felt. She may tell the same thing over and over, or there might be some slight variations as she incorporated a new image—something she heard, thought, saw, or smelled. It's still the re-experiencing of a flashback and few friends would leave her in this trance-induced state of reliving the event without bringing her back to the present, safe, moment.

Unfortunately, people do this all the time with PLR survivors. They allow the survivor to go into page-long explanations on blogs, reliving details of the relationship in flashbacks. Many blogs encourage survivors to tell their story as often and as detailed as needed. Friends and family call the survivor daily to ask, "What did he do to you today?" leading her directly into re-experiencing and engraining more deeply the neuro-pathways she is trying to avoid. She spends hours a day reading blogs and books about *My Life with a Psychopath* that is not discouraged by her therapist—all the while re-experiencing her own trauma while reading someone else's that was just like hers. She may visit chat forums seeking validation of her experiences which is simply a form of cognitive dissonance that creates more re-experiencing.

These un-moderated and even encouraged acts of re-experiencing flashbacks are not Trauma-Informed Care. Survivors will not only *not* get better engaging in these activities, they will strengthen their re-experiencing and cause far worse debilitation.

While therapists may miss that the PLR re-experiencing is often nightmares/flashbacks about positive experiences, blogger "experts" don't understand that allowing people to tell their stories, seek validation, and talk about their partners' Jekyll and Hyde features are, in fact, cooperating in someone's re-experiencing. Few would say to a friend who had been sexually assaulted, "Tell me again, tell me more."

As trauma is better understood, treatment changes to reflect these new understandings. More recent approaches, including trauma treatment that is more forward-facing, attempts to manage the symptoms of re-experiencing by reducing how much, and specifically how, re-experiencing is dealt with. This includes well-managed reliving of the experiences conducted in short therapy sessions, which allow for the trauma to be processed without excessive monologues about the experience that old trauma treatment used to do in a 'cataloguing of the trauma' type fashion. The point being, we now know *better* ways of dealing with the persistent symptom of re-experiencing and for a survivor with *two* forms of re-experiencing, it is even more critical because she has twice the amount to manage.

Some survivors vehemently maintain that telling their story repeatedly is what healed them, yet they are in the same social media group four years later, still discussing every detail of their story. In most cases, trauma survivors should be free of re-experiencing in a far shorter amount of time. Survivors who count the strength of the compulsive need to keep telling their story as proof that it's what they need to heal are like alcoholics who feel compulsively driven to drink. The only difference is that alcoholics in recovery have learned that the strong compulsion is something *not* to be heeded.

Wrapping This All Up

It is more than unfortunate that survivors are not getting what they need to recover because what they have experienced has been non-identified, misidentified, or dis-identified. Survivors who believe they are finding "what happened to me" on survivor sites and books, or with unknowing therapists, are getting -

- A non-identified diagnosis of something *else* when they really have a trauma disorder.
- A misinterpreted lexicon of aftermath symptoms as a normalized community experience, when in fact the symptoms are really trauma reactions that could be better identified as such.
- Permission to flashback/re-experience all over a blog, social media, chat forum, or in a non-trauma reducing therapy session.

Mis-identification

Survivors whose atypical PTSD is non-identified and whose emotion, behavior, and brain functioning are off, are often assumed to have *other disorders*. When Super Traits are assumed to be related to codependency, when a person's moods are unregulated and swing wildly, when behavior seems erratic, and when the self-concept is beaten down, a person may appear to be suffering from Borderline Personality Disorder, or the highs and lows of Bipolar Disorder. Normally high-functioning teachers, city transportation directors, and air traffic controllers who have not had mental health problems *prior* to the PLR have been mis-diagnosed as BPD or Bipolar. They are put on medications and into programs for conditions they don't have, all because the atypical presentation of trauma (and Super Traits) was mis-identified.

Dis-identification

Dis-identification of PLR-related trauma hides the identity and characteristics of a *formerly* high functioning individual who is having a *situational,* and totally normal, reaction to pathology. The historical view of who the survivor was *before* the PLR is disregarded in favor of the current symptoms in the aftermath. Instead of the view of a *situational* crisis with traumatic reactions, a therapist will make clinical assumptions based on the presentation of the survivor's identity and characteristics.

Dis-identified Symptoms of PLRs and Super Traits©

- Super Traits look like dependency/codependency.
- Mood problems that are associated with the anxiety and agitation of trauma look like Borderline Personality Disorder and Bipolar Disorder.
- Rumination can look like Borderline Personality Disorder or Bipolar Disorder.
- Cognitive dissonance can look like Borderline Personality Disorder or Bipolar Disorder.
- The erratic behavior of trying to get Darkness back, surveillance behavior, or relational craving looks like Borderline Personality Disorder.
- The poor view of self can look like various personality disorders.

Unfortunate? Yes. But I think the survivor partner would call it more than unfortunate. This dis-identification has, after all, robbed her of the very thing she has been seeking—her healing.

Survivor Work Page Questions:

Because of the PLR I have been diagnosed with:_____

_____.

___ Yes, I think this diagnosis is accurate.

___ No, I don't think it is accurate.

While it is clear that survivor partners have had, at a minimum, traumatic reactions, and at a maximum, some form of PTSD, the hallmark of PLRs is a debilitating symptom that is rarely treated. Let's examine why that could be.

Chapter Fifteen Endnotes

1, 2   Brown, Sandra L., The Institute (2007). Aftermath as Trauma in Pathological Love Relationships: Applying the Real Diagnosis. Agency raw data. Also prepared for The Institute's Therapist Training Program and Manual: Treating the Aftermath of Pathological Love Relationships.

3   Post-Traumatic Stress Disorder. https://www.nimh.nih.gov/health/topics/post-traumatic-stress-disorder-ptsd/index.shtml

4, 7, 9, 10, 11   Brown, Sandra L., The Institute (2007). Cognitive dissonance perceived as traumatic in Pathological Love Relationships. Raw data from a study; also in Women Who Love Psychopaths: Inside the Relationships of Inevitable Harm with Narcissists, Sociopaths & Psychopaths. Second Edition (2009). Mask Publishing.

5, 6   Brown, Sandra L. and Young, Jennifer, R., The Institute (2016). Cognitive dissonance's Enhancement of PTSD symptoms in Pathological Love Relationships: Case studies in qualitative research. Interagency data.

8, 12   Brown, Sandra L., The Institute (2015). Atypical trauma presentation in pathological love relationship survivors. An interagency report; also prepared for The Institute's Therapist Training Program and Manual: Treating the Aftermath of Pathological Love Relationships.

13   Brown, Sandra L., The Institute (2006). [Survivor symptom survey]. Agency raw data.

14   Brown, Sandra L. and Young, Jennifer R., The Institute (2015). Self-Perceptual Injuries from Pathological Love Relationships: Treatment Implications. Prepared for The Institute's Therapist Training Program and Manual: Treating the Aftermath of Pathological Love Relationships.

15, 16   Brown, Sandra L., The Institute (2016). Re-experiencing in Trauma-Related Cognitive Dissonance. Prepared for Women Who Love Psychopaths. Third Edition; and The Institute's Therapist Training Program and Manual: Treating the Aftermath of Pathological Love Relationships.

Chapter Sixteen

Cognitive Dissonance
Puzzle Piece #4™

In our examination of Puzzle Piece #4™ and the Extreme Aftermath Symptoms, we discuss the number one symptom affecting all survivors—cognitive dissonance.

Quick Survivor Review

- Approximately 90 percent of PLR survivors will have some sort of trauma with 50-75 percent having a form of PTSD.
- Survivor trauma is often non-, mis-, and dis-identified.
- Some of the nonidentification is due to how the DSM defines trauma.
- Some of the identification problems are because the survivor's trauma is atypical.

In the last chapter we noted that the survivor's atypical trauma was one of the factors that caused nonidentification, misidentification and dis-identification of the survivor's aftermath. This chapter identifies not only an often-missed symptom, but the symptom most in need of treatment.

What Is Cognitive Dissonance?

In 2006, in preparation for writing the second edition of *Women Who Love Psychopaths*, I began researching what constituted the unusual dynamics of "I love him/I loathe him" that seemed to enflame the trauma symptoms and the thinking turmoil survivors were experiencing. The 'mind mess' is called cognitive dissonance.[1]

The term cognitive dissonance is based on a theory in social psychology related to how people are motivated to deal with internal conflicts in beliefs and the machinations the mind goes through to resolve them.

Cognitive dissonance (CD) and its mental hostage taking mechanisms are best understood by looking at how CD operates in a survivor's life. First, let's look at what the words mean -

cognitive (n.) relating to being or involving conscious intellectual activity such as thinking, reasoning, or remembering.[2]

dissonance (n.) lack of agreement, especially the inconsistency between the beliefs one holds, or between one's actions.[3]

Cognitive dissonance (n.) a psychological conflict resulting from incongruous beliefs and attitudes that are held simultaneously.[4]

More simply put, cognitive dissonance is an inconsistency between a survivor's thoughts and/or her actions, resulting in internal conflict. Sounds simple enough to understand doesn't it? How complicated can it be to describe an internal war of sorts?

The whole concept of CD suffers from its own identity disturbance of being a huge theory, but one that is not well understood functionally. We are pointing this out as an explanation to why CD is not likely to have been treated up to this point, or even suggested by mental health professionals as part of a survivor's symptom package.

Today cognitive dissonance is the most widely studied social theory but has the least written about psychological treatment for this pervasive phenomenon that affects almost anyone with a conscience. The handful of theorists who threw their ideas in the ring had little to contribute toward the idea of cognitive dissonance *resolution* or even *reduction*. It comes down to the fact that the psychological theory with the biggest potential punch of menace is often associated with the fewest ideas about how to help others with this mental tug of war.

*H*ow CD Operates

Although dissonance is about inconsistency, that simple explanation doesn't begin to describe what a little inconsistency in thinking can do to the mind and what the mind will do to try to correct it. We probably don't realize how inconsistency can be so crazy making until we have had too much of it. Most people like consistency, and we call a lack of consistency 'drama'—the ups and downs and ins and outs of people who can't be consistent in their thinking, emotions, or behavior. But whether we realize it or not, we are even *more* fanatical about our *own* consistency or lack thereof.

That's because consistency produces predictability—we like it when we know what we can expect from others and especially from ourselves. Relationships and partners who are not consistent are chaotic. Their chaos feels like a contagion to others as they drag the chaos from their own inconsistency into the relationship. It is one thing when inconsistency is affecting Darkness, but it's another when it starts to affect survivors.

The Necessity of Consistency

Consistency also produces stability—knowing who we are and what we believe. We rarely recognize how important this is to our own well-being until our consistency is interrupted and we begin to feel 'all over the place' and not ourselves. We feel our best when our thinking, emotions and behavior reflect what we believe. That's when we are living our truth, when we are on point, when we feel settled and balanced.

The external consistency in our friends, family, work life, and partners produces stability which is perceived as internal stability in *oneself*.

Our perceived stability is also related to how consistent we are in our thinking and our emotions which guide our behavior. The disruption of this stability is produced by the inconsistency in those around us, in ourselves, or both. Therefore, normal people will always be affected by the dissonance of Darkness.

Inconsistency, whether from others or from within, changes our beliefs about ourselves, the partner, and even how we see the world. When we become destabilized by inconsistency, we lose our internal anchor. Suddenly the world is no longer about the Golden Rule, the moral compass needle is bent, and the structured edge of a belief system becomes a wavy line. What was once valued is murky, what we lived by is distorted, and what used to be done or never done is now the opposite. This makes the issue of consistency very important for most people.

The Power of Inconsistency

While we can see the importance of consistency, what becomes even more evident is the powerful disruption produced by inconsistency in a survivor's former functioning and well-being. Inconsistency can present itself in several ways -[5]

- Inconsistency in what she thinks (he's kind/he's sadistic)
- Inconsistency in what she feels (he's sometimes kind/but I feel so disrespected most of the time)
- Inconsistency in how she behaves (he's so unpredictable/ but I still stay)

The internal war begins when one or more of these become unbalanced.

Inconsistent Thinking

Dissonance begins first in the thinking when both sides of Darkness must be routinely dealt with. Her thinking must compare and contrast information, actions, and his emotions on both sides of the Jekyll/Hyde spectrum. She may think she concluded that he is, in fact, telling the truth or he does love her, when more information comes up that shows he was lying or was abusive.

- He's telling the truth/He's lying
- He's monogamous/I found five different texts
- He said he was married only once/Someone told me he was married four times

Inconsistent Feelings

From inconsistent thinking about both sides of Darkness comes the corresponding emotions with those thoughts. That makes dissonance also about conflicting feelings. Feelings of love produced in state dependent learning during love bombing are the bedrock of dissonance. These entrenched and subconscious feeling states defy rationalization. In the face of rational feelings—such as loathing his behavior—are the conflicted and unexplainable feelings of love, loyalty, and desire that are in contrast with the survivor's feelings of terror.

- He is my soul mate/He is a terrorist
- I trust him/I distrust him
- This is the happiest I've ever been/This is the most destroyed I have ever been

Inconsistent Behavior

Inconsistent thinking about both sides of Darkness and the corresponding emotions eventually lead to action or behavior. Remember the saying, "Your walk doesn't match your talk"? This is the behavioral form of CD created when the survivor's behavior isn't matching her value system or when she is tolerating something in his behavior that she shouldn't. All PLRs produce *behavior* in survivors that violate their innately driven conscientiousness Super Trait, which is responsible for the belief that their walk and talk *should* be aligned.

- A survivor knows it is against her belief system to tolerate infidelity. But she has.
- A survivor knows she is against someone dealing drugs. But he has.
- A survivor knows she does not normally engage in porn. But she has.
- A survivor knows she is against staying in a relationship with any kind of violence—psychological subterfuge or physical violence. But she has.

Inconsistent Thinking, Feeling, and Behavior

This makes CD about conflicted thinking, feelings, *and* behavior, meaning that every thought, emotion, and resulting behavior are all connected and twisted by cognitive dissonance. Not only does the survivor have dual thoughts, feelings, and behavior about the dissonant Darkness, each thought conflicts with feelings; each feeling conflicts with behavior; and each behavior conflicts with thinking.

$\mathcal{R}$eactions Produced by Cognitive Dissonance

Because cognitive dissonance is an unnatural state of being, anyone with dissonance will attempt to relieve her internal war in several ways. Sometimes this is a conscious process, but more often it is unconscious, almost an automatic response to try to return equilibrium to one's thinking. These are not necessarily functional or healthy ways in which to attempt to rebalance. It is largely through these failed attempts at internal conflict reduction that the person begins to realize the magnitude of the problem and their unsuccessful attempts to free themselves from the internal war.

Rebalancing Atempt: Selective Exposure

Cognitive dissonance is extremely hard to recognize in the beginning of its formation because it is well hidden behind our well-loved beliefs. It is when our beliefs are shattered that we experience dissonance. This form of selective-exposure dissonance is because everyone has beliefs and *people only (or mostly) pay attention to ideas they already believe.*[6]

Whether we realize it or not, we all have beliefs that influence our opinions. Those beliefs catch our attention more than other information, and people are naturally attached to ideas that they already believe. For instance, survivors already come with a natural predisposition towards optimism about human nature and tend to see others through who the survivors are. They begin dating Darkness with the belief that he is like them and, of course, Darkness plays to the twin-ship and mutuality in the love bombing state. He mirrors back her beliefs, mimicking and parroting them, which solidifies her belief that he is like her.

There is a difference between beliefs we have acquired through life, like political views which are taught or acquired and are largely conscious, and beliefs that have always been there, as seen in our predisposition in our personalities. For instance, we are aware we are a Republican or Democrat and can state why, but beliefs that are generated out of our naturally occurring personality are largely unconscious—they just *are*. A survivor's Super Trait of agreeableness means she is highly relationship invested and will *resist* the relationship-oriented internal conflict when she is faced with negative information that not only conflicts with her conscious beliefs about him but with her hard-wired personality, or who she is.

Survivors are not likely to go looking for information that he is not like them, even in the early stages of the relationship, because it is *already* conflicting with how she tends to see others.[7] A woman isn't avoiding doing a background check on her partner because she is desperate for a relationship. She doesn't do one because she naturally does not consider people to be motivated by evil—conducting a background check would run counter to her long-held belief systems. However, by the mid-relationship phase when information is found out that Darkness is, indeed, different than her belief that others are like her, dissonance is created from this conflicting reality.

When Darkness' mask begins to slip, she is going to be even *more* challenged in dissonance than someone without the extra strong personality predisposition because this new information is not merely violating a belief system, it is conflicting with an internal personality trait.[8]

What makes this form of dissonance particularly difficult is that selective exposure, unfortunately, delivers a double-edged sword -

> Not only do people tend to only pay attention to information that supports what they already believe, but *when they are given information that conflicts with that belief, they naturally reject the information.*

The scores of doctors listed on the Malpractice and Lost License website would not likely deter people from their basic belief that doctors are respectable. These long-held belief systems are stronger than incoming new information. In fact, the beliefs are so engrained that they are *automatic* belief systems—beliefs that are a personality default setting and so are largely unconscious.

Survivor Note:

Dissonance is created when one's perception meets a differing reality:
Agreeableness and/or conscientiousness traits

-vs-

A differing reality

=

cognitive dissonance[©]

The double-edged sword of selective exposure dissonance means she won't be *looking* for the information in the early phases and she won't *believe* the new information in the mid-phase. Avoiding the search for information and rejecting new information once it is presented are both defensive reactions which create dissonance.[9]

Survivor Work Page Question:
I had Selective Exposure Dissonance. ___ Yes ___ No

Rebalancing Atempt — Thought Dissonance 'Altering Reality'

To reduce the internal conflict of their inconsistent thinking, survivors will also tamper with their own thinking to stop the war. Dissonance can begin when thinking conflicts with behavior. The survivor experiences dissonance as a thinking war and will attempt to negotiate with her captor — ironically, which is herself. She will seek peace negotiations internally with herself to stop the war.

A survivor's first line of defense in an internal war with herself when her thinking/feeling/behavior is in conflict is to offer an olive branch to her internal war and change her thinking. It is the first line of defense because changing how one thinks about something is the easiest thing to change. If her thoughts are at war with her thoughts (He won't cheat again/He cheated again) she will change her thinking to try to focus on just the hopeful thought that he won't cheat again. When her thinking conflicts with her behavior (I'm dating a bad person) she will change her *thinking* about the negative behavior — "He's not *that* bad. He's not *worse* than the last guy I dated."

Choosing to change one's thinking as the easiest route is a temporary stopgap measure and only works until the next conflicted thought, feeling, or behavior arises. Then the process is repeated. But tampering with her thinking to focus on just the behaviors she hopes Darkness will continue with is altering how she notices reality. And reality is her only friend.

Rebalancing Atempt — Bothersome Behavior

Inconsistent thinking and feelings eventually result in action or behaviors that also reflect the internal war of dissonance.

For instance, abortion is a hotbed of debate, but what is not absent from the debate is the issue of cognitive dissonance that women experience in contemplating or having an abortion. Staying outside of the many psycho-emotional-political-religious issues of abortion, most people can agree that no one hopes to grow up one day and find themselves, for various reasons, terminating a pregnancy. It may be perceived as necessary, but it still produces dissonance when a woman's *thinking* that she would never be in this position conflicts with the *reality* that she is indeed in this position. There are beliefs, and then there is the *action* of termination, which is probably at war with the beliefs, no matter the perceived necessity.

In PLRs, conflicting behavior could mean doing things she is morally against, or it could simply involve staying in the relationship and not leaving when she knows she should. While the 'thinking dissonance' may be aligned with a survivor's high-normal agreeableness trait (optimism about human nature, trust, seeing others as she sees herself), her *behavior* is conflicting with her high-normal conscientiousness trait where long-term behavior is often generated.[10] When her behavior violates her values, she enters another round of dissonance. The more cycles she endures as her behavior bounces between wanting to act in accordance with her beliefs, but she doesn't behave in accordance with them, the deeper the dissonance becomes engrained.

Dissonance is created when a survivor's conscientiousness is confronted by her own out-of-character behavior—when what she truly believes conflicts with the reality of her behavior.

Table 16.1
What She Truly Believes vs. Reality

What She Truly Believes	vs. Reality
Partners should not be violent...	...but he is violent, and I am still here.
To have a happy relationship, people should be monogamous...	...but he is not, and I haven't ended it.
A healthy person would not accept this behavior...	...but I accept this behavior.

Changing her thinking about these conflicting pieces of information would reduce dissonance. Apply a little rationalization—and there, that feels better. But her behavior of remaining in the relationship—whether it is her pursuit of the relationship or other behaviors, like lying for him, stealing, or other violations of her moral code—will increase her dissonance on the other end as it relates to behavior and conscientiousness. This will make her feel much worse.[11]

===

Survivor Note:
Her high-normal conscientiousness means that values, beliefs, and corresponding behavior are priorities, and when her current behavior conflicts with how she normally lived before the PLR, the act of not living in accordance with her own value system in her behavior is going to cause significant dissonance©.

===

In fact, research has shown that people who have high levels of conscientiousness (which the survivors have) are at *most* risk of dissonance. People who are naturally guided by values and beliefs will have horrific conflict when they violate their own life principles.

Survivors often say that the worst part of dissonance is "who they became." Their behaviors in the PLR make them question this Super Trait of conscientiousness as they no longer live by their own compass.[12] Their compass was broken by coercion, and when their behavior was no longer aligned with their beliefs, their own behavior seemed to them to be out of control, an element noted in addiction. Survivors often perceive their radical change in behavior to be a relationship or sexual addiction because this is the only way they can explain the steps they took to reduce their internal war©.

Survivor Work Page Question:
I had 'Thought Dissonance' and 'Behavior Dissonance.'
___ Yes ___ No

Rebalancing Atempt— 'Post-Decision Dissonance'

As if fighting one's thinking, emotions, and behavior isn't difficult enough, more internal conflict and inconsistency can occur with each decision made. 'Post-decision dissonance,' yet another form of cognitive dissonance, is brought about by *distressing doubts concerning the wisdom of the survivor's decision after it's been made.*

The makeup and breakup cycles of PLRs are cycles of inevitable post-decision dissonance.[13] Dissonance is not just related to information a survivor *receives*, it is also related to the *decisions* she makes. In studies about post-decision dissonance it is noted that the need for reassurance to reduce dissonance is highest *the more the decision was important/difficult/irrevocable.*

A survivor may decide to leave her job for Darkness, loan him $50,000, give her children to their biological father so she can be with him, or marry him when she really feels like she shouldn't. Decisions that have produced life-altering consequences means the survivor will try to find positive reasons for the decision she made. The more the decision was important, difficult, irrevocable, or life altering, the more invested the survivor will be to *like* the decision she made even if it means changing her thinking about it. She will invest more time and energy to justify an important or irrevocable decision to reduce post-decision dissonance.

But afterwards, more thinking wars are the repercussions of her decisions.

- "Did I do the right thing? Yes, I love him/No, he's still behaving badly."
- "I never marry this quickly/Why did I marry this quickly?"

Post-decision dissonance creates yet another round of confusion and emotional pain regarding those important decisions that have violated her normal behavior.

While 'selective-exposure dissonance' is relegated to the beginning of the relationship when information is not sought, and in the middle parts of the relationship as contradictory information is introduced but avoided, there is dissonance throughout the relationship when decisions to stay/reinvest in the relationship occur again and again. This makes dissonance a reoccurring state that never seems to dissipate.[14]

Survivor Work Page Question:
I had 'post-decision dissonance.'
___ Yes ___ No

Rebalancing Atempt—'Post-Decision Validation' Dissonance

The next step in trying to reduce post-decision dissonance begins when a survivor's own attempts at focusing on the positive reasons for her decision are not enough. She then will seek outside validation to quiet her conflicting thoughts about whether she made the right decision. Post-decision dissonance and validation dissonance are therefore connected.

We've all seen the survivor blogs where readers strive to get validation for certain actions such as leaving the pathological partner. On the surface, it looks simple enough—she wants support for her decision. But this overt cry for validation demonstrates that the dissonance is not gone and is, in fact, in need of treatment.

- Her thinking hasn't reduced it.
- Her behavior so far hasn't reduced it.
- The decisions she has made about the relationship haven't reduced it.

- So, she thinks she will try to get validation from others to reduce it…

So, where does she go? She goes to sites that are not practicing trauma-informed care, populated by survivors who are chock full of the Super Traits of empathy, sympathy, and helpfulness. They're also full of perseverance and resourcefulness and will give never-ending validation. Validation is in plentiful supply with other survivors sharing their horror stories of PLRs, which produces more thinking conflicting with thinking for her, more flashbacks of her own situation, more relationship craving—wait![15] "Why isn't all this validation reducing my symptoms?"

Post-decision validation dissonance needs more than just validation from other readers and survivors to manage it. Months on a survivor blog getting validation from dozens of other survivors has still not reduced her need for even more validation. Ironically, it has all the earmarks of possibly causing a relapse and recontact with Darkness. The survivors who she thought were helping her by validating her experience may have caused the opposite response!

Let's explore why.

Survivor Work Page Question:
I had 'post-decision validation dissonance.'
___ Yes ___ No

'Post-Decision Validation' Boomerang

As we have seen, the reason dissonance has become so unmanageable is that the survivor develops methods for corralling dissonance that seem logical to her. She might not even be aware of her approaches, but they cause *other* problems within dissonance. Just like we saw as she tried to extinguish thinking dissonance by focusing on Darkness' positive behavior, this tactic caused her to notice her own behavior which produced *more* dissonance. Additionally, when selective exposure caused her to avoid new information, it produced *more* dissonance in her emotions.

In this form of 'post-decision validation' dissonance, the innocent need for reassurance about her decisions has the potential to boomerang back to her with an unrecognized side effect—sending her back to Darkness for the reassurance she is seeking. Seems counter-intuitive, doesn't it?

Most survivors don't notice post-decision validation dissonance since its identification seems counter intuitive. Woven into this form of dissonance is the misread symptom of needing reassurance as a way of calming the dissonance. This desire looks not only innocent on the surface, it also looks like proactive recovery—seeking support for the issue of struggling with decisions.[16]

Survivor Note:

But just as with other forms of dissonance, the subconscious use of methods to extinguish it are often the things that are fanning the flames of it.

When months of receiving validation in a forum or on a survivor blog does not consistently squelch the need for more validation, survivors looking for a way to stop the internal war often unconsciously migrate back to the source of pain.

The isolation imposed in a Pathological Love Relationship means that clear-thinking family and friends are likely to have been sidelined for Darkness to create the atmosphere necessary for control. A survivor's former circle of friends and family diminishes, rational outside support is nonexistent, and the validation she has gotten on survivor blogs or in on-line forums has not reduced the dissonance as she had hoped, so the last man standing for post-decision validation is Darkness. Even if she has decided to stay but has doubts about it, Darkness is there to support her decision. If she has decided to leave and has second thoughts, Darkness is there to support her doubts. The perceived failure of her validation on survivor sites has caused Plan B thinking in which she returns to Darkness to reduce her pain.

Survivor Note:

The machinations of fearing, loving, staying, leaving, and returning are seen in what is called 'betrayal and trauma bonding' and the repetition of those cycles and decisions connected to each bout of it are, in fact, dissonance©.

At *The Institute*, we believe that betrayal bonding is simply a symptom of dissonance and at play in the dynamics of staying/leaving as a form of post-decision validation dissonance.[17] In fact, betrayal and trauma bonding is probably better explained (and treated) as a natural reaction to dissonance than a separate reaction to trauma.

Post-decision validation, unrecognized as a form of dissonance, can be harmful to survivors, because as they continue to receive validation on blogs of their decisions to leave while the dissonance remains undealt with, they are more likely to seek validation from other sources which could include Darkness, *since their dissonance is not being reduced* by blogs or books.

- Just as in the 'thinking form' of dissonance, more thinking about it does *not* solve the problem long term.
- More intel ("If I find he cheated, THEN I will leave") does not solve the problem either.
- More selective exposure—rejecting new information—does not solve it.
- Nor does more post-decision validation solve it.

More facts, more thinking, and more misguided validation are part of the trap of dissonance as one is simply going in never ending circles.

These measures might provide temporary relief, but they eventually produce more dissonance. If they worked, why do survivors continue to need validation from other survivors that can span months or years? The vast number of available methods of trying to reduce dissonance causes a survivor to believe that more thinking, facts, or validation will help, when, in reality, this approach is dangerous, dysfunctional, and harmful.

"We cannot solve our problems with the same thinking we used when we created them."

~ Albert Einstein

$\mathcal{T}$he Layers of Cognitive Dissonance [©]

Dissonance does not revolve around just one issue. *The Institute* has noted in its own theory of The Layers of Cognitive Dissonance that it affects survivor partners on three levels -[18]

Table 16.2
The Layers of Cognitive Dissonance and
the Thoughts Associated with the Layer

Layers	Thoughts Associated with the Layer
Cognitive dissonance regarding *the partner*	He's Jekyll/He's Hyde I love him/I loathe him
Cognitive dissonance regarding *the relationship*	It's exciting/It's exhausting I want it/I hate it
Cognitive dissonance regarding *herself*	I'm happy/I'm miserable I am a good person/I do horrible things, I caused this

These layers of dissonance follow, to some degree, the relationship dynamics. The first likely experience of dissonance might occur in the early phase of the relationship when something he does doesn't mesh with what she thought she knew about him or when she finds out conflicting information. Her likely response with selective-exposure dissonance is normally about *him*.

By mid-relationship, when the mask slips, dissonance begins occurring about the *relationship*—questioning how healthy it is or why communication is so difficult in it.

By mid-relationship and well into the end of the relationship and afterwards, there will be dissonance about *herself*—questioning if **she** was the problem and why she now is so unrecognizable to herself.

By the end of the relationship and thereafter, *all* layers of dissonance are in action—the mind reviewing conflicting thoughts/feelings/behavior about him, while reviewing other conflicting thoughts and feelings about the relationship, while also having conflicting thoughts/feelings/behavior about herself.

It is important to note that the cognitive dissonance which is created about herself is one of the biggest factors in her choice to leave the relationship. During a group session with survivors, we posed this question: "When do women leave and why?" A client answered, "I left when who he was became intolerable to who I am." This is an important awareness and seems to attend to the idea that it is the destruction of the 'self' that is the most painful and disorienting to survivors. It is the destruction of the self that helps us understand the reason why women eventually leave. It is not based on one particular behavior or another of his, but the outcome to herself and her identity. Women leave when their sense of self has been destroyed to a point that she is suffering the loss of her once congruent self. And this is particularly true for those with Super Traits because they can tolerate and cope with a lot but, what they cannot tolerate (like most of us) is the destruction of the conscientious self.

These multilayers of dissonance, all occurring together, magnify the aftermath symptoms associated with neurological deterioration created by PTSD and is enflamed by cognitive dissonance.[19]

What happens to the mind and brain from this much negative mental activity is what we will discuss next.

Survivor Work Page Question:
I had _____ layers of cognitive dissonance.

$\mathcal{W}$rapping This All Up

While cognitive dissonance is common to all human beings with a conscience, the pathological disorders of Darkness and his conflicting responses mean that dissonance will almost always result from being in a relationship with someone who has such disorders. Not all bad relationships produce dissonance the way a PLR does with Darkness, nor do most 'bad relationships' contain the dissonant relationship dynamics of being both kind and vicious, love bombing and cheating. Nor do most partners have the unusual Super Traits of agreeableness and conscientiousness that contribute to dissonance, elevating it to cataclysmic levels.

Clearly, PLRs have unique aspects that produce dissonance in every corner, from the relationship, to the survivor, to the aftermath. But the impact of dissonance on the aftermath is yet another aspect to understand. This much negative and exhausting mental activity impacts mental functionality, and that becomes an aftermath symptom.

Chapter Sixteen Endnotes

1   Brown, Sandra L., *The Institute* (2007). Cognitive dissonance perceived as traumatic in Pathological Love Relationships. Raw data from a study; also, in *Women Who Love Psychopaths: Inside the Relationships of Inevitable Harm with Narcissists, Sociopaths & Psychopaths*. Second Edition (2009). Mask Publishing.

2   *cognitive.* www.merriam-webster.com/dictionary/cognitive

3   *dissonance.* www.merriam-webster.com/dictionary/dissonance

4   *Cognitive dissonance.* www.merriam-webster.com/dictionary/cognitive dissonance

5   Brown, Sandra L., *The Institute* (2010). Destabilization in cognitive dissonance in *The Institute's Therapist Training Program and Manual: Treating the Aftermath of Pathological Love Relationships*.

6-12 Brown, Sandra L. and Young, Jennifer R., *The Institute* (2014). Five Factor Form/ Five Factor Model Rating Form traits of agreeableness and conscientiousness in pathological love relationship dynamics. An interagency report; also prepared for *The Institute's Therapist Training Program and Manual: Treating the Aftermath of Pathological Love Relationships*.

13-17 Brown, Sandra L., *The Institute* (2010). Relationship Cycles and Its Impact on Cognitive Dissonance: An Outcome Study included in *The Institute's Therapist Training Program and Manual: Treating the Aftermath of Pathological Love Relationships*.

18, 19 Brown, Sandra L. and Young, Jennifer R., *The Institute* (2013). Tri-Dimensional Layers of Cognitive Dissonance in Pathological Love Relationships: Relational and Traumatic Examination.

Chapter Seventeen

Cognitive Dissonance and Cognitive Decline—The Other 'CD' Puzzle Piece #4™

Quick Survivor Review

- Cognitive dissonance is an internal war of inconsistency.
- It is related to inconsistency in thinking, feeling, and behavior.
- Dissonance produces reactions of Selective Exposure, Post Dissonance Decisions, and Post Decision Validation.
- Dissonance happens on three levels—about Darkness, about the relationship, and about herself.

Now that we understand what dissonance is, how it is created, and its layers, let's look at how it creates and further amplifies aftermath symptoms and the havoc that it wreaks.

*T*hinking Problems Arising from Cognitive Dissonance: Remembering, Judgment, and Reasoning

As we saw in the last chapter, cognitive dissonance is a web of emotional and thinking entanglements happening on three levels.[1] It is not only emotionally painful to experience, but it produces debilitating problems in the functionality of the survivor's mind which has already been impaired by trauma symptoms.

PLRs do significant damage to the main resource that everyone in a PLR needs, which is the ability to recognize, rally, and respond to Darkness' devastating impact. For instance, chemists, Department of Defense analysts, and public relations professionals rely on the *functionality* of their minds to both achieve their career goals and to have a sense of well-being. But they also need the functionality of their mind to recognize and respond to Darkness' deviance and to heal themselves after they have been in a PLR.

While cognitive dissonance produces inconsistent behavior, reactions, and internal conflicts in a survivor that are so unlike her, these are generated because of how cognitive dissonance impacts the mind's *performance* in several notable areas of functioning. Over time this can create a form of *cognitive decline*—the 'other' CD.

Survivor Note:

Cognitive decline is the reduction in the former functionality of memory, thinking skills, judgment, and reasoning.

Remembering

Cognitive dissonance is a thinking process in which remembering, judgment, and reasoning is inharmonious (or inconsistent) with the experience. Since PLRs are simply a reflection of the pathology in Darkness, who himself is -

- both Jekyll and Hyde,
- both charming and a tormenter,
- both kind and sadistic,
- both love bombing and cheating,

any survivor partner has two sets of memories—*two* separate judgments, and *two* explanations for him—the charming side and the pathological side. So, of course a survivor's thought process is going to be inharmonious, if not *intolerable*. They have had to simultaneously hold two differing belief systems—that he is good/bad, conjuring up positive remembrances/horrific remembrances—and they've had to look for answers as to why he is so kind but so vicious.

In most normal relationships, people don't struggle with two very *different* representations of the same person. This leads people who are in PLRs to try to find a harmonious (or consistent) middle ground of experience. Survivors with Super Traits, who are optimistic, and relationship invested, will try to resolve conflict, even the conflict of how they *experience or remember* the pathological partner.[2]

The emotional exhaustion, combined with constantly trying to process which person he is at any given moment—Jekyll or Hyde—and the gaslighting that further distorts the reality, keeps the survivor's brain working at warp speed. The mind cannot rest on one *remembrance* or *experience* of him from which to make conclusions and preparations. Remembering betrayal as a motivation to flee or remembering how to reach out for help can be impacted by dissonance, causing a cognitive decline in the mind's ability to *remember* and then *take* proactive action.[3]

And because PLRs have three layers of dissonance—centering on the pathological partner, the relationship, and herself—a survivor's decline in remembering is happening on all three levels.[4]

Survivor Work Page Question:
I experienced cognitive decline in remembering?
___ Yes ___ No

Judging

Dissonance impacts *judgment*, which is defined as 'the ability to make a decision or form an opinion objectively and wisely in matters of action, good sense, and discretion.'[5]

Just at the time a woman really needs to make clear decisions and judge the behavior of Darkness for her own self-protection, her judgment has become impaired from dissonance.

When in a PLR, executives who make split-second decisions in their work are unable to make a split-second judgment to not answer the phone when Darkness calls. That is because sound judgment, which is part of the conscientiousness trait that a survivor relies on in her job, has declined in her personal life. While she should be able to judge that repeated lying and infidelity makes a person a bad risk, the phone rings and the dissonance is set off. The mind is ping-ponging, cramming the brain full of too many conflicting memories requiring judgment. Her ability to judge the relationship or how she has changed because of the relationship is also disrupted.

> **Survivor Work Page Question:**
> I experienced cognitive decline in my judgment?
> ___ Yes ___ No

Reasoning

Dissonance also damages *reasoning*, 'the process of forming conclusions or inferences from facts or premises.'[6]

Police Detectives, whose job it is to form conclusions based on facts and to draw inferences based on premises, when in PLRs cannot make logical conclusions about their history with Darkness. Reasoning is predicated upon functional remembering and judging, which are derailed by dissonance and reduce the normally powerful reasoning skills that are part of a survivor's Super Trait of conscientiousness.[7] While she should be able to reason that if he cheated before, he will cheat again, and like that in her work of tracing criminals, the best predictor of future behavior is past behavior, this rational process is not easily accessible when it's needed to be applied to Darkness because she is having a decline in reasoning skills. Accurate reasoning about the relationship and about the potential harm to herself have also declined.

> **Survivor Work Page Question:**
> I experienced cognitive decline in my reasoning processes:
> ___ Yes ___ No

Thinking/Cognition

We can see that dissonance effects the thinking *process* of remembering, judging, and reasoning. But when these three components are not functional then a person's 'cognitive' ability to think has been damaged (but not broken). It is why they are said to be experiencing a decline, especially since dissonance has been damaging the person for months, years, or perhaps decades.

Thinking is required for action. The mind, instead of working to stabilize itself, is consumed by dissonance and, instead of using remembering, judging, and reasoning, the declining mind's functionality is trying to track down facts by breaking into his phone, conducting fly-bys on social media, contacting women suspected of being in the pipeline, and becoming an amateur private investigator. Instead of stabilization, paranoia increases, but the survivor can never settle on one conclusion because here comes the love bombing and carrot dangling to confuse the facts.

Survivor Note:
When the three components (remembering, judging, and reasoning) that support stabilized thinking are obstructed, the mind can't do its job, because it is in a state of cognitive decline.

Survivor Work Page Question:
I experienced cognitive decline in my thinking/cognition?
___ Yes ___ No

*T*hinking That's Affected by Both Trauma *and* Cognitive Dissonance

We can see right off the bat that the survivor is already vulnerable to functionality issues in the brain because of the impact of trauma and yet here comes dissonance also impacting very similar areas and functionality and enhancing the decline.

Remembering, judging, and reasoning are part of the thinking process related to the 'executive functioning' of the brain which helps organize and execute things that need to be done like leaving, finding a therapist, going no contact, performing work duties or remembering to exercise self-care. Survivors often complain about not being able to think a coherent thought, to remember to feed the children, or about having complete white outs of brain fog. Survivor partners have had significant trauma which is damaging to the executive functioning of the brain and reduces the mind's functionality in the areas of -

- Attention
- Restraint
- Memory
- Reasoning
- Decision making
- Problem solving
- Planning

These functions look a lot like the functions obstructed by dissonance (remembering, judgment, reasoning) which, unfortunately, are *similar* brain functions that are *concurrently being reduced* by trauma.

Damaging Effects of Trauma and Cognitive Dissonance on Executive Functioning[8]

Since trauma *and* dissonance affect similar areas, the disorientation that survivors experience includes cognitive decline in several functions. In the following checklist, check all that apply to you -

___ Not being able to focus at work (attention)

___ Behaving in ways that are not normal for a person, such as impulsivity (restraint)

___ The inability to remember important aspects of an experience (memory)

___ The inability to figure out what the problem is (problem solving)

___ The inability to formulate a reason to leave the partner (reasoning)

___ The inability to make the decision to leave (decision making)

___ The inability to follow through with a plan on how to recover (planning)

===

Survivor Note:

*This double impact of trauma **and** dissonance produces severe cognitive symptoms resulting in a form of cognitive decline — an increasing inability to make rational choices and judgments.*

===

As a trauma therapist, I was amazed at how severe these symptoms were in survivors and struggled to find the reason that highly professional women whose executive functioning had been important to their career success, were being debilitated by their own mind's dysfunctional performance. It took years for me to be able to understand the overlapping impact of both trauma *and* dissonance to the executive functioning areas of the mind that brought these thinking processes to a screeching halt. Teachers, CPAs, and paralegals were on disability or had taken time off because they could not perform their jobs and could not take care of their most basic day-to-day needs—balancing their checkbook, practicing daily self-care, etc. Their symptoms were often assumed to only be depression, yet the severity of the symptoms indicated much more than lingering sadness over the end of a relationship with Darkness. Although depression does impact cognitive functioning, it was apparent that this was more than just depression.

Survivor Work Page Question:
In the list above, how many items were applicable to you? _____

*B*rain Changes Impacting the Mind's Functionality

This impairment from both trauma *and* dissonance is doubly harmful in that beyond reducing the thinking processes, it can also affect the brain *as an organ*.

Survivor Note:
The changes to the mind from dissonance can lead to changes in the neurological condition of the brain.

Neuroscience has come to the rescue again in aiding how we understand what can happen to the brain, not just the mind, in relationships. Both brain *and* mind are involved in the emotions experienced in love, betrayal, and breakups, just as both brain *and* mind are involved in trauma and dissonance. Combining what we know about trauma, dissonance, and PLRs helps us understand which brain systems are likely affected.

Cognitive problems of remembering, judging, and reasoning that start from trauma during the PLR and explode like a bomb during the devaluing and discarding/rejection phase, no doubt *magnify* the problems already being produced from cognitive dissonance. Survivors struggle with the difficulty of the mind or brain to be a supportive agent in their recovery because of the changes the brain goes through while under stress from trauma and the layers of dissonance.[9]

Like any other organ in the body, the brain can be made vulnerable by physical problems just as the lungs or any other organ can be. One of the known factors in certain organ problems is the effects of accumulative stress. The brain is no different in that regard and is highly sensitive to stress and trauma. Ruminations and flashbacks, as well as jolts of adrenaline, cortisol, and other chemicals released during anxiety, eventually cause changes to the chemistry of the brain that produce symptoms of trauma and cognitive decline.[10] These stressors deplete the brain chemicals needed for a person to maintain a feeling of well-being or even normalcy.

These long-term changes to the mind's functionality, either from stress, dissonance, or the resulting chemical imbalances, cause the brain systems responsible for its smooth operation to decline -

- Areas of the brain that should be calm are anxious.
- Areas of the brain that should help with rational decision making are impaired.
- Areas of the brain that should stabilize feelings about the relationship are stimulated, producing craving for the traumatizing person who brought the survivor to this condition—a situation similar to betrayal and trauma bonding.

Survivor Note:

Long-term changes to various brain systems can change how the brain operates. So, we can see that -

Trauma + dissonance impacts → cognitive processes and the mind's functionality, which impacts → brain chemistry and a further decline in both the mind and brain functionality, which eventually → impacts entire brain systems.

This chain reaction highlights why survivors have experienced such extreme aftermath symptoms that appear complex and not amenable to the simple recovery suggestions you read about online.

Reactive Brain Systems in Rejection and Breakups

So, just what happens to the organ of the brain from all the trauma and dissonance produced in the PLR?

Helen Fisher, an anthropologist and human behavioral researcher is a leading expert on love and one of the most referenced scholars on the issues of love and its corresponding emotion—pain from breakups. She has researched and written extensively for decades and her work can be heard on the renowned TED Talks. Fisher's pioneering work about love, the brain, and the pain of breakups has laid the theoretical foundation from which other theories and research have been built.

Fisher identified systems in the brain impaired during love and breakups. While she depicts the brain problems occurring at the time of the once-and-for-all rejection itself, we at *The Institute* believe that since the PLR is merely one of many cycles of love bombing/aloofness and breaking up/making up, these brain systems may be activated *throughout* portions of the PLR and *not* just in the final and last phase of discarding.© This means that while these systems might be impaired at the end of a *normal* relationship and briefly cause distress *once* for a person, in a PLR they are likely to be impaired from the mid-relationship onward and experienced *continuously*, or at the very least, numerous times in the makeup and breakup cycles typical of a PLR. Once is bad enough but continuously is totally disorienting.

Fisher identifies **The Reward System** as activated following a breakup.[11] We believe this system is activated following the first betrayal, which is likely early on, and continues throughout the relationship. When operating correctly, this system guides people toward pleasure and away from pain. But it backfires when it becomes destabilized from trauma, breakups, or as we have seen, even dissonance. Instead of drawing a survivor away from pain (Darkness), Fisher says it produces a craving for the relationship, even in the face of facts. As we have noted, this craving-vs-facts *is* dissonance, and the reward system that should be leading a survivor toward the pleasure of the peace in recovery outside of the PLR relationship, instead leads her back toward Darkness.

When the Reward System is unstable, a person might find herself impulsively seeking out Darkness and trying to reunite with him despite her belief that it would be harmful for her to do so. Surveillance behaviors like fly-bys on social media, driving past his home, or hacking his computer or phone—all incredibly unlike her normal behavior—are ramped up by the destabilized reward center. The conscientious Super Traited survivor has found herself arrested for stalking, as her electrified reward system keeps returning her to the object of her love and craving. The Super Trait of agreeableness, with all its relationship investment facets, draws her back to try again. This vulnerable mind and brain system can lead to a neurochemical imbalance which also produces a form of cognitive decline.

Another system that's destabilized by rejection is **The Bonding System**.[12] When the Bonding System is operating correctly, it enables us to attach and bond—a necessity in any form of healthy attachment and intimacy. But when this system is destabilized, a person will desperately seek the object of her attachment—Darkness. Since this system is also associated with the Reward System that Fisher states produces craving, it not only produces the craving for, but the constant *pursuit of*, Darkness. Sometimes this results in the surveillance behavior mentioned earlier, but it certainly also includes the craving and mental pursuit found in the dissonance experienced in loving/loathing. Simultaneous love-bombing and betrayal creates dissonance, and the bonding system that could lead a survivor to detach from the relationship creates a stronger attachment to Darkness instead. The cycles of abuse, whether sexual, physical, emotional, or psychological, create the betrayal or trauma bond aspect of the Bonding System.[13] A survivor's agreeableness traits again seem to override her conscientiousness traits, which might have aided her in leaving. Instead, agreeableness traits, such as relationship investment, which support the bonding and craving system, lead to attempts to salvage the relationship. This destabilized mind and brain system can lead to a neurochemical imbalance, furthering cognitive decline.

Fisher also identifies **The Stress System** as another area that is destabilized during rejection.[14] The Stress System, when operating correctly, alerts us to incoming danger. The system is created for the occasional alert, however, and not for an ongoing fire alarm that never shuts off. During or after a PLR, the survivor might feel anxious, agitated, and with a pronounced startle reflex making her feel hyperalert. When the Stress System becomes hyperactivated in the PLR, disorders such as anxiety can lead to Acute Stress Disorder, PTSD, and C-PTSD. The system that is for the occasional alert is now on permanent alert, causing constant hypervigilance as seen in PTSD. People with high-normal agreeableness traits, with all their emotional sensitivity, are more at risk of stress disruptions. With additional high-normal conscientiousness traits, they are more *bothered* by their behavior, such as stress reactions, when it doesn't match their previous stable behavior. This disruption to the mind and brain system can also lead to a neurochemical imbalance in the brain, furthering cognitive decline.

The **Pain System**, when it is functioning, assists in keeping emotions related to disappointment and the loss of a relationship relatively stable. When this system is in its most disrupted state, a person may have depression or even suicidal or homicidal thoughts. Interestingly, Fisher notes that the Pain System does not distinguish between emotional and physical pain, so the physical and emotional sensations of relationship withdrawal are why survivors often feel the withdrawal as an *addiction*.[15] People with high-normal agreeableness traits are very relationship-invested and so intensely feel this loss of connection. Again, this destabilization can lead to a neurochemical imbalance in the brain causing further decline.

Survivor Note:

Fisher describes these disrupted brain systems in terms of what people in normal relationships might experience in a breakup. It makes sense that the probable brain impairment from a PLR would be greatly amplified when you add the cognitive impact of trauma and dissonance. The inevitable harm of cognitive decline occurs when the mind and brain are being obstructed in multiple ways through trauma, dissonance, neurochemistry imbalances, executive functioning problems, and destabilized brain systems and become like a line of tumbling dominoes, pulling the mind and the brain into decline and low functionality.

Survivor Work Page Question:
How many of your brain systems were impacted? _____

$\mathcal{M}$ind, Brain, Trauma, Dissonance, and the Body

Prolonged trauma and/or dissonance can also change the physical health of the body. A shockingly high percentage of people in long-term

PLRs have adrenal, thyroid, metabolic, and autoimmune disorders. Of course, medical conditions can also affect how well a survivor's stress response system works when their immune system is being assaulted by so much stress and corresponding wrong brain/body chemistry, in turn disrupting how well the mind and brain functions or, in a survivor's situation, how much it declines. Medical problems often associated with prolonged stress or trauma include -

- Endocrine
- Hypothalamus
- Pituitary
- Adrenal
- Thyroid
- Metabolic systems

It is therefore safe to say that cognitive dissonance as a neurological problem and enhancer of trauma is cataclysmic in nature and contributes significantly to the other CD—cognitive decline.

Thinking processes, brain chemistry, and functionality illuminate why survivors need trauma-informed care. The earlier the intervention, the better the outcomes.

$\mathcal{D}$issed Again

With a firestorm in the mind and brain, it is easy to see why survivors have a hard time finding the right kind of care and it is understandable that her bundle of symptoms can be misread by therapists, family, and friends who are trying to offer support.

It is easy to see why, for the first time in her career, she didn't get the promotion, or why friends can't follow her explanations, or why she has such difficulty in making the hard decisions about protection, leaving, or even what others think is obvious in Darkness' behavior. Her emotions seem erratic, her reasoning skewed, everyone can feel the throbbing craving for the relationship and fear she will relapse as her judgment seems so unlike her. Everyone is holding their breath for the old her, full of clarity and strong convictions, to return. But as we can see, a comeback, while possible, is going to take longer than she or others anticipate.

But cognitive decline is not the only disruption to the survivor.

Dissonance's Destruction to Self-Perception

My great enjoyment in working with survivors with Super Traits is that they couldn't have a better elevated trait than conscientiousness. This trait is a gold mine of resources that can help Super Traited survivors in their recoveries. Before it can return to the recovery resource it is, it will need some work from its assault from dissonance.

What has been clear after 30 years of work with survivors is that what they perceive they *want* is different from what they actually *miss*. Survivors want *symptom management*—to stop the neurological problems of obsession, rumination, concentration, and dysfunctionality, to stop the bouncing brain of cognitive dissonance, and the gut-wrenching craving caused by positive and negative remembering from atypical PTSD.[16]

And who wouldn't?

But what they really *miss* is the ability to recognize themselves again. This is where traditional trauma treatment can run amok. In the event the survivor can get diagnosed for the traditional PTSD symptoms she might have, most therapists assume the primary traumas to treat are those of the negative flashbacks and nightmares, avoidance, or anxiety. While those symptoms do need treatment, therapists often don't recognize that those may not be her most *debilitating* symptoms. Survivors who do not yet understand their cognitive dissonance may assume that the symptoms of dissonance will lessen with traditional PTSD treatment. It is why they perceive that what they *want* is to relieve the symptoms, believing that any reduction of their PTSD will lessen the unnamed symptoms of cognitive dissonance.[17]

When asked to identify which symptoms are the most traumatic to experience, few survivors ever name physical or sexual violence. When asked what has done the single most damage to themselves for which they need recovery help, when asked which event or symptom has caused them to be unrecognizable to themselves, or which symptom has reduced a strong sense of their former internal resources, they name *cognitive dissonance as the core trauma* once they are educated as to what that symptom *is*.[18]

===

Survivor Note:

Cognitive dissonance is named by most survivors as both the core trauma and the number one symptom in need of management.

===

Let's think about that a minute. It's not the beatings, not the other women in the pipeline, not emptying the bank accounts, not the humiliating sex. What has traumatized the survivor is the *disorientation* created by cognitive dissonance that has made her lack of functioning an unrecognizable aspect of herself. She is unable to access the once-strong internal resources that she knows used to comprise her personality. She misses her former conscientiousness as an aspect of her 'self' and her resources.[19]

In the earlier chapter on cognitive dissonance, we said that part of the destructiveness of dissonance was that it happened on three levels—cognitive dissonance regarding the partner, the relationship, and regarding *herself*. Dissonance as inconsistency means that a survivor's ability to see, feel, and act consistently with who she perceived herself to *be* has been derailed.[20]

===

Survivor Note:

While dissonance can occur on three levels at once, only one of these levels of dissonance depletes internal resources—the dissonance regarding the self.

===

Our internal resources are not only aspects of our personality, as we have seen in the section on Super Traits, they are also an aid in how one copes. The ability to cope by managing problems consistently is identified as *resiliency*, which is 'the ability to return to the original form after being bent, compressed, or stretched; the ability to recover; buoyancy.'[21] The loss of internal resources to cope can negatively affect resiliency when the survivor is stretched too thin and does not recover.

Healthy people rely on their known skills to handle life's stresses. We are comfortable in our knowledge that the best predictor about how we handle anything is how we have always handled most things. When we lose our job, we know we have skills and we will get another job. When we are told we must move from our apartment, we find another one.

Our personality and skill sets are what we fall back on. We understand that we are capable people who can handle what life throws at us. While life problems are hard for anyone, survivors find them *particularly* difficult because of their Super Traits. A survivor's repertoire of handling problems includes her straightforwardness, her valuing others, her aiming for achievement, her controlled impulses, her organization, and her persevering nature—in other words, her high-normal agreeableness but especially her conscientiousness.[22]

In the past, these internal resources have conquered whatever challenges life has dealt her. She did not tend to worry about the future because she always had herself, which had always been enough. The Super Traits may have given her an unfair advantage in confidence because they aided her in persevering through anything and coming out okay. Survivors, because of these trait elevations, had unusual and copious amounts of confidence in themselves. They didn't possess the anxiety about the future that plagues others without Super Traits, especially those with true codependency.[23]

Survivor Note:

Those with Super Traits did not rely on others to fix their problems; they relied on themselves because history had proven time and again that they would solve problems based on their own internal resources.

But the PLR, with all the damaging affects to the executive functioning of the brain, combined with the disorienting change in a survivor's former behavior, has left her unrecognizable to herself and temporarily without the internal resources she used to have. Let's examine those characteristics that she used to rely on, and what became of them.

Table 17.1
The Institute's **Chart of Former Super Traits After Destructive Impact**
The Institute © 2015

Super Trait Facet	When Impacted, Becomes:
Self-confident	Lacking in self-confidence
Straight forward	Reticent
Trusting	Paranoid
Valuing others	Avoiding others
Cooperative	Uncooperative
Purposeful	Listless, confused
Dependable	Undependable or inconsistent
Organized	Disorganized
Having controlled impulses	Impulsive
Possessing moral guidelines	Feels immoral

Super Trait Facet	When Impacted, Becomes:
Friendly	Reserved
Tolerant	Reactive, intolerant
Emotionally stable	Erratic

The source of these considerable changes from how a survivor knew herself to what she becomes in a PLR are largely traumatic reactions, cognitive dissonance, or the changes in her brain. But knowing that she isn't herself is a far cry from understanding the severity of the problem or what to do about it. The resources she seeks to try to regain her resiliency may help somewhat, such as understanding the pathological partner's disorder or her aftermath symptoms, but these attempts normally fall short of dealing with the true *originating* source of her trauma — the impact of cognitive dissonance on her *self-perception*.[24]

Since 2007, when *The Institute* began producing information about the original trauma in these survivors, cognitive dissonance being widely named on blogs has fallen victim to non-scrutiny and wrong approaches along the path of nonidentification, misidentification, and dis-identification.

- IF she was lucky enough to be identified as having trauma reactions, the treated traditional trauma still does not resolve the cognitive dissonance.
- IF she was lucky enough to be identified with neurochemistry disruptions, medication still does not resolve the cognitive dissonance.
- IF she was lucky enough to be identified with cognitive dissonance, most survivor blogs and even therapists may have labeled the symptom but don't address the treatment and mostly focus on the survivor's cognitive dissonance about him and his pathology but not about herself.[25]

Injuries to her self-perception are the greatest source of the reduction in her resiliency and overall decline due to no longer being able to recognize herself or her internal resources.[26]

Survivor Work Page Question:

I have untreated Self-Perception Injuries©

___ Yes ___ No

It is no wonder then that a survivor often asks, "Am I disordered, too?" The changes in her neurological condition, along with trauma and aftermath symptoms, make her feel as erratic as Darkness is.

The DSM defines what a normal and abnormal 'self' can and cannot do. A survivor's natural personality—full of conscientiousness—is how she operated in life, as seen in the left column below. But with dissonance from the PLR, trauma, and neurological changes, a survivor's healthy self-identity, direction, and corresponding emotion and behavior has been seriously scrambled and she sees herself operating similarly like Darkness, as shown in the right column.

Table 17.2

The Institute's Chart of Changes to Super Traits
that Produce Injuries to Self-Perception
The Institute © 2015

Healthy Self-Identity and Direction in Non-Personality Disordered Persons	Disordered Self-Identity and Direction in Personality Disordered Persons
Can recognize and appraise self-characteristics	Distorted sense of self-characteristics
Has clear sense of boundaries	Poor sense of boundaries
Can experience, regulate, and tolerate a full range of emotions	Can't experience or stabilize emotions
Can establish and achieve reasonable expectations of herself	Can't establish reasonable expectations of herself
Sets personal goals and standards of conduct	Lacks realistic goals and standards of conduct
Can appraise strengths and weaknesses	Unrealistic view of strengths and weaknesses
Can reflect on internal experiences	Can't reflect on internal experiences
Can attain fulfillment and satisfaction in life	Can't currently attain true fulfillment and satisfaction

The damaging assault of cognitive dissonance removes her *recognition* of those Super Trait personality characteristics, primarily conscientiousness.[27] The former ability to know she would make the right decisions, would bounce back from emotional upheaval, or she could reasonably anticipate her behavior convinces her she was either disordered all along and didn't realize it, or she will never be herself again.

Survivor Work Page Question:
What has disoriented me most deeply is the change in how I see myself?
___ Yes ___ No

The reasons that survivors cannot harness their minds for assistance to disengage from Darkness and fully focus on recovery are due in part to the decline in the very brain they desperately need to move forward. Seen in this light, cognitive dissonance is more than -

- A social theory related to an internal conflict about someone
- A set of behaviors that survivors can't seem to break
- The annoying obsessing about Darkness that family/friends complain about
- Just "No Contact" as a way of recovery
- A wrong attribution of codependency as the issue

In fact, this unusual overlap of the neurological disruption of trauma *and* dissonance, combined with atypical PTSD and an assumption of codependency, illustrates why treatment has been minimal at best and nonexistent at worst.

Wrapping this All Up

Cognitive dissonance deserves its credit for being the trauma enhancer, mind-mangler, and cognitive decline-producer behind much of the aftermath that survivors have experienced—which is why it has taken *The Institute* years of study to identify the psychological and traumatic injury done to survivors.[28] This complicated web of Darkness' pathology, the dynamics of the relationship, the survivor's Super Traits, her trauma, the derailed brain, and the resulting aftermath—including dissonance—has been a process of untangling all the pieces of the puzzle.

I am often infuriated by the oversimplification that is often spouted on websites and in books on the subject as it does a horrible injustice to the reality of the aftermath of a PLR and does not validate the survivor's debilitation because of it. What has become clear to us at *The Institute* is that this is a treatment issue of the highest order. Survivors deserve far more than the nonidentification, misidentification, and dis-identification that has plagued them. But there is still another impairment to examine.

Chapter Seventeen Endnotes

1, 3, 4, 19   Brown, Sandra L. and Young, Jennifer R., *The Institute* (2013*)*. Tri-Dimensional Layers of Cognitive Dissonance in Pathological Love Relationships: Relational and Traumatic Examination.

2, 7, 19, 20, 22, 27   Brown, Sandra L. and Young, Jennifer R., *The Institute* (2014). Five Factor Form/Five Factor Model Rating Form traits of agreeableness and conscientiousness in pathological love relationship dynamics. An interagency report; also prepared for *The Institute's Therapist Training Program and Manual: Treating the Aftermath of Pathological Love Relationships.*

5   *judgment.* www.dictionary.com/judgment

6   *reasoning.* www.collinsdictionary.com/dictionary

8   Brown, Sandra (2017). Damaging Effects of Trauma & Cognitive Dissonance on Executive Functioning. An interagency report; also prepared for *The Institute's Therapist Training Program and Manual: Treating the Aftermath of Pathological Love Relationships.*

9, 18, 25, 28   Brown, Sandra L. and Young, Jennifer, R., *The Institute* (2016). Cognitive Dissonance's Enhancement of PTSD symptoms in Pathological Love Relationships: Case studies in qualitative research. Interagency data.

10   van der Kolk, B. (2015). *The Body Keeps the Score: Brain, Mind and Body in the Healing of Trauma.* Penguin Books.

11   Fisher, H. E., Brown, L. L., Aron, A., Strong, G., & Mashek, D. (2010). Reward, Addiction, and Emotion Regulation Systems Associated with Rejection in Love. *Journal of Neurophysiology, 104,* 51–60. https://doi.org/10.1152/jn.00784.2009

12   Acevedo, B. P., Aron, A., Fisher, H. E., & Brown, L. L. (2011). Neural correlates of long-term intense romantic love. *Social Cognitive and Affective Neuroscience,* 7(2), 145–159. https://doi.org/10.1093/scan/nsq092

13   Carnes, P. (1997). *The Betrayal Bond: Breaking Free of Exploitive Relationships.* Health Communications, Inc.

14, 15   Fisher, H. (2004, February). Dumped! *Science and Technology News,* 40–43
Fisher, H. (2006). Broken hearts: The nature and risks of romantic rejection. In *Romance and Sex in Adolescence and Emerging Adulthood: Risks and Opportunities* (pp. 3–28). https://doi.org/10.4324/9781410617361

16, 17   Brown, Sandra L., *The Institute* (2015). Atypical trauma presentation in pathological love relationship survivors. An interagency report; also prepared for *The Institute's Therapist Training Program and Manual: Treating the Aftermath of*

Pathological Love Relationships.

21   *resiliency.* www.dictionary.com/resiliency

23   Brown, Sandra L., and Young, Jennifer R., *The Institute* (2016). Misidentification of Super Traits in Pathological Love Relationships—Stop Calling it Codependency. Prepared for *Women Who Love Psychopaths. Third Edition*; and *The Institute's Therapist Training Program and Manual: Treating the Aftermath of Pathological Love Relationships.*

24, 26 Brown, Sandra L. and Young, Jennifer R., *The Institute* (2015). Self-Perceptual Injuries from Pathological Love Relationships: Treatment Implications. Prepared for *The Institute's Therapist Training Program and Manual: Treating the Aftermath of Pathological Love Relationships.*

Chapter Eighteen

Inconsistent Intuition Puzzle Piece #4™

Continuing with our discussion about Puzzle Piece #4™ and the Extreme Aftermath Symptoms is the much-needed discussion about what happens to intuition from trauma.

Quick Survivor Review

- The PLR has created trauma, which impacts the mind and the brain's functionality.
- Cognitive dissonance has amplified trauma's impact on the mind and the brain's functionality.
- Any breakup impacts the mind and the brain's functionality, especially someone in a PLR who *already has* cognitive dissonance.
- The brain's Reward, Pain, Bonding, and Stress Systems are destabilized.
- These destabilized brain systems can set off a firestorm in her emotional systems, changing her brain chemistry.
- Brain and body chemistry changes, if untreated, can cause medical issues.

*T*rust Your Gut, That's All There Is to It

According to many blogs, books, and coaches, to be safe again, out there in the world against the 1 in 5 with personality disorders and the 1 in 100 with no conscience, all you must do is trust your gut, remember what you learned from the experience of a PLR, or tune into your red flags.

There, isn't that simple?

This dangerous advice is not educated in the facts of the personality science of survivors—the unusual personality trait combinations that raise their risk levels for being exactly who Darkness seeks. It fails to recognize what trauma does to the intuition they hope to trust, now or in the future.

Intuition is 'the ability to understand something immediately, without the need for conscious reasoning.'[1] It's one of those words that is hard to explain so, in many ways, is left unexplained. It's thought of as the primal impulse of the mind, so it's not only related to thinking. It's 'knowing' without knowing why you know; a direct apprehension of something that is occurring, or a function of perception that sorts through conscious and unconscious information. It's sort of having an eye to the background material of what is happening or the ability to sense the hidden meaning in something or someone.

Lots of empaths and INFJs (Myers-Briggs Introversion, Intuition, Feeling, and Judging personality types) and people who work in the energy field claim to have higher intuition that functions like an extension of sensory functioning. Things we see and hear are our senses, but what we perceive is our intuition. Some equate it with a spiritual (but not necessarily religious) functioning.

Intuition can, of course, have a protective function in being able to 'intuit' danger, and that's what survivors are really concerned with — "don't let this happen to me again!" Risk analyst Gavin de Becker, author of *The Gift of Fear*,[2] explains that the primal emotion of fear even without facts *is* the action of intuition — a knot in the stomach, an uneasiness, or the hair on your body standing up. Fear as instinct, and intuition as sensing, are largely primal and are an awareness of something below the level of consciousness or the thinking mind.

But many people, and especially trauma survivors, have had the messages of their fear response hijacked and replaced with anxiety which are not the same things. Real fear is protective. Anxiety is a counterfeit and often sees phantom possible events that don't happen and distracts from sensing legitimate fear signals.

Anxiety is a state characterized by the expectation and preparation for danger — even if it's an unknown event — while fear implies a specific object to be feared in the *here/now*.

Survivor Note:

Anxiety is, "He MIGHT harm me again." where fear is, "He IS harming me with his fist, words, and actions in this moment."
Fear is based in the moment—anxiety is based in the future.

So, it would seem that the only thing survivors need to do to tap back into the protection of their intuition is to hum, have a Zen moment, and come back into their bodies to feel the primal fear and then RESPOND. The next time her gut wrenches when she meets a new guy, all she needs to do is high-tail it. But de Becker states that, while most of us do have a primal fear response as part of our intuition, many of us have experienced tampering with this mechanism from trauma and anxiety, and from willfully overriding it.

De Becker discusses that, in the animal kingdom, for instance, if a wolf walks into an unknown den and finds a bear who growls (or even if he doesn't growl), the wolf's consistent fear instinct is to back out of the den. Animals react to the intuitive signal of danger. They don't have internal dialogue with themselves like, "What did that mean? Why did he say that? I don't like that behavior—I wonder if he was abused as a child?" They simply run. You don't see animals stuck in abusive mating environments. When survivors respond to the flash of true fear or intuition, they aren't left having a commentary with themselves. De Becker states that unlike any other living creature, humans will sense danger, yet *still* walk right into it.

There are other things, though, than just the ability to *get* an intuitive feeling that predicts *how* protective our intuition will *be*.

$\mathcal{H}$ow Intuition Becomes Inconsistent

Back to Oprah-ology for a moment… There seems to be a universal belief that everyone has *good* intuition, that all we need to do is tap in more or take a class from one of the gurus.

Intuition being that sort of hard-to-name *quality*—with all its primal (and who can explain that?) unconscious and instinctive impulses, with all its not fully understood processes, with all its etherealness of it lives 'in here' which is somewhere mysterious, straddling the worlds between spirit and the mind—makes it hard to know whether it is produced by angels, a reptilian brain, the roll of the dice in personality, a brain chemistry lotto, or a combo pack of all of the above. And if we can't even tie down this wispy-natured mystery, how do we ever know when something goes wrong with it?

Like anything else that even remotely has to do with the mind, brain, and personality, there are plenty of things in those realms that can influence the coveted receptors of the primal and ethereal message.

Overriding the Signal

Our tendency, as cultured people, tends to put political correctness in front of responding to messages of fear because to do otherwise would be perceived as rude. De Becker used a story as an example –

You're in a hallway waiting for an elevator late at night. The elevator door opens and there's a guy inside. You feel a flash of true fear, an intuition that you should not step in. You don't know why, but you definitely had a flash of fear and the message was "Do Not Enter."

Many women will stand there and look at that guy and say to themselves, "Oh, I don't want to think like that. I don't want to be the kind of person who lets the door close in his face. I don't want him to think I think he's dangerous when he might be a really nice guy."

De Becker states, "And so human beings will get into a steel soundproof chamber with someone they're afraid of, while there isn't an animal in nature that would even consider it."

Survivor Note:
According to de Becker, women can impair or make their own intuition unreliable by overriding and ignoring an intuition when they receive one.

The more often she ignores it, she's retraining her brain to ignore the fear signal. Once rewired, the incoming intuition is merely a blip on the radar screen that used to be a flashing red alert. In the case of a PLR that lasted months or years, that's a lot of overrides.

The question is, is there a personality trait responsible for some women thinking "I don't want him to think I think he is dangerous"?

Personality and the Signal

Well, to answer the question just posed above—yes, there is a trait. It's called Harm Avoidance. As we have seen with the Super Traits, not all people come with the same amount of each personality trait, meaning some of us have more (or less) of certain traits, which causes problems for survivors because of their own elevated traits. In the personality realm, we don't all come wired with the same ability to pick up incoming intel of red flags. Some of us miss the intel more than others because some have less of the harm avoidance trait, which has a protective measure to it.

The personality trait of harm avoidance includes facets of:[3]

- Excessive worrying
- Pessimism
- Shyness
- Fearful doubt/fear of uncertainty
- Becoming easily fatigued by others

Hmmm... that **doesn't** sound like the Super Traits of agreeableness and conscientiousness, does it? Just as a refresher, here are some of the agreeableness and conscientious traits compared to the harm avoidance traits -

Table 18.1

Harm Avoidance Traits vs. Agreeableness/Conscientiousness Traits

Harm Avoidance	Agreeableness/Conscientiousness
Anticipatory/excessive worrying	Open and warm
Pessimism	Optimistic about human nature
Fearful doubt/fear of uncertainty	Self-confident/acceptance
Easily fatigued	Persevering, diligent

It is hard to imagine that someone with high harm avoidance with all that pessimism being anything like the 'optimistic about human nature' person. Or the 'easily fatigued' person being anything like the 'persevering' one.

That's because the survivors **aren't.**

From the survivor's high-normal agreeableness and conscientious-

373

ness we learned that being *over* the bell curve has caused her some problems with Darkness. Now we are going to look at what being *under* the bell curve can do to her ability to sense red flags.

Low Harm Avoidance

On the TCI, half of the survivors tested as having *low* harm avoidance.[4] That means that their naturally occurring personality is prone to the following -

- They were *not* having excessive worrying (because they had a lot of self-confidence)
- They were *not* prone to pessimism (because they had a lot of optimism about human nature)
- They were *not* fearful (due to self-confidence and resourcefulness)
- They were *not* easily fatigued by others (due to perseverance and diligence)

Being low in a personality trait has its crosses to bear. It means there isn't a balanced amount of the trait for optimal protection.

- A little suspicious nature can go a long way toward not being optimistic about *all* human nature or stepping into an elevator at night with a man you don't know.
- A little worry that people aren't always who they say they are could be preventative.
- A little fear and uncertainty of someone's actions could open the trap door for escape sooner.
- A little fatigue from someone wearing one out with their constant drama might set more boundaries.

Being low in harm avoidance as a naturally occurring personality trait places survivors at risk because, not only are they not suspicious *enough*, the little bit of incoming intel they might pick up on is also met with their agreeableness — all that empathy, tolerance, and blind trust — seeing others through who she is, etc. In a nanosecond, all those affiliated facets of Super Traits can alter the potential response of the red flags.[5] That's not good news for survivors because it shows just how unconscious our filters of personality can be. For the woman getting ready to step into the elevator, her Super Trait of agreeableness did a huge number on the intuition she had just a second before.

Those with normal amounts of harm avoidance may become a victim of a PLR *less* often because their intuition helps them read and perceive the intel differently than someone with low harm avoidance.[6]

==

Survivor Note:
Having low harm avoidance, then, is as much a risk factor for survivors as having high normal agreeableness and conscientiousness. This means risk factors that predators likely seek include high-normal agreeableness, high-normal conscientiousness, and low harm avoidance.[6]

==

So, as opposed to what the gurus tout, you may not be able to *permanently* and *consistently* raise your level of intuition in your *personality* when it is structured otherwise. You can sit in a lotus position and conjure up from the other side of the spirit world or wherever it is generated "out there," but you might not be getting more of it from the here and now in your *personality*.

There may be some things you can do to supplement it but know that there is not a permanent and consistent repair in the personality. The safest thing you can do is to know you have a personality that is naturally lower in harm avoidance so that you make accommodations for it, and approach it differently in the future. While some recovery approaches lead us to believe that we just tune in, or that these primal and ethereal signals are not connected at all to personality because the intuition is thought to be only spirit generated, it is dangerous for survivors to misunderstand their own personality wiring which can affect how well their intuition is responded to. It is important that they know, in their here and now personality, there are propensities for a lack of responding to signals like the story of the woman and the elevator. They should act in ways that protect these low areas of personality functioning and refrain from believing that the past PLR has rewired their personality to know better in the future. Sure, you might *know*, but will your harm avoidance trait *respond*?

There are also other reasons why some survivors might misread the cues of fear, or be slow in responding…

*H*arm Avoidance and Hypervigilance

To make things even more confusing, the trait of harm avoidance can do strange and unusual things after a PLR, trauma, and/or unrelenting stress. Many survivors find themselves exactly LIKE the harm avoidance traits listed above after a PLR.

Harm avoidance in a personality is a measurement of *anxiety*. Those traits of worrying, fear, shyness, and fatigability are often associated with anxiety. Before the PLR (or before earlier traumas, like childhood adversity, if they existed), it is likely the survivor's natural personality configuration was *low* in anxiety. That makes sense with all that conscientiousness full of self-directed behavior, acceptance and confidence, and with the resourcefulness traits. With agreeableness—of being tolerant and giving, optimistic and trusting—there just isn't a lot of naturally occurring anxiety.[7]

Until the PLR.

As noted in earlier chapters, aftermath symptoms *are* trauma symptoms. Acute stress disorder, PTSD, and C-PTSD are identified in the DSM under *anxiety* disorders. Survivors coming out of a PLR most likely have an anxiety disorder of some magnitude. Trauma disorders including PTSD and C-PTSD have hypervigilance as symptoms.

---

hypervigilance

noun

an enhanced state of sensory sensitivity accompanied by an exaggerated intensity of behaviors whose purpose is to detect activity. It may bring about a state of increased anxiety which can cause exhaustion. Other symptoms include abnormally increased arousal, a high responsiveness to stimuli, and a constant scanning of the environment to search for sights, sounds, people, behaviors, smells, or anything else that is reminiscent of activity, threat, or trauma.[8]

It would be easy to mistake hypervigilance which is an 'enhanced state of sensory sensitivity' with intuition that is described as a 'direct apprehension of something that is occurring, or an extended sensory function.' And it's even easier to misread why hypervigilance feels like throbbing intuition.

Survivors who began life *low* in harm avoidance and absent of excessive anxiety now find themselves completely the opposite with many of the features of what is now *high* harm avoidance—anxiety-ridden and full of hypervigilance. Now they feel they do match the traits of harm avoidance—brimming with excessive worrying, pessimistic, fear of uncertainty, and fatigued. They can't even remember when their personality was low in harm avoidance because by the mid-relationship phase in the PLR, they were into high harm avoidance, and have been ever since.[9]

Consequently, they are completely suspicious of everyone's motives and fear a psychopath behind every tree, fear the future, and obsessing that they will never feel like themselves again. What most survivors want is a return to their previous worldview. They want again to be optimistic about human nature, to see others through who they are, to trust, and to come home to who they always were. Many of them ask, "When will I trust others again? I hate being suspicious!" They want a return to low harm avoidance.

The PLR has raised their anxiety, creating a sensation of having heightened intuition from hypervigilance.[10] From the hypervigilance comes a belief they have (consistent and reliable) intuition because they feel keenly in tune with all aspects of their suspicion. But this altered state of *high* harm avoidance, complete with enough paranoia to now invoke conditional trust and a perceived heightened intuition, is most likely only *temporary*. The trauma that has adjusted her low harm avoidance into high harm avoidance may give the survivor an artificial sense of protection that, since she is so hypervigilant she will see it coming next time because she is now suspicious of everything.

However, even hypervigilance is not a remedy to the problem of intuition, because distortions in incoming intel happen when anxiety sets off the glugs of neurochemistry, like adrenaline, which can cause survivors to overreact as if everything is a threat. Most survivors have had experiences when they were hypervigilant (often from adrenaline) that, things they thought were happening, they later realized were not. They wrongly misread the situation, and wrongly assumed their anxiety was a true intuitive fear reaction like de Becker warned when he said anxiety is a counterfeit reaction.

Survivor Note:

Anxiety can be a counterfeit reaction that masks true intuitive fear.

Hypervigilance as a trauma reaction normally reduces with treatment. What was once her perceived edge to see it coming will not always be there (hopefully) if she gets the correct kind of treatment. But survivors don't realize that as the hypervigilance decreases, so does the artificial or counterfeit protection it provided in the adjustment to their naturally occurring low harm avoidance.[11]

She cannot afford to assume that hypervigilance will always be there. Misinformed bloggers who are telling her to just trust her gut or red flags are committing an act of leading the lamb to the slaughter to suggest she has a skill that her personality has not equipped her with in balanced proportions, or that untreated trauma has altered in a risky way.

Before she returns to her previous personality configuration, there is also another impact to her intuition she needs to be aware of—how trauma further impacts intuition.

Harm Avoidance, Hypo-vigilance, and Emotional Numbing

We discussed how trauma causes hypervigilance to become highly elevated which makes her cautious about everyone entering her life or the motives of others. The example of hypervigilance that can temporarily raise her sensory perceptions of incoming intel is not the only way intuition is altered by trauma. There is the opposite—hypo or low vigilance.

Trauma disorders, specifically PTSD and C-PTSD have the symptom called 'emotional numbing.' Emotional numbing means that a person is not feeling or sensing emotions or bodily sensations that are often clues to danger. As we have seen, intuition is highly predicated on a functioning sensing system.

De Becker reminds us how the *correct* sensing of fear is hijacked by the masked symptom of anxiety. Anxiety can cause one to misread or not sense danger. The issue of people *already* having been previously traumatized can change how they react to lurking potential danger and may be why they didn't see Darkness coming in the first place. Therefore, not everyone may have the same reaction to red flags, especially those with preexisting trauma.

Trauma science has taught us that having had previous trauma changes how we read incoming information in the brain. For survivors who had early childhood adversity or adult trauma prior to the PLR, who wonder how they didn't see it coming, their ability to perceive may have been obstructed in receiving the correct *perception* of him because of emotional numbing. The emotional numbing that is common in trauma is not just the absence of the ability to feel joy. It can also change the way survivors perceive or intuit red flag emotions and bodily reactions like a pounding heart or a rush of adrenaline that should tell them they are in danger.

This means untreated trauma can place survivors at high risk for not correctly reading the incoming intel as changes to the brain occur from trauma, reducing the brain's ability to read and *react* appropriately (covered in a previous chapter related to the executive functioning of the brain). Since trauma disorders alter brain reactions to incoming information, it is why some sexual assault victims, for instance, are MORE at risk of not reading danger signals *after* they were victimized because emotional numbing has disrupted the way they read incoming intel and has slowed reaction time.

To complicate it further, survivors can move in and out of hypervigilance and emotional numbing or hypo-vigilance—sometimes being on high alert and paranoid (feeling their intuition is abuzz with sensitivity), and other times, being numb or dissociated from what is happening around them. During times of hypervigilance they may feel competent to see it coming while not realizing they may later cycle through numbing or hypo-vigilance that will place them at risk.[12] This is one of the big reasons why we advise survivors not to date while they still have a trauma disorder!

When our intuition is not impaired by personality trait functioning, when it doesn't have to go through our filters of past trauma, or when it isn't tainted by lots of neurological changes to our brain from a PLR, it's a pretty good mechanism. But as we can see, there are lots of things that can, and do, influence the functionality of intuition.

*I*ntuition and Future Aftermath

The issue of inconsistent intuition has everything to do with potential future aftermath[13] and cannot be stressed enough. Survivors might look back at the beginning of the PLR and remember when they did have red flags and those red flags turned out to be true. They surmise that -

Red flags + they were true = I have fully functioning intuition©

The belief that she will see it next time is shortsighted about the natural propensity and predisposition of personality. She didn't have just *one* red flag. This wasn't *a* single act of ignoring intuition. Over the years in the PLR she had hundreds of red flags that continued to be met with her core beliefs of her personality. Those intuitions were overridden again and again—so much so that it produced cognitive dissonance. Her natural tendency, even in the face of intuition and then later the facts—was still to try to believe the best. Her optimism about human behavior, her relationship investment, and her cognitive dissonance reaction was still stronger than reality.

It is often years until something breaks through the grip of the Super Traits and the cognitive dissonance (let's call it grace and mercy), that lets her finally respond *differently* to intuitive fear transmitted months or years earlier.[15] This is the ongoing risk of Super Trait influenced intuition.

Inconsistent Intuition

While we can cheer that the survivor did notice the red flags eventually, it is still a long way from confidently assuming that her intuition is *consistently* responded to. The fact that there were hundreds of red flags before she reacted differently is a sample of how inconsistent a Super Traited person's response to intuition can be.

I use the analogy of Attention Deficit Hyperactivity Disorder (ADHD) as an example. While ADHD is not related to the personality (so is different than Super Traits), it can serve as an example. In ADHD, there doesn't seem to be a space between thinking and behavior. If someone with ADHD thinks it, they do it or say it. Therapeutic work with these patients is about trying to create a big enough space between a thought and choosing the way they want to respond, not simply reacting.

In my thinking, the power of naturally occurring personality is like that. Personality filters and the automatic reactions, even to intuition, seem not to leave space to react differently. The space between receiving an intuition and the immediacy of Super Traits reconfiguring the response to that intuition through filters of agreeableness, conscientiousness, and low harm avoidance happens in a nanosecond.[16]

It takes a lot of work to help survivors learn to operate differently—but not just from a traumatic reaction of *that can't happen to me again* because that doesn't work. However, learning, when they are involved with people they don't know, their Super Traits are going to want to go back to their natural default to what feels comfortable to them, therefore, their entire *lifestyle* of approach must change.

This is not a behavioral quick fix. The lengthy work which requires creating that space between Super Traits immediacy, often completely opposite of what they would normally and automatically do, takes time. It's not that their intuition is never correct, it's that the immediacy and filters of their Super Traits are likely to hijack the message and send it back to its default setting.[17]

==

Survivor Note:

What is important to recognize is that inconsistency in intuition is far more than not having any intuition. As we have seen, many survivors do have intuition, but what they do with the incoming intel is the problem. The risk is that it only takes one time of inconsistency in their intuition, or their Super Traits jumping in front of incoming information, for them to make the same mistake again. Who wants to trust that it will never happen again?

==

Wrapping This All Up

Intuition is meant to be our safety mechanism. Everyone needs it— it's a crazy world out there. It's been years of *The Institute* teaching one of our seminars, *How to Spot a Dangerous Man Before You Get Involved*, to recognize that we can *teach* the signs of pathology, but if someone is naturally predisposed to having low harm avoidance, all the signs in the world may not be enough protection for them to consistently *respond* to those signs without some work on that issue.

Just like many of the assumptions that have plagued survivors that I have discussed in the Preface and Foreword—of being mis-, dis-, and nonidentified—the issue of inconsistent intuition can be placed on the pile of things not understood by the survivor, therapists, nor from whomever they are getting their pathology education. Not understanding low harm avoidance can lead to assumptions that survivors are naive or that their reactions are codependent, stemming from the low self-esteem of not wanting to confront the red flags because of needing to be accepted.

The duck's quack of inconsistent intuition may not be related to learned helplessness or other family dynamics but by something as simple, yet deeply innate, as her personality configuration, or as powerful as her untreated trauma.

Treating a survivor's trauma for symptom reduction may bring relief, but without the work on intuition, she will never be supplied with the safety mechanism that will keep her out of future PLRs. She comes into this world already targeted due to her Super Traits because Darkness knows how to find her. With inconsistent intuition from either personality or trauma, how could she see him coming?

Chapter Eighteen Endnotes

1, 6-16 Brown, Sandra L., *The Institute* (2017). Inconsistent Intuition in Survivors of Pathological Love Relationships: Impact of Super Trait Personality Elevations and Trauma. Prepared for *Women Who Love Psychopaths, Third Edition* and *The Institute's Therapist Training Program and Manual: Treating the Aftermath of Pathological Love Relationships.*

2 de Becker, Gavin (1998). *The Gift of Fear: Survival Signals That Protect Us from Violence.* Random House Publishing Group.

3 Cloninger, R., Przybeck, T., Svrakic, D., & Wedel, R. (1994). *TCI-Guide to Its Development and Use.* Center for Psychobiology of Personality, Washington University, (July). https://www.worldcat.org/title/temperament-and-character-inventory-tci-a-guide-to-its-development-and-use/oclc/32133789

4 Brown, Sandra L. and Leedom, Liane J., *The Institute* (2007). Temperament and Character Inventory Outcomes of Women's Super Traits: Elevations in Pathological Love Relationships in *Women Who Love Psychopaths: Inside the Relationships of Inevitable Harm. First Edition (2008); also, in *Women Who Love Psychopaths Second Edition (2009).*

5 Brown, Sandra L. and Young, Jennifer R., *The Institute* (2014). Five Factor Form/Five Factor Model Rating Form traits of agreeableness and conscientiousness in pathological love relationship dynamics. An interagency report; also prepared for *The Institute's Therapist Training Program and Manual: Treating the Aftermath of Pathological Love Relationships.*

Section Five

Puzzle Piece #5™
The Finished Puzzle

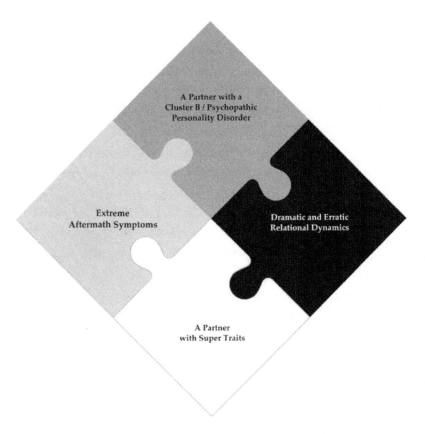

Figure 19.1
Puzzle Piece #1-4™

Chapter Nineteen: The Basics of a Recovery Model

Chapter Nineteen

The Basics of a Recovery Model
The Finished Puzzle

We have completed all the puzzle pieces that show all aspects of a PLR. Now we'll discuss recovery from a PLR since we understand the four puzzle pieces that comprise them.

Quick Survivor Review

- There are societal assumptions about everyone having functional intuition.
- Intuition can be affected by personality traits such as harm avoidance.
- Intuition can be inconsistent due to overriding it, anxiety, personality traits, and trauma reactions.

We've finally reached the topic that every survivor wants to know about—how to recover. What should now be apparent is that PLRs are comprised of a unique set of problems that are both severe and not well understood. Amidst a psychology field that has never had a true theory for this type of relationship and aftermath, survivors are at a loss for how to heal. Many of their symptoms go unidentified or misdiagnosed. Some approaches have made their symptoms worse, while no treatment at all has left them with symptoms which have not gotten better.

Each person's unique care plan is beyond the scope of this book and is something that should be left for trained mental health professionals; however, over the past several decades we have found that there are universal needs which all survivors must include in their steps to recovery and should be aware of. All survivors need -

- Awareness
- Education
- The ability to find meaning in their suffering

- Validation which is not steeped in post-decision dissonance
- Symptom management/trauma treatment
- Super Trait specialized education and intervention
- Life restructuring

Survivors can address many of these needs in their steps to recovery. However, other steps require finding Trauma-Informed Care. But let's examine each of these universal needs individually and present some guidelines for what a survivor should be looking for to meet each of them.

Steps to Recovery from a Pathological & Toxic Relationship©

Understanding the Unique Needs of PLRs Compared to Other Recovery Models

PLRs, as a unique category of relationship-wounding and trauma, create specific types of challenges that survivors should be aware of. There are various recovery approaches, some which compliment PLR recovery. Most people are aware of recovery models like the 12 Steps, that can be applied to a variety of issues—drugs, alcohol, spending, gambling, and sexual acting out. Millions have found sanity in rooms around the world that teach their version of the 12 Steps for recovery.

Likewise, many people are familiar with the Grief Recovery Model and its Five Stages of Grief—denial and isolation, anger, bargaining, depression, and acceptance. There is certainly a grief process in recovery from PLRs and survivors may find themselves going through those stages.

Survivors may simultaneously use the 12 Steps and the Grief Recovery Model in their recovery. The 12 Steps can help with out-of-control self-medicating while recovering, and grief stages are probably applicable to almost everyone as they grieve the loss of a feigned relationship.

PLRs, because of their unique traumatic impact, require *additional* specialized types of recovery that focus specifically on the aftermath caused by Darkness. Survivors may go through denial, anger, bargaining, depression, and eventually acceptance. These are related to the loss of the relationship, whether it was the survivor's decision or her partners to end it. While understanding these stages helps move her through the sensation of a loss, for recovery to occur, it does not address the unique elements of a PLR that need additional focus.

While grief is focused on loss, and the 12 Steps address managing life-altering behaviors, neither of them focuses on the exposure to someone else's pathology and the trauma it caused. That's why PLR Steps to Recovery adds the missing elements for a well-rounded recovery. We encourage survivors to use the 12 Steps and Grief Recovery methods if they need them, in conjunction with PLR Steps to Recovery.

Below are the steps that *The Institute* makes sure is in every recovery plan. While these steps can seem like 'do this' then 'do that,' recovery is never that linear. The steps are really processes that survivors will need to address, and they often overlap or occur simultaneously while working on recovery. For instance, pathology education is likely to occur throughout trauma treatment as will a clinical form of validation. So, while we list them as steps to make them relevant to what survivors might already know through 12 steps or grief recovery steps, some of these can occur while working on other items in the process.

Step One: Awareness

Step One of the 12 Steps and Stage One of Grief Recovery attempts to address an *awareness* of the problem. Step One of the 12 Steps says "we became aware we were powerless" over what had taken over our lives. Grief Recovery notes that "denial is an absence of awareness." Both deal with the need for awareness in order to proceed with recovery.

In PLRs, effective public pathology education draws attention to the unique elements of a PLR. "You can't fix what you don't identify." So, until a survivor understands what kind of relationship she was in, she may be barking up the wrong tree by acquiring information for relationships that are dysfunctional for other reasons.

All awareness is not created equal, though. I am often saddened while reading some of the blogs, websites and social media pages moderated by those who are not trauma-informed professionals. I read things like, "Cluster Bs are delusional or psychotic," which is usually incorrect. Or, "The best way to heal is to tell your story until it feels like you don't want to tell it anymore," which, as you have read, creates more trauma symptoms!

The *quality* of the awareness to which a survivor is exposed is one of the foundations on which she will build a recovery, so it matters if the information is correct or not. While awareness is not the totality of education, getting off on the wrong foot can lead the survivor into problems in the next step of recovery—pathology education.

Step Two: Pathology Education

In the 12 Steps, education is part of the recovery process—people learn about compulsive behavior. All the step work in the 12 Steps has an educational thread woven into it. In Grief Recovery, it's less obvious where education is part of the process until the acceptance phase, in which, during the natural process of grieving, a breakthrough happens as a result of the education. In these two recovery approaches, the person must receive some type of education to understand her experiences and recover.

Awareness that is based and built on accurate information will heighten a survivor's receptivity to finding out more about PLRs and will lead to even more in-depth education. Perhaps she saw a meme, or a blurb, or someone's website, and that heightened her curiosity to learn more.

PLR *education*, as identified by *The Institute*, includes the four components of PLRs—the puzzle pieces covered in the earlier parts of the book:

1. Information about personality disorders/psychopathy as related to the survivor's partner.
2. The unique relationship dynamics in PLRs that differs from merely bad, abusive, codependent, or addictive relationships, and why.
3. Based on *The Institute*'s research with Purdue University, the elevated personality traits of the survivor which attract pathological partners, add to the relationship dynamics, and perpetuate difficulty in identifying the incoming pathological partner and disengaging from him.
4. The aftermath trauma, which is comprised of a mixture of typical and atypical symptoms including cognitive dissonance, self-perception-based injuries, impacted intuition, and difficulty knowing how to heal.

What she learns, and from where she learns it, is important. The quality of the education she acquires has everything to do with the core misinformation or disinformation she is going to try to build her recovery on. You can't adequately heal from something when you have a mishmosh of incorrect information presented by someone who does not correctly understand the issue. The survivor will be trying to heal based on incorrect education. Many survivors we work with are those who found their sources of information mostly from other survivors, and their education must be totally dismantled and rebuilt.

What is needed is education that is research based, has a foundation established in mental health principles related to pathology and relationships, and that is based on a survivor's specific type of trauma. If it matters enough for a survivor to dig for accurate information, she should go to an accurate source. Failure to understand what she has lived through will impact the next existentially crucial step of finding meaning in the suffering she has lived through.

Step Three: Finding Meaning in Suffering

One of a 12 Step group's slogans is *never regret what you lived through to get you where you are today*. This core need to find meaning in suffering is experienced after the disastrous effects of a compulsive behavior that led a person to hit rock bottom, and to finally build a life of abstinence.

Working through grief also focuses on finding meaning in the life lesson of loss. People who have suffered the pain of divorce, a job loss, the death of a friend, or a PLR, all share this need to convert suffering into something useful, even something that is redemptive. The comprehensive view of all four puzzle pieces of a PLR's destruction helps to bring a more rounded view of finding meaning in the totality of the experience, not just the gaslighting, the trickery, or the eventual discarding.

The act of finding meaning is not only the mindful reconstitution of something awful into something insightful, it is a necessary hurdle in the process of recovery. Otherwise, a survivor's eye is only on that which is lost, and she lives perpetually as a victim. Although no survivor would ever say she was glad she went through it, she becomes convinced that what others meant as harm can be converted into good, at least for her. In some ways, this step toward finding meaning is akin to a level of spiritual work.

This focus of finding meaning was a catalyst in my own recovery following my father's murder and it is what led me to my life's work. While I could reduce my PTSD symptoms, I still struggled to understand the place that homicide played in my life. And until I did, I was stuck in the recovery process.

The need to turn this around, not just for the survivor but for others, is so universal—especially in survivors with Super Traits who are resourceful, empathetic, and optimistic—that it is the leading reason why survivors flock to the field of pathology education to pay it forward.

Step Four: Validation

In 12 Step rooms around the world, people support each other as they validate one another's struggles from life-altering behavior. Likewise, grief survivors validate each other's experience in the stages of loss. Clearly, validation is a part of most recovery processes.

The word *validation* means 'to substantiate or confirm.' PLR survivors need to find out if what they lived through is a PLR and if they are crazy, which many have been told they are. Most will find a website and compare/contrast a staggering number of descriptions that could have nothing to do with the *true* elements of a PLR—not every bad breakup is the result of a PLR, and not every abuser or jerk is a Cluster B/psychopath. But these are rarely differentiated.

There are clinical criteria that need to be met to discuss a potential diagnosis of Cluster B and to provide a conclusive "yes" to validate a survivor's experience as a PLR. It is tantalizing for her to find a website full of women telling their own stories that sound a lot like hers, and she can spend hours and days digesting it. It feels like an oasis of understanding. And yes, she does need to find validation that gaslighting and coercion is real, that cognitive dissonance is a real symptom, and that, no, there was nothing she could have done to have a happily ever after ending with a psychopath. Validation is a necessary and concrete step in recovery.

Validation, though, is more than a survivor agreeing with her or sharing a similar story. In PLRs, what's needed is a *clinical* validation of her trauma symptoms and a clinical discussion about his suspected diagnosis.

As we have seen in the chapter on cognitive dissonance, validation seeking is also a form of unresolved dissonance searching for resolution. Many sites are what we call 'sit and spin' sites, where survivors are encouraged, or at least allowed, to continue to tell their story repeatedly. while ingraining rumination and cognitive dissonance symptoms. The stories of others trigger trauma reactions in the survivor who is then up for days with symptoms that are set on fire by participating in a setting that is not guided by Trauma-Informed Care—care which is created under a structure that understands what makes trauma worse and adheres to standards that do no further harm.

We receive many crisis contacts from survivors who have found these online oases of unmoderated storytelling that have ignited their PTSD symptoms. As we have seen from the information on the neurological impact to the brain, what happens to the condition of the brain is very real. Much of this is perpetrated by excessive reading of material about *My Life with a Psychopath,* or by sitting in chat forums reading one story after the next, fueling the survivor's own trauma and increasing the symptoms she hoped she was trying to heal.

Validation in PLRs, as opposed to the 12 Steps and Grief support, needs to be more than "Yes, that happened to me too," or support acquired from other still-recovering survivors. The survivor needs to disengage from the topic of pathology *except* in guided forms of public pathology education that adhere to Trauma-Informed Care or while verbally processing the PLR in a therapy session. Only in this way will a survivor be able to reduce her trauma symptoms.

Since the need for continued validation is often a *symptom* of cognitive dissonance, survivor bloggers may read this symptom as a need to spend more time on the issue, which increases cognitive dissonance and the neurological impact on the survivor. The duck's quack of needing validation doesn't mean it is always just that. Validation, as the bedrock of support in recovery, needs to adhere to Trauma-Informed Care practices to be effective and not to retraumatize the survivor.

Step Five: Symptom Management and Trauma Treatment

In the 12 Steps, much of the focus is how to manage the desire to relapse. This form of symptom management is woven throughout the recovery process. Grief recovery also uses symptom management techniques for managing the symptoms of loss. In compulsive behavior or loss, symptom management is important to recovery.

In PLRs, what survivors want most is a reduction or elimination of their symptoms, which can include intrusive thoughts, anxiety, panic, cognitive dissonance, rumination, not feeling like their former selves, and distrust of their judgment and intuition. They want the craving for the relationship to stop and the flashbacks of both the good and bad memories to be gone—in other words, they want their trauma symptoms abated.

Over 90 percent of survivors have some form of trauma symptoms, a trauma disorder, or an acute stress disorder. Some will have full blown *active* PTSD, and some will have Complex PTSD with symptoms that may be with them for months or years. All forms of trauma are *treatable,* not *coachable* disorders. They require a trauma therapist who is trained in Trauma-Informed Care and who knows not only how to reduce the symptoms through treatment, but how to not cause the symptoms *to increase.*

Symptom management for trauma is related to mental health counseling approaches and comes from Evidence Based Practices, meaning that therapists use not only what is known to help but, just as importantly, what is known not to further trigger or harm.

Treatment can contain -

- Trauma therapy
- Cognitive behavioral therapy (CBT)
- Dialectical behavioral counseling (DBT)
- Stress reduction
- Eye Movement Desensitization and Reprocessing (EMDR)
- Other specialized approaches that are taught in graduate school and through specialization training

Symptom management is *a therapeutic process* that prepares the survivor with a toolbox of therapeutic techniques and skills to reduce her symptoms. The process takes time to gain mastery over triggers through technique building. It is, however, not the be-all and end-all of the recovery process. There is more work to be done after symptom management, but survivors will not continue in recovery if they don't feel reasonably safe in managing the symptoms they do have before unearthing more issues to deal with. Symptom management that is done right will give survivors the confidence to continue in treatment, so they can realize a more completed recovery.

Just like a percentage of 12 Step group members are going to need detox treatment, and many Grief Recovery members may need a Grief Therapist, over half of survivors of PLRs are going to need more than education and validation. They are going to need a trauma specialist.

Step Six: Super Trait Education and Management Specialization for Recovery

People using the 12 Steps, who need to overcome life-threatening compulsive behaviors such as substance-abuse addictions, are not likely to go to a career counselor for help. People suffering from grief are not likely to go to a neuropsychologist. Why? Because what they need is a specialized approach to what they are trying to conquer. Specialized treatment helps people be successful in their recovery by addressing what is unique to their situation.

In PLRs, the core issues surrounding why a survivor was targeted are related to what a pathological predator *hunts*—Super Traits. We know this from our research and the testing we have done, and that has been discussed throughout this book.

Survivors will never be able to guard against future pathological partners if their treatment approaches have not addressed what is really the culprit. Receiving help for codependency when you don't have it is like going to a career counselor for assistance with alcoholism.

Super traits must be addressed to prepare the survivor not only to date again, but to safeguard those traits that others may seek to exploit in all areas of the survivors' lives. Therefore, a large amount of recovery work involves this specialization of working with Super Traits as they affect symptom management. PLR survivors who have not received this type of support, and who have instead invested in empath understanding or codependency counseling, have missed the life-saving work that can specifically help with their personality and intuition issues.

One result of a survivor's configuration of Super Traits is the impact of cognitive dissonance on her Self-Perceptual Injuries©. This is the other portion of Super Traits recovery work that can relieve much of the cognitive dissonance, and can help, not only to reduce symptoms, but reunite the survivor with core beliefs about herself—her true internal resources. Super Traits and Self-Perceptual Injury work comprise a significant portion of recovery, and without it survivors will never experience a return to themselves.

Step Seven: Life Restructuring

The goal in the 12 Steps is to regain sanity and to stop life-threatening compulsive behavior. In Grief Recovery, the goal is to live a life that is free of the chronic pain of loss. The goal of every recovery is to get over the pain of *something*, and to get back one's life.

In PLRs, the part that survivors want to jump to without doing all the other steps is life restructuring. They want to get their life back and get

.e. They want to get back out there and find a normal partner, ✓hich is possible as a process and in a specific order. But there are ✓r steps that must be taken first to prepare the survivor for success in ebuilding a life that is recovery focused.

People in 12 Step groups don't jump to Step 12 and begin helping others when they haven't even mastered Step 1—admitting they are powerless over alcohol. People in grief recovery can't embrace acceptance when they aren't even out of denial.

Many survivors think that merely making the symptoms go away is what they are after. This may have been advised by whatever type care provider they are utilizing—when the symptoms are gone they are ready to get back out there in the dating pool without having done the work involved for recovery to be successful and to learn how to have friendships or date partners more safely in the future.

Life restructuring is how their recovery will play out and will ensure that self-care and a structure for managing their symptoms is in place should issues arise in the future. This is the rest of the work for the survivor—the day-to-day practice of recovery principles in a structured, recovery-focused way that includes Super Trait awareness, self-care, symptom management, and learning to live a life that prevents relapse and retargeting. It is a life and recovery *style* that is attuned to a survivor's proclivities and the at-risk personality traits that predators seek.

Many people live the 12 Step recovery model forever. That is the goal: to change their lives for the better and to continue to use their recovery tools to stay abstinent from pathology for life. As the AA *Big Book* says, "Half measures availed us nothing." It does no good to simply change one's life only to relapse. The focus is on living one's best life—forever and always.

In PLRs, life restructuring focuses on getting appropriate support. The object is to achieve a gentle life in which the survivor recognizes the hyper vigilant trauma her mind and body have been through with an eye toward self-care, making mental and physical health a priority, and rebuilding those parts of her life that were ravaged by pathology. Specific steps for creating the structure of a supported life is taught and monitored until all the recovery principles have been incorporated into daily living.

$\mathcal{T}$he Good News in Recovery

This book has thus far catalogued a wide range of types of serious harm to survivors. It can be discouraging to see the breadth and depth of the trauma and then conclude that recovery isn't possible from something of this magnitude. But nothing could be further from the truth. Let's understand what is working in the survivor's favor and get a better understanding of trauma treatment.

Trauma is Treatable

Trauma and its various forms of reactions—acute stress, PTSD, and C-PTSD—are clinical disorders that can be successfully improved with the correct treatment. Every year we gain a better understanding of the effects of trauma on the brain and behavior. Treatment approaches are always improving based on our new information and understanding, and I can tell you that today's treatment is light years ahead of the not-so-effective ways trauma was treated in the 1980s when I was going through it. So that is great news. Today there are some highly effective techniques for symptom reduction.

Some of the more effective techniques within trauma treatment include Eye Movement Desensitization Reprocessing (EMDR), brain mapping, brain spotting, neuro feedback, Emotional Freedom Technique (EFT), and medication. Finding a trauma-certified therapist who incorporates these techniques, as opposed to only talk therapy, will result in more effective and less triggering treatment. Finding a trauma therapist who is willing to learn about PLRs is also a great step in your recovery.

With that said, the good news is trauma *is* treatable and *should* be treated. But what every survivor needs to know is that trauma can become worse over time when it is **not** treated. As discussed in earlier chapters, trauma thinking becomes an engrained and reactive way of thinking without intervention and treatment. Trauma, having both hyper and hypo brain impact, is not a likely situation for simply pulling yourself up by the bootstraps. Ignoring it and trying to get back to your old life will not relieve these symptoms, which become more entrenched as they are left untreated. However, trauma treatment brings symptom relief—the earlier the intervention, the better the outcome.

Your Super Traits Will Aid Your Recovery!

If you have come to hate your Super Traits with a passion for putting a target on your back with Darkness, hold up! You are naturally endowed with some hefty and positive stuff. Remember all that outwardly focused empathy? It's available for your own recovery if you point it in the other direction—toward yourself. It is the same with facets like tolerance and compassion. And the Super Trait of conscientiousness is just brimming with Recovery Boot Camp skills. It brings all that determination and aiming for achievement right to your doorstep of recovery. The conscientiousness trait alone is chock full of characteristics we try to develop in others in recovery who don't possess Super Traits, but you have them naturally!

Let's review some of the characteristics that you can draw on in recovery:

Table 19.1
Characteristics You Can Draw on in Recovery

Conscientiousness	Agreeableness
Anticipatory/excessive worrying	Open and warm
Pessimism	Optimistic about human nature
Fearful doubt/fear of uncertainty	Self-confident/acceptance
Easily fatigued	Persevering, diligent
Self-confidence	Empathy
Purposefulness, goal-directed behavior	Compassion
Controlled impulses	Prone to assisting, not attacking
Self-acceptance	Tolerance
Resourcefulness, perseverance	

These naturally occurring traits are who you are. Although they have been beaten down from the PLR, they are still in you and are ready to be resurrected and focused on your own recovery. Resourcefulness for finding the tools you need, persevering on your journey to recovery, exhibiting recovery-directed behavior, showing self-compassion, and assisting yourself—these are all excellent resources.

It has made survivors of PLRs a dream to work with because, when those Super Traits are pointed inward, plenty of internal resources are available.

Trauma Symptoms Are Reduceable Over Time

Survivors who have been in pain from the inevitable harm of a PLR are in a hurry to feel like themselves again. Symptoms of trauma are reduceable with the help of trauma therapists using evidence-based practices, but survivors are not often realistic about the time parameters of the treatment needed for this much harmful impact. Survivors with Super Traits of resourcefulness are likely to remember all the other times they pulled themselves out of bad situations and believe that recovery from aftermath is similar. Websites that promote their Three Steps to Recovery are likely to have greatly simplified this process. Aftermath, with all its traumatic reactions, cognitive dissonance, and neurological impact, is not addressed in just a few weeks' time. Work on self-perceptual injuries and understanding Super Traits takes longer than the site's suggestion to just have no contact with the partner. A combination of Trauma-Informed Care and PLR-specific recovery practices need to be employed for symptoms to be reduced.

Trauma Symptoms Are Improved by Trauma Informed Self-Help Measures

There is much that survivors can do to help their recovery along. First and foremost is to *do no further harm*. As we saw in the section on reexperiencing, survivors can harm their neurological processes by participating in actions that are not Trauma-Informed approaches, causing treatment to be more difficult and often taking longer. On the other hand, survivors can learn self-help methods that will aid in the work their trauma therapist is already doing. *The Institute*'s on-line *Living Recovery Program* is a type of Trauma-Informed Care that provides an excellent way to learn symptom reduction and self-care which will aid in recovery. However, for those with PTSD and C-PTSD, self-help alone or in lieu of counseling is not likely to be enough and may delay recovery as symptoms worsen. Self-help is best used in addition to counseling.

PLR Treatment is Effective

Earlier in this book we talked about the percentage of survivors who were different from those we studied in our Super Trait research. These were people who, unlike most in our group, had previous histories of early childhood abuse and neglect, alcoholic or pathological parents, and true histories of dependency and codependency. Since the length of trauma treatment is related to the length and breadth of previous trauma, those who experienced early childhood adversity also often require treatment before, or in addition to, PLR treatment. In addition, a survivor's personality has a lot to do with the internal resources she has to draw on. True codependency requires the acquisition of certain skills in order to face the rest of the recovery work, whereas survivors with more resiliency seem to have shorter and easier recoveries. Those with preexisting untreated trauma, topped off with a PLR, have more to work on than a survivor with just a PLR.

We experienced outcomes in a shorter period of time with -

- Survivors who did not have early childhood adversity
- Survivors who did not have true dependency or codependency
- Survivors who *consistently* used a trauma-trained professional
- Survivors who used additional PLR resources and PLR self-help materials
- Survivors who practiced doing no further harm regarding reexperiencing
- Survivors who did not have long histories of preexisting depression, anxiety, PTSD, or other mood disorders
- Survivors who did not relapse with Darkness or immediately jump into another relationship

These survivors could expect -

- From professional trauma treatment—trauma symptom reduction (not total symptom extinction) within six months to a year, including better neurological functioning
- From professional PLR interventions—a reduction in cognitive dissonance within six months
- From professional PLR interventions—a return to consistent self-care in six to nine months
- From professional PLR interventions—an understanding of how to work with their own Super Traits to prevent future damaging relationships within a year

- From professional PLR interventions—healing Self-Perceptual Injuries and reclaiming the pre-trauma self, within one to two years.

Some of this work is done concurrently.

As we can see, being run over by the Pathology Train is not as quick a fix as one would like, but then, most underestimate the harm caused by Darkness. However, recovery *is* possible when survivors make the right choices about treatment. Let's take a look at what a survivor needs to know when looking for competent help.

$\mathcal{W}$hat to Look for in Competent Care

Finding competent care according to the survivors is like looking for the Holy Grail. They find a therapist their insurance will cover only to find s/he doesn't know anything about personality disorders. They find someone hanging a shingle out that says they know PLRs only to find they are a highly traumatized survivor blogger trying to lead someone else somewhere she hasn't gone herself. They find a trauma therapist who, instead of diagnosing her with a trauma disorder, diagnoses her as codependent. Or they find a therapist who wants to try reunification marriage counseling even when Darkness has been diagnosed as psychopathic.

So frequent are these horror stories of finding competent care that *The Institute* did a data survey on Finding Competent Care. Over 300 persons took the survey. What we found out about their journey of trying to find someone, *anyone*, that possessed knowledge about PLRs and how to treat its trauma -

Finding Competent Care Survey Outcomes

Therapist Type, Length, and Experience

- 53.7% saw a therapist on an average of 4-9 times
- 38.7% spent $1k-5k on counseling
- 68% saw a psychologist
- 51% saw a Marriage and Family Therapist
- 49% of the therapists were not effective at spotting Darkness' pathology

- 51% of the therapists were not effective at identifying her symptoms as trauma
- 59.3% of the therapists were not effective at recognizing that the relational dynamics were harmful
- 50% of survivors tried to educate their therapist on PLRs
- 32.3% said their efforts did not help
- 49.7% were diagnosed as having PTSD
- 10.7% were diagnosed as having C-PTSD
- 45% were diagnosed (or concurrently diagnosed) as having codependency

Self-Help Measures

- 40.3% of survivors used self-help methods along with counseling
- 23.3% used self-help or online programs in lieu of counseling

Coaches

- Survivors spent an average of more than one year in coaching with a survivor coach-helper
- 51.2% found coaches were not effective or worsened their trauma symptoms

This data was compelling and certainly validated what survivors have been saying about finding the Holy Grail of both knowledgeable and professional care. And it's not a good testament about what is out there for care. It takes to task the psychology field for being so far behind in psychopathology training instead of Oprah-ology training. Help is coming soon on this through our Association for therapists.

So, we recognize all the problems and barriers to competent care. Most survivors want *The Institute* to be down the street from their house, crammed full of PLR-trained therapists and with PLR-trained attorneys, judges, and CPS workers on staff. Once a survivor has had a little PLR education, she is sure that this is the cause of her trauma and she wants to talk in detail about it to someone who gets it. But let's hit the reality button here. As you are well aware, PLR-trained therapists are not that plentiful *yet*, and it's why you can't find someone down the street from your house.

While we are pretty sure you might end up with a therapist who doesn't understand the totality of personality disorders, PLRs, and/or the unique aspects of your aftermath symptoms, it doesn't mean you can't work with these therapists. The key is to start with the *right kind* of therapist. In our survey, very few survivors started with the right kind of therapist, which began the problem of the therapist not identifying her symptoms as traumatic.

1. Find a Trauma Therapist

This book has made it apparent that what you experienced is *trauma*. Therefore, you need a trauma therapist. Trauma therapists haven't experienced every kind of trauma that their patients bring to them, but they still manage to help their clients reduce their symptoms, even if, for instance, they personally didn't experience 9/11 or were not sexually assaulted but their clients were.

That's because how traditional trauma impacts people is relatively the same. (PLR trauma has some differences.) Just because therapists may not be familiar with the lingo of PLRs (word salad, monkey-mind, crazy-making, etc.) doesn't mean they can't treat your symptoms if you stay away from PLR lingo. They may need this book to understand atypical PTSD symptoms to understand how to treat them, but they do understand trauma treatment and can learn to adapt their approach to PLR recovery. If you get hung up on wanting them to know exactly and in detail what you have been through, you will have missed the benefits of why you are there—to make the symptoms go away!

In a perfect world, every therapist would know about PLRs, but we don't have that just yet. So, presenting your symptoms of trauma will help them match them up with the known PTSD symptoms and be able to treat your issues.

2. Find a Trauma Therapist Trained in EMDR

Eye Movement Desensitization Reprocessing (EMDR) is a gentle type of trauma treatment that processes the trauma (thus reducing the symptoms) so that it does not further traumatize you. Therapists who use old-school methods of trauma treatment are, I believe, behind on the neuroscience of what we know causes more symptoms. Traditional talk therapy without EMDR can bring reexperiencing of symptoms, as can re-exposure therapy. You should interview therapists who are willing to use EMDR on your most stubborn reoccurring memories, thoughts, and dreams (of both positive/negative memories). You can find trained EMDR therapists online at emdr.org.

3. Ask the Therapist If He or She is Willing to Read About PLRs

Trauma therapists know they haven't experienced everything a patient has been through, and are usually willing to research and study the specific traumatic experiences of different populations. Provide them with this book. Or send them to our Association website—survivortreatment. com—where they can get information about our upcoming online training. If he/she isn't willing to learn your specifics, evaluate how important that is to you and decide if he/she is the appropriate therapist for you.

4. Seek Pathology Education Elsewhere If Needed

Since a therapist may not understand PLRs the way you do, find accurate pathology education elsewhere—through *The Institute* or other reputable sources of information on PLRs—to supplement your therapy. This can support your treatment until your trauma therapist gets up to speed on how to provide educational information to you about your trauma.

The Institute's year-long on-line self-study course, *The Living Recovery Program*™, provides a wealth of information on pathology education, Super Traits, and aftermath—visit our website for more information. There are other well-informed websites on pathology as well.

5. Find Additional PLR Support If Needed

Survivors can also find other forms of PLR support beyond educational materials, such as therapist-led telephone support groups, online seminars, or supplemental tele-counseling, if your trauma therapist feels PLR additional support is warranted. Check our website for some of these support options.

6. Seek Mindfulness Training

As this book has suggested, what has happened from the PLR has a lot to do with the neurological impact on your mind caused by gaslighting, PTSD, and cognitive dissonance. Mindfulness work *is not optional*. Your strung-out-on-adrenaline system needs to refocus, and mindfulness training will help. Every *Institute* program either teaches mindfulness, or refers survivors to a program to learn it. You need your mind for recovery, so learn mindfulness and use it daily. There are many free programs online.

7. Do No Further Harm

It's wrong to hold a trauma therapist accountable for not reducing your symptoms fast enough if you are creating them faster than s/he can extinguish them. If you are on social media, websites, or chat forums that are not Trauma-Informed Care—stop it. Stop it right now! If you are freely talking with family/friends/survivors about every detail of the PLR—stop it! Story-telling, seeking validation, and reading excessively are all trauma symptoms of re-experiencing that you are increasing by continuing. Give the therapist a chance to really help you by cooling your brain and stopping the re-experiencing problem behavior.

If you aren't currently dating, stay there! The midst of a trauma disorder is not the time to be seeking a partner. You have a year or more that necessitates your whole focus on recovery. With the trauma symptoms, the inconsistent intuition, and an un-reclaimed self, there is much work to be done. Your trauma therapist will discuss when it's time. We advise a lot of work on your Super Traits before even casually dating. Dating now could cause further trauma if it ends badly with another PLR.

8. Self-Care Basics

The PLR has made an impact on your body, mind, and spirit. Trauma recovery is just as much about getting your energy back, cooling the state of the 'brain-on-fire', and restoring the body that has been damaged by too much adrenaline as it is about reducing flashbacks. Self-care is also not optional, and I can always tell who *isn't* doing it by how well they are *not* doing in overall recovery.

You need to focus all your attention on your recovery. You need a daily structure that helps you heal, especially your disorganized and cognitively dissonant brain.

Back to the basics -

1. Do no further harm to yourself.
2. Eat good food—not junk food.
3. Exercise to reduce adrenaline and stabilize your mood.
4. Practice mindfulness training at least 15 minutes daily, as well as drama avoidance.
5. Get 20 minutes a day of sunshine, face up to the sun, baby! It helps the mood.

6. Sleep—read about sleep rituals and develop one you use nightly.
7. Practice stress reduction/relaxation techniques—after all, you *do* have a stress disorder.
8. Spirituality—reconnect. Find a spiritual practice or religious expression that produces hope for the future and your recovery. Various research studies have shown that people who engage in some form of spiritual practice do better in recovery than those who don't. We are, after all, mind, body, and *spirit*.
9. Take vitamin supplements for whatever symptoms you are having.
10. HAVE FUN! Remember what that is? Include it in your daily schedule. It helps to create positive neurochemistry and helps to rewire the brain.

One of *The Institute*'s first steps in working with survivors is to get them on a daily self-care plan. We check in with them about self-care in every session. Being other-oriented, survivors tend to meet others' needs before ever considering their own. The mind, body, and spirit cannot recover from this amount of harm without a serious daily focus on healing all three of these aspects of the self. Sometimes work on the trauma or PLR cannot *begin* until a survivor is *consistently* involved in daily self-care to support the next level of work to be done.

These basic self-care practices are what every survivor can start doing today, while hunting for a therapist, and should be done daily to create structure and physical health for the lagging brain and body. Making these 10 practices a priority will show your trauma therapist that you are already on the road to recovery. And these self-care basics build the structure for the step of life restructuring that you will do in the future. These are NOT care steps for when you are in crisis, they are care steps you should practice forever if you want to stay out of poor mental or physical health in the future.

*T*he Kinds of Care You Should Avoid

As tempting as it for survivors to migrate to other survivors for help (as has already been explained about this level of trauma and mind/brain mangle), it warrants trauma care. As was displayed in the survey data above, even some non-trauma therapists have gotten it wrong on several levels, so I can't imagine a formerly traumatized survivor feeling they are equipped to tackle severe trauma. But they do, and more so-called 'experts' are springing up every week. Here is what you need to know about the advertised competent care you are likely to see out there as you are searching for your recovery method -

Survivor Helper #1: The Avoidant

Although we alone have lived through, and triumphed over, our own crises and disasters, this does not necessarily make us technically capable to help others master their own pain. That sounds like an oxymoron. But victimization does not always produce healers. Sometimes it produces victims who avoid their own recovery by plunging headfirst into frantic efforts of helping others in order to backpedal away from their own unprocessed trauma. For help-seeking survivors, this type of helper spells disaster.

Caution: In the search for help, one might find survivors who are offering things they call victim services, mentoring, or coaching who may have not done day one of true (or maybe effective) therapy with a mental health professional. Or they might have done a little and declared themselves well, even if the therapist did not agree. They produce no indication or measurement that they themselves have undergone any type of healing.

However, these same avoidant survivors, who have not worked on their own healing with professionals, may consider themselves healed because they have spent hundreds of hours on chat forums about pathology, submerged in reliving their own pathological relationships. Or perhaps they feel they are healed because they have read a lot of books about the topic and believe that, since they have invested hundreds of hours in chatting or reading, they are ready to be a helper in the field. Some unhealed survivors start their own programs trying to lead other survivors where they haven't gone themselves.

Newly traumatized survivors who have fallen into nonprofessional coaching are often harmed by approaches such as those offered by these avoidant survivors, which can be counter-productive for those with stress disorders.

Well-meaning coaches have been sued by clients who have ended up in psych units, who have self-harmed after sessions, or who feel they are much worse from the coaching experience as indicated in our survey on Finding Competent Care. This is where a survivor's own personal experience is not experience enough for helping someone else. It is why mental health professionals have spent six years or more in training to do *effective* treatment.

Survivor Helper #2: The Faux Therapist

Some survivors feel that they can help others because they have, after all, according to them, spent their entire life in therapy and feel they are a better helper than their therapist was to them.

Caution: Survivors who have spent many years in counseling may have some type of chronic mental health issue. Most mental health disorders which are not chronic are treatable, and clients are in and out of counseling within a couple of years at the maximum. Those who have spent most of their adult lives in counseling, however, usually have a type of disorder that requires monitoring or frequent intervention.

While it might be obvious to others that a survivor with a long history of mental health problems shouldn't be a coach to someone else, these are often the very types of survivors who will try to give back through their existential need to create meaning out of their own pain and so do not disclose that they have a long history of mental health problems, which may eventually become obvious.

Survivor Helper #3: The Pseudo Paraprofessional

Some survivors have gone through some training for general coaching. General relationship or life coaching training provides a good way to access the basic rules of working with others, but it would never be sufficient to work with those who have significant crises and likely current mental health issues such as PTSD.

Caution: Coaching organizations that teach Peer Coaching offer certification in the basics of how to coach. The problem exists when survivors take coaching certification that is meant for issues unrelated to the severity of the aftermath of PLRs, PTSD, etc. and apply it to these situations. It's unethical to offer a level of care that is not equal to the level of need.

The Institute briefly offered coaching training to nonprofessionals for PLRs. After frantic calls from coaches not knowing what to do when working with clients who were triggered/in flashbacks/dissociating/having suicidal ideation, our staff ending up working with the coach's clients to stabilize them. We very quickly discontinued these trainings because the coaches were freaked out, the clients were freaked out, and we were freaked out. We soon realized that over 75 percent of clients who request coaching services have active PTSD.

In fact, even though survivors don't usually know they have PTSD, it is the PTSD that is propelling them to seek help.

Seeking the least restrictive and most cost-effective route to recovery, survivors often pick coaching. It seems less threatening, and there is the relatability factor —those doing the coaching are survivors themselves. However, with over three quarters or more of those seeking help and who have PTSD, it became clear that PLR coaching is not practical or even safe without a mental health professional doing it.

Additionally, most coaches who do not have a mental health background do not know the difference between the merely symptomatic behaviors of the PLR and those of recurring PTSD, which need more intense treatment, normally in a face-to-face format.

Sometimes coaching training or symptom reduction training (learning one technique for one symptom and using it in all the coaching situations) can give the client the feeling that the coach has the skills to handle anything. But a handful of techniques and some generalized coaching skills are not enough to deal with this type of trauma.

Survivor Helper #4: The Spiritual Counselor

Some survivors who have found solace in spirituality seek to bring that path of healing to others no matter what the survivor needs—currently and/or psychologically. Whether or not the client is exhibiting a host of PTSD symptoms, if she comes to a spiritual counselor, spiritual guidance is what she is going to get.

Caution: Spiritual counselors often come with a certification that is not a degree and is acquired elsewhere. Much like paraprofessional counselors, they have some training in how to work with others, but their approach is clearly spiritually based. The helper can be of any religion; many have pastoral or self-proclaimed theological backgrounds.

While spirituality is almost always part of a survivor's recovery, it is not the *only* part. It is often best incorporated *after* PTSD treatment or symptom management has been effective. However, when spiritual coaching is the only tool in the toolbox, it isn't necessarily, nor always helpfully, the only approach. Spiritual recovery is important and should be addressed in the proper order of a treatment plan but cannot and should not replace trauma treatment.

Survivor Helper #5: The 12 Stepper

God bless the 12 Steps, which have restored the sanity of millions and are arguably the best peer support program on the planet! I love the 12 Steps, and I believe in them. They can be a great additional tool in a survivor's arsenal of helpful approaches in recovery.

Caution: Coaches who work only with the 12 Steps as peer support face the same challenges that other coaches do—at the time the survivor reaches out, she is often suffering from PTSD or other stress reactions. If the survivor is using substances, of course a 12-Step group can, and should, address that.

However, the rest of the trauma that the survivor is experiencing is a treatment issue, not only a 12-Step problem. Admitting that one is powerless by overdrinking to medicate the aftermath (Step One) is not the same as symptom management for PTSD. The 12 Steps are a wonderful ancillary support system during the aftermath. This spiritual and structural program has helped millions in crisis, and urges them to pass it forward to others, but it cannot replace other needed trauma recovery approaches.

Survivor Helper #6: The Support Groupie

For many people in recovery, support groups can be life savers. These groups can vary from churches, to survivors' meetings, to professionals offering various types of groups for different topics and issues. There are even Meet Up support groups, found on the Internet, for almost any type of victimization that you can name.

Caution: While it is enormously appealing to find groups of other survivors who 'get' what a survivor has been through, these groups face the same problems discussed previously; they can be run by survivors who may or may not be healed or trained and don't have the true ability to run such a group effectively. Having a passion about understanding pathology is admirable but is a long way from being able to handle the traumatic reactions that can occur in a group when someone is disclosing the details of their PLR which sets off other survivors' reactions. Mental health professionals are trained in group dynamics and how to facilitate discussions in a manner that minimizes traumatic reactions. Since we don't know the true capability of a nonprofessional who runs a group for PLRs, we only refer survivors to other professionals. Some survivors run groups based on a curriculum and assume that, if they stick to it, nothing bad can happen. That isn't always true. Survivors should know the risk of church, survivor, and Meet Up support groups.

Survivor Helper #7: The Blogger

Bloggers can fall into some of the other helper categories listed above—from those who have worked on their recovery to those who haven't had five minutes of recovery. A blog that started out to be information on PLRs or personality disorders and which develops a massive following can quickly jump from the helpful presentation of information to over-confident coaching where the blogger believes that marketing numbers must be an indicator of their ability and effectiveness.

Caution: It is hard to ignore the successful effects of Internet marketing on your business when your list of clients, followers, or supporters grows to 10,000 or more. That means that you have hit on a popular topic and you know how to market it well. But it doesn't mean that you are qualified or ethically trained to coach over half of the people on your list who have a trauma disorder.

Bloggers, like other helpers, probably don't recognize the covert signs of atypical PTSD, and if a survivor is earnestly seeking help, the blogger has her own recovery method to fall back on when offering advice. A book, an e-book, a mini-book, a newsletter, and a chat room that is crammed full may lend credence to successful marketing but not to the trauma-support ability of the blogger. While bloggers may claim they are not treating trauma, they often may be unaware that a follower is indeed suffering from PTSD.

Helper #8—Hardly a Survivor: The Pathological

If you ever want to see the power of trauma bonding, look at how many survivors flock to the books, websites, and coaching offered by self-proclaimed, or legitimately diagnosed, narcissists or psychopaths. Trauma reenactment as a form of trauma bonding draws survivors to other people with pathological disorders as a continued form of interacting with someone similar to the person who harmed them.

Caution: I don't need to name names; you've probably already found their websites. For $100 you can talk to, and get a glimpse of, the menacing mind of someone diagnosed with narcissistic personality disorder or psychopathy. You may feel it will help you understand why Darkness hurt you. Or you can buy a whole series of books written by Darkness to reexperience, through reading, the trauma of someone who damaged you. Are we surprised that Darkness would make his living by further harming survivors while, on the surface, looking helpful? Are we surprised that the power of trauma bonding and the trauma reaction of reenactment leads survivors to expose themselves to more pathology? Well, certainly not. But it happens all the time. Driven not only by curiosity but also the power of trauma bonding and reenactment, survivors seek restoration from the same disorder that destroyed them.

Wrapping This All Up

This chapter has helped to delineate what kind of competent care you should seek, what you should avoid, and what you can expect. I want to reiterate that *recovery is possible,* or *The Institute* would not continue to exist and grow as a service provider for survivors of PLRs. Survivors with true Super Traits bring many great internal resources to the task of recovery. While this certainly isn't a quick fix, with the right team of professionals, survivors not only have significant trauma symptom reduction, they have the ability, through education and prevention techniques, to guard against future PLRs. I encourage all survivors to get a competent team for the best recovery.

The previous chapters that comprised Puzzle Piece #4™ Extreme Aftermath Symptoms has drawn a haunting picture of the effects of someone else's pathology on another human being. Not only are these effects inhumane, they have been consistently and largely undetected or misunderstood. With all the DSM has had to say about personality disorders, it is incomprehensible, at least to me, that the relationships haven't been better recognized as causing inevitable harm and the survivor's trauma hasn't been expected by professionals and others. It should seem obvious, with 60 million people in the United States alone being negatively impacted by others' pathology, that survivors should have other choices than traumatized bloggers or marriage counselors working toward reunification with the source of her trauma.

There is another group of professionals for whom I have a final word…

Chapter Twenty

An Epilogue of Sorts—A Call to Action for Our Societal Systems

I am on a bird-filled, stream-babbling mountain in the middle of nowhere as I finish this book. This is the first time I have worked on a book for *years*. I have been digging out archived information I have collected over decades of work—pulling every last vestment of information out to include in anticipation of this being my last full-length book about PLRs.

Remembering and reading the archives has made writing difficult—like a very long flashback of remembering my clients, the stories that filled me with fury from the moment I started in this field, the pervasive paradoxes of pathology that both penetrated my life through the death of my father and through the lives of the women and children I have helped. I have been flooded with memories of the faces, the stories, and their personal pain, which rekindled the fire of my youth about how long it has taken to make inroads for survivors and why I have been so perturbed about it.

Consequently, I have swallowed buckets of adrenaline in the writing—ferocity for breakfast, as I banged out these chapters while remembering survivor's pain; indignation for lunch, in knowing historically how little has been there for survivors; and acrimony for dinner, that the universe is always strangely tilted to Darkness' benefit while the societal systems turn a blind eye. I have relived the decades long beliefs held by my career field, and labels about this work when *The Institute* began developing a new theory about PLRs—being labeled everything from 'juvenile enthusiasm' to 'philosophical idealism' and my frustration from the unconquerable laziness of societal systems. When I began writing this book, I wanted to quit many times. Even though I wanted to liberate the survivors from oblivion and injustice, it was profoundly painful to remember how *many* survivor stories and so *many* examples of failed justice; how long they have had to wait for real help, and the *resistance* they have encountered in trying to have systems recognize what pathology does to souls and societies.

What has always guided my work and my motivation is the power of real recovery that I witnessed in my own mother, Joyce, who made a come-back from soul destruction to live her last days in joy and peace, in art and travel, in love (yes, she met someone!), in life on a beach, in pottery and painting and sculpting, and in a wide, deep, and pulsating community of friendships. (See the Dedication section.)

Her life after a PLR affirmed the indisputable value of recovery—the attainable miracle of getting a great life despite Darkness' ethical and moral depravity and the soul-destruction of the aftermath. I wasn't merely a philosophical idealist to think that PLRs could be understood, that a theory could be built, or a treatment model created—I was a first-row *witness* to the fertile use of recovery to build back a life of profound beauty—a yummy carbohydrate-filled life of soul-satisfying living, love, interests, and connections that could produce her declaration on her death bed that "16 good years lived right is enough." Yes. That's what I believed could be created for survivors once the whole PLR was clinically and soulfully understood. That's the indisputable value of recovery that I have sought like the Holy Grail and worked to recreate for other survivors.

My front-row seat to my mother's destruction, and yet epic phoenix-rising recovery, fueled my curiosity that these survivors were made of some different *stuff*. And indeed, they are—an indominable spirit that has been briefly silenced but whose DNA has wired them, most definitely, for Joyce's epic phoenix-rising ability. The souls of the women, with whom I have been privileged to be a small part of their recovery, are full of warm eloquence and Super Trait fabulosity. They have provided a far more timeless corrective view of the rest of humanity than just the pretension and vanity of the pathology that I witnessed. They balanced my worldview, which was drastically close to being lost in the hopelessness of the world as being largely pathological.

I knew immediately when working with these survivors that Joyce was not some rogue DNA fluke—the traits I had seen in her I was seeing again in these women. The traits were both the source of their targeting and the source of their *potential*. To that end, this has been hatching the great embryonic work

413

of understanding the puzzle pieces of PLRs so that a recovery model could be birthed—a recovery model of real understanding and real hope.

But the buckets of adrenaline I swallowed in the writing of this book are due in part to the aerial view of where we began, where we are now, and where this needs to go for society to be safe from Darkness. This book wouldn't be complete without acknowledging that everything about recognizing Darkness still needs work—there are many miles to go before victims are truly safe, society is enlightened, and societal systems are not only trained, but *responsive*.

Societal Systems: A Rant

As someone who has taken up the cause to speak for the 60 million people in the United States destroyed by someone else's pathology, I have earned the right to rant about our societal systems that are aiding and abetting pathological partners by forcing their victims into these systems that remain unresponsive to the inevitable harm being done. Like the prophets who ranted and raved like madmen, begging people to see the error of their ways and change their behavior, I willingly rant like a madman, too.

The Internet is home to over eight hundred websites (and growing), and social media pages encompassing *millions* of survivors devoted to the issue of the abuse of victims by their pathological partners. Abuse by proxy—when other people and systems *are used as accomplices* to continue Darkness' coercive control and abuse—is only one example of how Darkness continues his reign of terror. When Darkness can't get his friends to perpetuate harm, he turns to the systems in which his victim is engaged.

Hundreds of thousands of survivors have taken to the Internet to force change in our courts, law enforcement system, Guardians Ad Litem programs, psychological evaluator systems, and child protective services, seeking to inform these broken and inept systems of the reality of the damage that Darkness can inflict on them, their children, and the systems they drag others into.

Abuse by proxy is a form of continued domestic violence and psychological terrorism in which Darkness, hiding behind his socially acceptable mask, can manipulate his victims through these ineffective systems that are *supposed* to protect victims and children, but which seem clueless about how Darkness operates.

Legal Abuse Syndrome, a form of PTSD, is a psychological descriptor of what happens to survivors and children when Darkness, unregulated, uses systems to continue to terrorize his victims. This is especially prevalent in the court systems, which he uses for simultaneously entertaining himself and continuing forced contact and coercive control with the survivor. This can go on for years, producing a form of court-induced PTSD on victims and which the court should be protecting against.

While I may have offered a hall pass to these systems in the past for not knowing that Darkness (with his mask of sanity) was hiding among us, that hall pass has been *revoked*. The hundreds of thousands of survivors who have taken to the Internet *already* offer (to these systems) examples of what is happening, and yet the systems have remained unresponsive.

Over the years, *The Institute* has trained many of these blinded systems, including judges. In a symposium titled *What the Neuroscience of a Batterer's Brain Can Teach Us About Recidivism*, the "aha" moment was clear on their faces, but the gist of the responses was, "While we understand this, it would mean we would have to revamp an entire court system." Um . . . yes, it would, so get up and do it and stop acting as if current neuroscience, personality assessments, brain imaging knowledge, and millions of survivors haven't told you what is happening. It's your system. Fix it. Or get out of the way and let others fix it.

Law enforcement, you have no hall pass either. You, more than others, know the habits and characteristics of the antisocial personalities who live within your system and to those whose damage to their partners and children and yet you turn a blind eye.

State representatives and Senators, we suggest that you stop ignoring the changes we ask you to make to tighten access to victims and their children. Listen to Domestic Violence Coalitions when they ask you for what they need. You aren't the expert, they are.

Psychological Evaluators—since people with personality disorders are those *most* likely to abduct children, stalk ex-partners, violate custody orders, and murder their family members, how about learning how to identify them and including personality disorder assessments in your arsenal of testing instruments? They are frequently missed on your standard and archaic assessments.

And Child Protective Services—why are you so ineptly trained in personality disorders and psychopathy when these disorders comprise your main *repeating* cases? Email us—we will gladly train you. How about hiring only social workers who have been specifically trained in psychopathology? Stop destroying children!

Guardians Ad Litem and Mediators—get your butts to pathology training and stop advising courts to share custody! Psychopaths simply cannot be turned into soccer dads.

And counties—why do you not have Inter-Agency Collaborative Committees who meet regularly and share high-conflict cases? Those same repeating cases are in all your agencies and will likely seriously harm the survivor and her children. This isn't rocket science. All counties should have agencies who meet and talk about Darkness and what he's doing in each of their agencies as he gaslights and coerces, and how he is masking the impending doom he is creating for his partner.

Therapists—60 million people out there are looking for someone to help them. Get trained, get updated, take another psychopathology class, update your skills, and be part of the solution.

Am I frustrated? Beyond...

Decades of finding treatment approaches and trying to help survivors heal, and all the work keeps getting torn apart by these broken, reckless, and clueless systems. I work to patch 'em up, they tear 'em apart.

We will not be able to consistently help victims until all societal systems that are being manipulated by Darkness are on the same page. The work we do will find no lasting effect with victims and their children until these systems step up and get educated and make the effort to change their system to remove the power, access, and damage from Darkness.

With the advent of neuroscience, personality assessments, and brain imaging, there is no longer *any* excuse for believing that all parents should share custody simply because they provided the DNA. There is no remaining loophole for this asinine belief system. There is only apathy and laziness in systems, resulting in the torture of children who must live with pathological parents who have already produced PTSD in their partners. How will Darkness *not* produce PTSD in young developing psyches?

And so here is my prophetic warning:

If the societal systems, starting with the courts and Child Protective Services, don't stop the willful participation in Darkness' terror on their for-

mer partners and children, we will see the next generation of unmitigated PTSD in the children who are becoming young adults. They will be traumatized and acting out, forever impacted by Darkness' disturbed view of the world that has been parented into these children. These young adults will flood our societal systems either as victims or perpetrators, creating a system overload and melt down. Our already over-burdened systems will become overrun with more cases like Darkness, producing more victims and more children broken by him which will either become like Darkness in perpetrating harm, or become another PTSD victim targeted by others. Our court and CPS systems will largely exist to funnel pathological relationship perpetrators and victims through their revolving door—into CPS and out through the court system only to go back through CPS, either in this generation or the next, and into the court system again, stuck on the hamster wheel for years to come. Our community mental health system will combust from the 60 million people seeking help for themselves or their children as they are held hostage in court and CPS systems. The $560 BILLION per year that Darkness costs us now will be a drop in the bucket in comparison to the bill society will have to cover in the future.

I wish there was a phrase stronger than *shame on you,* which doesn't sufficiently admonish the inexcusable behavior I see in these systems, whose representatives now know better but refuse to change. The news is full of the horror stories of these broken, castrated, and impotent systems throughout every state who refuse the evidence of hundreds of thousands of victims, of neuroscience and brain imaging, and who refuse to believe the stories behind dead children.

The Institute, as a forum for public pathology education *for all*—and this includes you, O Systems of Destruction—is out to educate everyone. We are coming:

- Armed with science
- Armed with 60 million survivors as evidence
- Armed with the broken children
- Armed with fury

A Long and Winding Road

I began this journey with questions that didn't have answers, despite not having a Ph.D., not being a researcher, not being a lot of things. *The Institute* has slowly excavated one answer at a time and cracked the code by putting together the puzzle pieces of who the survivor is, why she is targeted, what her damage is, and how she can heal.

It has taken decades of work, research, digging, writing, treating survivors, hunting for answers under the rock piles of psychology—honestly, an exhausting level of work. While this has been my life's work, it has come with enormous personal sacrifice but it's a sacrifice I do not regret.

And here we are now—with workable information for a survivor's recovery -

- We've debunked outdated and archaic theories that did not describe her.
- We've challenged status quo assumptions and pop psychology approaches.
- We've identified the mind mess of cognitive dissonance and correctly associated it with the survivor's trauma.
- We've mapped out relational dynamics.
- We've created trauma treatment approaches specific to this type of survivor, and effectively applied them in the recoveries of thousands of survivors.
- We've identified atypical PTSD.
- We've developed an understanding of the risks of inconsistent intuition.
- We've identified the traumatizing aspects of self-perceptual injuries.
- And most importantly, we've unearthed the Mother Lode of the Super Traits.

With the remaining time I'll be spending in the field, I have created the first professional *Association for Narcissistic Personality Disorder/ Psychopathy Survivor Treatment, Research & Education*, with the goal of training mental health professionals in this new emerging genre of counseling. Scientific and trauma-specific approaches will dispel myths and positive psychology approaches that survivors have been plagued with. A Board of Directors will keep the Association training going long after it is fully operational.

None of this would have been possible without what I learned from the survivors who taught me, and who bravely bared their wounds to me so that I could understand. You are the heroes of this new emerging genre of counseling.

I have been privileged to spend decades in a field with the amazing strength of Super-Traited women. The burn-out would have done me in if it weren't for the beauty I saw in the hearts and Super Traits of survivors. What else could have kept me in it this long if it weren't for being awe-struck at the character and fortitude I was honored to witness daily?

Lastly, I want to say that, what I see woven into these Super Traits and true survivorship, is tenacity and resiliency. While these were not technically traits in agreeableness and conscientiousness in the Five Factor Model, I think that after thousands of counseling hours I get to add my two cents and declare that these traits should be included.

Tenacity

Tenacity is 'the quality or fact of being able to grip something firmly.' The joy of working with survivors of PLRs is their ability to not only grasp the concepts of pathology but the Super Traits that imbue them with an intrinsic desire and hunger for recovery. The self-perceptual injuries© that have robbed so much of their lives, turning them into someone they no longer recognize, create a longing to return (with protection) to the beautiful selves they knew themselves to be. They are tenacious in their approach to win back what trauma has taken from them, to not only live again but to thrive. Most of the survivors we have worked with astound us with the amount of work they are willing to do—to grip the hope of recovery and not let it go until they succeed.

Resiliency

Resilience is 'the process of adapting well in the face of adversity, trauma, tragedy, threats or significant sources of stress' — such as family and relationship problems, serious health problems or workplace and financial stressors. It means *bouncing back from difficult experiences.*

The mystery of resiliency has been so pursued in psychology because it's more valuable than ginseng and truffles. The psychology field wishes it had a magic wand to produce it in all people, especially children in difficult and adverse situations, because it's pretty much the path to

419

recovery. *How* to get more of it, unlike ginseng and truffles that can be planted, is what all the research has been about. Sure, there are lots of theories about how to cultivate it, improve it, or hunt it like the Holy Grail, but I sort of suspect that, like Super Traits, it's a personality factor that some people have more of and some people have less. I can tell you that most survivors of PLRs have it in abundance.

I am convinced that there is no way to survive the mind mangle of Darkness, the neurological changes from PLRs, the monkey mind of cognitive dissonance, and the wallop of atypical PTSD without having *serious* resilience, because it is completely disorienting. Survivors who have had to go on disability from PTSD and cognitive dissonance still manage to claw their way back to functionality—that is sheer resilience.

Resiliency aids with the ability to bounce back from adversity and in the desire to not get lost in despair. Resilient people not only tend to heal, they tend to heal faster than those without resiliency. And, while the road back from PLRs can take a while, these survivors never stop reaching to recover their lives. To that degree, it's a delight to witness first hand their amazing resilience—to see a formerly devastated person resume the helm in her career, to go on to find lasting love with a healthy partner, and to again find meaning and purpose in life. I have great hope for most survivors' ability to heal with the right treatment precisely because of the enormous of amount of *resilience* they have.

With that said, I encourage every survivor to rustle the branches of their resilience and keep seeking competent professional treatment and recovery so that you understand what you have lived through and why, and to grab hold of the recovered life like Joyce did, filled with beauty, joy, and protection.

To the survivors: thank you for the honor and privilege of being my life's work.

With much hope for your healing, and unwavering allegiance to change all systems,

– Sandra L. Brown, MA

About The Authors

Sandra L. Brown, M.A.

Sandra L. Brown, M.A., is the founder of The Institute for Relational Harm Reduction & Public Pathology Education. She is a former psychotherapist, community educator on pathological love relationships, clinical lecturer and trainer, TV and radio guest, and an author. Sandra is recognized for her pioneering work in women's issues related to relational harm from dangerous and pathological partners. She specializes in the development of Pathological Love Relationship training for other professionals and the development of survivor-based support services. *The Institute* is the only formal Model-of-Care approach for survivors and offers the largest available array of products and services related to this population. Her books and other training materials have been used as curriculum in drug rehabs, women's organizations and shelters, women's jail and prison programs, school and college-based programs, inner city projects, psychology and sociology programs. Her books have been translated into several languages and are distributed in almost every country of the world.

Sandra is most noted for being the first to research the effects of male psychopathy on female partners which has ignited interest in training by mental health professionals for this new and emerging genre of counseling. Her research on women's personality trait elevations as an element of trait-targeting by pathological partners was conducted in collaboration with Purdue University. *The Institute's* research has largely impacted the treatment field through the systematic approaches to recovery for women. Her collaborative research in the field was presented at the Ruth Ginsberg Lecture Series', Women and The Law on Domestic Violence, at End Violence Against Women International, at the Society for the Scientific Study of Psychopathy, the US Army Family Advocate Training, San Diego Psychology Association's Staying Ahead of the Curve in Domestic Violence Training, and the State of Georgia Commission on Family Violence during which her unique focus on Pathological Love Relationships has been featured.

She is currently a writer for Psychology Today and is a frequent radio and TV personality regarding dangerous relationships, high lethality cases and psychopathy. She has been on over 100 radio shows including NPR and over 50 TV shows including Anderson Cooper. She hosts a weekly radio show, *Relational Harm Reduction Radio*, that is focused on the topics of *The Institute's* message, services, and books.

She is the founder and current president of The Association for NPD/Psychopathy Survivor Treatment, Research & Education, a mental health professional training association for trauma-specific treatment approaches for Pathological Love Relationships.

Sandra L. Brown, M.A. has also published the following books:

- *Counseling Victims of Violence*, First Edition
- *The Moody Pews*
- *How to Spot a Dangerous Man Before You Get Involved*
- *How to Spot a Dangerous Man Before You Get Involved* Workbook
- *Counseling Victims of Violence: A Handbook for Helping Professionals*, Second Edition
- *Women Who Love Psychopaths: Inside the Relationships of Inevitable Harm with Narcissists, Sociopaths, & Psychopaths*, First Edition
- *Women Who Love Psychopaths: Inside the Relationships of Inevitable Harm with Narcissists, Sociopaths, & Psychopaths*, Second Edition

Jennifer R. Young, L.M.H.C.

Jennifer R. Young, L.M.H.C. is the Director of Counseling and Survivor Support Services with *The Institute for Relational Harm Reduction & Public Pathology Education*, a Certified Clinical Trauma Professional and a trained clinician in Forward-Facing Trauma Treatment. She has been instrumental in providing the Clinical Model of Care approach with *The Institute's* clients through in-person, tele-mental health, and retreat formats. Jennifer has provided therapist training services for *The Institute* and was a lead team-member for The Institute with our collaborative research with Purdue University. Jennifer has worked in domestic violence prevention, legal advocacy support, substance abuse treatment, and is currently in private practice in the Tampa Bay area. She is a member of the Pinellas County (Florida) Fatality Review Team and The Suncoast Mental Health Counseling Association. She is a writer for *The Institute's* website and newsletter and co-host of *The Institute's Relational Harm Reduction Radio Show* on Blog Talk Radio.

Printed in Great Britain
by Amazon

26080548R00238